Lecture Notes in Artificial Intelligence   12833

Subseries of Lecture Notes in Computer Science

Series Editors

Randy Goebel
University of Alberta, Edmonton, Canada
Yuzuru Tanaka
Hokkaido University, Sapporo, Japan
Wolfgang Wahlster
DFKI and Saarland University, Saarbrücken, Germany

Founding Editor

Jörg Siekmann
DFKI and Saarland University, Saarbrücken, Germany

More information about this subseries at http://www.springer.com/series/1244

Fairouz Kamareddine · Claudio Sacerdoti Coen (Eds.)

Intelligent Computer Mathematics

14th International Conference, CICM 2021
Timisoara, Romania, July 26–31, 2021
Proceedings

 Springer

Editors
Fairouz Kamareddine
Heriot-Watt University
Edinburgh, UK

Claudio Sacerdoti Coen 🆔
University of Bologna
Bologna, Italy

ISSN 0302-9743   ISSN 1611-3349   (electronic)
Lecture Notes in Artificial Intelligence
ISBN 978-3-030-81096-2   ISBN 978-3-030-81097-9   (eBook)
https://doi.org/10.1007/978-3-030-81097-9

LNCS Sublibrary: SL7 – Artificial Intelligence

This Springer imprint is published by the registered company Springer Nature Switzerland AG
The registered company address is: Gewerbestrasse 11, 6330 Cham, Switzerland

Preface

With the continuing, rapid progress of digital methods in communications, knowledge representation, processing, and discovery, the unique character and needs of mathematical information require unique approaches. Its specialized representations and capacity for creation and proof, both automatically and formally as well as manually, set mathematical knowledge apart.

The Conference on Intelligent Computer Mathematics (CICM) was initially formed in 2008 as a joint meeting of communities involved in computer algebra systems, automated theorem provers, and mathematical knowledge management, as well as those involved in a variety of aspects of scientific document archives. It has offered a venue for discussing, developing, and integrating the diverse, sometimes eclectic, approaches and research. Since 2008, CICM has been held annually: Birmingham (UK, 2008), Grand Bend (Canada, 2009), Paris (France, 2010), Bertinoro (Italy, 2011), Bremen (Germany, 2012), Bath (UK, 2013), Coimbra (Portugal, 2014), Washington D. C. (USA, 2015), Bialystok (Poland, 202016), Edinburgh (UK, 2017), Linz (Austria, 2018), Prague (Czech Republic, 2019) and Bertinoro (Italy, 2020). This latter edition, which was originally scheduled to be held in Bertinoro, Italy, was hosted online due to the COVID-19 pandemic. This year's meeting was supposed to be held in Timisoara, Romania, but again due to the pandemic, it was held online (July 26–31, 2021).

This year's meeting exposed advances in formalizations, automatic theorem proving, applications of machine learning to mathematical documents and proof search, search and classifications of mathematical documents, teaching and geometric reasoning, and logic and systems, among other topics. This volume contains the contributions to this conference. From 38 formal submissions, the Program Committee (PC) accepted 20 papers including 12 full research papers, 7 shorter papers describing software systems or datasets and 1 paper highlighting development of systems and tools in the last year. All papers were reviewed by at least three PC members or external reviewers. The reviews were single-blind and included a response period in which the authors could respond and clarify points raised by the reviewers. In addition to the main sessions, the conference included a doctoral program, chaired by Yasmine Sharoda, which provided a forum for PhD students to present their research and get advice from senior members of the community. Additionally, the following workshops were scheduled:

- The 31st OpenMath Workshop, organized by James Davenport and Michael Kohlhase.
- The 2nd Workshop on Natural Formal Mathematics (NatFoM 2021), organized by Peter Koepke and Dennis Müller.
- The 5th Workshop on Formal Mathematics for Mathematicians (FMM 2021), organized by Jasmine Blanchette and Adam Naumowicz.

- The 2nd Workshop on Formal Verification of Physical Systems (FVPS 2021), organized by Sofiene Tahar, Osman Hasan and Adnan Rashid.
- The 13th Workshop on Mathematical User Interaction (MathUI 2021), organized by Andrea Kohlhase.

Finally, the conference included four invited talks:

- Alessandro Cimatti (Fondazione Bruno Kessler, Italy): "Logic at work, and some research challenges for computer mathematics".
- Michael Kohlhase (FAU Erlangen-Nürnberg, Germany): "Referential Semantics – a Concept for Bridging between Representations of mathematical/technical Documents and Knowledge".
- Laura Kovacs (TU Vienna, Austria): "Induction in Saturation-Based Reasoning".
- Angus McIntyre (Emeritus Professor, Queen Mary University of London, UK): "Doing classical number theory in weak axiomatic systems".

A successful conference is due to the efforts of many people. We thank Madalina Erascu and her colleagues at the West University of Timisoara, Romania, for the difficult task of organizing a conference with the expectation of it being held face to face but with the dynamics of COVID-19 making it difficult to accommodate in person meetings. We are grateful to Serge Autexier for his publicity work. We also thank the authors of submitted papers, the PC for their reviews, and the organizers of the workshops, as well as the invited speakers and the participants of the conference.

June 2021

F. Kamareddine
C. Sacerdoti Coen

Organization

Program Committee Chairs

Fairouz Kamareddine   Heriot-Watt University, UK
Claudio Sacerdoti Coen   University of Bologna, Italy

Program Committee

Akiko Aizawa	National Institute of Informatics, Japan
Mauricio Ayala-Rincón	Universidade de Brasilía, Brasil
Frédéric Blanqui	Inria, France
Jacques Carette	McMaster University, Canada
Howard Cohl	NIST, USA
James H. Davenport	University of Bath, UK
Catherine Dubois	ENSIIE-Samovar, France
Jacques Fleuriot	The University of Edinburgh, UK
Osman Hasan	National University of Sciences and Technology, Pakistan
Jan Jakubuv	Czech Technical University, Czech Republic
Mateja Jamnik	University of Cambridge, UK
Moa Johansson	Chalmers University of Technology, Sweden
Cezary Kaliszyk	University of Innsbruck, Austria
Manfred Kerber	University of Birmingham, UK
Andrea Kohlhase	University of Applied Sciences Neu-Ulm, Germany
Adam Naumowicz	Institute of Informatics, University of Bialystok, Poland
Olga Nevzorova	Kazan Federal University, Russia
Markus N. Rabe	Google, USA
Florian Rabe	FAU Erlangen-Nürnberg, Germany
Moritz Schubotz	Universität Konstanz, Germany
Stephan Schulz	DHBW Stuttgart, Germany
Volker Sorge	University of Birmingham, UK
Olaf Teschke	FIZ Karlsruhe, Germany
Joe Wells	Heriot-Watt University, UK
Makarius Wenzel	sketis.net, Germany
Wolfgang Windsteiger	RISC Institute, Austria
Richard Zanibbi	Rochester Institute of Technology, USA

Additional Reviewers

Thaynara Arielly de Lima
Ciaran Dunne
André Greiner-Petter
Alexander Kirillovich
Artur Korniłowicz
Dennis Müller
Miroslav Olšák
Stanisław Purgał

Adnan Rashid
Max Rapp
Colin Rothgang
Philipp Scharpf
Jonas Schopf
Philipp Smola
René Thiemann
Josef Urban

Invited Talks

Logics at Work, and Some Challenges for Computer Mathematics

Alessandro Cimatti![ORCID]

Fondazione Bruno Kessler
cimatti@fbk.eu

Formal verification aims at the exhaustive analysis of the behaviours of a system, to ensure that the expected properties are universally met. Formal verification has been applied in many sectors including control software, relay interlocking, space, avionics, hardware circuits, and production plants. We informally distinguish systems in discrete systems and hybrid systems.

Symbolic Verification of Transition Systems. In case of discrete systems, a behaviour can be seen as a sequence of valuations to a set of state variables. We focus on symbolic verification, where logical methods are used to represent and explore the system model. In the case of transition systems, a state is represented as an assignment to a set of logical variables V. Logical formulae are used to represent sets of states, so that $I(V)$ represents the (initial) states satisfying I, and $T(V, V')$ represents sets of transitions, with V' being the next state variables. In the finite-state case, V is a vector of Boolean variables. Symbolic algorithms for automated verification [8], originally based on Binary Decision Diagrams [7], have progressively been replaced by verification based on satisfiability checking (SAT) [5]. SAT-based model checking techniques include Bounded Model Checking [4], induction [19], interpolation [17] and IC3 [6].

In case of infinite-state transition systems, the state variables may have infinite range, and I and T are generally expressed as formulae in first-order logic, in the framework of Satisfiability Modulo Theories (SMT) [3]. SMT extends the propositional case by allowing for functions and relations between individual variables, with interpretations over relevant theories. These include linear and non-linear real and integer arithmetic (LRA, NRA, LIA, NIA). The algorithms for the analysis of infinite-state transition systems, also referred to as Verification Modulo Theories [11], are not only obtained by replacing SAT solvers with SMT solvers in SAT-based verification approaches [2, 14]. A fundamental role is played by abstractions, most notably predicate abstraction [16]. Abstractions are dynamically refined based on the analysis of abstract counterexamples [13], and can be either computed explicitly, or implicitly [20], in tight integration with verification algorithms such as IC3 [10]. Particularly relevant for non-linear theories is the case of incremental linearization [9], where the abstract space is built by treating non-linearities as uninterpreted functions with piecewise-linear bounds.

Verification of Hybrid Systems. In the case of continuous time, the situation is significantly more complex. In fact, hybrid systems are composed of interacting discrete and continuous subsystems. Within the reference modeling framework of Hybrid Automata [1], two kinds of transitions exist: discrete transitions, where the system instantaneously switches from a discrete mode to the next, and continuous transitions, where time elapses while in one mode, with continuous variables evolve according to the specified laws. With respect to the case of transition systems, the semantics of hybrid automata comes with an implicit elapse of time, during which continuous variables evolve according to specific laws defined by differential equations, subject to invariants that must hold throughout the continuous transitions. The traditional approaches are based on an explicit enumeration of the modes and the analysis of the differential equations in the various modes. We focus on symbolic, logic-based approaches [12, 15, 18], where deductive methods are used to analyze the continuous dynamics.

In this setting, we can identify several interesting challenges.

Satisfiability Modulo Theories. At the level of SMT engines, a key problem is to provide efficient and effective theory solvers for non-linear theories, to be integrated within the standard online SMT search schema [3]. In addition to incrementality and the ability to construct theory lemmas, a fundamental requirement could be referred to as "non-constructive satisfiability", i.e. the ability to prove the satisfiability of a set of constraints without actually having to produce a model. Algorithms for incomplete theory reasoning, providing efficiently sufficient conditions for satisfiability or for unsatisfiability, would also be very useful.

Verification Modulo Theories. At the level of verification of transition systems over non-linear and transcendental theories, most techniques are oriented to prove universal properties, whereas existential properties have been devoted less attention. Non-constructive satisfiability would be an important tool in abstraction refinement, to prove the existence of infinite behaviours. In fact, traces can not be finitely presented in lasso-shape form as for the finite-state case.

Hybrid Automata. A key challenge is to integrate within the existing symbolic algorithms the large body of work on characterizing, checking, and finding differential invariants that has been developed in the setting of dynamical systems. Depending on the nature of the system (e.g. linear, non-linear polynomial, or featuring transcendental functions), different invariants could be found (e.g. polynomial equalities and inequalities).

In some cases, hybrid automata can be reduced to the analysis of infinite-state transition systems, so that the SMT-based approaches can be leveraged. Such precise encodings rely on the existence of a closed-form exact solution. Even in such subcases, an important challenge is to improve the quantifier-free encoding of invariant conditions [12].

Finally, it would be interesting to support the direct reasoning at the level of differential equations in the verification algorithm, in the style of [15], but to more advanced algorithms such as IC3. The requirement is to identify procedures for the checks of induction (and relative induction) under the differential equations.

References

1. Alur, R., Courcoubetis, C., Henzinger, T.A., Ho, P.H.: Hybrid automata: an algorithmic approach to the specification and verification of hybrid systems. In: Grossman, R.L., Nerode, A., Ravn, A.P., Rischel, H. (eds.) HS 1992, HS 1991. LNCS, vol. 736, pp. 209–229. Springer, Heidelberg (1993). https://doi.org/10.1007/3-540-57318-6_30
2. Audemard, G., Bozzano, M., Cimatti, A., Sebastiani, R.E.: Verifying industrial hybrid systems with MathSAT. Electron. Notes Theor. Comput. Sci. **119**(2), 17–32 (2005)
3. Barrett, C.W., Sebastiani, R., Seshia, S.A., Tinelli, C.: Satisfiability modulo theories. In: Handbook of Satisfiability, vol. 185. Frontiers in AI and Applications, pp. 825–885. IOS Press (2009)
4. Biere, A., Cimatti, A., Clarke, E., Zhu, Y.: Symbolic model checking without BDDs. In: Cleaveland, W.R. (eds.) TACAS 1999. LNCS. Vol. 1579, pp. 193–207. Springer, Heidelberg (1999). https://doi.org/10.1007/3-540-49059-0_14
5. Biere, A., Heule, M., van Maaren, H., Walsh, T. (eds.): Handbook of Satisfiability, vol. 185. Frontiers in AI and Applications. IOS Press (2009)
6. Bradley, A.R.: SAT-Based model checking without unrolling. In: Jhala, R., Schmidt, D. (eds.) VMCAI 2011. LNCS, vol. 6538, pp. 70–87. Springer, Heidelberg (2011). https://doi.org/10.1007/978-3-642-18275-4_7
7. Bryant, R.E.: Graph-based algorithms for Boolean function manipulation. IEEE Trans. Comput. 35(8), 677–691 (1986)
8. Burch, J., Clarke, E.M., McMillan, K.L., Dill, D.L., Hwang, L.J.: Symbolic model checking: $10^{\wedge}20$ states and beyond. Inf. Comput. **98**(2), 142–170 (1992)
9. Cimatti, A., Griggio, A., Irfan, A., Roveri, M., Sebastiani, R.: Incremental linearization for satisfiability and verification modulo nonlinear arithmetic and transcendental functions. ACM Trans. Comput. Log. **19**(3), 19:1–19:52 (2018)
10. Cimatti, A., Griggio, A., Mover, S., Tonetta, S.: Infinite-state invariant checking with IC3 and predicate abstraction. Formal Methods Syst. Des. **49**(3), 190–218 (2016). https://doi.org/10.1007/s10703-016-0257-4
11. Cimatti, A., Griggio, A., Tonetta, S. Verification modulo theories: language, benchmarks and tools (2011). http://vmt-lib.fbk.eu/
12. Alessandro Cimatti, Sergio Mover, and Stefano Tonetta. Quantifier-free encoding of invariants for hybrid systems. Formal Methods Syst. Des. **45**(2), 165–188, 2014.
13. Clarke, E.M., Grumberg, O., Jha, S., Lu, Y., Veith, H.. Counterexample-guided abstraction refinement for symbolic model checking. J. ACM, **50**(5), 752–794 (2003)
14. de Moura, L., Rueß, H., Sorea, M.: Lazy theorem proving for bounded model checking over infinite domains. In: Voronkov, A. (eds.) CADE 2002. LNCS, vol. 2392, pp. 438–455. Springer, Heidelberg (2002). https://doi.org/10.1007/3-540-45620-1_35
15. Eggers, A., Fränzle, M., Herde, C.: SAT modulo ODE: a direct SAT approach to hybrid systems. In: Cha, S.., Choi, J.Y., Kim, M., Lee, I., Viswanathan, M. (eds.) ATVA 2008. LNCS, vol. 5311, pp. 171–185. Springer, Heidelberg (2008). https://doi.org/10.1007/978-3-540-88387-6_14
16. Graf, S., Saidi, H.: Construction of abstract state graphs with PVS. In: Grumberg, O. (eds.) CAV 1997. LNCS, vol. 1254, pp. 72–83. Springer, Heidelberg (1997). https://doi.org/10.1007/3-540-63166-6_10
17. McMillan, K.L.: Interpolation and model checking. In: Clarke, E., Henzinger, T., Veith, H., Bloem, R. (eds.) Handbook of Model Checking, pp. 421–446. Springer, Cham (2018). https://doi.org/10.1007/978-3-319-10575-8_14

18. Platzer, A.: Logical Foundations of Cyber-Physical Systems. Springer, Cham (2018). https://doi.org/10.1007/978-3-319-63588-0

19. Sheeran, M., Singh, S., Stålmarck, G.: Checking safety properties using induction and a SAT-solver. In: Hunt, W.A., Johnson, S.D. (eds.) FMCAD 2000. LNCS, vol. 1954, pp. 108–125. Springer, Heidelberg (2000). https://doi.org/10.1007/3-540-40922-X_8

20. Tonetta, S.: Abstract Model checking without computing the abstraction. In: Cavalcanti, A., Dams, D.R. (eds.) FM 2009. LNCS, vol. 5850, pp. 89–105. Springer, Heidelberg (2009). https://doi.org/10.1007/978-3-642-05089-3_7

Induction in Saturation-Based Reasoning

Laura Kovács

TU Wien, Austria
laura.kovacs@tuwien.ac.at

Keywords: Automated reasoning · Theorem proving · Induction

Extended Abstract

Seminal works on automating induction mainly focus on inductive theorem proving [1, 2]: deciding when induction should be applied and what induction axiom should be used. Further restrictions are made on the logical expressiveness, for example induction over only universal properties [1, 13] and without uninterpreted symbols [10], or only over term algebras [5, 8]. Inductive proofs usually rely on auxiliary lemmas to help proving an inductive property. In [3] heuristics for finding such lemmas are introduced, for example by randomly generating equational formulas over random inputs and using these formulas if they hold reasonably often. Recent advances related to automating inductive reasoning, such as first-order reasoning with inductively defined data types [9], inductive strengthening of SMT properties [12], structural induction in superposition [4, 5, 6, 8, 11], open up new possibilities for automating induction. In this talk, we describe our extensions to first-order theorem proving in support of automating inductive reasoning.

It is common in inductive theorem proving, that given a formula/goal F, try to prove a more general goal instead [1, 2]. Such an approach however does not apply in the context of saturation-based first-order theorem proving, which is not based on a goal-subgoal architecture. In our work we therefore integrate induction directly into saturation-based proof search. We do so by turning applications of induction into inference rules of the saturation process and adding instances of appropriate induction schemata. To this extent, we pick up a formula F in the search space and add to the search space new induction axioms, that is instances of induction schemata, aiming at proving $\neg F$, or sometimes even a more general formula than $\neg F$. Our recent works [6, 7] investigated such an approach, introducing new inference rules for induction in saturation-based first-order theorem proving.

Our inference rules for induction in saturation capture the application of induction to inductive formulas to be proved. However, this is insufficient for efficient theorem proving. Modern saturation-based theorem provers are very powerful not just because of the logical calculi they are based on, such as superposition. What makes them powerful and efficient are (i) redundancy criteria and pruning search space, (ii) strategies for directing proof search, mainly by clause and inference selection, and recent results on (iii) theory-specific reasoning, for example with inductive data types. We overview our results in mechanizing mathematical induction in saturation-based first-order theorem proving in an efficient way. In particular we describe induction in saturation by generalizing inductive formulas [6] with/without recursive functions and integers [7].

Acknowledgements. The results described in this talk are based on joint works with Márton Hajdú, Petra Hozzvá, Johannes Schoisswohl and Andrei Voronkov. We acknowledge funding from the ERC CoG ARTIST 101002685, the ERC StG 2014 SYMCAR 639270, the EPSRC grant EP/P03408X/1 and the Austrian FWF research project LogiCS W1255-N23.

References

1. Boyer, R.S., Moore, J.S.: A Computational Logic Handbook, Perspectives in Computing, vol. 23. Academic Press (1979)

2. Bundy, A., Stevens, A., van Harmelen, F., Ireland, A., Smaill, A.: Rippling: a heuristic for guiding inductive proofs. Artif. Intell. **62**(2), 185–253 (1993)

3. Claessen, K., Johansson, M., Rosén, D., Smallbone, N.: HipSpec: automating inductive proofs of program properties. In: Proceedings of the ATx/WinG, pp. 16–25 (2012)

4. Cruanes, S.: Superposition with structural induction. In: Dixon, C., Finger, M., (eds.) FroCoS 2017. LNCS, vol. 10483, pp. 172-188. Springer, Cham (2017). https://doi.org/10.1007/978-3-319-66167-4_10

5. Echenheim, M., Peltier, N.: Combining induction and saturation-based theorem proving. J. Autom. Reason. 64, 253–294 (2020). https://doi.org/10.1007/s10817-019-09519-x

6. Hajdú M., Hozzová, P., Kovács, L., Schoisswohl, J., Voronkov, A.: Induction with generalization in superposition reasoning. In: Benzmüller, C., Miller, B. (eds.) CICM 2020. LNCS, vol 12236, pp. 123–137. Springer, Cham (2020). https://doi.org/10.1007/978-3-030-53518-6_8

7. Hozzová, P., Kovács, L., Voronkov, A.: Integer induction in saturation. In: Proceedings of the CADE (2021, to appear)

8. Kersani, A., Peltier, N.: Combining superposition and induction: a practical realization. In: Fontaine, P., Ringeissen, C., Schmidt, R.A. (eds.) FroCoS 2013. LNCS, vol. 8152, pp. 7–22. Springer, Heidelberg (2013). https://doi.org/10.1007/978-3-642-40885-4_2

9. Kovács, L., Robillard, S., Voronkov, A.: Coming to terms with quantified reasoning. In: Proceedings of the POPL. pp. 260–270 (2017)

10. Passmore, G., et al.: The Imandra automated reasoning system (system description). In: Peltier, N., Sofronie-Stokkermans, V. (eds.) IJCAR 2020. LNCS, vol. 12167, pp. 464–471. Springer, Cham (2020). https://doi.org/10.1007/978-3-030-51054-1_30

11. Reger, G., Voronkov, A.: Induction in saturation-based proof search. In: Fontaine, P., (eds.) CADE 2019. LNCS, vol. 11716, pp. 477–494. Springer, Cham (2019). https://doi.org/10.1007/978-3-030-29436-6_28

12. Reynolds, A., Kuncak, V.: Induction for SMT solvers. In: D'Souza, D., Lal, A., Larsen, K.G. (eds.) VMCAI 2015. LNCS, vol. 8931, pp. 80–98. Springer, Heidelberg (2015). https://doi.org/10.1007/978-3-662-46081-8_5

13. Sonnex, W., Drossopoulou, S., Eisenbach, S.: Zeno: an automated prover for properties of recursive data structures. In: Flanagan, C., König, B. (eds.) TACAS 2012. LNCS, vol. 7214, pp. 407–421. Springer, Heidelberg (2012). https://doi.org/10.1007/978-3-642-28756-5_28

Doing Number Theory in Weak Systems
of Arithmetic

Angus Macintyre

University of Edinburgh
a.macintyre@qmul.ac.uk

Abstract. Although Godel's Theorem shows that even ZFC is incomplete for unsolvability of diophantine equations, nothing explicit of any real interest to number theorists has ever been shown to be unprovable. I will consider various important statements about solvability modulo all prime powers, and exhibit a wide class which get decided by PA (first order Peano Arithmetic) using serious algebraic geometry inside nonstandard models of PA. So although PA is often misrepresented as very weak, it is rather strong for basic results of 20th century number theory.

Keywords: Number theory · Weak arithmetic

Contents

Search and Classification

Teaching and Geometric Reasoning

Logic and Systems

Formalizations

A Modular First Formalisation
of Combinatorial Design Theory

Chelsea Edmonds[(✉)] and Lawrence C. Paulson

Department of Computer Science and Technology, University of Cambridge,
Cambridge, UK
{cle47,lp15}@cam.ac.uk

Abstract. Combinatorial design theory studies set systems with certain balance and symmetry properties and has applications to computer science and elsewhere. This paper presents a modular approach to formalising designs for the first time using Isabelle and assesses the usability of a locale-centric approach to formalisations of mathematical structures. We demonstrate how locales can be used to specify numerous types of designs and their hierarchy. The resulting library, which is concise and adaptable, includes formal definitions and proofs for many key properties, operations, and theorems on the construction and existence of designs.

Keywords: Isabelle/HOL · Combinatorics · Formalisation · Interactive proof assistants · Combinatorial design theory · Block designs · Locales

1 Introduction

The formalisation of mathematics is an area of increasing interest, with benefits including verifying correctness, deeper insights into proofs, and automation. This has lead to substantial development of formal mathematical libraries across several different proof assistants covering a notable portion of undergraduate mathematics. However, one area of mathematics that remains underrepresented is combinatorics. In particular, the field of combinatorial design theory has not previously been formalised in any system.

Combinatorial design theory is the study of systems of finite sets which meet certain balance and symmetry properties. Many results in design theory have been driven by applications to fields such as communications and security, where formal verification is of increasing interest. This paper presents a general formal library for design theory using a modular approach in Isabelle/HOL.

Locales are Isabelle's module system, and are well suited to the problem of managing the complex hierarchy of design classes. While locales have been

The first author is supported by a Cambridge Australia Scholarship and a Cambridge Department of Technology Qualcomm Premium Research Scholarship. The work is also supported by the ERC Advanced Grant ALEXANDRIA (Project GA 742178).

F. Kamareddine and C. Sacerdoti Coen (Eds.): CICM 2021, LNAI 12833, pp. 3–18, 2021.
https://doi.org/10.1007/978-3-030-81097-9_1

available in the current form since the early 2000s, they typically have been used sparingly in mathematical contexts, or alongside other tools such as type classes and records. This project presented the opportunity to explore a locale-centric approach to formalising mathematical structures, building on Ballarin's prior work in algebra [3], and using ideas from Noschinski's graph theory library [13].

We focus on balanced and block designs to define BIBDs, the most extensively studied class of designs, but also explore how easy it is to extend the formalisation to other design classes and graph theory. Our library includes the formal definitions for many key properties and operations on designs generally. It also explores the formal proof process for theorems on the construction and existence of designs with certain parameters, two basic questions in design theory.

This paper begins with (2) the necessary background on design theory and locales, then presents (3) the formalisation of fundamental concepts on designs, followed by (4) the development of the BIBD locale hierarchy and (5) extending the formalisation beyond BIBDs. We conclude (6) with a discussion on the locale-centric approach to formalising mathematical structures.

2   Background

2.1   Mathematical Background

Designs are one of many different combinatorial structures which have emerged in the last century. Formally, a design is defined as follows [16]:

Definition 1 (Design). *A design is a pair (V, B) where V is a (finite) set of points and B is a (finite) collection of non-empty subsets of V called* blocks.

Designs are also referred to as *incidence structures* [5] and more specifically, *incidence set systems*. There are four sets defined on key set system properties which can be restricted to impose structural conditions on a design [8].

i) The set K of all block sizes in the design.
ii) The set R of replication numbers for points in the design, where the *point replication number* r_x is the number of blocks the point x occurs in.
iii) The set Λ_t of t-indices for $t \geq 0$ the design. For any t subset of points, the *t points index* is the number of blocks that subset occurs in.
iv) The set I of intersection numbers. For two blocks in a design, the *intersection number* is the number of points the blocks intersect on.

Using different structural restrictions results in numerous classes of designs. The designs of most interest mathematically usually involve the combination of several restrictions, such as *balanced incomplete block designs (BIBD)*.

Definition 2 (BIBD). *Let v, k, and λ, be positive integers such that $2 \leq k < v$. A (v, k, λ)-design is a design with v points where every block has k elements and where every pair of points occurs in exactly λ blocks.*

The balance and uniformity properties of a BIBD, as well as properties like resolvability and symmetry, lead to further design variations such as group divisible designs (GDDs), pairwise balanced designs (PBDs), triple systems, and resolvable designs [8].

Most open questions in design theory concern either the existence of a design with certain parameters or the construction of certain designs for which existence is already known [16]. Numerous operations have been defined to reason on the construction of designs, several of which this paper explores. Proofs in design theory often draw on other fields of mathematics, and combinatorial counting techniques, which present interesting formalisation challenges.

Set systems are the underlying construct of a design, and are the basis for numerous other structures such as hypergraphs, matrices, geometries, codes, and graphs [8]. As such, designs have close links to these fields, and they are often used in proofs on designs. For example, it can be seen that an undirected simple graph is a design, where the vertices are points and edges are 2-blocks. The design of a graph is normally not interesting from a design theoretic standpoint, as it often lacks the structure of many design classes. However, a r-regular graph can be thought of as a design with replication number r. Graphs are also useful for representing other design properties such as resolvability [6].

2.2 Isabelle and Locales

Isabelle/HOL is an interactive proof assistant built on higher order logic [14]. It has extensive libraries of formalised mathematics, including the largest number of results related to combinatorics from a survey of several proof assistants. These libraries, combined with powerful built-in tools such as the Isar proof language and Sledgehammer, make Isabelle an ideal choice for this formalisation work.

Locales are an important extension of the Isar proof language. They act as a module system within Isabelle, providing persistent contexts which can be used across numerous theories drawing on similar structures [1]. In the simplest form, a locale declaration introduces parameters and assumptions. Each parameter has a specified type and can even have associated syntax. Once defined, a locale can be extended with definitions, notation and theorems within its context.

Locale expressions were designed to support multiple inheritance and thus offer extensive flexibility. Existing locales can be combined to create a new locale and extended by adding new parameters and assumptions [1]. The locale hierarchy can be transformed using the **sublocale** command, which is used to show indirect inheritance between two separately specified locales. It is also possible to instantiate locale parameters and instances through locale expressions and interpretations. A full tutorial introduction on locales is available with Isabelle [2].

3 The Basic Design Formalisation

Formalising design theory presents a number of initial challenges. Of particular note is (i) notation and definition inconsistencies in the literature, (ii) the significant number of definitions and properties, and (iii) the complex relations between different classes of designs, as well as other combinatorial structures.

To narrow the focus of the formalisation, addressing (ii), initial formalisation efforts focussed on defining BIBDs and operations commonly found in computational libraries for designs such as GAP [15]. Proofs focused on enabling reasoning on common design properties, constructions, and existence requirements.

To address (i), key decisions were made early in the formalisation process covered below and in Sect. 4. For consistency, the Handbook of Combinatorial Designs was the primary reference for definitions, with publications from well known researchers such as Stinson [16] serving as alternatives when needed. Challenge (iii) is the motivation for our locale-centric approach to formalising fundamental definitions and operations for general designs, discussed below.

3.1   Pre-designs

First, a locale representing a general incidence system is defined, which introduces the core components of a design: a block collection formalised using multisets, a point set, and a well-formed assumption:

> **locale** incidence-system =
> **fixes** point-set :: $'a$ set $(\mathcal{V})$ **and** block-collection :: $'a$ set multiset $(\mathcal{B})$
> **assumes** wellformed: b $\in\# \mathcal{B} \Longrightarrow$ b $\subseteq \mathcal{V}$

Definition 1 (see Sect. 2.1) states designs are finite, which is added as an assumption in the *finite-incidence-system* locale. Lastly, a design often has the additional condition that blocks must be non-empty [16]:

> **locale** design = finite-incidence-system +
> **assumes** blocks-nempty: bl $\in\# \mathcal{B} \Longrightarrow$ bl $\neq \{\}$

Some design definitions further impose the condition that a design must be non-empty [15]. This is important for some classes of designs, but constrains others unnecessarily, and hence is defined separately in the locale *proper-designs*.

3.2   Basic Design Properties

The four key properties on elements of a set system are block size, intersection numbers, point indices, and replication numbers. These are defined outside of a locale context, as they are properties on components of the set system, rather than the entire structure. The definition of the points index property is below:

> **definition** points-index :: $'a$ set multiset $\Rightarrow$ $'a$ set $\Rightarrow$ nat **where**
> points-index B ps $\equiv$ size $\{\#b \in\# B \ . \ ps \subseteq b\#\}$

Numerous lemmas for reasoning on these properties can be defined in the context of incidence systems and designs. Using these properties, the four key sets outlined in (2) can be defined within the general *incidence_system* locale. The definition of the point indices set is given below:

definition point-indices :: int $\Rightarrow$ int set **where**
point-indices t $\equiv$ { points-index $\mathcal{B}$ ps | ps. int (card ps) = t $\wedge$ ps $\subseteq$ $\mathcal{V}$}

Lastly, the basic design locale includes a number of abbreviations to mirror terminology in the literature: design supports, multiplicity of blocks, incomplete blocks, design order v (number of points), and design size b (number of blocks). The multiplicity and design support abbreviations are used to establish a new locale for *simple-designs*, where block multiplicity is at most 1.

3.3 Basic Design Operations

Designs are often constructed by building on pre-existing designs through operations. The three main operations considered for the formalisation are design complements, multiples, and combinations. The *complement* of a design (V, B) is the design $(V, \{V - bl.bl \in B\})$, where $V - bl$ is the *block complement* of the block bl. A *multiple* of a design multiplies the block multiset by some constant $n \geq 0$, and *combining* designs is simply the union of the point set and addition of the block multisets. The formal definitions for these operations are defined within the incidence system locale, such as the complement operation below, along with a number of relevant lemmas.

definition complement-blocks :: ′a set multiset **where**
complement-blocks $\equiv$ {# block-complement bl . bl $\in\#$ $\mathcal{B}$ #}

Numerous basic lemmas are shown for all three operations. In particular, *multiple* and *combine* are shown to be closed under the design conditions, and *complement* will result in a design if the original blocks are incomplete. We additionally formalised a number of simple computational operations, such as addition and deletion of points, which are useful when constructing new designs.

4 The Block Design Hierarchy

By Definition 2, a BIBD could be easily defined in a single locale with parameters for block size, index, and replication number, as well as assumptions on balance, constant replication, and uniformity conditions. However, this approach would have significant limitations. Although a replication number is widely used in proofs of a BIBD, its value is implied by the other parameters, hence the assumption is unnecessary. Additionally, this could result in a significant amount of rework if more general designs than BIBDs need to be formalised.

The approach taken in this formalisation uses the idea of little and tiny theories [7,9], discussed in Sect. 6. Each locale definition adds a single concept, and lemmas on properties and operations are introduced in the most general locale possible. This section explores the process of building up the locale hierarchy to BIBDs through the gradual specification of more general locales.

4.1   Restricting Block Size

The first new parameter in a BIBD is k, the uniform size of a design's blocks. Formally, it is introduced through the block design locale:

> **locale** block-design = proper-design +
> **fixes** u-block-size :: int (k)
> **assumes** uniform [simp]: bl $\in\# \mathcal{B} \implies$ block-size bl = k

A key design decision was to let uniform parameters such as block size be integers. While these are clearly positive and could be natural numbers, proofs often require manipulating algebraic expressions involving subtraction on the parameters, which is notably simpler to do using integers in Isabelle.

A number of lemmas are defined within the *block_design* locale. Recurring themes on proofs throughout the formalisation include proving inequality relationships on parameters, such as $k \leq v$, and that the three main operations defined in (3.3) result in another type of this design given certain conditions. For a block design, *multiple* and *combine* are clearly closed, whereas *complement* requires an additional assumption. Two main proof strategies are used for these lemmas: a direct proof using introduction rules, and the more expressive **interpret** proof structure, discussed in Sect. 6.4.

A *K-design* is a generalisation of a k-design which limits the size of blocks to a finite set of positive integers. An important specialisation of a block design is an *incomplete design* where all blocks are incomplete, i.e. $k < v$.

4.2   Balanced Designs

The balance property and its variations are widely used across different design classes. The most general balanced design is a t-wise balanced design or tBD, where for some $1 \leq t \leq v$, the points index of a t-sized subset of points equals λ_t.

> **locale** twise-balance = proper-design +
> **fixes** grouping :: int (t) **and** index :: int (Λ_t)
> **assumes** t-non-zero: t $\geq$ 1 **and** t-lt-order: t $\leq$ v
> **and** balanced [simp]: ps $\subseteq \mathcal{V} \implies$ card ps = t $\implies$ points-index $\mathcal{B}$ ps = Λ_t

Note that as λ is reserved in Isabelle, Λ is used in its place. Also, as the parameters t and λ_t and their assumptions are linked, there is no sensible way to further break down the locale. Within the locale context it can easily be shown that combining two designs with the same point set, or applying the multiple operation, results in another tBD. A t-wise balanced design can include a set K of valid block sizes, which is formalised by combining the tBD and K block design locales.

BIBDs are interested in pairwise balance, where $t = 2$. A PBD is a clear specialisation of a tBD which can be defined formally using the *for* command in a locale definition to instantiate one parameter and simplify syntax.

> **locale** pairwise-balance = t-wise-balance $\mathcal{V} \mathcal{B}$ 2 Λ
> **for** point-set ($\mathcal{V}$) **and** block-collection ($\mathcal{B}$) **and** index (Λ)

There are several variations on PBDs in the literature depending on block size properties and the value of λ, which are easy to specify by combining locales and the use of the sublocale declaration, following the functor proof pattern [3].

4.3   T-Designs

An important generalisation of BIBDs are t-designs. Given the modular structure of the existing locale declarations, they can be easily specified by combining locales on incomplete block designs and t-wise balanced designs. Additionally, an extra assumption is required on the relationship of the parameters t and k.

> **locale** tdesign = incomplete-design + t-wise-balance +
> **assumes** block-size-t: t ≤ k

In addition to t-designs, the related concepts of t-covering and t-packing designs are also formalised, where λ_t has a slightly different meaning, a typical example of design notation inconsistencies. A t-covering design is a relaxed version of a tBD where, for all point subsets of size t, λ_t is a lower bound on the points index. A t-packing design mirrors this with an upper bound. Given the different meaning of the parameter λ_t, these designs build only on block designs. If a design is incomplete, t-packing and t-covering, then it is a t-design.

Additionally, a locale is declared for *Steiner systems*: t-designs where $\lambda_t = 1$. Then it can be proven that all blocks in a Steiner system have a multiplicity of 1. Hence it can be shown that Steiner systems are simple designs using sublocales.

4.4   Uniform Replication Number

When every point in a design has the same replication number, r is known as the replication number of the design.

> **locale** constant-rep-design = proper-design +
> **fixes** design-rep-number :: int (r)
> **assumes** rep-number [simp]: x ∈ $\mathcal{V}$ ⟹ $\mathcal{B}$ rep x = r

As with the other locales, we can prove that $r > 0$, and that the complement, multiple, and combination operators result in another constant replication design under certain conditions within the locale's context.

4.5   BIBDs and Proofs

The final BIBD locale declaration builds on the t-design locale and is now simple to define using the **for** command to instantiate $t = 2$, as with PBDs.

> **locale** bibd = t-design $\mathcal{V}$ $\mathcal{B}$ k 2 Λ **for** point-set ($\mathcal{V}$) **and** block-collection ($\mathcal{B}$)
> **and** u-block-size (k) **and** index (Λ)

Figure 1 gives an overview of the final locale hierarchy for BIBDs, with sublocale relationships represented by a dotted line. Using this structure, we used

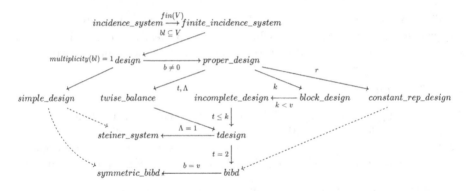

Fig. 1. The BIBD locale hierarchy

BIBDs as case study for doing more involved proofs on both existence and construction. Many of these proofs required formalising a counting proof, the full details of which are out of scope of this paper.

There are two necessary conditions on BIBD existence, which therefore must hold in the locale context. These define important relationships between parameters: $r(k-1) = \lambda(v-1)$ and $vr = bk$. Notably, this uses the design replication number, which is not yet defined in the BIBD context. However, the first condition can still be shown to hold for each point's replication number r_x, which in turn proves r is constant. This results in the following sublocale declaration.

sublocale bibd ⊆ constant-rep-design $\mathcal{V}$ $\mathcal{B}$ $(\Lambda * (v-1)$ div $(k-1))$
  using r-constant-2 **by** (unfold-locales) simp-all

These necessary conditions enable proofs of useful lemmas on inequalities between parameters, and set up the formalisation for further construction proofs.

As with previous locales, it is simple to prove the combination and multiple operations result in another BIBD with simply defined parameters assuming equal point sets. The complement of a (v, k, λ)-design is a $(v, v-k, b+\lambda-2r)$-design. These parameters are more complicated and so are their proofs. The final proof for the main *complement-bibd* lemma is a good example of how constructive design proofs can be presented with little effort using interpretation and the Isar proof language (see Sect. 6).

4.6   BIBD Extensions

Symmetric BIBDs are an extension of BIBDs where $b = v$, as shown in Fig. 1. An important theorem on symmetric designs is the *intersection property*: the intersection number of any two blocks in the design is equal to the design index λ. We have formalised its delicate counting proof, making use of the necessary conditions on a BIBD.

The BIBD locale also includes definitions and lemmas on residual and derived designs, which are common constructions specific to BIBDs. The formal definitions of these operations resolve some ambiguities in the literature which use set comprehensions and notation to describe operations on multisets. Using the intersection property, it is possible to prove that the derived and residual designs of a symmetric BIBD are also BIBDs. The intersection property and sublocale command can also be used to show that symmetric designs are simple.

5 Extending the Formalisation

This section investigates the ease of extending the formalisation to a number of other structures in design theory and graph theory.

5.1 Resolvable Designs

A *resolution class* of a design is a partition of the point set using blocks. A partition of the blocks into resolution classes is known as a *resolution*, and a design with a resolution is *resolvable*. While set partitions are well covered in Isabelle, we had to formalise multiset partitions. The concepts of a resolution class and resolution were then easily defined within *incidence-system*. A resolvable design is represented by a new locale building on designs:

locale resolvable-design = design +
    fixes partition :: 'a set multiset multiset $(\mathcal{P})$
    assumes resolvable: resolution $\mathcal{P}$

Further classes of resolvable designs were defined by combining this locale with block designs and BIBDs. The resolvable specification enables us to prove a number of new relations between the parameters of these designs, such as $k|v$ in a resolvable block design. A proof was also completed for an alternate statement of Bose's inequality on resolvable BIBDs based on Stinson's approach [16].

5.2 Group Divisible Designs

GDDs are closely related to PBDs and are often studied simultaneously. As such, they were an ideal case study for extending the BIBD hierarchy. A GDD is a design which has a non-empty group G which partitions the point set, and a points index of λ or 0 for each pair depending on if points occurs together in G.

Continuing with the little theories approach, the definition is split into two locales. Firstly, a *group-design* locale is declared, which introduces the parameter G and the partition assumption. Within this locale a number of properties of the group in GDDs are defined. sThis includes the concept of group types, which represent a GDDs structure by the size of the sets in G. A GDD locale then introduces the index parameter and assumptions:

locale GDD = group-design + **fixes** index :: int $(\varLambda)$
    assumes index-ge-1 : $\varLambda \geq 1$
    assumes index-together: $[\![G \in \mathcal{G}; \ x \in G; \ y \in G; \ x \neq y \ ]\!] \implies$ points-index $\mathcal{B} \ \{x, y\} = 0$ **and** index-distinct: $[\![G1 \in \mathcal{G}; \ G2 \in \mathcal{G}; \ G1 \neq G2; \ x \in G1; \ y \in G2]\!] \implies$ points-index $\mathcal{B} \ \{x, y\} = \varLambda$

As with PBDs, GDDs are defined in different ways, commonly combined with K block designs, or certain instantiated parameters, which can easily be formalised using locales. Operations such as adding and deleting points, or combining the group sets and blocks are common on both PBDs and GDDs. For example, combining the group of a K-GDD with its blocks results in a PBD with the same point set, a block collection containing both groups and blocks of the original GDD, and a size set K. Authors often use these constructions without proofs and lacking necessary assumptions.

5.3   Design Isomorphisms

Two designs (V, B) and (V', B') are *isomorphic* if there exists a bijection π such that $V' = \pi(V)$ and $B' = \{\pi(bl).bl \in B'\}$. There are two obvious ways of formalising this relation: through a number of definitions, or through another locale. The second approach enables direct and concise reasoning on an isomorphism relation by using two labelled instances of the same locale:

> **locale** incidence-system-isomorphism = source: incidence-system $\mathcal{V}$ $\mathcal{B}$ + target: incidence-system $\mathcal{V}'$ $\mathcal{B}'$ **for** $\mathcal{V}$ **and** $\mathcal{B}$ **and** $\mathcal{V}'$ **and** $\mathcal{B}'$ + **fixes** bij-map (π)
> **assumes** bij: bij-betw π $\mathcal{V}$ $\mathcal{V}'$ **and** block-img: image-mset (('') π) $\mathcal{B} = \mathcal{B}'$

Within the locale, it is easy to show how elements in (V, B) map to (V', B'), and that π^{-1} also defines an isomorphic relation. Furthermore, by extending the locale to design instances, the four key properties on set systems are proven to be identical for isomorphic designs. Even with a locale approach, it is still easy to work with isomorphisms outside of the locale if required: below, we define the concept of isomorphic designs on set systems using the locale definition.

> **definition** isomorphic-designs (**infixl** $\cong_D$ 50) **where** $\mathcal{D} \cong_D \mathcal{D}' \longleftrightarrow$
> ($\exists$ π . design-isomorphism (points $\mathcal{D}$) (blocks $\mathcal{D}$) (points $\mathcal{D}'$) (blocks $\mathcal{D}'$) π)

5.4   Graph Theory

Graph theory proves an interesting case study when looking at extending the design hierarchy. As discussed in Sect. 2, simple graphs are designs. Can we link the design locale hierarchy to an existing formalisation, such as the general graph theory library in the AFP? This appears to present a number of challenges: (i) the graph theory library was developed in 2013 by a different author, (ii) the library includes digraphs, which are not designs, and (iii) the locale approach for graph theory uses records, which are not used for designs.

Despite these challenges, the flexibility of locales made it straightforward to prove that a simple graph is a design, as well as a number of other properties. Figure 2 shows the resulting links made between the design theory and graph theory locale developments, using sublocales.

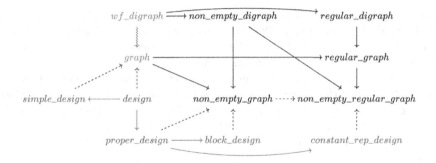

Fig. 2. Interaction between graph and design locales

To show that a graph is a design, we must convert the ordered edge representation to an unordered block. The *arcs-blocks* definition manages the transformation within the *graph* locale, which defines a simple graph by declaring the edge set to be symmetric without multiples or loops. A few lemmas ensure the translation is valid, from which it follows that a graph is a sublocale of a design.

sublocale graph $\subseteq$ design verts G arcs-blocks

Clearly, a non-empty graph is also a block design with $k = 2$, which is represented by another sublocale relationship. Additionally, we extended the existing graph theory library to define the concept of a *regular-digraph* and *regular graph*, which are of particular interest in design theory. In particular, a non-empty regular graph is a sublocale of a constant representation number design.

sublocale non-empty-reg-graph$\subseteq$constant-rep-design verts G arcs-blocks r

6   The Modular Approach

This paper has thus far demonstrated how locales can be used to build up an extensive hierarchy to formally reason on designs. This section discusses the benefits and limitations of the approach taken and recurring reasoning techniques.

6.1   The Formal Design Hierarchy

This paper presents seemingly the first formalisation of design theory. As such, initial investigations focused on examining the approach taken by similar libraries on mathematical structures. There does exist a formalisation of Latin squares [4] in Isabelle. While these are a very specific type of design, their formalisation does not reflect this and is not extendable to designs generally. Rather, it highlights the need for flexibility when defining different design classes.

Type classes [10] were briefly considered, however the constraints on parameters meant they didn't offer the same flexibility as locales. The "record + locale" approach first considered in (3.1) is based on Noschinski's graph theory library and the HOL-Algebra library. This approach uses a record to define structural elements and definitions, and locales for supporting concise syntax by parameter annotation [3]. It was originally designed when definitions could not be declared within a locale and is still widely used. Changes to locales in 2009 [11] however, enabled local theory specification, so definitions are now possible within a local context while still globally accessible. As such, structures can now be defined over a number of parameters within a locale without any noticeable limitations. This reduces the need for records and the required workarounds, while also simplifying notation and definitions for the structure.

The small AFP development on matroids, another combinatorial structure, uses this more locale-centric approach [12], but more interesting is Ballarin's take to formalising algebra [3]. He uses locales to define structures as well as operations and relationships on multiple instances of a locale, similar to the design isomorphism definition.

The final locale hierarchy of the design library can be seen in Fig. 3, with some minor omissions. Figure 3 presents the numerous types of designs available in the formalisation and the complex inheritance network. The final formalisation defines 36 purely design related locales, as well as five new locales on graph theory. The larger graph theory library used only 21 locales.

6.2   The Little Theories Approach

Using the little theories approach, and drawing on ideas from the more radical tiny theories approach where suitable, each new locale declaration in the design library does some of three things: (i) combines multiple pre-existing locales, (ii) adds new parameters and assumptions related to a single new concept, or (iii) instantiates one or more parameters to a concrete value.

This approach drew inspiration from both Noschinski and Ballarin [3,13], and yielded a number of benefits, preventing unnecessary duplication when new

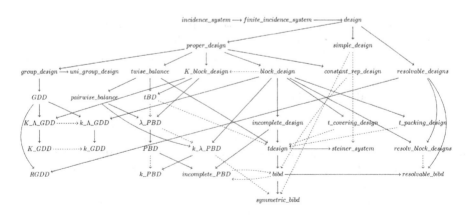

Fig. 3. Design theory locale development

designs were introduced. More importantly, it increased the flexibility and extensibility of the library. As can be seen from the case studies in Sect. 5 where the formalisation was extended, it was easy to integrate locales from the original hierarchy with new concepts. The sublocale command proved particularly useful in manipulating the hierarchy. Additionally, each extension took significantly less time than the original development due to the inherited material.

6.3 Notational Benefits

One of the key benefits that Ballarin discussed when comparing the locale-centric algebra approach with the existing library was notation, and its readability in comparison to a textbook [3]. The locale-centric approach yields similar results for design theory. For example, in mathematical literature, a t-design is referred to as a t-(v, k, λ_t)-*design*. In Isabelle, it would be represented by t-*design* V B k Λ_t, where v can still be used to refer to the cardinality of V.

In fact, all the usual single letter parameters are available with a design context, and definitions were done in locales where possible, thus the majority are simple and readable as is. The **for** command further increased readability by removing unnecessary parameters from specialisations. Overall, this results in concise notation both within a locale context and on instances of a locale, which should be readable for anyone familiar with design theory. Such notation also simplifies lemma statements, avoiding repeated assumptions, as well as proof goals. We expect that further extensions to different structures such as hypergraphs could benefit from locale notation features such as **rewrites**.

6.4 Reasoning on Locales

The flexibility of locales offers many benefits for reasoning. However, it is worth noting a number of proof patterns specific to working with locale definitions.

Locales come with two proof tactics: *unfold-locales*, which unfolds all the assumptions in the current context hierarchy, and *intro-locales*, which unfolds to the axiomatic definitions of each locale in the current hierarchy. The *intro-locales* tactic was often used on proofs on the combine and multiple operations, which avoided the need to unfold all axioms for each proof.

Interpretations are likely the most powerful proof tool for locales, and can decrease the complexity of proofs by providing an instance of a locale to refer to. The *complement-bibd* lemma described in (4.5) is an example.

lemma complement-bibd:
  assumes k ≤ v − 2
  shows bibd $\mathcal{V}$ (complement-blocks) (v − k) (b + Λ − 2 ∗ r)
proof −
  interpret des: incomplete-design $\mathcal{V}$ (complement-blocks) (v − k)
    using assms complement-incomplete **by** blast
  show ?thesis **proof** (unfold-locales, simp-all)
    show 2 ≤ des.v **using** assms block-size-t **by** linarith
    show $\bigwedge$ps. ps ⊆ $\mathcal{V}$ ⟹ card ps = 2 ⟹
    points-index (complement-blocks) ps = b + Λ −
    2 ∗ (Λ ∗ (des.v − 1) div (k − 1)) **using** complement-bibd-index **by** simp
    show 2 ≤ des.v − k **using** assms block-size-t **by** linarith
  qed

The **interpret** command yields an instance of an incomplete-design with the complement parameters. To prove the conclusion, after applying *unfold-locales* and simplification, we get three sub-goals instead of the 10 *unfold-locales* gives without interpretation. This is both easy to approach and read.

Another useful pattern that assists automation is defining custom introduction rules, particularly around reverse sublocale relationships. For example, an introduction rule can be proven stating that parameters which satisfy the axioms of *t*-covering and *t*-packing designs also satisfy the *t*-design axioms. Ballarin's functor pattern [3], which connects two linear locale hierarchies related by a functor using a series of sublocale declarations, is also used in the formalisation. An example of this can be seen from the GDD variations in Fig. 3.

Lastly, we also note the ease of reasoning on multiple labelled instances of a locale, within another locale. The prime example of this is in the *design-isomorphism* theory. This is a technique that could be explored further for other operations and relationships, such as the concept of *sub-designs*.

6.5   Limitations

A few limitations of the locale-centric approach to mathematics are worth noting. First, locale specifications were not designed to be used extensively outside of the locale. However, the approach requires this, which particularly causes issues with sublocales. A sublocale proof does not generate any additional facts, and as such cannot be referenced; to reference this relationship for reasoning outside of the locale, one must define a separate lemma with a nearly identical proof.

While the **interpret** command within proofs is incredibly useful, it would be beneficial to see extensions to locale proof tactics to aid automation and proof structure. Many **interpret** declarations are trivial consequences of known facts, but they must be written out in full.

Lastly, the little theories approach can cause locale hierarchies to become complex. We need ways to keep track of relationships between locales during development. In particular, sublocale relationships must be maintained and added carefully when frequently combining locales at different levels in the hierarchy.

7   Conclusion and Future Work

Through the use of locales, this paper demonstrates how the complex hierarchy of design theoretic structures can be formalised in a proof assistant, presenting the first such formalisation for this field. It is intended that this library will be used to further explore some of the unique challenges combinatorial proofs currently pose to formalisation. The locale-centric modular approach discussed has proven to be an effective method of concisely and accurately defining numerous fundamental properties and classes of designs, and reasoning on key theorems and inheritance relationships. Additionally, the case studies presented in Sect. 5 demonstrates the formalisation's flexibility and extensibility for future work on design theory and other related combinatorial structures, fulfilling the aim of establishing a general adaptable library for designs. This library will be made available in full through the Isabelle Archive of Formal Proofs. Beyond the obvious potential to continue formalising new classes of designs, other future work includes further exploring locale-centric proof techniques and improvements, experimenting with links to hypergraphs, and investigating the formalisation of theorems on designs which involve more advanced and varied proof techniques.

References

1. Ballarin, C.: Locales and locale expressions in Isabelle/Isar. In: Berardi, S., Coppo, M., Damiani, F. (eds.) TYPES 2003. LNCS, vol. 3085, pp. 34–50. Springer, Heidelberg (2004). https://doi.org/10.1007/978-3-540-24849-1_3
2. Ballarin, C.: Tutorial to locales and locale interpretation. In: Contribuciones Científicas en Honor de Mirian Andrés Gómez, pp. 123–140. University of Rioja (2010). https://dialnet.unirioja.es/servlet/articulo?codigo=3216664
3. Ballarin, C.: Exploring the structure of an algebra text with locales. J. Autom. Reason. **64**(6), 1093–1121 (2020)
4. Bentkamp, A.: Latin square. Isabelle Archive of Formal Proofs (Dec 2015). http://isa-afp.org/entries/Latin_Square.html
5. Beth, T., Jungnickel, D., Lenz, H.: Design Theory, Encyclopedia of Mathematics and Its Applications, vol. 1, 2nd edn. Cambridge University Press, Cambridge (1999)
6. Cameron, P.J., van Lint, J.H.: Designs, Graphs, Codes and Their Links, London Mathematical Society Student Texts. vol. 22. Cambridge University Press, Cambridge (1996)
7. Carette, J., Farmer, W.M., Jeremic, F., Maccio, V., O'Connor, R., Tran, Q.M.: The MathScheme Library: Some Preliminary Experiments. arXiv:1106.1862 (Jun 2011)
8. Colbourn, C.J., Dinitz, J.H.: Handbook of Combinatorial Designs, 2nd edn. Chapman & Hall/CRC, Boca Raton (2007)
9. Farmer, W.M., Guttman, J.D., Javier Thayer, F.: Little theories. In: Kapur, D. (ed.) CADE 1992. LNCS, vol. 607, pp. 567–581. Springer, Heidelberg (1992). https://doi.org/10.1007/3-540-55602-8_192
10. Haftmann, F., Wenzel, M.: Constructive type classes in Isabelle. In: Altenkirch, T., McBride, C. (eds.) TYPES 2006. LNCS, vol. 4502, pp. 160–174. Springer, Heidelberg (2007). https://doi.org/10.1007/978-3-540-74464-1_11

11. Haftmann, F., Wenzel, M.: Local theory specifications in Isabelle/Isar. In: Berardi, S., Damiani, F., de'Liguoro, U. (eds.) TYPES 2008. LNCS, vol. 5497, pp. 153–168. Springer, Heidelberg (2009). https://doi.org/10.1007/978-3-642-02444-3_10
12. Keinholz, J.: Matroids. Isabelle Archive of Formal Proofs (Nov 2018). https://www.isa-afp.org/entries/Matroids.html
13. Noschinski, L.: A graph library for Isabelle. Math. Comput. Sci. **9**(1), 23–39 (2015)
14. Paulson, L.C.: Computational logic: its origins and applications. Proc. R. Soc. A **474**(2210), 20170872 (2018)
15. Soicher, L.H.: Designs, groups and computing. In: Detinko, A., Flannery, D., O'Brien, E. (eds.) Probabilistic Group Theory, Combinatorics, and Computing. Lecture Notes in Mathematics, vol. 2070, pp. 83–107. Springer, London (2013). https://doi.org/10.1007/978-1-4471-4814-2_3
16. Stinson, D.: Combinatorial Designs: Constructions and Analysis. Springer, New York (2004). https://doi.org/10.1007/b97564

Beautiful Formalizations
in Isabelle/Naproche

Adrian De Lon$^{(\boxtimes)}$ ⓘ, Peter Koepke ⓘ, Anton Lorenzen ⓘ, Adrian Marti ⓘ,
Marcel Schütz ⓘ, and Erik Sturzenhecker

University of Bonn, Bonn, Germany
adelon@uni-bonn.de, koepke@math.uni-bonn.de
https://www.math.uni-bonn.de/ag/logik/

Abstract. We present short example formalizations of basic theorems
from number theory, set theory, and lattice theory which ship with the
new Naproche component in Isabelle 2021. The natural proof assistant
Naproche accepts input texts in the mathematical controlled natural
language ForTheL. Some ForTheL texts that proof-check in Naproche
come close to ordinary mathematical writing. The formalization examples demonstrate the potential to write mathematics in a natural yet
completely formal language and to delegate tedious organisatorial details
and obvious proof steps to strong automated theorem proving so that
mathematical ideas and the "beauty" of proofs become visible.

1 Introduction

In informal mathematical discourse one frequently encounters appraisals of theorems and proofs as "intuitive", "elegant", "interesting", "simple", or indeed
"beautiful". Following Paul Erdős, perfect proofs by these criteria would be
entered in God's BOOK of proofs [12]. Although mathematicians often agree
about the beauty of particular proofs, mathematical beauty in principle appears
as elusive as the concept of beauty in general. Discussions of beauty by eminent
mathematicians exhibit a spectrum of ad hoc theories and personal opinions (see,
e.g., [18,22]). A popular view that fits the perspective of this paper is expressed
in [13, p. 22], (but observe [6]):

> *Mathematicians have customarily regarded a proof as beautiful if it con-
> formed to the classical ideals of brevity and simplicity.*

This explains that completely formal proofs as studied in formal mathematics
are widely viewed as being the opposite of "beautiful". Reuben Hersh [5, p. 52],
writes:

> *We prefer a beautiful proof with a serious gap over a boring hyper-correct
> one.*

Formal mathematicians themselves acknowledge difficulties with their proofs.
Lawrence Paulson writes:

F. Kamareddine and C. Sacerdoti Coen (Eds.): CICM 2021, LNAI 12833, pp. 19–31, 2021.
https://doi.org/10.1007/978-3-030-81097-9_2

> *However, existing theorem provers are unsuitable for mathematics. Their*
> *formal proofs are unreadable.* [17]

A closer look, however, reveals that informal proofs usually contain a considerable amount of formality, and that current proof assistants are moving towards proof languages and proof presentations that are at least "readable" by human experts. The natural proof assistant Naproche attempts to close the gap between informal and formal mathematics. Some texts which are proof-checked by Naproche come close to ordinary mathematical writing. This is further emphasized by a new LaTeX dialect of the Naproche input language ForTheL which allows immediate mathematical typesetting of input files. The Naproche project aims at providing comfortable editing of natural mathematical texts with integrated automated proof checking.

Naproche is included as a bundled component in the latest edition of the Isabelle prover platform. ForTheL texts in the classic `.ftl` format or the new `.ftl.tex` format can be edited in Isabelle/jEdit and are automatically checked by Naproche. In this paper we present some formalization examples which are included in Isabelle 2021. These short texts demonstrate the potential for writing mathematics in a natural yet completely formal language and to delegate tedious detail to strong automated theorem proving. The examples present proofs that can be considered "beautiful". Some of them follow proofs in THE BOOK [12].

The examples are contained in the folder `contrib/naproche-*/examples` within the Isabelle 2021 folder. They cover

- Cantor's diagonal argument (`cantor.ftl.tex`, Sect. 3);
- König's Theorem from cardinal arithmetic (`koenig.ftl.tex`, Sect. 4);
- the infinitude of primes according to Euclid (`euclid.ftl.tex`, Sect. 5)
- ... and according to Furstenberg (`fuerstenberg.ftl.tex`, Sect. 6);
- the Knaster–Tarski fixpoint theorem (`tarski.ftl.tex`, 7).

Some of these formalizations go back to example texts that Andrei Paskevich included with his original SAD system ([15] and [16]). The files can be opened in Isabelle, and PDF-versions are provided for immediate reading. Note that we have made a few superficial typographic changes to the examples in this paper to increase legibility. There is always room for further improvements to the typesetting of texts.

In conclusion: we are certain that natural proof assistants will facilitate the eventual acceptance of formal mathematics in the wider mathematical community. Ideally, proofs should be beautiful *and* formally correct.

2   Naproche, ForTheL, and LaTeX

The Naproche proof assistant stems from two long-term efforts aiming towards naturalness: the Evidence Algorithm (EA)/System for Automated Deduction (SAD) projects at the universities of Kiev and Paris [15,16,20,21], and the Naproche project at Bonn [1,3,9,11]. In Naproche, the ForTheL input language of SAD has been extended and embedded in LaTeX, allowing mathematical type-setting; the original proof-checking mechanisms have been made more efficient and varied.

The mathematical controlled language ForTheL has been developed over several decades in the Evidence Algorithm (EA)/System for Automated Deduction (SAD) project. It is carefully designed to approximate the weakly typed natural language of mathematics whilst being efficiently translatable to the language of first-order logic. In ForTheL, standard mathematical types are called *notions*, and these are internally represented as predicates with one distinguished variable, whilst the other variables are considered as parameters ("types as dependent predicates"). Compared to most type systems of proof assistants, this yields a more flexible dependent type system where number systems can be cumulative ($\mathbb{N} \subseteq \mathbb{Q} \subseteq \mathbb{R}$), and notions can depend on parameters (subsets of $\mathbb{N}$, divisors of n).

Technically, Naproche shares several features with the Mizar system. Mizar has a soft type system and pretyping of variables. It is, however, difficult to read and understand Mizar texts due to Mizar's unnatural input language and the need to include small proof details that in Naproche are found automatically. As an example one might compare our proof of Cantor's Theorem in the next section to the Mizar article http://www.mizar.org/JFM/Vol1/card_1.miz.html, Theorem 29.

In Naproche, first-order languages of notions, constants, relations, and functions can be introduced and extended by *signature* and *definition* commands. The formalization of Euclid's theorem to be discussed later, sets out like:

Signature. A natural number is a small object.
Let $\ldots m, n \ldots$ denote natural numbers.
Signature. 0 is a natural number.
...
Signature. $m + n$ is a natural number.

We require natural numbers to be *small* objects, so that we can later form sets of natural numbers. This is due to the present ontology of Naproche where elements of sets have to be small. Future versions will provide a choice between several standard ontologies.

We have extended Naproche to support a `.ftl.tex` format, in addition to the original `.ftl` format. Files in `.ftl.tex` format can be processed by Naproche for logical checking and by LaTeX for typesetting.

The LaTeX tokenizer ignores everything except what is inside ForTheL environments of the form

```
\begin{forthel}
    % Insert what you want Naproche to process here
\end{forthel}
```

Inside a ForTheL environment, standard LaTeX syntax can be used for declaring text environments for theorems and definitions.

In Naproche, users can define their own operators and phrases through *patterns* of words and symbols. This mechanism has been adapted to allow LATEX constructs in patterns. In the Euclid example we shall use the pattern `\Set{p}{1}{r}` for the finite set $\{p_1, \ldots, p_r\}$. By also defining `\Set` as a LATEX macro we can arrange that the ForTheL pattern will be printed out in familiar set notation:

```
\newcommand{\Set}[3]{\{#1_{#2},\dots,#1_{#3}\}}
```

There are some primitive concepts in Naproche, such as the logical operators $\vee$, $\wedge$, $\exists$ that are directly recognized in the LATEX source and expanded to corresponding internal tokens.

3   Example: Cantor's Theorem

In this section we prove Cantor's famous theorem, by which the powerset of a set has strictly greater cardinality than the given set. The proof rests on Cantor's beautiful diagonal argument which is also used in THE BOOK [12] to show that the set of real numbers is not countable.

Our formalization is so short, that we can include it in its entirety and use it to remark on further features of Naproche and ForTheL. More information can be found in a short tutorial introduction to Naproche in the file `TUTORIAL.ftl.tex` in the examples folder.

[synonym subset/-s] [synonym surject/-s]

Let M denote a set. Let f denote a function.

Axiom 1. *M is setsized.*

Axiom 2. *Let x be an element of M. Then x is setsized.*

Let the value of f at x stand for $f(x)$. Let f is defined on M stand for $\text{Dom}(f) = M$. Let the domain of f stand for $\text{Dom}(f)$.

Axiom 3. *The value of f at any element of the domain of f is a set.*

Definition 1 (Subset). *A subset of M is a set N such that every element of N is an element of M.*

Definition 2. *The powerset of M is the class of subsets of M.*

Axiom 4. *The powerset of M is a set.*

Definition 3. *f surjects onto M iff every element of M is equal to the value of f at some element of the domain of f.*

Theorem 1 (Cantor). *No function that is defined on M surjects onto the powerset of M.*

Proof. Proof by contradiction. Assume the contrary. Take a function f that is defined on M and surjects onto the powerset of M. Define

$$N = \{x \in M \mid x \notin f(x)\}.$$

Take an element z of M such that $f(z) = N$. Then

$$z \in N \leftrightarrow z \notin f(z) = N.$$

Contradiction. ∎

Remarks:

1. This formalization, like the subsequent examples, is a self-contained natural language representation of a collection of first-order assumptions and consequences. Except for some built-in notions and axioms the whole logical scenario has to be set up explicitly. Future versions of Naproche will contain libraries of foundational theories which can be imported into formalizations.
2. The simple grammar of Naproche and ForTheL is directed towards the identification of first-order logical content. Writing grammatically correct English is possible (and encouraged) but not enforced by the system. [synonym subset/-s] is a parser command that identifies the token "subsets" with the token "subset". This allows to choose the correct grammatical number in statements. One might increase the "beauty" of texts by printing parser commands as footnotes. Note that Naproche does not have a predefined English vocabulary but works with arbitrary alphabetic tokens. Future versions may use standard linguistic algorithms for plural formation or other grammatical modifications.
3. The notions of "set" and "function" are already coded into Naproche. Variables like M or f can be pretyped with those notions by, e.g., "Let M denote a set."
4. A rudimentary set- and class-theory is built into Naproche. Since classes can only contain "setsized" elements, we stipulate that every set is setsized by the axiom: "M is setsized." Also elements of sets are setsized by Axiom 2.
5. Naturalness requires to have alternative phrases available for the same logical entity, so that one may speak of the "value of f at x" instead of $f(x)$. Such alternatives are introduced by "Let ... stand for ..." commands.
6. Definitions 1 and 2 define new notions dependent on the pre-typed variable M for a set.
7. Axiom 4 is the well-known powerset axiom.
8. The short proof of Cantor's theorem uses the same language as undergraduate texts on basic set theory. A mathematical context is created by "Assume ...", "Take ...", or "Define ..." statements. At proof time Naproche checks that all terms and statements are type-correct: the term $f(x)$, e.g., spawns the obvious prover task derived from the assumptions in the definition of $f(x)$; namely that $x \in \text{Dom}(f)$. This task is given to the background ATP eprover which is able to prove it within the local proof context.

9. Abstraction terms {...} are already built into the syntactic mechanisms of Naproche.
10. Naproche supports familiar proof methods like proofs by cases, by induction, or, in this case, by contradiction. Internally, these methods influence the construction of proof tasks.
11. Mathematical typesetting is an important ingredient of the "beauty" of mathematical texts. Naproche mostly treats LaTeX commands as irrelevant to the logical content of a text and ignores them during parsing. This allows common layout features like prominently displaying the definition of N or the final equivalence by \[... \] commands.

4   Example: König's Theorem

The next example presents an important set-theoretical result about the arithmetic of cardinals which was proved by Julius König in 1905 [10] The global proof structure is again a Cantorean diagonal argument.

Mathematical notation greatly contributes to the brevity and aesthetics of mathematical texts. The "big operator" notation for multiple sums ($\sum$) or products ($\prod$) with their 2-dimensional arrangement of arguments represents typical mathematical symbolism.

These terms can be typeset by LaTeX macros which by the generous pattern mechanisms of ForTheL simultaneously stand for first-order functions. The sum macro is defined by:

```
\newcommand{\Sum}[2]{\sum_{i \in #2} \val{{#1}_{i}}{}}
```

\Sum{_}{_} is simultaneously used as a ForTheL pattern for an internal binary function. The instance \Sum{\kappa}{D} of the pattern typesets as $\sum_{i \in D} \kappa_i$.

The LaTeX interpretation of certain ForTheL patterns and the orthogonality of most LaTeX commands to the logical interpretation allow many typographical effects, according to taste and style.

Theorem. *Let κ, λ be sequences of cardinals on D. Assume that for every element i of D $\kappa_i < \lambda_i$. Then*

$$\sum_{i \in D} \kappa_i < \prod_{i \in D} \lambda_i.$$

Proof. Proof by contradiction. Assume the contrary. Then

$$\prod_{i \in D} \lambda_i \leq \sum_{i \in D} \kappa_i.$$

Take a function G such that $\bigcup_{i \in D} \kappa_i$ is the domain of G and $\times_{i \in D} \lambda_i$ is the image of G. Indeed $\times_{i \in D} \lambda_i$ has an element.

Define

$$\Delta(i) = \{G((n, i))(i) \mid n \text{ is an element of } \kappa_i\} \text{ for } i \text{ in } D.$$

For every element f of $\times_{i\in D}\lambda_i$ for every element i of D $f(i)$ is an element of λ_i. For every element i of D λ_i is a set. For every element i of D for every element d of $\Delta(i)$ we have $d \in \lambda_i$. For every element i of D $\Delta(i)$ is a set.

(1) For every element i of D $|\Delta(i)| < \lambda_i$.

Proof. Let i be an element of D. Define

$$F(n) = G((n,i))(i) \text{ for } n \text{ in } \kappa_i.$$

Then $F[\kappa(i)] = \Delta(i)$. qed.

Define

$$f(i) = \text{ choose an element } v \text{ of } \lambda_i \setminus \Delta(i) \text{ in } v \text{ for } i \text{ in } D.$$

Then f is an element of $\times_{i\in D}\lambda_i$. Take an element j of D and an element m of κ_j such that $G((m,j)) = f$. $G((m,j))(j)$ is an element of $\Delta(j)$ and $f(j)$ is not an element of $\Delta(j)$. Contradiction. ∎

5   Example: Euclid's Theorem

We formalize the very first proof in THE BOOK [12], Euclid's theorem that there are infinitely many prime numbers. Before the proof the example sets up the axiomatic background: a language and axioms for natural numbers, arithmetic, divisibility and prime numbers, some set theory, and finite sets, sequences and products. Here we only present the concluding proof, juxtaposing the BOOK proof (left) and the Naproche proof (right) in order to demonstrate their similarity:

Signature. $\mathbb{P}$ *is the class of prime natural numbers.*

Theorem (Euclid). $\mathbb{P}$ *is infinite.*

Euclid's Proof.

For any finite set $\{p_1, \ldots, p_r\}$ of primes,

Proof.

Assume that r is a natural number and p is a sequence of length r and $\{p_1, \ldots, p_r\}$ is a subclass of .

(1) p_i is a nonzero natural number for every i such that $1 \leqslant i \leqslant r$.

consider the number $n = p_1 p_2 \cdots p_r + 1$.

Consider $n = p_1 \cdots p_r + 1$.

This n has a prime divisor p.

Take a prime divisor q of n.

But p is not one of the p_i:

Let us show that $q \neq p_i$ for all i such that $1 \leqslant i \leqslant r$.

otherwise

Proof by contradiction. Assume that $q = p_i$ for some natural number i such that $1 \leqslant i \leqslant r$.

p would be a divisor of n and of the product $p_1 p_2 \cdots p_r$, and thus also of the difference

$$n - p_1 p_2 \cdots p_r = 1,$$

which is impossible. So a finite set $\{p_1, \ldots, p_r\}$ cannot be the collection of *all* prime numbers. ∎

q is a divisor of n and q is a divisor of $p_1 \cdots p_r$ (by factor property, 1). Thus q divides 1. Contradiction. qed. Hence $\{p_1, \ldots, p_r\}$ is not the class of prime natural numbers. ∎

6   Example: Furstenberg's Topological Proof

In 1955 Hillel Furstenberg published another proof of the infinitude of primes using the language of topology [4]. Paskevich provided a version of this proof as a ForTheL example in SAD [14] which we translated to ForTheL's LaTeX dialect in the course of the release of Isabelle 2021 [7]. Here is the concluding theorem and proof, taken directly from the example file in Isabelle 2021.

Theorem. (Fuerstenberg). *Let $S = \{r\mathbb{Z} + 0 \mid r \text{ is a prime}\}$. S is infinite.*

Proof. Proof by contradiction. S is a family of integer sets.

We have $\overline{\bigcup S} = \{1, -1\}$.
Proof. Let us show that for any integer n n belongs to $\bigcup S$ iff n has a prime divisor. Let n be an integer.

If n has a prime divisor then n belongs to $\bigcup S$.
Proof. Assume n has a prime divisor. Take a prime divisor p of n. $p\mathbb{Z} + 0$ is setsized. $p\mathbb{Z} + 0 \in S$. $n \in p\mathbb{Z} + 0$. Qed.

If n belongs to $\bigcup S$ then n has a prime divisor.
Proof. Assume n belongs to $\bigcup S$. Take a prime r such that $n \in r\mathbb{Z} + 0$. Then r is a prime divisor of n. Qed. End. Qed.

Assume that S is finite. Then $\bigcup S$ is closed and $\overline{\bigcup S}$ is open.

Take p such that $p\mathbb{Z} + 1 \subseteq \overline{\bigcup S}$.

$p\mathbb{Z} + 1$ has an element x such that neither $x = 1$ nor $x = -1$.
Proof. $1 + p$ and $1 - p$ are integers. $1 + p$ and $1 - p$ belong to $p\mathbb{Z} + 1$. Indeed $1 + p = 1 \pmod{p}$ and $1 - p = 1 \pmod{p}$. $1 + p \neq 1 \wedge 1 - p \neq 1$. $1 + p \neq -1 \vee 1 - p \neq -1$. Qed.

We have a contradiction.   ∎

In 2020 Manuel Eberl published an Isar version of Furstenberg's proof in the Archive of Formal Proofs [2]. In this section we will discuss the formalization in ForTheL's LaTeX dialect and compare it with Eberl's Isar version.
Let us start with the statement.

Theorem. *There are infinitely many primes.*

Despite its apparent simplicity, it is not as easy as it seems to formalize it. Even the *natural* formal language ForTheL cannot capture it. The problem is the quantification "there are infinitely many". We reformulate the statement in terms of the cardinality of the set of primes as in the Isar formalization:

Theorem. *infinite* $\{p{::}nat.\ prime\ p\}$

Here we have a unary predicate *infinite* with an argument $\{p{::}nat.\ prime\ p\}$. In ForTheL however we cannot pass class terms as parameters to predicates, hence we cannot adopt the Isar statement literally to ForTheL. So what we have to state instead is the following:

Theorem. *Let* $S = \{r \mid r$ *is a prime*$\}$. S *is infinite.*

In fact, Paskevich's formalization of Furstenberg's proof does not provide a full axiomatization of integers or even a general notion of infinity, and rather proves the infinitude of the set $\{p\mathbb{Z} \mid p$ is a prime$\}$. The ForTheL theorem thus reads:

Theorem. *Let* $S = \{r\mathbb{Z} + 0 \mid r$ *is a prime*$\}$. S *is infinite.*

Note that we cannot write $r\mathbb{Z}$ instead of $r\mathbb{Z} + 0$. For our formalization introduces the pattern $q\mathbb{Z} + a$ for arbitrary integers a, q (where q is supposed to be non-zero). If we would additionally define the pattern $q\mathbb{Z}$ as $q\mathbb{Z} + 0$ then Naproche could not figure out the meaning of $q\mathbb{Z} + 0$. It could either refer to the pattern $(x\mathbb{Z} + y)[q/x, 0/y]$ or to the pattern $(x + y)[q\mathbb{Z}/x, 0/y]$, where $[t/x, t'/y]$ denotes substitution of x by t and of y by t'. Future versions of Naproche shall have mechanisms to disambiguate such overloadings.

Let us continue our comparison of the Isar version of Furstenberg's proof with the ForTheL version. The Isar proof begins with the following statements:

assume *fin*: *finite* $\{p{::}nat.\ prime\ p\}$
define A **where** $A = (\bigcup p \in \{p{::}nat.\ prime\ p\}.\ arith\text{-}prog\text{-}fb\ 0\ p)$
have *closed* A
...
hence *open* $(-A)$

Here *arith-prof-fb* $0\ p$ denotes the set $p\mathbb{Z} + 0$ and $-A$ denotes the complement of A in $\mathbb{Z}$. In ForTheL we can directly write $p\mathbb{Z} + 0$ which allows for a better intuitive understanding of the proof text:

Let $S = \{r\mathbb{Z} + 0 \mid r$ is a prime$\}$.
...
Assume that S is finite. Then $\bigcup S$ is closed and $\overline{\bigcup S}$ is open.

Up to now both proof texts are quite similar (if we ""identify" a prime p with the set $p\mathbb{Z} + 0$), except that ForTheL uses natural language constructs like subject-predicate-object sentences. The central part of Furstenberg's proof is to show that

$$\bigcup\{p\mathbb{Z} + 0 \mid p \text{ is prime}\} = \mathbb{Z} \setminus \{1, -1\}$$

(as in the Isar version) or, equivalently, that

$$\bigcup\{r\mathbb{Z} + 0 \mid r \text{ is a prime}\} = \{n \in \mathbb{Z} \mid n \text{ has a prime divisor}\}$$

(as in the ForTheL version). Let us first have a look at how the statement $\mathbb{Z} \setminus \{1, -1\} \subseteq \bigcup\{p\mathbb{Z} + 0 \mid p \text{ is prime}\}$ is proven in the Isar text.

fix $x::int$ **assume** $x : x \in -\{1, -1\}$

...

show $x \in (\bigcup p \in \{p::nat. \ prime \ p\}. \ arith\text{-}prog \ 0 \ p)$

...

obtain p **where** $p : \ prime \ p \ p \ dvd \ x$
using $prime\text{-}divisor\text{-}exists[of \ x]$ **and** $\langle |x| \neq 1 \rangle$ **by** $auto$
hence $x \in arith\text{-}prog \ 0 \ (nat \ p)$ **using** $prime\text{-}gt\text{-}0\text{-}int[of \ p]$
by $(auto \ simp: \ arith\text{-}prog\text{-}def \ cong\text{-}0\text{-}iff)$
thus $?thesis$ **using** p
by $(auto \ simp: \ A\text{-}def \ intro!: \ exI \ [of \ - \ nat \ p])$

On the other hand the proof of the statement $\{n \in \mathbb{Z} \mid n \text{ has a prime divisor}\} \subseteq \bigcup\{p\mathbb{Z} + 0 \mid p \text{ is prime}\}$ looks like the following in ForTheL.

Let n be an integer.

...

If n has a prime divisor then n belongs to $\bigcup S$.
Proof. Assume n has a prime divisor. Take a prime divisor p of n. $n \in p\mathbb{Z}+0$.
Qed.

Note that in both versions we silently assumed that $x \neq 0$ and $n \neq 0$, respectively.

In principle, both proofs are similar. But whereas Isabelle uses proof tactics to search for proofs, Naproche relies on an external ATP. Users of Isabelle can steer proof search efficiently by commands like

by $(auto \ simp: \ A\text{-}def \ intro!: \ exI \ [of \ - \ nat \ p])$

On the other hand one would not want to see such technicalities in a natural or even "beautiful" proof à la Naproche. As a future project we shall investigate whether Naproche can reach a similar prover efficiency by using sledgehammer methods to steer external ATPs.

Finally, let us compare the statement discussed above to its original formulation in THE BOOK [12]:

Since any number $n \neq 1, -1$ has a prime divisor p, and hence is contained in $N_{0,p}$, we conclude

$$\mathbb{Z} \setminus \{1, -1\} = \bigcup_{p \in \mathbb{P}} N_{0,p}.$$

Here $\mathbb{P}$ denote the set of prime numbers and $N_{0,p}$ the set $p\mathbb{Z} + 0$. Obviously, this is a very elegant formulation compared to Isar and ForTheL, paying the price of a quite complicated sentence structure as a combination of three statements with internal dependencies:

Since φ, and hence ψ, we conclude χ.

Moreover, there are hidden variables, e.g. n occurs in ψ without being explicitly mentioned, and implicit variable bindings, e.g. p is not free in ψ as it might seem if we consider ψ being independent from φ. Parsing such sentences is beyond the possibilities of the current Naproche, and it will have to be discussed if one would even want this level of grammatical complication in an efficient controlled natural language for mathematics.

7   Example: The Knaster–Tarski Theorem

We conclude with an example from lattice theory about fixed points of monotone functions. Bronisław Knaster and Alfred Tarski established it in 1928 for the special case of power set lattices [8]. The more general result was stated by Tarski in 1955 [19]. It states that the set of fixpoints of a monotone function on a complete lattice is also a complete lattice. In particular, we can take the supremum or the infimum of the empty set in order to get the biggest or the smallest fixpoint.

The full formalization starts by defining a complete lattice, a monotone function and a fixpoint. The formalized proof relies on automation to achieve a natural brevity.

Theorem. (Knaster–Tarski). *Let U be a complete lattice and f be a monotone function on U. Let S be the class of fixed points of f. Then S is a complete lattice.*

Proof. Let T be a subset of S.
Let us show that T has a supremum in S.
Define

$$P = \{x \in U \mid f(x) \leqslant x \text{ and } x \text{ is an upper bound of } T \text{ in } U\}.$$

Take an infimum p of P in U. $f(p)$ is a lower bound of P in U and an upper bound of T in U. Hence p is a fixed point of f and a supremum of T in S.
End.
Let us show that T has an infimum in S.
Define

$$Q = \{x \in U \mid f(x) \leqslant x \text{ and } x \text{ is an lower bound of } T \text{ in } U\}.$$

Take a supremum q of Q in U. $f(q)$ is an upper bound of Q in U and a lower bound of T in U. Hence q is a fixed point of f and an infimum of T in S.
End. ∎

8 Outlook

The Naproche project will continue to expand the methods presented in this paper. We shall enlarge our grammar to capture more natural language phrases. Recurrent notions and notations will be predefined in library files. Tuning the background ATP for the demands of Naproche checking will allow to make further proof steps implicit and make it easier to follow existing natural texts.

This approach will have to prove its value by further, more comprehensive formalizations and by interlinked libraries of natural formalizations.

References

1. Cramer, M.: Proof-checking mathematical texts in controlled natural language. PhD thesis, University of Bonn (2013)
2. Eberl, M.: Furstenberg's topology and his proof of the infinitude of primes. Archive of Formal Proofs (March 2020). https://isa-afp.org/entries/Furstenberg_Topology.html
3. Frerix, S., Koepke, P.: Automatic proof-checking of ordinary mathematical texts. In: Proceedings of the Workshop Formal Mathematics for Mathematicians (2018)
4. Furstenberg, H.: On the infinitude of primes. Am. Math. Monthly **62**(5), 353 (1955)
5. Hersh, R.: What is Mathematics, Really?. Oxford University Press, Oxford (1997)
6. Inglis, M., Aberdein, A.: Beauty is not simplicity: an analysis of mathematicians' proof appraisals. Philosophia Math. **23**, 87–109 (2014)
7. Isabelle contributors. The Isabelle 2021 release (February 2021)
8. Knaster, B., Tarski, A.: Un théorème sur les fonctions d'ensembles. Annales de la Société Polonaise de Mathématique **6**, 133–134 (1928)
9. Koepke, P.: Textbook mathematics in the Naproche-SAD system. In: Joint Proceedings of the FMM and LML Workshops (2019)
10. König, J.: Mathematische Annalen. Zum Kontinuumsproblem **60**, 177–180 (1905)
11. Kühlwein, D., Cramer, M., Koepke, P., Schröder, B.: The Naproche system (2009)
12. Ziegler, G.M., Aigner, M.: Proofs from THE BOOK. 4th edition, Springer, Berlin (2009)
13. McAllister, J.W.: Mathematical beauty and the evolution of the standards of mathematical proof. In: Emmer, M. (ed) The Visual Mind II, pp. 15–34. MIT Press, Cambridge (2005)
14. Paskevich, A.: Furstenberg's proof in SAD (2008). http://nevidal.org/cgi-bin/sad.cgi?ty=txt&ln=en&link=fuerst.ftl
15. Paskevich, A.: Méthodes de formalisation des connaissances et des raisonnements mathématiques: aspects appliqués et théoriques. PhD thesis, Université Paris (12, 2007)
16. Paskevich, A.: The syntax and semantics of the ForTheL language (2007)
17. Paulson, L.C.: Alexandria: Large-scale formal proof for the working mathematician (2018)
18. Rota, G.-C.: The phenomenology of mathematical beauty. Synthese **111**(2), 171–182 (1997)
19. Tarski, A.: A lattice-theoretical fixpoint theorem and its applications. Pac. J. Math. **5**(2), 285–309 (1955)

20. Verchinine, K., Lyaletski, A., Paskevich, A.: System for automated deduction (SAD): a tool for proof verification. In: Pfenning, F. (ed.) CADE 2007. LNCS (LNAI), vol. 4603, pp. 398–403. Springer, Heidelberg (2007). https://doi.org/10.1007/978-3-540-73595-3_29

21. Verchinine, K., Lyaletski, A., Paskevich, A., Anisimov, A.: On correctness of mathematical texts from a logical and practical point of view. In: Autexier, S., Campbell, J., Rubio, J., Sorge, V., Suzuki, M., Wiedijk, F. (eds.) CICM 2008. LNCS (LNAI), vol. 5144, pp. 583–598. Springer, Heidelberg (2008). https://doi.org/10.1007/978-3-540-85110-3_47

22. Wells, D.: Are these the most beautiful? Math. Intell. **12**, 37–41 (1990)

Formalizing Axiomatic Systems for Propositional Logic in Isabelle/HOL

Asta Halkjær From[(✉)] [ID], Agnes Moesgård Eschen, and Jørgen Villadsen[ID]

DTU Compute - Department of Applied Mathematics and Computer Science,
Technical University of Denmark, Kongens Lyngby, Denmark
{ahfrom,jovi}@dtu.dk, s151952@student.dtu.dk

Abstract. We formalize soundness and completeness proofs for a number of axiomatic systems for propositional logic in the proof assistant Isabelle/HOL.

Keywords: Propositional logic · Axiomatic systems · Isabelle/HOL · Completeness · Soundness

1 Introduction

With the proof assistant Isabelle/HOL [10] we can create canonical reference documents for logics and their metatheory. The formal language of Isabelle/HOL, namely higher-order logic, is precise and unambiguous. This means every proof can be mechanically checked. We consider here two (functionally complete) fragments of propositional logic and various axiomatic systems for these fragments. Table 1 gives an overview of the systems and fragments. Our focus is mostly syntactic and we showcase the benefits of doing this work in Isabelle. We write down both the syntax and semantics of our languages, with infix syntax and abbreviations as desired. Furthermore we specify various inference systems by their rules and axioms. The systems here are all axiomatic but the techniques work for proof systems in general.

This sets the stage for our investigations. We can easily verify that the proof systems are sound with respect to the semantics, with Isabelle doing almost all the work. We can verify completeness by adapting a formalization for a similar system or by finding derivations for the axioms of one system in the other one (and similarly for the rules). Here, Isabelle helps out: instead of painstakingly writing down each derivation, a sometimes daunting task in an axiomatic system, we can let one of its sophisticated proof methods prove its existence for us. We can even let Isabelle find the right proof method and a suitable collection of needed axioms and previously derived formulas for us with its *Sledgehammer* technology. With these tools at hand we can verify historical claims such as how some axiom can be omitted because it follows from the others.

As an example we formalize Łukasiewicz's shortest axiom for implicational propositional logic and provide, in full, his derivation of Wajsberg's axioms, for

© Springer Nature Switzerland AG 2021
F. Kamareddine and C. Sacerdoti Coen (Eds.): CICM 2021, LNAI 12833, pp. 32–46, 2021.
https://doi.org/10.1007/978-3-030-81097-9_3

Table 1. The formalized axiomatic systems. The first three are formalized in the theory *System-W* and use $\perp, \rightarrow$ as primitive symbols. The last three are formalized in the theory *System-R* and use $\neg, \bigvee$ as primitives, with the abbreviation $p \rightarrow q \equiv \neg p \bigvee q$.

System	Source	Page [3]	Axioms
Axiomatics	Wajsberg 1937	159	$p \rightarrow (q \rightarrow p)$ $(p \rightarrow q) \rightarrow (q \rightarrow r) \rightarrow (p \rightarrow r)$ $((p \rightarrow q) \rightarrow p) \rightarrow p)$ $\perp \rightarrow p$
FW	Wajsberg 1939	163	$p \rightarrow (q \rightarrow p)$ $(p \rightarrow (q \rightarrow r)) \rightarrow (p \rightarrow q) \rightarrow (p \rightarrow r)$ $((p \rightarrow \perp) \rightarrow \perp) \rightarrow p)$
WL	Łukasiewicz 1948	159	$((p \rightarrow q) \rightarrow r) \rightarrow ((r \rightarrow p) \rightarrow (s \rightarrow p))$ $\perp \rightarrow p$
Axiomatics	Rasiowa 1949	157	$p \bigvee p \rightarrow p$ $p \rightarrow p \bigvee q$ $(p \rightarrow q) \rightarrow (r \bigvee p) \rightarrow (q \bigvee r)$
RB	Russell 1908, Bernays 1926	157	$p \bigvee p \rightarrow p$ $p \rightarrow p \bigvee q$ $p \bigvee q \rightarrow q \bigvee p$ $(p \rightarrow q) \rightarrow (r \bigvee p) \rightarrow (q \bigvee r)$
PM	Whitehead & Russell 1910	–	$p \bigvee p \rightarrow p$ $p \rightarrow q \bigvee p$ $p \bigvee q \rightarrow q \bigvee p$ $(p \bigvee (q \bigvee r)) \rightarrow (q \bigvee (p \bigvee r))$ $(p \rightarrow q) \rightarrow (r \bigvee p) \rightarrow (q \bigvee r)$

which we have formalized completeness. In this example we also show how to seamlessly use his notation in Isabelle and have the proof assistant translate it to the more familiar one. As another example we consider the exchangeability of two axioms.

We reproduce parts of our formalizations in the paper. The full Isabelle/HOL formalizations, 669 lines (535 sloc, source lines of code, not counting blank lines) in file `System_W.thy` and 631 lines (510 sloc) in file `System_R.thy`, are available here:

https://github.com/logic-tools/axiom

The paper strives to be self-contained so consulting the formalizations is optional. However, the availability enables the reader to investigate the formalizations on their own and, if curious, to look up anything we have omitted for reasons of space. The files can also be extended with other proof systems or taken as inspiration for different fragments of propositional logic or expansions to other logic. To verify properties of some new axiomatic system, it could be shown equivalent to one formalized here, so that soundness and completeness can be carried over. All of this with automation available to aid the process and a trusted kernel that guarantees correctness.

We modify our existing work [5] to formalize completeness of the axiomatic systems we consider. The existing completeness proof uses Henkin's synthetic technique based on maximal consistent sets of formulas to build a model for underivable formulas. We have adapted this proof to two representatives of the fragments we consider in this paper (the two systems dubbed *Axiomatics* in Table 1). A lot of this work involves showing that the proof system can derive certain formulas that are used in the completeness proof. Similarly, to reuse the completeness result for the other axiomatic systems for the same fragment, we show that certain formulas can be derived using their axioms. In short, much of this work is about proving that specific formulas can be derived. The classic book by Church [3] has been an excellent source for relevant formulas and instead of fiddling with instantiating the axioms ourselves and finding the right sequence of rule applications, we call upon Isabelle's tool *Sledgehammer* [2]. Often the built-in provers *meson* and *metis* can assemble the pieces for us.

Unfortunately, we are not always lucky enough to find a proof in the first attempt and *Sledgehammer* simply times out. We are then faced with a choice: either make a manual attempt to derive the formula or take a guess that some other formula should be derived first. We generally prefer the latter approach since it lets the proof assistant do more of the menial work for us, while leaving the more creative role of finding the right stepping stones to us.

In cases where we need to derive more than one formula to aid us, we typically mark each one of them with **sorry** before trying to prove them. This *fake proof* is accepted by Isabelle, so that *Sledgehammer* will pick up the lemma as usable in further derivations, but provides no guarantee that the formula can actually be derived. It saves time because we can make sure that the formulas marked by **sorry** are actually useful for our derivation before we try to find derivations for them in turn.

The paper is organized as follows. We continue with a discussion of the closest related work (Sect. 2). We move on to formalize the first three systems (Sect. 3) including the completeness of Lukasiewicz's single shortest axiom. We follow up by formalizing the remaining three systems (Sect. 4) for our other fragment of propositional logic and discuss historical concerns about the independence of certain axioms. Finally we describe the main challenges and benefits of using the proof assistant Isabelle/HOL (Sect. 5) and we conclude (Sect. 6) by placing our work in the context of the IsaFoL (Isabelle Formalization of Logic) project.

2   Related Work

We see two main pieces of related work explained below: that of Michaelis and Nipkow [9] and of Fitelson and Wos [4,13]. We distinguish ourselves by considering completeness of a number of systems based on different primitives using the same approach.

- Michaelis and Nipkow [9] formalized a number of proof systems for propositional logic in Isabelle/HOL: resolution, natural deduction, sequent calculus and an axiomatic system. They used a much larger syntax with falsity, negation, conjunction, disjunction and implication. They both gave a syntactic completeness proof for the sequent calculus and showed completeness of the other systems by translations, but also showed completeness of the sequent calculus and axiomatic system with a Henkin-style [5] proof akin to ours. They only considered an axiomatic system similar to the Wajsberg axioms from 1939, where we consider the range of systems in Table 1. Their larger scope also means they go into fewer details than us, especially regarding the role of Isabelle in deriving formulas.

- Fitelson and Wos [4,13] used the OTTER theorem prover to find axiomatic proofs for a range of formulas, similar to our use of Isabelle. They start from a clause with the disjunction of the negated Wajsberg 1937 axioms and a clause consisting of the Łukasiewicz 1948 axiom. Then they ask OTTER to derive the empty clause, causing it to derive each of the Wajsberg axioms along the way. We take a different approach and verify the correctness of the inference steps given by Łukasiewicz directly in Isabelle. Moreover, we show how to use Łukasiewicz's notation directly, instead of translating it into the clausal form of OTTER. Finally, Isabelle allows us to formalize semantics as well as proof systems.

We have recently [5] presented the details of a direct Henkin-style completeness proof for the Wajsberg axioms from 1939. In the present paper we elaborate on our use of derivations and equivalences instead of describing the Henkin-style completeness proof. We have used preliminary versions of our formalizations in the files `System_W.thy` and `System_R.thy` in our course on automated reasoning in 2020 and 2021 with, respectively, 27 and 37 MSc computer science students. The focus of the exercises was on our approach to formalization of syntax, semantics and axiomatic systems using Isabelle/HOL. As an introductory example we included a very brief description of the approach in our paper [6] about our main Isabelle/HOL tools for teaching logic, namely the Natural Deduction Assistant (NaDeA) and the Sequent Calculus Verifier (SeCaV), both much larger developments for first-order logic with functions.

3   Implication and Falsity

We start by considering Wajsberg's axioms for the fragment of propositional logic built from propositional symbols, implication and falsity.

3.1   Language

The following datatype *form* embeds our syntax into Isabelle:

datatype *form* = *Falsity* (⟨⊥⟩) | *Pro nat* | *Imp form form* (**infix** ⟨→⟩ *0*)

Vertical bars separate the three constructors. The first one introduces ⊥ as a primitive, the next one propositional symbols with natural numbers as identifiers and the final one is implication between two formulas, with the infix symbol →.

Besides these primitive connectives, Isabelle allows us to introduce abbreviations as we would do with pen and paper. Here for the trivially true formula and for negation:

abbreviation *Truth* (⟨⊤⟩) **where** ⟨⊤ ≡ (⊥ → ⊥)⟩
abbreviation (*input*) ⟨*Neg* p ≡ (p → ⊥)⟩

To give our syntax meaning, we write a primitive recursion function in higher-order logic that uses an interpretation of the propositional symbols to map a formula into a truth value:

primrec *semantics* (**infix** ⟨⊨⟩ *0*) **where**
⟨(I ⊨ ⊥) = *False*⟩ |
⟨(I ⊨ (*Pro n*)) = I n⟩ |
⟨(I ⊨ (p → q)) = (*if* I ⊨ p *then* I ⊨ q *else True*)⟩

We use Isabelle's *if-then-else* to interpret implication but we could also use the built-in higher-order logic implication (⟶).

We can define what it means for a formula to be valid by quantifying over all interpretations:

definition ⟨*valid* p ≡ ∀ I. (I ⊨ p)⟩

3.2 Wajsberg 1937

Consider first Wajsberg's proof system from 1937 [3, p. 159]:

inductive *Axiomatics* (⟨⊢⟩) **where**
⟨⊢ q⟩ **if** ⟨⊢ p⟩ **and** ⟨⊢ (p → q)⟩ |
⟨⊢ (p → (q → p))⟩ |
⟨⊢ ((p → q) → ((q → r) → (p → r)))⟩ |
⟨⊢ (((p → q) → p) → p)⟩ |
⟨⊢ (⊥ → p)⟩

The ⊢ predicate holds for a given formula if it can be derived from the specified rule and axioms. Notably, the axioms are schemas, where p and q can be instantiated for any formula. The only rule, here and later, is modus ponens (*MP*). The first axiom (*Imp1*) corresponds to the K combinator, the second (*Tran*) expresses transitivity of implication and the third (*Clas*), Peirce's law, implies the law of the excluded middle. Finally we have the principle of explosion (*Expl*).

As an example, we can derive ⊤ from this last axiom:

theorem ⟨⊢ ⊤⟩ **using** *Axiomatics.intros*(5) .

Isabelle automatically instantiates the given axiom correctly.

Since we have specified the meaning of our formulas in Isabelle, we can verify the soundness of the proof system:

theorem *soundness*: ⟨⊢ p ⟹ I ⊨ p⟩
by (*induct rule*: *Axiomatics.induct*) *auto*

The proof works by induction over the proof system, an induction principle that Isabelle automatically provides. The proof method *auto* discharges each of the resulting proof obligations. Such checks are cheap and easy in Isabelle, helping to prevent typos or other mistakes.

Completeness follows the synthetic recipe due to Henkin and, together with soundness, results in the following theorem:

theorem *main*: ⟨*valid p* = ⊢ *p*⟩
proof
  assume ⟨*valid p*⟩
  with *completeness* **show** ⟨⊢ *p*⟩
    unfolding *valid-def* .
next
  assume ⟨⊢ *p*⟩
  with *soundness* **show** ⟨*valid p*⟩
    unfolding *valid-def* **by** (*intro allI*)
qed

The proof is shown in its entirety to showcase features of the Isabelle syntax.

3.3   Wajsberg 1939

Consider a later proof system by Wajsberg with different axioms [3, p. 163]:

inductive *FW* (⟨⊩⟩) **where**
  ⟨⊩ *q*⟩ **if** ⟨⊩ *p*⟩ **and** ⟨⊩ ($p \rightarrow q$)⟩ |
  ⟨⊩ ($p \rightarrow (q \rightarrow p)$)⟩ |
  ⟨⊩ (($p \rightarrow (q \rightarrow r)$) $\rightarrow$ (($p \rightarrow q$) $\rightarrow$ ($p \rightarrow r$)))⟩ |
  ⟨⊩ ((($p \rightarrow \bot$) $\rightarrow \bot$) $\rightarrow p$)⟩

We still have the *Imp1* axiom corresponding to the K combinator, but as second axiom we now have a correspondence to the S combinator (both axioms used by Frege). Finally, with the abbreviation for *Neg*, we see that this last axiom eliminates a double negation.

We can now verify that the two systems prove the same formulas:

theorem *Axiomatics-FW*: ⟨⊢ *p* ⟷ ⊩ *p*⟩
proof
  have *∗*: ⟨⊩ (($p \rightarrow q$) $\rightarrow$ (($q \rightarrow r$) $\rightarrow$ ($p \rightarrow r$)))⟩ **for** *p q r*
    by (*metis FW.intros(1−3)*)
  then have *∗∗*: ⟨⊩ ((($p \rightarrow q$) $\rightarrow p$) $\rightarrow p$)⟩ **for** *p q*
    by (*metis FW.intros(1−4)*)
  show ⟨⊩ *p*⟩ **if** ⟨⊢ *p*⟩
    using *that* **by** *induct* (*use Imp1 Imp2 Neg Axiomatics.intros in meson*)+
  show ⟨⊢ *p*⟩ **if** ⟨⊩ *p*⟩
    using *that* **by** *induct* (*use ∗ ∗∗ FW.intros in meson*)+
qed

As part of the proof we find derivations for the transitivity principle (*Tran*) and Peirce's law in the latter system.

3.4 Shortest Axiom

Considering the fragment of classical logic with implication but without a symbol for falsity, Łukasiewicz found a shortest single axiom from which you can derive the rest [12].

To obtain completeness for our fragment with a symbol for falsity, we also need the principle of explosion [3, p. 159]:

inductive *WL* (⟨≫⟩) **where**
⟨≫ q⟩ **if** ⟨≫ p⟩ **and** ⟨≫ ($p \to q$)⟩ |
⟨≫ ((($p \to q$) $\to r$) $\to$ (($r \to p$) $\to$ ($s \to p$)))⟩ |
⟨≫ ($\bot \to p$)⟩

Łukasiewicz writes $C\ p\ q$ for $p \to q$. This prefix notation allows him to avoid parentheses. We can use it in Isabelle via the following specification:

abbreviation (*input*) C :: ⟨*form* $\Rightarrow$ *form* $\Rightarrow$ *form*⟩ (⟨C - -⟩ [*0, 0*] *1*) **where**
⟨($C\ p\ q$) $\equiv$ ($p \to q$)⟩

We set the symbol C up with the mixfix specification $[0,0]$, 1, giving the two arguments higher precedence (0) than the full expression (1). This means that e.g. $C\ C\ p\ q\ r$ is parsed correctly into $(p \to q) \to r$. Since we specified the abbreviation as *input* only, any Isabelle output will display the formulas in the conventional $\to$-notation.

Łukasiewicz shows in 29 lines how to derive the Wajsberg axioms (*Axiomatics* above). With our abbreviation we reproduce his derivations almost verbatim in Figs. 1 and 2 on pages 14 and 15. The formalization follows the original faithfully: each line is only derived from the specified lines and modus ponens as passed to the *meson* prover. Łukasiewicz carefully describes how to instantiate each previous formula in order to arrive at the current formula but we leave this to Isabelle to figure out. While Łukasiewicz's paper must be hand-checked to ensure there are no errors, Isabelle instantly verifies the correctness of our formalization. Given those derivations we can prove equivalence between this proof system and the first Wajsberg axioms:

theorem *equivalence*: ⟨≫ p ⟷ ⊢ p⟩
proof
  have ∗: ⟨⊢ ((($p \to q$) $\to r$) $\to$ (($r \to p$) $\to$ ($s \to p$)))⟩ **for** $p\ q\ r\ s$
    using *completeness* **by** *simp*
  show ⟨⊢ p⟩ **if** ⟨≫ p⟩
    using *that* **by** *induct* (*auto simp*: ∗ *intro*: *Axiomatics.intros*)
  show ⟨≫ p⟩ **if** ⟨⊢ p⟩
    using *that* **by** *induct* (*auto simp*: *l27 l28 l29 intro*: *WL.intros*)
qed

We use the completeness of the Wajsberg axioms to show that Łukasiewicz's formula can be derived. In the other direction we use the formulas in lines 27–29 of Fig. 2.

lemma *l1*: ⟨≫ $(C\ C\ C\ p\ q\ r\ C\ C\ r\ p\ C\ s\ p)$⟩
  using *WL.intros(2)* .

lemma *l2*: ⟨≫ $(C\ C\ C\ C\ r\ p\ C\ s\ p\ C\ p\ q\ C\ r\ C\ p\ q)$⟩
  using *l1* **by** *(meson WL.intros(1))*

lemma *l3*: ⟨≫ $(C\ C\ C\ r\ C\ p\ q\ C\ C\ r\ p\ C\ s\ p\ C\ t\ C\ C\ r\ p\ C\ s\ p)$⟩
  using *l1 l2* **by** *(meson WL.intros(1))*

lemma *l4*: ⟨≫ $(C\ C\ C\ p\ q\ p\ C\ s\ p)$⟩
  using *l3 l1* **by** *(meson WL.intros(1))*

lemma *l5*: ⟨≫ $(C\ C\ C\ s\ p\ C\ p\ q\ C\ r\ C\ p\ q)$⟩
  using *l1 l4* **by** *(meson WL.intros(1))*

lemma *l6*: ⟨≫ $(C\ C\ C\ r\ C\ p\ q\ C\ s\ p\ C\ t\ C\ s\ p)$⟩
  using *l1 l5* **by** *(meson WL.intros(1))*

lemma *l7*: ⟨≫ $(C\ C\ C\ t\ C\ s\ p\ C\ r\ C\ p\ q\ C\ u\ C\ r\ C\ p\ q)$⟩
  using *l1 l6* **by** *(meson WL.intros(1))*

lemma *l8*: ⟨≫ $(C\ C\ C\ s\ q\ p\ C\ q\ p)$⟩
  using *l7 l1* **by** *(meson WL.intros(1))*

lemma *l9*: ⟨≫ $(C\ r\ C\ C\ r\ p\ C\ s\ p)$⟩
  using *l8 l1* **by** *(meson WL.intros(1))*

lemma *l10*: ⟨≫ $(C\ C\ C\ C\ C\ r\ q\ p\ C\ s\ p\ r\ C\ t\ r)$⟩
  using *l1 l9* **by** *(meson WL.intros(1))*

lemma *l11*: ⟨≫ $(C\ C\ C\ t\ r\ C\ C\ C\ r\ q\ p\ C\ s\ p\ C\ u\ C\ C\ C\ r\ q\ p\ C\ s\ p)$⟩
  using *l1 l10* **by** *(meson WL.intros(1))*

lemma *l12*: ⟨≫ $(C\ C\ C\ u\ C\ C\ C\ r\ q\ p\ C\ s\ p\ C\ t\ r\ C\ v\ C\ t\ r)$⟩
  using *l1 l11* **by** *(meson WL.intros(1))*

lemma *l13*: ⟨≫ $(C\ C\ C\ v\ C\ t\ r\ C\ u\ C\ C\ C\ r\ q\ p\ C\ s\ p\ C\ w\ C\ u\ C\ C\ C\ r\ q\ p\ C\ s\ p)$⟩
  using *l1 l12* **by** *(meson WL.intros(1))*

lemma *l14*: ⟨≫ $(C\ C\ C\ t\ r\ C\ s\ p\ C\ C\ C\ r\ q\ p\ C\ s\ p)$⟩
  using *l13 l1* **by** *(meson WL.intros(1))*

lemma *l15*: ⟨≫ $(C\ C\ C\ r\ q\ C\ s\ p\ C\ C\ r\ p\ C\ s\ p)$⟩
  using *l14 l1* **by** *(meson WL.intros(1))*

Fig. 1. Lines 1–15 of Łukasiewicz's derivation.

lemma *l16*: ⟨≫ (*C C r C s p C C C r q p C s p*)⟩
   using *l15 l9* **by** (*meson WL.intros(1)*)

lemma *l17*: ⟨≫ (*C C C C C p q r t C s p C C r p C s p*)⟩
   using *l16 l1* **by** (*meson WL.intros(1)*)

lemma *l18*: ⟨≫ (*C C C C r p C s p C C C p q r t C u C C C p q r t*)⟩
   using *l1 l17* **by** (*meson WL.intros(1)*)

lemma *l19*: ⟨≫ (*C C C C s p q C r p C C C p q r C s p*)⟩
   using *l18* **by** (*meson WL.intros(1)*)

lemma *l20*: ⟨≫ (*C C C C r p p C s p C C C p q r C s p*)⟩
   using *l14 l19* **by** (*meson WL.intros(1)*)

lemma *l21*: ⟨≫ (*C C C C p r q q C C q r C p r*)⟩
   using *l20 l15* **by** (*meson WL.intros(1)*)

lemma *l22*: ⟨≫ (*C p p*)⟩
   using *l5 l4* **by** (*meson WL.intros(1)*)

lemma *l23*: ⟨≫ (*C C C p q r C C r p p*)⟩
   using *l20 l22* **by** (*meson WL.intros(1)*)

lemma *l24*: ⟨≫ (*C r C C r p p*)⟩
   using *l8 l23* **by** (*meson WL.intros(1)*)

lemma *l25*: ⟨≫ (*C C p q C C C p r q q*)⟩
   using *l15 l24* **by** (*meson WL.intros(1)*)

lemma *l26*: ⟨≫ (*C C C C p q C C q r C p r C C C p r q q C C C p r q q*)⟩
   using *l25* **by** (*meson WL.intros(1)*)

lemma *l27*: ⟨≫ (*C p C q p*)⟩
   using *l8* **by** (*meson WL.intros(1)*)

lemma *l28*: ⟨≫ (*C C C p q p p*)⟩
   using *l25 l22* **by** (*meson WL.intros(1)*)

lemma *l29*: ⟨≫ (*C C p q C C q r C p r*)⟩
   using *l21 l26* **by** (*meson WL.intros(1)*)

Fig. 2. Lines 16–29 of Łukasiewicz's derivation.

4   Disjunction and Negation

We now wipe the slate clean and consider Rasiowa's axioms for a different fragment of propositional logic built from propositional symbols, negation ($\neg$) and disjunction ($\bigvee$).

4.1   Language

Again we specify the syntax as a datatype in Isabelle:

datatype *form* = *Pro nat* | *Neg form* | *Dis form form* (**infix** ⟨$\bigvee$⟩ *0*)

We regain implication through its classical interpretation:

abbreviation *Imp* (**infix** ⟨$\rightarrow$⟩ *0*) **where** ⟨$(p \rightarrow q) \equiv (Neg\ p \bigvee q)$⟩

We again define the trivially true formula, this time more abstractly since we no longer have $\bot$ available (in Isabelle/HOL, by formulation, each type has one designated value that is *undefined* but we do not know which value it is):

abbreviation *Truth* (⟨$\top$⟩) **where** ⟨$\top \equiv (undefined \rightarrow undefined)$⟩

Given $\top$, however, defining $\bot$ becomes simple:

abbreviation *Falsity* (⟨$\bot$⟩) **where** ⟨$\bot \equiv Neg\ \top$⟩

We specify the semantics similarly to before:

primrec *semantics* (**infix** ⟨$\models$⟩ *0*) **where**
⟨$(I \models Pro\ n) = I\ n$⟩ |
⟨$(I \models Neg\ p) = (if\ I \models p\ then\ False\ else\ True)$⟩ |
⟨$(I \models (p \bigvee q)) = (if\ I \models p\ then\ True\ else\ (I \models q))$⟩

4.2   Rasiowa 1949

Consider the following proof system by Rasiowa [3, p. 157]:

inductive *Axiomatics* (⟨$\vdash$⟩) **where**
⟨$\vdash q$⟩ **if** ⟨$\vdash p$⟩ **and** ⟨$\vdash (p \rightarrow q)$⟩ |
⟨$\vdash ((p \bigvee p) \rightarrow p)$⟩ |
⟨$\vdash (p \rightarrow (p \bigvee q))$⟩ |
⟨$\vdash ((p \rightarrow q) \rightarrow ((r \bigvee p) \rightarrow (q \bigvee r)))$⟩

To aid readability we write the rules using the abbreviation for implication introduced above $(p \rightarrow q \equiv Neg\ p \bigvee q)$, but we recall that it is not a primitive. If we expand the abbreviation for the modus ponens rule *(MP)*, it infers $\vdash q$ from $\vdash p$ and $\vdash \neg p \bigvee q$.

The first axiom *(Idem)* expresses idempotence of disjunction. The second *(AddR)* builds a disjunction from a given formula by adding an arbitrary formula on the right-hand side. Finally, the last axiom *(Swap)* does two things: it replaces the formula on right-hand side of the disjunction with an implied formula and then it swaps the two sides of the disjunction.

The principle of explosion is not a built-in axiom but Isabelle can quickly find a derivation:

theorem ⟨⊢ (⊥ → p)⟩ **using** *Axiomatics.intros* **by** *metis*

We can just as quickly verify the soundness:

theorem *soundness*: ⟨⊢ p ⟹ I ⊨ p⟩
  by (*induct rule*: *Axiomatics.induct*) *auto*

The axiom *AddR* forms a disjunction with the given formula on the left and an arbitrary one on the right. We might wonder if this is essential or whether we could add the arbitrary formula on the left instead (i.e. *AddL*). Isabelle can help answer this question:

proposition *alternative-axiom*: ⟨⊢ (p → (p ∨ q))⟩ **if** ⟨⋀p q. ⊢ (p → (q ∨ p))⟩
  by (*metis MP Idem Swap that*)

We see that *AddR* can be derived from *AddL* (in Isabelle given after **if** and referred to as *that*) alongside the remaining proof system. Note that *AddR* is not made available to *metis*.

Likewise, we can derive *AddL* from the full proof system:

lemma *AddL*: ⟨⊢ (p → (q ∨ p))⟩
  by (*metis MP Idem Swap AddR*)

Thus, we can quickly answer questions about different variants of the axioms.

A notable derivable formula is the following that substitutes a formula on the right-hand side of a disjunction with an implied formula:

lemma *SubR*: ⟨⊢ ((p → q) → ((r ∨ p) → (r ∨ q)))⟩
  by (*meson MP SwapCon Swap*)

Again, we can prove the completeness of the system:

theorem *main*: ⟨valid p = ⊢ p⟩
  (proof omitted)

4.3   Russell 1908 and Bernays 1926

Consider now another proof system over the same fragment [3, p. 157]:

inductive *RB* (⟨⊪⟩) **where**
  ⟨⊪ q⟩ **if** ⟨⊪ p⟩ **and** ⟨⊪ (p → q)⟩ |
  ⟨⊪ ((p ∨ p) → p)⟩ |
  ⟨⊪ (p → (q ∨ p))⟩ |
  ⟨⊪ ((p ∨ q) → (q ∨ p))⟩ |
  ⟨⊪ ((p → q) → ((r ∨ p) → (r ∨ q)))⟩

Here we have first *Idem* and *AddL*, then a permutation or commutativity principle for disjunction (*Perm*) and finally *SubR*. We only need the derived *SubR* to show equivalence:

theorem *Axiomatics-RB*: ⟨⊢ p ⟷ ⊩ p⟩
proof
  show ⟨⊢ p⟩ **if** ⟨⊩ p⟩
    using *that* **by** *induct* (*use SubR Axiomatics.intros* **in** *meson*)+
  show ⟨⊩ p⟩ **if** ⟨⊢ p⟩
    using *that* **by** *induct* (*use RB.intros* **in** *meson*)+
qed

4.4 Whitehead and Russell 1910

Consider next the system for propositional logic that appears in the first volume of the three-volume *Principia Mathematica* (often abbreviated PM):

inductive *PM* (⟨≫⟩) **where**
  ⟨≫ q⟩ **if** ⟨≫ p⟩ **and** ⟨≫ $(p \rightarrow q)$⟩ |
  ⟨≫ $((p \lor p) \rightarrow p)$⟩ |
  ⟨≫ $(p \rightarrow (q \lor p))$⟩ |
  ⟨≫ $((p \lor q) \rightarrow (q \lor p))$⟩ |
  ⟨≫ $((p \lor (q \lor r)) \rightarrow (q \lor (p \lor r)))$⟩ |
  ⟨≫ $((p \rightarrow q) \rightarrow ((r \lor p) \rightarrow (r \lor q)))$⟩

    Here we have *Idem*, *AddL*, *Perm*, a distributivity principle and *SubR*. We can easily show that we can derive at least as many formulas when we have the extra axiom:

proposition *PM-extends-RB*: ⟨⊩ p ⟹ ≫ p⟩
  by (*induct rule*: *RB.induct*) (*auto intro*: *PM.intros*)

    To show the equivalence in both directions, we use the completeness of *RB* to prove the existence of a derivation for the extra axiom:

theorem *equivalence*: ⟨≫ p ⟷ ⊢ p⟩
proof
  have *∗*: ⟨⊢ $((p \lor (q \lor r)) \rightarrow (q \lor (p \lor r)))$⟩ **for** p q r
    using *completeness* **by** *simp*
  show ⟨⊢ p⟩ **if** ⟨≫ p⟩
    using *that* **by** *induct* (*use ∗ SubR Axiomatics.intros* **in** *meson*)+
  show ⟨≫ p⟩ **if** ⟨⊢ p⟩
    using *that* **by** *induct* (*use PM.intros* **in** *meson*)+
qed

5 Challenges and Benefits

Isabelle helped enormously in adapting the completeness proof to each of the two fragments, since it is easy to define abbreviations for non-primitive connectives and the proof assistant gives an error everywhere something needs to be changed. What the proof assistant cannot tell us, is what sub-derivations are needed to derive a key formula. This proved a particular challenge for the Rasiowa axioms for the fragment $\neg, \bigvee$. Those axioms are concerned with these two operators but we usually think in terms of implication, $\rightarrow$, and want to derive formulas like the Wajsberg 1937/1939 axioms (cf. Table 1). However, the starting point does not give us much help. For instance, to derive the following transitivity of implication, a useful lemma for further derivations, we must first derive several other formulas:

lemma *Tran*: $\langle\vdash ((p \rightarrow q) \rightarrow ((q \rightarrow r) \rightarrow (p \rightarrow r)))\rangle$

One of the formulas we found useful is the following, somewhat unintuitive, *SwapAnte* lemma:

lemma *SwapAnte*: $\langle\vdash (((p \bigvee q) \rightarrow r) \rightarrow ((q \bigvee p) \rightarrow r))\rangle$

Luckily, Isabelle makes it easy to quickly derive a range of formulas (or pretend to derive them with **sorry**) and figure out which ones are useful after the fact. As we have shown throughout the paper, this allows us to quickly investigate connections between various proof systems, with Isabelle keeping track of the details for us.

6   Conclusion

We have seen two languages and a range of axiomatic proof systems with various derivations and equivalences. To our knowledge, most of the systems have been formalized here for the first time with soundness and completeness proofs.

Our work is part of the IsaFoL (Isabelle Formalization of Logic) project [1] which aims at developing formalizations in Isabelle/HOL of logics, proof systems, and automatic/interactive provers. Other work in the same line includes completeness of epistemic [7] and hybrid [8] logic and an ordered resolution prover for first-order logic [11]. The project collects formalizations such as ours that can be used as reference documents to verify historical claims, in teaching logic, or to aid in the formalization of other logics and potentially executable provers. Our own formalization could serve as starting point for a student project to formalize the completeness of some other axiomatic proof system.

A notable thing about our approach is that while we show that several formulas are derivable in one system or another, we do not give the derivation itself. Instead, we let an automated prover like *metis* or *meson* find it. This allows us to move quickly and at a higher level than if we spelled out each step in full: faced with a formula that is hard to derive we can experiment with simpler formulas that the automation can handle and try to piece things together afterwards. As mentioned, this was exactly how we worked to derive many of the formulas. However, it also means that even if we prove that a formula can be derived, we have no derivation to inspect; we must simply trust Isabelle that it exists. Meanwhile, we argue that Isabelle is at least as trustworthy as a human author whose work we might not check in the first place. If we do wish to spell out the derivation, Isabelle can help us do so, by proving that derivations exist for our stepping stones.

The ability to introduce abbreviations can provide interesting perspectives on formulas. Consider the usual axiom for disjunction elimination:

lemma $DisE$: $\langle\vdash ((p \rightarrow r) \rightarrow ((q \rightarrow r) \rightarrow ((p \bigvee q) \rightarrow r)))\rangle$

We might think of it as "if both p and q imply r, then if we know either then we know r." In the language with disjunction and negation, the implication is an abbreviation and expanding the inner ones gives us:

$$(\neg p \bigvee r) \rightarrow (\neg q \bigvee r) \rightarrow (p \bigvee q) \rightarrow r$$

This has another natural reading: "either p is false or r holds, and either q is false or r holds, but either p or q is in fact true, so r must hold." An interactive system like Isabelle makes it simple to hide away details like the abbreviation for implication but also to peek at them if we want to.

Acknowledgements. We thank Alexander Birch Jensen, Frederik Krogsdal Jacobsen, Osman Hasan and the anonymous reviewers for comments on drafts.

References

1. Blanchette, J.C.: Formalizing the metatheory of logical calculi and automatic provers in Isabelle/HOL (invited talk). In: Mahboubi, A., Myreen, M.O. (eds.) Proceedings of the 8th ACM SIGPLAN International Conference on Certified Programs and Proofs, CPP 2019, 14–15 January 2019, Cascais, Portugal, pp. 1–13. ACM (2019)
2. Blanchette, J.C., Böhme, S., Paulson, L.C.: Extending sledgehammer with SMT solvers. J. Autom. Reason. **51**(1), 109–128 (2013). https://doi.org/10.1007/s10817-013-9278-5
3. Church, A.: Introduction to Mathematical Logic. Princeton University Press, Princeton (1956)
4. Fitelson, B., Wos, L.: Finding missing proofs with automated reasoning. Studia Logica **68**(3), 329–356 (2001). https://doi.org/10.1023/A:1012486904520
5. From, A.H.: Formalizing Henkin-style completeness of an axiomatic system for propositional logic. In: Proceedings of the Web Summer School in Logic, Language and Information (WeSSLLII) and the European Summer School in Logic, Language and Information (ESSLLI) Virtual Student Session (2020), pp. 1–12, preliminary paper. https://www.brandeis.edu/nasslli2020/pdfs/student-session-proceedings-compressed.pdf#page=8. Accepted for Springer post-proceedings
6. From, A.H., Villadsen, J., Blackburn, P.: Isabelle/HOL as a meta-language for teaching logic. In: Quaresma, P., Neuper, W., Marcos, J. (eds.) Proceedings 9th International Workshop on Theorem Proving Components for Educational Software, ThEdu@IJCAR 2020, 29th June 2020, Paris, France. EPTCS, vol. 328, pp. 18–34 (2020). https://doi.org/10.4204/EPTCS.328.2
7. From, A.H.: Epistemic logic: completeness of modal logics. Archive of Formal Proofs, October 2018. https://devel.isa-afp.org/entries/Epistemic_Logic.html, Formal proof development

8. From, A.H.: Formalizing a Seligman-style tableau system for hybrid logic. Archive of Formal Proofs, December 2019. https://isa-afp.org/entries/Hybrid_Logic.html, Formal proof development

9. Michaelis, J., Nipkow, T.: Formalized proof systems for propositional logic. In: Abel, A., Forsberg, F.N., Kaposi, A. (eds.) 23rd International Conference on Types for Proofs and Programs, TYPES 2017, 29 May–1 June 2017, Budapest, Hungary. LIPIcs, vol. 104, pp. 5:1–5:16. Schloss Dagstuhl - Leibniz-Zentrum für Informatik (2017)

10. Nipkow, T., Wenzel, M., Paulson, L.C. (eds.): Isabelle/HOL. LNCS, vol. 2283. Springer, Heidelberg (2002). https://doi.org/10.1007/3-540-45949-9

11. Schlichtkrull, A., Blanchette, J., Traytel, D., Waldmann, U.: Formalizing Bachmair and Ganzinger's ordered resolution prover. J. Autom. Reason. **64**(7), 1169–1195 (2020)

12. Łukasiewicz, J.: The shortest axiom of the implicational calculus of propositions. Proc. Royal Irish Acad. Sect. A: Math. Phys. Sci. **52**, 25–33 (1948)

13. Wos, L., Pieper, G.W.: Automated Reasoning and the Discovery of Missing and Elegant Proofs. Rinton Press, Princeton (2003)

Formalization of RBD-Based Cause Consequence Analysis in HOL

Mohamed Abdelghany$^{(\boxtimes)}$ and Sofiène Tahar$^{(\boxtimes)}$

Department of Electrical and Computer Engineering,
Concordia University, Montreal, QC, Canada
{m_eldes,tahar}@ece.concordia.ca

Abstract. Cause consequence analysis is a safety assessment technique that is traditionally used to model the causes of subsystem failures in a critical system and their potential consequences using Fault Tree and Event Tree (ET) dependability modeling techniques, combined in a graphical Cause-Consequence Diagram (CCD). In this paper, we propose a novel idea of using Reliability Block Diagrams (RBD) for CCD analysis based on formal methods. Unlike Fault Trees, RBDs allow to model the success relationships of subsystem components to keep the entire subsystem reliable. To this end, we formalize in higher-order logic new mathematical formulations of CCD functions for the RBD modeling of generic n-subsystems using HOL4. This formalization enables universal n-level CCD analysis, based on RBDs and ETs, by determining the probabilities of multi-state safety classes, i.e., complete/partial failure and success, that can occur in the entire complex systems at the subsystem level.

Keywords: Cause-Consequence Diagram · Reliability Block Diagram · Event Tree · Higher-order logic · Theorem proving

1 Introduction

Since the late 60's, various types of dependability modeling techniques have been developed to determine the safety assessment of safety-critical systems, such as smart grids and automotive industry. These include predominantly graph theory based approaches such as Fault Trees (FT) [18], Reliability Block Diagrams (RBD) [7] and Event Trees (ET) [14]. FTs mainly provide a graphical model for analyzing the factors causing a complete system failure upon their occurrences. On the other hand, RBDs provide a schematic structure for analyzing the success relationships of system components that keep the entire system reliable. In contrast to FTs and RBDs, ETs provide a tree model for all possible complete/partial failure and success scenarios at the system-level so that one of these possible scenarios can occur [14]. More recently, an approach has been proposed to conduct ET analysis in conjunction with FTs to identify all subsystem failure events in a critical system and their cascading dependencies on the entire system [16]. This analysis method is known as cause-consequence analysis, using a combined hierarchical structure of Cause-Consequence Diagrams (CCD) [16].

© Springer Nature Switzerland AG 2021
F. Kamareddine and C. Sacerdoti Coen (Eds.): CICM 2021, LNAI 12833, pp. 47–64, 2021.
https://doi.org/10.1007/978-3-030-81097-9_4

Traditionally, CCD analysis based on FTs and ETs is carried out by using paper-and-pencil approaches (e.g., [5]) or computer simulation tools (e.g., [20]). The major limitations of the manual analysis approach are its human-error proneness and scalability to handle large complex systems [19]. On the other hand, simulation-based analysis approaches, such as MATLAB Monte-Carlo Simulation (MCS), can be used for CCD analysis for faster computation. They, however, lack the rigor of detailed proof steps and absolute accuracy (i.e., results approximation) due to an explosion of the test cases [20]. A more practical way to remedy the shortcomings of informal reasoning approaches of cause-consequence analysis is to use formal generic mathematical formulations that can analyze large-scale CCD graphs. Only a few works have previously considered using formal methods for cause-consequence analysis. For instance, Ortmeier et al. in [13] developed a formal framework for Deductive Cause-Consequence Analysis (DCCA) using the SMV model checker to formally verify probabilistic properties for CCD analysis. However, according to the authors of [9], there is a scalability problem of showing the completeness of DCCA due to the exponential growth of the number of proof obligations with large complex CCD graphs. For that reason, to overcome the above-mentioned limitations, we endeavor to solve the scalability problem of CCDs by using theorem proving, in particular the HOL4 proof assistant [10], which provides the ability of verifying generic expressions constructed in higher-order logic (HOL).

Prior to this work, there were three notable projects for building formal infrastructures in HOL to formally model and analyze FTs, RBDs and ETs. For instance, Ahmad [4] used the HOL4 theorem prover to formalize ordinary (static) FT and RBD structures. Elderhalli [8] had formalized dynamic versions of FTs and RBDs in HOL4. These formalizations have been used for the reliability analysis of several engineering systems. However, they formally analyze either a critical system static/dynamic failure or static/dynamic success only. Therefore, in [2], we developed a HOL4 theory to reason about ETs considering all failure and success events of system-level components simultaneously. We proposed a new datatype EVENT_TREE consisting of ET basic constructors that can build large scale ET diagrams and provides us with the ability to obtain a verified system-level failure/operating expression. Moreover, in [3], we proposed a formal approach for state-of-the-art CCD analysis using the above static FT and ET formalizations, which enables safety analysts to perform formal failure analysis for n-level subsystems of a complex system and obtain all possible complete/partial failure and success consequences events that can occur in HOL4. However, in order to identify potential areas of poor reliability, safety analysts often require a reliability model that is close to the hierarchical structure of the subsystem components. For that reason, we propose in this paper a novel approach to conduct a CCD analysis based on RBDs rather than FTs. In particular, we develop new formulations of CCDs based on RBD and ET theories, and provide their formalization using HOL theorem proving.

Unlike FT-based CCD analysis, RBDs allow to model all success relationships of n-subsystems to keep them reliable and obtain multi-state consequence safety classes, i.e., complete/partial failure and complete/partial success, that can occur in the entire critical system at the subsystem level. To the best of our knowledge, the idea of using RBD modeling in conjunction with the graph theory of CCDs has not been proposed before. We propose new mathematical formulations that can analyze scalable CCDs associated with different RBD configurations to n-subsystems. In order to check the correctness of the newly-proposed equations, we verified them within the sound environment of the HOL4 theorem prover. To this end, we formalize in HOL4 cause-consequence functions for the formal modeling of the graph theory of RBDs corresponding to generic n-subsystems. Also, our proposed formalization enables the formal probabilistic assessment of large scale n-level CCD structures based on any probabilistic distribution, which makes our work the first of its kind.

The rest of the paper is organized as follows: In Sect. 2, we describe some preliminaries of RBDs and ETs to facilitate understanding of the rest of the paper. Section 3 presents the proposed formalization of CCDs based on RBDs and ETs, including the newly introduced probabilistic formulations and their verification in the HOL4 theorem prover. Lastly, Sect. 4 concludes the paper.

2   Preliminaries

In this section, we summarize the fundamentals of existing RBD and ET formalizations in HOL4 to facilitate the reader's understanding of the rest of the paper.

2.1   RBD Formalization

Reliability Block Diagram [7] (RBD) analysis is one of the commonly used safety assessment techniques for critical systems. It mainly provides a schematic diagram for analyzing the success relationships of subsystem components that keep the entire subsystem reliable. An RBD structure consists of blocks that represent the subsystem components and connectors that indicate the connections between these components. An RBD has two main types of configuration patterns *series* and *parallel*. The reliability of a subsystem when its components are connected in series configuration is considered to be reliable at time t only if all of the components are functioning reliably at time t, then the overall reliability $\mathcal{R}$ of the subsystem can be mathematically expressed as [7]:

$$\mathcal{R}_{series}(t) = Pr\left(\bigcap_{i=1}^{N} X_i(t)\right) = \prod_{i=1}^{N} \mathcal{R}_i(t) \tag{1}$$

Similarly, the reliability of a subsystem where its components connected in parallel will continue functioning at a specific time t as long as at least one of its components remains functional, which can be mathematically expressed as [7]:

$$\mathcal{R}_{parallel}(t) = Pr\left(\bigcup_{i=1}^{N} X_i(t)\right) = 1 - \prod_{i=1}^{N}(1 - \mathcal{R}_i(t)) \tag{2}$$

Ahmad et al. in [4] presented the RBD formalization by defining a new datatype rbd, in HOL4 as:

Hol_datatype rbd = series of (rbd list) | parallel of (rbd list) | atomic of (event)

The RBD constructors series and parallel are recursive functions on rbd-typed lists, while the RBD constructor atomic operates on an rbd-type variable. A semantic function is then defined over the rbd datatype that can yield mathematically the corresponding RBD diagram as:

Definition 1
⊢ rbd_struct p (atomic X) = X ∧
   rbd_struct p (series []) = p_space p ∧ rbd_struct p (parallel[]) = {} ∧
   rbd_struct p (series (X::XN)) =
   rbd_struct p X ∩ rbd_struct p (series XN) ∧
   rbd_struct p (parallel (X::XN)) =
   rbd_struct p X ∪ rbd_struct p (parallel XN)

The function rbd_struct takes a single event X, identified by a basic type constructor atomic, and returns the given event X. If the function rbd_struct takes an arbitrary list of type rbd, identified by a type constructor series, then it performs the intersection of all elements after applying the function rbd_struct on each element of the given list. Similarly, if the function rbd_struct takes an arbitrary list of type rbd, identified by a type constructor parallel, then it returns the union of all elements after applying the function rbd_struct on each element of the list X_N. The formal verification in HOL4 for the reliability series and parallel probabilistic expressions Eq. 1 and Eq. 2, respectively, is presented in Table 1 [4]. These mathematical expressions (Theorems 1–2) are verified under the constraints that (a) all associated events in the given list X_N are drawn from the events space p ($X_N \in$ events p); (b) p is a valid probability space (prob_space p); and lastly (c) the events in the given list X_N are independent (MUTUAL_INDEP p X_N). The function PROB_LIST takes an arbitrary list $[Z_1, Z_2, Z_3, \ldots, Z_N]$ and returns a list of probabilities associated with the

Table 1. RBD probabilistic theorems [4]

RBD Connection	Probabilistic Theorem
Input X₁ — X₂ —ᴺ--- Xₙ Output	**Theorem 1:** prob p (rbd_struct p (series X_N)) = ∏ (PROB_LIST p X_N)
Input X₁ X₂ X₃ ⋮N Xₙ Output	**Theorem 2:** prob p (rbd_struct p (parallel X_N)) = 1 − ∏ (PROB_LIST p (COMPL_LIST p X_N))

elements of the list [`prob p` Z_1,`prob p` Z_2,`prob p` Z_3,..., `prob p` Z_N], while the function `COMPL_LIST` takes a list $[X_1, X_2, X_3, ..., X_N]$ and returns the complement of all elements in the list $[(1 - X_1), (1 - X_2), (1 - X_3), ..., (1 - X_N)]$. The function $\prod$ takes a list $[Y_1, Y_2, Y_3, ..., Y_N]$ and returns the product of the list elements $Y_1 \times Y_2 \times Y_3 \times \cdots \times Y_N$.

2.2   ET Formalization

Event Tree [14] (ET) is a widely used dependability modeling technique that can model all possible system-level components failure and success states and their cascading dependencies on the entire system in the form of a tree structure. An ET diagram starts by an *Initiating Node* from which all possible consequence scenarios of a sudden event that can occur in the system are drawn as *Branches* connected to *Proceeding Nodes* so that *only one* of these scenarios can occur, i.e., all possible ET consequence paths are disjoint (mutually exclusive) and distinct. These ET constructors were formally modeled using a new recursive datatype `EVENT_TREE`, in HOL4 as [2]:

Hol_datatype `EVENT_TREE` = `ATOMIC of (event)` | `NODE of (EVENT_TREE list)` | `BRANCH of (event) (EVENT_TREE)`

The type constructors `NODE` and `BRANCH` are recursive functions on `EVENT_TREE`-typed. A semantic function is then defined over the `EVENT_TREE` datatype that can yield a corresponding ET diagram as:

Definition 2
⊢ `ETREE (ATOMIC Y) = Y` ∧ `ETREE (NODE []) = {}` ∧
   `ETREE (NODE (X::XN)) = ETREE X` ∪ `(ETREE (NODE XN))` ∧
   `ETREE (BRANCH Y Z) = Y` ∩ `ETREE Z`

The function `ETREE` takes a success/fail event `Y`, identified by an ET type constructor `ATOMIC` and returns the event `Y`. If the function `ETREE` takes a list `XN` of type `EVENT_TREE`, identified by a type constructor `NODE`, then it returns the union of all elements after applying the function `ETREE` on each element of the given list. Similarly, if the function `ETREE` takes a success/fail event `X` and a proceeding ET `Z`, identified by a type constructor of `EVENT_TREE` type, then it performs the intersection of the event `X` with the ET `Z` after applying the function `ETREE`. For the formal probabilistic assessment of each path occurrence in the ET diagram, HOL4 probabilistic properties for `NODE` and `BRANCH` ET constructors are presented in Table 2 [2]. These expressions are formally verified under the same RBD constraints, i.e., $X_N \in$ `events p`, `prob_space p`, `MUTUAL_INDEP p` X_N, as well as the ET constraints defined by Papazoglou [14] (*distinct, disjoint, finite*), i.e., `ALL_DISTINCT` X_N and `disjoint` X_N to ensure that each pair of elements in a given list X_N is distinct and mutually exclusive, respectively. The elements in a list are intrinsically finite and thus all ET constraint requirements are satisfied. The function $\sum$ takes a list $[X_1, X_2, X_3, ..., X_N]$ and returns the sum of the list elements $X_1 + X_2 + X_3 + \cdots + X_N$.

Table 2. ET probabilistic theorems [2]

ET Constructor	Probabilistic Theorem
Initiating Node X1 N XN	**Theorem 3:** prob p (ETREE (NODE X_N)) = $\sum$ (PROB_LIST p X_N)
Branch Z1 N Y ← ZN Proceeding Node	**Theorem 4:** prob p (ETREE (BRANCH Y (NODE Z_N))) = (prob p Y) × $\sum$ (PROB_LIST p Z_N)

3   Cause-Consequence Diagram Formalization

The graph theory of CCDs [21] uses three basic constructors *Decision box, Consequence path* and *Consequence box* [6]. The detailed description of the CCD constructors is illustrated in Table 3. To present a clear understanding of these concepts, the traditional FT/ET-based CCD analysis for n-subsystems is described in Fig. 1a. As shown in Fig. 1a, FT *logic*-gates, such as AND (models the complete failure of the subsystem if all of the input failure events occur at the same time) and OR (models the complete failure of the subsystem if any of the input failure events occurs alone), are associated with all decision boxes to model the failure of generic n-subsystems. It can be noticed from Fig. 1a that the output of each NO BOX for all decision boxes is equal to the subsystem FT model (FT_X), while the YES BOX is the complement of the FT model ($\overline{FT_X}$). Analogously to

Table 3. CCD symbols and functions [3]

CCD Symbol	Function
Traditional Decision Box Subsystem Functions Correctly YES | NO FT *Proposed Decision Box* Subsystem Functions Correctly YES | NO RBD	Decision Box: represents the status of functionality for a component or subsystem. (1) NO Box: describes the subsystem failure operation. An FT or RBD of the subsystem is connected to this box that can be used to determine the failure probability, i.e., $\mathcal{P}_{NO} = \mathcal{P}_{FT} = 1 - \mathcal{P}_{RBD}$ (2) YES Box: represents the correct functioning of the subsystem or reliability, which can be calculated by simply taking the complement of the failure operation, i.e., $\mathcal{P}_{YES} = 1 - \mathcal{P}_{FT} = \mathcal{P}_{RBD}$
⌐⌐↓	Consequence Path: models the next possible scenarios due to the occurrence of subsystem failure or reliability
⬡	Consequence Box: models the final outcome event due to a particular sequence of events for all connected subsystems

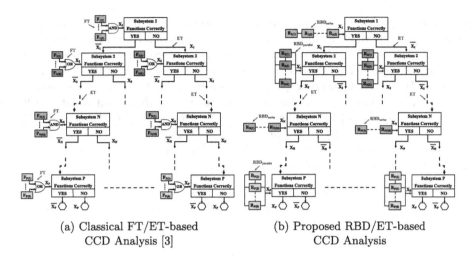

(a) Classical FT/ET-based
CCD Analysis [3]

(b) Proposed RBD/ET-based
CCD Analysis

Fig. 1. Cause consequence analysis models

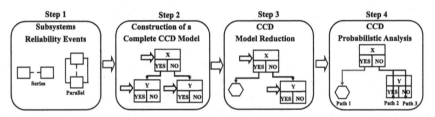

Fig. 2. Overview of RBD-based CCD analysis [3]

Fig. 1a, Fig. 1b illustrates the proposed RBD/ET-based CCD analysis, where different RBD configurations, such as *series* (models the complete success of the subsystem if all of the input success events occur at the same time) and *parallel* (models the complete success of the subsystem if any of the input success events occurs alone), are associated with all CCD decision boxes to model the reliability of generic n-subsystems. As shown in Fig. 1b, the output of each YES BOX for all decision boxes is equal to the RBD outcome (RBD_X), while the NO BOX is the complement of the RBD model ($\overline{RBD_X}$).

Figure 2 depicts the overview of the developed *four* steps of cause-consequence safety analysis for complex systems [5]: (1) *Subsystems reliability events*: identify the success events for all subsystems using RBD models that keep the subsystems reliable in a complex system; (2) *Construction of a complete CCD*: build a full CCD diagram using its basic constructors (see Table 3) considering that the order of components should follow the temporal action of the system; (3) *CCD model reduction*: remove the unnecessary decision boxes in the system to obtain its minimal CCD model representing the actual functional behavior of the complex system and reduce the number of test cases; and (4) *CCD probabilistic analysis*: determine the probabilities of all CCD consequence paths, which represent the likelihood of specific sequence scenarios that are possible to occur in a system so that *only one* scenario can occur [19]. This implies that all consequences in a CCD are mutually exclusive [6]. As an example, consider a Wind Turbine system [15] consisting of two main subsystems: Induction Generator (IG) and Power Converter (PC), as shown in Fig. 3a [11]. An IG consists of three components *Stator*, *Rotor* and *Brushes* [12], while a PC consists of four components *Rotor Side AC/DC Converter* (RSC), *DC Filter*, *Grid Side DC/AC Converter* (GSC) and *Control Unit* (CU) [17]. The *four* main steps of the above-mentioned RBD/ET-based cause-consequence analysis for the wind turbine system can be done as follows:

1. *Components reliability events*: Assign an RBD series configuration to each subsystem in the wind turbine, i.e., $\mathcal{R}_{IG}$, $\mathcal{R}_{PC}$, as shown in Fig. 3b [11], which can be expressed mathematically as:

$$\mathcal{R}_{IG} = \mathcal{R}_{stator} \times \mathcal{R}_{rotor} \times \mathcal{R}_{brushes} \qquad (3)$$

$$\mathcal{R}_{PC} = \mathcal{R}_{RSC} \times \mathcal{R}_{filter} \times \mathcal{R}_{GSC} \times \mathcal{R}_{CU} \qquad (4)$$

2. *Construction of a complete CCD*: Draw a complete CCD model of the wind turbine system, as shown in Fig. 4a. For instance, if the condition of the IG decision box is either YES or NO, then the next subsystem PC is taken into consideration. Each consequence path in the CCD analysis ends with either a wind turbine success (WT_S) or a wind turbine failure (WT_F).

3. *CCD model reduction*: Apply the reduction operation on the constructed complete CCD model. For instance, if the condition of the IG decision box (IG functions correctly) is not satisfied, i.e., NO box, then the wind turbine fails regardless of the status of PC. Figure 4b represents the minimal RBD/ET-based cause consequence analysis of the wind turbine operation.

4. *CCD probabilistic analysis*: The probabilistic assessment of the two consequence boxes WT_S and WT_F in Fig. 4b can be expressed mathematically as:

$$P(Consequence\_Box_{WT_S}) = P(IG_{YES}) \times P(PC_{YES}) \qquad (5)$$

$$P(Consequence\_Box_{WT_F}) = P(IG_{YES}) \times P(PC_{NO}) + P(IG_{NO}) \qquad (6)$$

where $P(X_{YES})$ is the reliability function outgoing from a subsystem decision box, i.e., $\mathcal{R}_X$ model, and $P(X_{NO})$ is the unreliability function or the probability of failure, i.e., the complement of the $\mathcal{R}_X$ model ($\overline{\mathcal{R}_X}$).

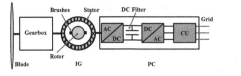

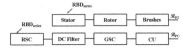

(a) WT Structure   (b) RBD Models of WT Subsystems

Fig. 3. Wind turbine system [11]

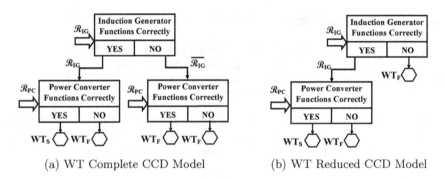

(a) WT Complete CCD Model   (b) WT Reduced CCD Model

Fig. 4. Wind turbine cause consequence analysis

3.1   Formal CCD Modeling

The CCD basic constructors *Decision box*, *Consequence path* and *Consequence box*, as described in Table 3, were formally developed, in HOL4, respectively, as [3]:

Definition 3
⊢ DECISION_BOX p X Y = if X = 1 then FST Y else if X = 0 then SND Y
                       else p_space p

where Y is an ordered pair (FST Y, SND Y) representing the reliability and unreliability functions in a decision box, respectively. The condition X = 1 represents the YES Box while X = 0 represents the NO Box. If X is neither 1 nor 0, for instance, X = 2, then this represents the irrelevance of the decision box, which returns the probability space p to be used in the CCD reduction process.

Secondly, the CCD *Consequence path* is defined by recursively applying the BRANCH ET basic constructor (see Sect. 2.2) on a given n-list of decision boxes (DECISION_BOX$_\mathcal{N}$) using the HOL4 recursive list function FOLDL as:

Definition 4
⊢ CONSEQ_PATH p (DECISION_BOX$_1$::DECISION_BOX$_\mathcal{N}$)
  = FOLDL (λa b. ETREE (BRANCH a (ATOMIC b))) DECISION_BOX$_1$ DECISION_BOX$_\mathcal{N}$

Finally, the CCD *Consequence box* is defined by mapping the function CONSEQ_PATH on a given *two-dimensional* list of consequence paths L$_\mathcal{M}$ using the HOL4 mapping function MAP, then apply the NODE ET constructor:

Definition 5
⊢ CONSEQ_BOX p L$_\mathcal{M}$ = ETREE (NODE (MAP (λa. CONSEQ_PATH p a) L$_\mathcal{M}$))

Using the above-mentioned CCD *generic* definitions, we can formally construct a complete CCD model (*Step 2* in Fig. 2) for the wind turbine shown in Fig. 4a, in HOL4 as:

⊢ Wind_Turbine_Complete_CCD $\mathcal{R}_{IG}$ $\mathcal{R}_{PC}$ =
  CONSEQ_BOX p
   [[DECISION_BOX p 1 $(\mathcal{R}_{IG},\overline{\mathcal{R}_{IG}})$; DECISION_BOX p 1 $(\mathcal{R}_{PC},\overline{\mathcal{R}_{PC}})$];
   [DECISION_BOX p 1 $(\mathcal{R}_{IG},\overline{\mathcal{R}_{IG}})$; DECISION_BOX p 0 $(\mathcal{R}_{PC},\overline{\mathcal{R}_{PC}})$];
   [DECISION_BOX p 0 $(\mathcal{R}_{IG},\overline{\mathcal{R}_{IG}})$; DECISION_BOX p 1 $(\mathcal{R}_{PC},\overline{\mathcal{R}_{PC}})$];
   [DECISION_BOX p 0 $(\mathcal{R}_{IG},\overline{\mathcal{R}_{IG}})$; DECISION_BOX p 0 $(\mathcal{R}_{PC},\overline{\mathcal{R}_{PC}})$]]

In cause-consequence safety analysis [19], *Step 3* in Fig. 2 is to minimize the complete CCD model in the sense that the unnecessary decision boxes should be eliminated to decrease the number of test cases and model the accurate functional behavior of systems. Upon this, the reduced CCD model that actually represents the wind turbine system, as shown in Fig. 4b, can be constructed formally by assigning X with neither 1 nor 0 options, for instance, X = 2, which represents the irrelevance of the decision box, in HOL4 as:

⊢ Wind_Turbine_Reduced_CCD $\mathcal{R}_{IG}$ $\mathcal{R}_{PC}$ =
  CONSEQ_BOX p
   [[DECISION_BOX p 1 $(\mathcal{R}_{IG},\overline{\mathcal{R}_{IG}})$; DECISION_BOX p 1 $(\mathcal{R}_{PC},\overline{\mathcal{R}_{PC}})$];
   [DECISION_BOX p 1 $(\mathcal{R}_{IG},\overline{\mathcal{R}_{IG}})$; DECISION_BOX p 0 $(\mathcal{R}_{PC},\overline{\mathcal{R}_{PC}})$];
   [DECISION_BOX p 0 $(\mathcal{R}_{IG},\overline{\mathcal{R}_{IG}})$; DECISION_BOX p 2 $(\mathcal{R}_{PC},\overline{\mathcal{R}_{PC}})$]]

Also, we can formally verify the above minimal CCD model of the wind turbine system after reduction, in HOL4 as:

⊢ Wind_Turbine_Reduced_CCD $\mathcal{R}_{IG}$ $\mathcal{R}_{PC}$ =
  CONSEQ_BOX p
   [[DECISION_BOX p 1 $(\mathcal{R}_{IG},\overline{\mathcal{R}_{IG}})$; DECISION_BOX p 1 $(\mathcal{R}_{PC},\overline{\mathcal{R}_{PC}})$];
   [DECISION_BOX p 1 $(\mathcal{R}_{IG},\overline{\mathcal{R}_{IG}})$; DECISION_BOX p 0 $(\mathcal{R}_{PC},\overline{\mathcal{R}_{PC}})$];
   [DECISION_BOX p 0 $(\mathcal{R}_{IG},\overline{\mathcal{R}_{IG}})$]]

3.2 Formal CCD Analysis

The last step in the cause-consequence analysis is to evaluate the probability of each path occurrence in the CCD model [6]. For that purpose, we propose the following novel CCD probabilistic mathematical formulations, based on RBD and ET modeling techniques, which have the capability to determine the probability of *n-level* CCD paths corresponding to n-subsystems in a critical system, where each subsystem consists of an arbitrary list of RBD events. Then, we provide the formalization of the proposed new formulas in HOL4.

One Decision Box: Figure 5 depicts a single CCD decision box associated with either a series or a parallel RBD pattern. It can be observed that the YES BOX of the former CCD diagram with a series RBD model is the outcome of Eq. 1 and its NO BOX is the complement of Eq. 1. Similarly, the YES BOX of the later CCD diagram with a parallel RBD model is the outcome of Eq. 2 and its NO BOX is the complement of Eq. 2. The probability of a consequence path for each CCD decision box assigned with a *generic* RBD model consisting of n-events, i.e., series or parallel, as shown in Fig. 5, is verified under the constraints described in Table 1 (Sect. 2.1), respectively, in HOL4 as:

Theorem 5

⊢ let $\text{RBD}_{\text{series}}$ = rbd_struct p (series X_N)
   in prob_space p ∧ X_N ∈ events p ∧ MUTUAL_INDEP p X_N ⇒
   prob p (CONSEQ_PATH p [DECISION_BOX p J ($\text{RBD}_{\text{series}}$,COMPL p ($\text{RBD}_{\text{series}}$))])
     = if J = 1 then $\prod$ (PROB_LIST p X_N)
   else if J = 0 then 1 - $\prod$ (PROB_LIST p X_N) else 1

Theorem 6

⊢ let $\text{RBD}_{\text{parallel}}$ = rbd_struct p (parallel Y_M)
   in prob_space p ∧ Y_M ∈ events p ∧ MUTUAL_INDEP p Y_M ⇒
   prob p (CONSEQ_PATH p [DECISION_BOX p K ($\text{RBD}_{\text{parallel}}$,COMPL p($\text{RBD}_{\text{parallel}}$))])
     = if K = 1 then 1 - $\prod$ (PROB_LIST p (COMPL_LIST p Y_M))
   else if K = 0 then $\prod$ (PROB_LIST p (COMPL_LIST p Y_M)) else 1

where the function COMPL is defined to take a set X, which is the output of the RBD function rbd_struct, and returns the complement of the set X in the probability space p. For a complex graph of CCDs consisting of n-level decision boxes, where each decision box is associated with a series/parallel RBD model consisting of an arbitrary list of success events, we define *three* types A, B and C with all possible CCD consequence scenarios that can occur.

N Decision Boxes (Type A): The probability of n-level decision boxes assigned to a consequence path corresponding to n-subsystems of a complex system, where each decision box is associated with a *generic* RBD model consisting of an arbitrary list of k-events in a *series* connection, can be expressed mathematically for *three* cases as:

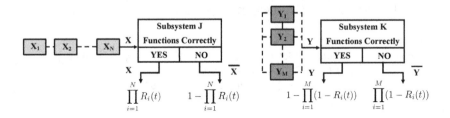

Fig. 5. CCD decision boxes with RBD connections

(A1) All outcomes of n decisions boxes are YES

$$\mathcal{R}_{A1}(t) = \prod_{i=1}^{n}\prod_{j=1}^{k} \mathcal{R}_{ij}(t) \tag{7}$$

(A2) All outcomes of n decisions boxes are NO

$$\mathcal{R}_{A2}(t) = \prod_{i=1}^{n}(1 - \prod_{j=1}^{k} \mathcal{R}_{ij}(t)) \tag{8}$$

(A3) Some outcomes of m decisions boxes are YES and the rest outcomes of p decisions boxes are NO, as shown in Fig. 6a, respectively, as follows:

$$\mathcal{R}_{A3}(t) = \left(\prod_{i=1}^{m} \prod_{j=1}^{k} \mathcal{R}_{ij}(t) \right) \times \left(\prod_{i=1}^{p} (1 - \prod_{j=1}^{k} \mathcal{R}_{ij}(t)) \right) \tag{9}$$

To formalize the above-proposed new cause-consequence mathematical formulations in HOL4, we formally define two *generic* functions $\mathcal{SS}_{series}^{YES}$ and $\mathcal{SS}_{series}^{NO}$ that can recursively generate the outcomes YES and NO of the RBD function `rbd_struct`, identified by the RBD basic constructor `series`, for a given arbitrary list of subsystems (SS) events, respectively as:

Definition 6
⊢ $\mathcal{SS}_{series}^{YES}$ p (SS1::SSN) =
   rbd_struct p (series (rbd_list SS1))::$\mathcal{SS}_{series}^{YES}$ p SSN

Definition 7
⊢ $\mathcal{SS}_{series}^{NO}$ p (SS::SSN) =
   COMPL p (rbd_struct p (series (rbd_list SS1)))::$\mathcal{SS}_{series}^{NO}$ p SSN

Using the above defined functions, we can verify *two-dimensional* and *scalable* CCD probabilistic properties corresponding to the proposed formulas Eq. 7, Eq. 8 and Eq. 9, respectively, in HOL4 as:

Theorem 7
⊢ prob_space p ∧ MUTUAL_INDEP p SSN ∧ ∀y. y ∈ SSN ⇒ y ∈ events p ∧ ⇒
   prob p (CONSEQ_PATH p ($\mathcal{SS}_{series}^{YES}$ p SSN)) =
      ∏ (MAP (λ a. ∏ (PROB_LIST p a)) SSN)

Theorem 8
⊢ prob_space p ∧ MUTUAL_INDEP p SSN ∧ ∀y. y ∈ SSN ⇒ y ∈ events p ∧ ⇒
   prob p (CONSEQ_PATH p ($\mathcal{SS}_{series}^{NO}$ p SSN)) =
      ∏ (MAP (λ b. (1 - ∏ (PROB_LIST p b))) SSN)

Theorem 9
⊢ prob_space p ∧ MUTUAL_INDEP p (SSM ++ SSP) ∧
   ∀y. y ∈ (SSM ++ SSP) ⇒ y ∈ events p ∧ ⇒
   prob p (CONSEQ_PATH p [CONSEQ_PATH p ($\mathcal{SS}_{series}^{YES}$ p SSM);
                          CONSEQ_PATH p ($\mathcal{SS}_{series}^{NO}$ p SSP)]) =
      ∏ (MAP (λ a. ∏ (PROB_LIST p a)) SSM) ×
      ∏ (MAP (λ b. (1 - ∏ (PROB_LIST p b))) SSP)

where the assumptions of Theorems 7–9 are similar to the ones used in Theorems 1–4 (see Sect. 2).

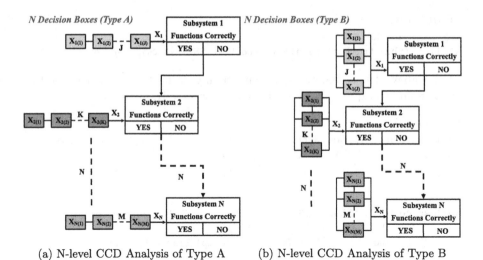

(a) N-level CCD Analysis of Type A   (b) N-level CCD Analysis of Type B

Fig. 6. Proposed N-level decision boxes for CCD analysis

N Decision Boxes (Type B): Similarly, the probabilistic assessment of n-level decision boxes assigned to a CCD consequence path, where each decision box is associated with a *generic* RBD model consisting of k-events connected in *parallel*, can be expressed mathematically for *three* cases: (B1) All outcomes of n decisions boxes are YES; (B2) All outcomes of n decisions boxes are NO; and (B3) Some outcomes of m decisions boxes are YES and some outcomes of p decisions boxes are NO, as shown in Fig. 6b, respectively, as follows:

$$\mathcal{R}_{B1}(t) = \prod_{i=1}^{n}(1 - \prod_{j=1}^{k}(1 - \mathcal{R}_{ij}(t))) \tag{10}$$

$$\mathcal{R}_{B2}(t) = \prod_{i=1}^{n}\prod_{j=1}^{k}(1 - \mathcal{R}_{ij}(t)) \tag{11}$$

$$\mathcal{R}_{B3}(t) = \left(\prod_{i=1}^{m}(1 - \prod_{j=1}^{k}(1 - \mathcal{R}_{ij}(t)))\right) \times \left(\prod_{i=1}^{p}\prod_{j=1}^{k}(1 - \mathcal{R}_{ij}(t))\right) \tag{12}$$

To verify the correctness of the above-proposed new CCD mathematical formulas in HOL4, we define two *generic* functions $\mathcal{SS}_{parallel}^{YES}$ and $\mathcal{SS}_{parallel}^{NO}$ to recursively generate the outcomes YES and NO of the function `rbd_struct`, identified by the RBD constructor `parallel`, for a given list of subsystems events.

Definition 8
$\vdash \mathcal{SS}_{parallel}^{YES}$ `p (SS1::SSN) =`
    `rbd_struct p (parallel (rbd_list SS1))::`$\mathcal{SS}_{parallel}^{YES}$ `p SSN`

Definition 9
⊢ $SS^{NO}_{parallel}$ p (SS::SSN) =
COMPL p (rbd_struct p (parallel (rbd_list SS1)))::$SS^{NO}_{parallel}$ p SSN

Using above defined functions, we can formally verify three *scalable* properties corresponding to Eq. 10, Eq. 11, and Eq. 12, respectively, in HOL4 as:

Theorem 10
⊢ prob_space p ∧ MUTUAL_INDEP p SSN ∧ ∀y. y ∈ SSN ⇒ y ∈ events p ∧ ⇒
  prob p (CONSEQ_PATH p ($SS^{YES}_{parallel}$ p SSN)) =
    ∏ (MAP (λ a. (1 - ∏ (PROB_LIST p (compl_list p a)))) SSN)

Theorem 11
⊢ prob_space p ∧ MUTUAL_INDEP p SSN ∧ ∀y. y ∈ SSN ⇒ y ∈ events p ∧ ⇒
  prob p (CONSEQ_PATH p ($SS^{NO}_{parallel}$ p SSN)) =
    ∏ (MAP (λ b. ∏ (PROB_LIST p (compl_list p b))) SSN)

Theorem 12
⊢ prob_space p ∧ MUTUAL_INDEP p (SSM ++ SSP) ∧
  ∀y. y ∈ (SSM ++ SSP) ⇒ y ∈ events p ∧ ⇒
  prob p (CONSEQ_PATH p [CONSEQ_PATH p ($SS^{YES}_{parallel}$ p SSM);
                         CONSEQ_PATH p ($SS^{NO}_{parallel}$ p SSP)]) =
    ∏ (MAP (λ a. (1 - ∏ (PROB_LIST p (compl_list p a)))) SSM) ×
    ∏ (MAP (λ b. ∏ (PROB_LIST p (compl_list p b))) SSP)

N Decision Boxes (Type C): The probabilistic assessment of n-level decision boxes assigned to a consequence path for a very complex system, where some m decision boxes are associated with *generic* RBD models consisting of k-events connected in *series*, while other p decision boxes are associated with *generic* RBD models consisting of z-events connected in *parallel*, as shown in Fig. 1b, can be expressed mathematically for *nine* cases as:
(C1) All outcomes of m and p decisions boxes are YES.

$$\mathcal{R}_{C1}(t) = \left(\prod_{i=1}^{m}\prod_{j=1}^{k}\mathcal{R}_{ij}(t)\right) \times \left(\prod_{i=1}^{p}(1 - \prod_{j=1}^{z}(1 - \mathcal{R}_{ij}(t)))\right) \tag{13}$$

(C2) All outcomes of m and p decisions boxes are NO.

$$\mathcal{R}_{C2}(t) = \left(\prod_{i=1}^{m}(1 - \prod_{j=1}^{k}\mathcal{R}_{ij}(t))\right) \times \left(\prod_{i=1}^{p}\prod_{j=1}^{z}(1 - \mathcal{R}_{ij}(t))\right) \tag{14}$$

(C3) All outcomes of m decisions boxes are YES and all outcomes of p decisions boxes are NO.

$$\mathcal{R}_{C3}(t) = \left(\prod_{i=1}^{m}\prod_{j=1}^{k}\mathcal{R}_{ij}(t)\right) \times \left(\prod_{i=1}^{p}\prod_{j=1}^{z}(1 - \mathcal{R}_{ij}(t))\right) \tag{15}$$

(C4) All outcomes of m decisions boxes are NO and all outcomes of p decisions boxes are YES.

$$\mathcal{R}_{C4}(t) = \left(\prod_{i=1}^{m} (1 - \prod_{j=1}^{k} \mathcal{R}_{ij}(t)) \right) \times \left(\prod_{i=1}^{p} (1 - \prod_{j=1}^{z} (1 - \mathcal{R}_{ij}(t))) \right) \qquad (16)$$

(C5) Some outcomes of s out of m decisions boxes are YES, some outcomes of u out of m decisions boxes are NO and all outcomes of p decisions boxes are YES.

$$\mathcal{R}_{C5}(t) = \left(\prod_{i=1}^{s} \prod_{j=1}^{k} \mathcal{R}_{ij}(t) \right) \times \left(\prod_{i=1}^{u} (1 - \prod_{j=1}^{k} \mathcal{R}_{ij}(t)) \right) \times \left(\prod_{i=1}^{p} (1 - \prod_{j=1}^{z} (1 - \mathcal{R}_{ij}(t))) \right)$$
$$(17)$$

(C6) Some outcomes of s out of m decisions boxes are YES, some outcomes of u out of m decisions boxes are NO and all outcomes of p decisions boxes are NO.

$$\mathcal{R}_{C6}(t) = \left(\prod_{i=1}^{s} \prod_{j=1}^{k} \mathcal{R}_{ij}(t) \right) \times \left(\prod_{i=1}^{u} (1 - \prod_{j=1}^{k} \mathcal{R}_{ij}(t)) \right) \times \left(\prod_{i=1}^{p} \prod_{j=1}^{z} (1 - \mathcal{R}_{ij}(t)) \right)$$
$$(18)$$

(C7) Some outcomes of s out of p decisions boxes are YES, some outcomes of u out of p decisions boxes are NO and all outcomes of m decisions boxes are YES.

$$\mathcal{R}_{C7}(t) = \left(\prod_{i=1}^{m} \prod_{j=1}^{k} \mathcal{R}_{ij}(t) \right) \times \left(\prod_{i=1}^{u} \prod_{j=1}^{z} (1 - \mathcal{R}_{ij}(t)) \right) \times \left(\prod_{i=1}^{s} (1 - \prod_{j=1}^{z} (1 - \mathcal{R}_{ij}(t))) \right)$$
$$(19)$$

(C8) Some outcomes of s out of p decisions boxes are YES, some outcomes of u out of p decisions boxes are NO and all outcomes of m decisions boxes are NO.

$$\mathcal{R}_{C8}(t) = \left(\prod_{i=1}^{m} (1 - \prod_{j=1}^{k} \mathcal{R}_{ij}(t)) \right) \times \left(\prod_{i=1}^{u} \prod_{j=1}^{z} (1 - \mathcal{R}_{ij}(t)) \right)$$
$$\times \left(\prod_{i=1}^{s} (1 - \prod_{j=1}^{z} (1 - \mathcal{R}_{ij}(t))) \right) \qquad (20)$$

Using Theorems 5–12, we formally *verify* in HOL4 all the above-newly proposed formulas from Eq. 13 to Eq. 20 for RBD/ET-based cause consequence safety analysis (see Theorems 13–20, respectively, in [1]), which is evidence for the correctness of the proposed mathematical formulations.

(C9) Some outcomes of s out of m decisions boxes are YES, some outcomes of u out of m decisions boxes are NO, some outcomes of v out of p decisions boxes are YES and some outcomes of w out of p decisions boxes are NO.

$$\mathcal{R}_{C9}(t) = \left(\prod_{i=1}^{s} \prod_{j=1}^{k} \mathcal{R}_{ij}(t) \right) \times \left(\prod_{i=1}^{u} (1 - \prod_{j=1}^{k} \mathcal{R}_{ij}(t)) \right)$$
$$\times \left(\prod_{i=1}^{v} (1 - \prod_{j=1}^{z} (1 - \mathcal{R}_{ij}(t))) \right) \times \left(\prod_{i=1}^{w} \prod_{j=1}^{z} (1 - \mathcal{R}_{ij}(t)) \right) \quad (21)$$

Theorem 21

```
⊢ prob p (CONSEQ_PATH p [CONSEQ_PATH p (SS_series^YES  p SSs);
                         CONSEQ_PATH p (SS_series^NO   p SSu);
                         CONSEQ_PATH p (SS_parallel^YES p SSv);
                         CONSEQ_PATH p (SS_parallel^NO  p SSw)]) =
    ∏ (MAP (λ a. ∏ (PROB_LIST p a)) SSs) ×
    ∏ (MAP (λ b. 1 - ∏ (PROB_LIST p b)) SSu) ×
    ∏ (MAP (λ c. (1 - ∏ (PROB_LIST p (compl_list p c)))) SSv) ×
    ∏ (MAP (λ d. ∏ (PROB_LIST p (compl_list p d))) SSw)
```

A Consequence Box: Lastly, we verify a *generic* probabilistic formulation of a CCD CONSEQ_BOX for a certain event occurrence in the given system as the sum of all individual probabilities of all $\mathcal{M}$ CCD paths ending with that event:

Theorem 22

```
⊢ Let PATHS L_M = MAP (λa. CONSEQ_PATH p a) L_M)
   in prob_space p ∧ MUTUAL_INDEP p L_M ∧ disjoint (PATHS L_M) ∧
   ALL_DISTINCT (PATHS L_M) ⇒
   prob p (CONSEQ_BOX p L_M) = ∑ (PROB_LIST p (PATHS L_M))
```

where the assumptions of the above-theorem are quite similar to those used in Theorems 3 and 4 (see Sect. 2.2). The verification of all the above-mentioned theorems was a bit challenging as we are dealing with all four types of different RBD configurations, i.e., series, the complement of series, parallel, and the complement of parallel, where each type is consisting of *generic* n-decision boxes and each decision box is associated with *generic* m-events, simultaneously in HOL4. The proof-script of the formalization work presented in this section amounts to about 5,500 lines of HOL4 code and can be downloaded from [1].

4   Conclusion

In this paper, we proposed novel formulations of cause-consequence analysis, based on RBDs and ETs dependability modeling techniques, for the safety assessment of large systems. We provided a HOL4 formalization for the proposed equations that enables the formal probabilistic assessment of scalable CCD models associated with different RBD configurations and based on any probabilistic distribution and failure rates. Moreover, the proposed RBD/ET-based CCD formalization in HOL4 solves the scalability problem of n-level CCD analysis. Our proposed new formulations provide the *first mechanical computation* of complex *n-level* cause-consequence probabilistic analysis ever, augmented with the rigor of the HOL4 theorem prover. As future work, we plan to use the proposed CCD formalization in performing the formal RBD/ET-based cause consequence analysis of real-world complex systems, such as a smart grid or a nuclear power plant system, to verify their probabilistic expressions for all possible safety classes of consequence events at the subsystem level.

References

1. RBD/ET based Cause-Consequence Formalization in HOL4 (2021). https://github.com/hvg-concordia/CCD_RBD
2. Abdelghany, M., Ahmad, W., Tahar, S.: Event tree reliability analysis of safety critical systems using theorem proving. IEEE Syst. J. (2021). https://doi.org/10.1109/JSYST.2021.3077558
3. Abdelghany, M., Tahar, S.: Cause-consequence diagram reliability analysis using formal techniques with application to electrical power networks. IEEE Access **9**, 23929–23943 (2021)
4. Ahmad, W.: Formal dependability analysis using higher-order-logic theorem proving. Ph.D. thesis, National University of Sciences & Technology, Pakistan (2017)
5. Andrews, J., Ridley, M.: Reliability of sequential systems using the cause consequence diagram method. Part E J. Process Mech. Eng. **215**(3), 207–220 (2001)
6. Andrews, J., Ridley, M.: Application of the cause-consequence diagram method to static systems. Reliab. Eng. Syst. Saf. **75**(1), 47–58 (2002)
7. Brall, A., Hagen, W., Tran, H.: Reliability block diagram modeling-comparisons of three software packages. In: Reliability and Maintainability Symposium, pp. 119–124 (2007)
8. Elderhalli, Y.: Dynamic dependability analysis using HOL theorem proving with application in multiprocessor systems. Ph.D. thesis, Concordia University, Canada (2019)
9. Güdemann, M., Ortmeier, F., Reif, W.: Using deductive cause-consequence analysis (DCCA) with SCADE. In: Saglietti, F., Oster, N. (eds.) SAFECOMP 2007. LNCS, vol. 4680, pp. 465–478. Springer, Heidelberg (2007). https://doi.org/10.1007/978-3-540-75101-4_44
10. HOL Theorem Prover (2021). https://hol-theorem-prover.org
11. Jaiswal, S., Pahuja, G.: Effect of reliability of power converters in productivity of wind turbine. In: Conference on Power Electronics, pp. 1–6. IEEE (2014)
12. Muller, S., Deicke, M., De Doncker, R.: Doubly fed induction generator systems for wind turbines. Ind. Appl. Mag. **8**(3), 26–33 (2002)
13. Ortmeier, F., Reif, W., Schellhorn, G.: Deductive cause-consequence analysis. IFAC Proc. Vol. **38**(1), 62–67 (2005)
14. Papazoglou, I.A.: Mathematical foundations of event trees. Reliab. Eng. Syst. Saf. **61**(3), 169–183 (1998)
15. Porté-Agel, F., Bastankhah, M., Shamsoddin, S.: Wind-turbine and wind-farm flows: a review. Bound.-Layer Meteorol. **174**(1), 1–59 (2020)
16. Ridley, M.: Dependency modelling using fault-tree and cause-consequence analysis. Ph.D. thesis, Loughborough University, UK (2000)
17. Shepherd, W., Zhang, L.: Power Converter Circuits. CRC Press, Boca Raton (2004)
18. Towhidnejad, M., Wallace, D.R., Gallo, A.M.: Fault tree analysis for software design. In: NASA Goddard Software Engineering Workshop, pp. 24–29 (2002)

19. Vyzaite, G., Dunnett, S., Andrews, J.: Cause-consequence analysis of non-repairable phased missions. Reliab. Eng. Syst. Saf. **91**(4), 398–406 (2006)
20. Wadi, M., Baysal, M., Shobole, A., Tur, R.: Reliability evaluation in smart grids via modified Monte Carlo simulation method. In: International Conference on Renewable Energy Research and Applications, pp. 841–845. IEEE (2018)
21. Xin, B., Wan, L., Yu, J., Dang, W.: Basic event probability determination and risk assessment based on cause-consequence analysis method. J. Phys. **1549**, 052094 (2020)

Automatic Theorem Proving
and Machine Learning

Online Machine Learning Techniques for Coq: A Comparison

Liao Zhang[1,3(✉)], Lasse Blaauwbroek[1,2], Bartosz Piotrowski[1,4],
Prokop Černý[1], Cezary Kaliszyk[3,4], and Josef Urban[1]

[1] Czech Technical University, Prague, Czech Republic
[2] Radboud University, Nijmegen, The Netherlands
[3] University of Innsbruck, Innsbruck, Austria
[4] University of Warsaw, Warsaw, Poland

Abstract. We present a comparison of several online machine learning techniques for tactical learning and proving in the Coq proof assistant. This work builds on top of Tactician, a plugin for Coq that learns from proofs written by the user to synthesize new proofs. Learning happens in an online manner, meaning that Tactician's machine learning model is updated immediately every time the user performs a step in an interactive proof. This has important advantages compared to the more studied offline learning systems: (1) it provides the user with a seamless, interactive experience with Tactician and, (2) it takes advantage of locality of proof similarity, which means that proofs similar to the current proof are likely to be found close by. We implement two online methods, namely approximate k-nearest neighbors based on locality sensitive hashing forests and random decision forests. Additionally, we conduct experiments with gradient boosted trees in an offline setting using XGBoost. We compare the relative performance of Tactician using these three learning methods on Coq's standard library.

Keywords: Interactive theorem proving · Coq · Machine learning · Online learning · Gradient boosted trees · Random forest

1 Introduction

The users of interactive theorem proving systems are in dire need of a digital sidekick, which helps them reduce the time spent proving the mundane parts of their theories, cutting down on the man-hours needed to turn an informal theory into a formal one. The obvious way of creating such a digital assistant is using machine learning. However, creating a practically usable assistant comes

This work was supported by the ERC grant no. 714034 *SMART*, by the European Regional Development Fund under the project AI&Reasoning (reg. no. CZ.02.1.01/0.0/0.0/15_003/0000466), and by the Ministry of Education, Youth and Sports within the dedicated program ERC CZ under the project POSTMAN no. LL1902.

F. Kamareddine and C. Sacerdoti Coen (Eds.): CICM 2021, LNAI 12833, pp. 67–83, 2021.
https://doi.org/10.1007/978-3-030-81097-9_5

with some requirements that are not necessarily conducive to the most trendy machine learning techniques, such as deep learning.

The environment provided by ITPs is highly dynamic, as it maintains an ever-changing global context of definitions, lemmas, and custom tactics. Hence, proving lemmas within such environments requires intimate knowledge of all the defined objects within the global context. This is contrasted by—for example—the game of chess; even though the search space is enormous, the pieces always move according to the same rules, and no new kinds of pieces can be added. Additionally, the interactive nature of ITPs demands that machine learning techniques do not need absurd amounts of time and resources to train (unless a pre-trained model is highly generic and widely applicable across domains; something that has not been achieved yet). In this paper, we are interested in online learning techniques that quickly learn from user input and immediately utilize this information. We do this in the context of the Coq proof assistant [26] and specifically Tactician [5]—a plugin for Coq that is designed to learn from the proofs written by a user and apply that knowledge to prove new lemmas.

Tactician performs a number of functions, such as proof recording, tactic prediction, proof search, and proof reconstruction. In this paper, we focus on tactic prediction. For this, we need a machine learning technique that accepts as input a database of proofs, represented as pairs containing a proof state and the tactic that was used to advance the proof. From this database, a machine learning model is built. The machine learning task is to predict an appropriate tactic when given a proof state. Because the model needs to operate in an interactive environment, we pose four requirements the learning technique needs to satisfy:

1. The model (datastructure) needs to support dynamic updates. That is, the addition of a new pair of a proof state and tactic to the current model needs to be done in (near) constant time.
2. The model should limit its memory usage to fit in a consumer laptop. We have used the arbitrary limit of 4 GB.
3. The model should support querying in (near) constant time.
4. The model should be persistent (in the functional programming sense [11]). This enables the model to be synchronized with the interactive Coq document, in which the user can navigate back and forth.

1.1 Contributions

In this work, we have implemented two online learning models. An improved version of the locality sensitive hashing scheme for k-nearest neighbors is described in detail in Sect. 3.1. An implementation of random forest is described in Sect. 3.2. In Sect. 4, we evaluate both models, comparing the number of lemmas of Coq's standard library they can prove in a chronological setting (i.e., emulating the growing library).

In addition to the online models, as a proof of concept, we also experiment in an offline fashion with boosted trees, specifically XGBoost [8] in Sect. 3.3. Even though the model learned by XGBoost cannot be used directly in the online setting described above, boosted trees are today among the strongest learning methods. Online algorithms for boosted trees do exist [27], and we intend to implement them in the future.

The techniques described here require representing proof states as feature vectors. Tactician already supported proof state representation using simple hand-rolled features [4]. In addition, Sect. 2 describes our addition of more advanced features of the proof states, which are shown to improve Tactician's performance in Sect. 4.

2 Tactic and Proof State Representation

To build a learning model, we need to characterize proof states and the tactics applied to them. To represent tactics, we first perform basic decompositions and simplifications and denote the resulting atomic tactics by their hashes [4].

Tactician's original proof state features [4] consist merely of identifiers and adjacent identifier pairs in the abstract syntax tree (AST). Various other, more advanced features have been considered for automated reasoning systems built over large formal mathematical knowledge bases [9,14,20]. To enhance the performance of Tactician, we modify the old feature set and define new features as follows.

Top-Down Oriented AST Walks. We add top-down oriented walks in the AST of length up to 3 with syntax placeholders. For instance, the unit clause $f(g(x))$ will contain the features:

f : AppFun , g : AppFun , x : AppArg , f : AppFun (g : AppFun) ,
g : AppFun (x : AppArg) , f : AppFun (g : AppFun (x : AppArg))

The feature g : AppFun indicates that g is able to act as a function in the term tree, and x : AppArg means that x is only an argument of a function.

Vertical Abstracted Walks. We add vertical walks in the term tree from the root to atoms in which nonatomic nodes are substituted by their syntax roles. For the term $f_1(f_2(f_3(a)))$, we can convert each function symbol to AppFun whereas the atom a is transformed to a : AppArg as above. Subsequently, we can export this as the feature AppFun(AppFun(AppFun(a : AppArg))). Such abstracted features are designed to better capture the overall abstract structure of the AST.

Top-Level Structures. We add top-level patterns by replacing the atomic nodes and substructures deeper than level 2 with a single symbol X. Additionally, to separate the function body and arguments, we append the arity of the function to the corresponding converted symbol. As an example, consider the term $f(g(b,c),a)$ consisting of atoms a,b,c,f,g. We first replace a,f,g with X because they are atomic. We further transform f and g to X2 according to the number of their arguments. However, b and c break the depth constraint and should be merged to a single X. Finally, the concrete term is converted to an abstract structure X2(X2(X),X). Abstracting a term to its top-level structure is useful for determining whether a "logical" tactic should be applied. As an illustration, the presence of $X \wedge X$ in the goal often indicates that we should perform case analysis by the split tactic. Since we typically do not need all the nodes of a term to decide such structural information, and we want to balance the generalization with specificity, we use the maximum depth 2.

Premise and Goal Separation. Because local hypotheses typically play a very different role than the conclusion of a proof state, we separate their feature spaces. This can be done by serially numbering the features and adding a sufficiently large constant to the goal features.

Adding Occurrence Counts. In the first version of Tactician, we have used only a simple boolean version of the features. We try to improve on this by adding the number of occurrences of each feature in the proof state.

3   Prediction Models

3.1   Locality Sensitive Hashing Forests for Online k-NN

One of the simplest methods to find correlations between proof states is to define a metric or similarity function $d(x, y)$ on the proof states. One can then extract an ordered list of length k from a database of proof states that are as similar as possible to the reference proof state according to d. Assuming that d does a good job identifying similar proof states, one can then use tactics known to be useful in a known proof state for an unseen proof state. In this paper, we refer to this technique as the k-nearest neighbor (k-NN) method (even though this terminology is somewhat overloaded in the literature).

Our distance function is based on the features described in Sect. 2. We compare these features using the Jaccard index $J(f_1, f_2)$. Optionally, features can be weighted using the TfIdf statistic [18], in which case the generalized index $J_w(f_1, f_2)$ is used.

$$J(f_1, f_2) = \frac{|f_1 \cap f_2|}{|f_1 \cup f_2|} \quad \text{tfidf}(x) = \log \frac{N}{|x|_N} \quad J_w(f_1, f_2) = \frac{\sum_{x \in f_1 \cap f_2} \text{tfidf}(x)}{\sum_{x \in f_1 \cup f_2} \text{tfidf}(x)}$$

Here N is the database size, and $|x|_N$ is the number of times feature x occurs in the database. In previous work, we have made a more detailed comparison of similarity functions [4].

A naive implementation of the k-NN method is not very useful in the online setting because the time complexity for a query grows linearly with the size of the database. Indexing methods, such as k-d trees, exist to speed up queries [3]. However, these methods do not scale well when the dimensionality of the data increases [17]. In this work, we instead implement an approximate version of the k-NN method based on Locality Sensitive Hashing (LSH) [16]. This is an upgrade of our previous LSH implementation that was not persistent and was slower. We also describe our functional implementation of the method in detail for the first time here.

The essential idea of this technique is to hash feature vectors into buckets using a family of hash functions that guarantee that similar vectors hash to the same bucket with high probability (according to the given similarity function).

To find a k-NN approximation, one can simply return the contents of the bucket corresponding to the current proof state. For the Jaccard index, the appropriate family of hash functions are the MinHash functions [7].

The downside of the naive LSH method is that its parameters are difficult to tune. The probability that the vectors that hash to the same bucket are similar can be increased by associating more than one hash function to the bucket. All values of the hash functions then need to pair-wise agree for the items in the bucket. However, this will naturally decrease the size of the bucket, lowering the number of examples k (of k-NN) that can be retrieved. The parameter k can be increased again by simply maintaining multiple independent bucketing datastructures. Tuning these parameters is critically dependent on the size of the database, the length of the feature vectors, and the desired value of k. To overcome this, we implement a highly efficient, persistent, functional variant of Locality Sensitive Hashing Forest [2] (LSHF), which is able to tune these parameters automatically, leaving (almost) no parameters to be tuned manually. Below we give a high-level overview of the algorithm as it is modified for a functional setting. For a more in-depth discussion on the correctness of the algorithm, we refer to the previous reference.

LSHFs consist of a forest (collection) of tries $\mathcal{T}_1 \ldots \mathcal{T}_n$. Every trie has an associated hash function h_i that is a member of a (near) universal hashing family mapping a feature down to a single bit (a hash function mapping to an integer can be used by taking the result modulus two). To add a new example to this model, it is inserted into each trie according to a path (sequence) of bits. Every bit of this path can be shown to be locally sensitive for the Jaccard index [2]. The path of an example is calculated using the set of features that represents the proof state in the example.

$$\text{path}_i(f) = \text{sort}(\{h_i(x) \mid x \in f\})$$

For a given trie $\mathcal{T}$, the subtrie starting at a given path $b_1 \ldots b_m$ can be seen as the bucket to which examples that agree on the hashes $b_1 \ldots b_m$ are assigned. Longer paths point to smaller buckets containing less similar examples, while shorter paths point to larger buckets containing increasingly similar examples. Hence, to retrieve the neighbors of a proof state with features f, one should start by finding examples that share the entire path of f. To retrieve more examples, one starts collecting the subtrees starting at smaller and smaller prefixes of $\text{path}_i(f)$. To increase the accuracy and number of examples retrieved, this procedure can be performed on multiple tries simultaneously, as outlined in Algorithm 1.

Tuning the LSHF model consists mainly of choosing the appropriate number of tries that maximizes the speed versus accuracy trade-off. Experiments show that 11 trees is the optimal value. Additionally, for efficiency reasons, it is a good idea to set a limit on the depth of the tries to prevent highly similar examples from creating a deep trie. For our dataset, a maximum depth of 20 is sufficient.

3.2   Online Random Forest

Random forests are a popular machine learning method combining many randomized decision trees into one ensemble, which produces predictions via

---

Algorithm 1. Querying the Locality Sensitive Hashing Forest

1: **function** QUERYLSHF($\mathcal{F}$, f) $\triangleright$ $\mathcal{F}$ a forest, f a feature set
2:     $\mathcal{P} \leftarrow \langle \text{path}_i(f) : i \in [1..|\mathcal{F}|] \rangle$
3:     neighbors $\leftarrow$ FILTERDUPLICATES(SIMULTANEOUSDESCEND($\mathcal{F}$, $\mathcal{P}$))
4:     Optionally re-sort neighbors according to real Jaccard index
5: **function** SIMULTANEOUSDESCEND($\mathcal{F}$, $\mathcal{P}$)
6:     $\mathcal{F}_{\text{rel}} \leftarrow \langle$ if head($\mathcal{P}$) then left(T) else right(T) : $T \in \mathcal{F}$ when not leaf(T) $\rangle$
7:     $\mathcal{F}_{\text{irrel}} \leftarrow \langle$ if leaf(T) then T elseif head($\mathcal{P}$) then right(T) else left(T) : $T \in \mathcal{F}$ $\rangle$
8:     **if** $\mathcal{F}_{\text{rel}}$ is empty **then**
9:         neighbors $\leftarrow$ empty list
10:    **else**
11:        $\mathcal{P}' \leftarrow \langle \text{tail}(\mathcal{P}_i) : i \in [1..n] \rangle$
12:        neighbors $\leftarrow$ SIMULTANEOUSDESCEND($\mathcal{F}_{\text{rel}}$, $\mathcal{P}'$)
13:    **if** $|\text{neighbors}| \geq k$ **then**
14:        **return** neighbors
15:    **else**
16:        **return** APPEND(neighbors, CONCATENATE($\langle$ COLLECT($T : T \in \mathcal{F}_{\text{irrel}}$)$\rangle$))

---

voting [6]. Even though the decision trees are not strong learners on their own, because they are intentionally decorrelated, the voting procedure greatly improves on top of their individual predictive performance. The decision trees consist of internal nodes labeled by decision rules and leaves labeled by examples. In our case, these are tactics to be applied in the proofs.

Random forests are a versatile method that requires little tuning of its hyperparameters. Their architecture is also relatively simple, which makes it easy to provide a custom OCaml implementation easily integrable with Tactician, adhering to its requirement of avoiding mutable data structures. Direct usage of existing random forest implementations is impossible due to challenges in Tactician's learning setting. These challenges are: (1) numerous sparse features, (2) the necessity of online learning, as detailed in the next two paragraphs.

The decision rules in nodes of the decision trees are based on the features of the training examples. These rules are chosen to maximize the *information gain*, i.e., to minimize the *impurity* of the set of labels in the node.[1] There are more than $37,000$ binary and sparse features in Tactician. Since the learner integrated with Tactician needs to be fast, one needs to be careful when optimizing the splits in the tree nodes.

Random forests are typically trained in an offline manner where the whole training data is available at the beginning of the training. In Tactician this would be quite suboptimal. To take advantage of the locality of proof similarity and to be able to use data coming from new proofs written by a user, we want to immediately update the machine learning model after each proof.

There are approaches to turn random forests into online learners [10,25] which inspired our implementation. The authors of [10] propose a methodology

---

[1] If we have labels $\{a, a, b, b, b\}$, ideally, we would like to produce a split which passes all the examples with label a to one side and the examples with b to the other side.

Algorithm 2. Adding training a example e to a decision tree $\mathcal{T}$

1: **function** ADDEXAMPLETOTREE($\mathcal{T}$, e)
2:    **match** $\mathcal{T}$ **with**
3:       Node($\mathcal{R}$, $\mathcal{T}_l$, $\mathcal{T}_r$):   ▷ $\mathcal{R}$ – binary rule, $\mathcal{T}_l$, $\mathcal{T}_r$ – left and right subtrees
4:          **match** $\mathcal{R}(e)$ **with**
5:             Left: **return** Node($\mathcal{R}$, ADDEXAMPLETOTREE($\mathcal{T}_l$, e), $\mathcal{T}_r$)
6:             Right: **return** Node($\mathcal{R}$, $\mathcal{T}_l$, ADDEXAMPLETOTREE($\mathcal{T}_r$, e))
7:       Leaf(l, $\mathcal{E}$):   ▷ l – label/tactic, $\mathcal{E}$ – examples
8:          $\mathcal{E} \leftarrow$ APPEND($\mathcal{E}$, e)
9:          **if** SPLITCONDITION($\mathcal{E}$) **then**
10:            $\mathcal{R} \leftarrow$ GENERATESPLITRULE($\mathcal{E}$)
11:            $\mathcal{E}_l$, $\mathcal{E}_r \leftarrow$ SPLIT($\mathcal{R}$, $\mathcal{E}$)
12:            $l_l \leftarrow$ label of random example from $\mathcal{E}_l$
13:            $l_r \leftarrow$ label of random example from $\mathcal{E}_r$
14:            **return** Node($\mathcal{R}$, Leaf(l_l, $\mathcal{E}_l$), Leaf(l_r, $\mathcal{E}_r$))
15:         **else**
16:            **return** Leaf(l, $\mathcal{E}$)

---

where new training examples are passed to the leaves of the decision trees, and under certain statistical conditions, the leaf is split and converted to a new decision node followed by two new leaves. We take a similar approach, but deciding a split in our implementation is simpler and computationally cheaper.

The pseudocode describing our implementation is presented below. Algorithm 2 shows how the training examples are added to the decision trees. A new training example is passed down the tree to one of its leaves. The trajectory of this pass is governed by binary decision rules in the nodes of the tree. Each rule checks whether a given feature is present in the example. Once the example reaches a leaf, it is saved there, and a decision is made whether to extend the tree (using function SPLITCONDITION). This happens only when the Gini Impurity measure [21] on the set of examples in the leaves is greater than a given impurity threshold i (a hyperparameter of the model). When the split is done, the leaf becomes an internal node with a new split rule, and the collected examples from the leaf are passed down to the two new leaves. The new rule (an output from GENERATESPLITRULE) is produced in the following way. N features are selected from the features of the examples, where N is the square root of the number of examples. The selection of the features is randomized and made in such a way that features that are distinguishing between the examples have higher probability: First, we randomly select two examples from the leaf, and then we randomly select a feature from the difference of sets of features of the two examples. Among such selected features, the one maximizing the *information gain* [21] of the split rule based on it is selected. The two new leaves get labels randomly selected from the examples belonging to the given leaf.

When adding an example to a random forest (Algorithm 3), first, a decision is made whether a new tree (in the form of a single leaf) should be added to the forest. It happens with probability $\frac{1}{n}$, where n is the number of trees in the forest under the condition that n is lower than a given threshold.

Algorithm 3. Adding a training example e to a random forest $\mathcal{F}$

1: **function** ADDEXAMPLETOFOREST($\mathcal{F}$, e, n_{max}) ▷ n_{max} – max number of trees
2:    $n \leftarrow$ number of trees in $\mathcal{F}$
3:    $m \leftarrow$ random number from $\{1, \ldots n\}$
4:    $\mathcal{F}_{updated} \leftarrow$ empty list
5:    **if** n $< n_{max}$ and $m = 1$ **then**
6:       $\mathcal{T} \leftarrow$ leaf labeled by tactic used in e
7:       $\mathcal{F}_{updated} \leftarrow$ APPEND($\mathcal{F}_{updated}$, $\mathcal{T}$)
8:    **for all** $\mathcal{T} \in \mathcal{F}$ **do**
9:       $\mathcal{T} \leftarrow$ ADDEXAMPLETOTREE($\mathcal{T}$, e)
10:      $\mathcal{F}_{updated} \leftarrow$ APPEND($\mathcal{F}_{updated}$, $\mathcal{T}$)
11:   **return** $\mathcal{F}_{updated}$

Algorithm 4. Predicting labels for unlabeled e in the random forest $\mathcal{F}$

1: **function** PREDICTFOREST($\mathcal{F}$, e)
2:    $\mathcal{P} \leftarrow$ empty list ▷ $\mathcal{P}$ – predictions
3:    **for all** $\mathcal{T} \in \mathcal{F}$ **do**
4:       $t \leftarrow$ PREDICTTREE(e)
5:       append t to $\mathcal{P}$
6:    $R \leftarrow$ VOTE($\mathcal{P}$) ▷ R – ranking of tactics
7:    **return** R
8: **function** PREDICTTREE($\mathcal{T}$, e)
9:    **match** $\mathcal{T}$ **with**
10:      Node($\mathcal{R}$, $\mathcal{T}_l$, $\mathcal{T}_r$):
11:         **match** $\mathcal{R}(e)$ **with**
12:            Left: **return** PREDICTTREE($\mathcal{T}_l$, e)
13:            Right: **return** PREDICTTREE($\mathcal{T}_r$, e)
14:      Leaf(l, $\mathcal{E}$): **return** l

Predicting a tactic for a given example with a random forest (Algorithm 4) is done in two steps. First, the example is passed to the leaves of all the trees and the labels (tactics) in the leaves are saved. Then the ranking of the tactics is made based on their frequencies.

Tuning Hyperparameters. There are two hyperparameters in our implementation of random forests: (1) the maximal number of trees in the forest and (2) the impurity threshold for performing the node splits. To determine the influence of these parameters on the predictive power, we perform a grid search. For this, we randomly split the data that is not held out for testing (see Sect. 4.1) into a training and validation part. The results of the grid search are shown in Fig. 1. The best numbers of trees are 160 (for top-1 accuracy) and 320 (for top-10 accuracy). We used these two values for the rest of the experiments. For the impurity threshold, it is difficult to see a visible trend in performance; thus we selected 0.5 as our default.

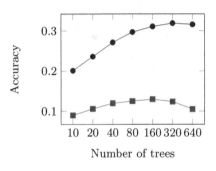 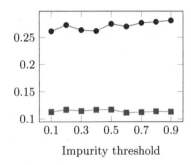

Fig. 1. Results of hyperparameter tuning for random forests. The blue circle corresponds to top-10 accuracy (how often the correct tactic was present in the first 10 predictions) whereas the red square corresponds to top-1 accuracy. (Color figure online)

3.3 Boosted Trees

Gradient boosted decision trees are a state-of-the-art machine learning algorithm that transforms weak base learners, decision trees, into a method with stronger predictive power by appropriate combinations of the base models. One efficient and powerful implementation is the XGBoost library. Here, we perform some initial experiments in an offline setting for tactic prediction. Although XGBoost can at the moment not be directly integrated with Tactician, this gives us a useful baseline based on existing state-of-the-art technology. Below, we illustrate a procedure of developing our XGBoost model based on binary logistic regression.

The input to XGBoost is a sparse matrix containing rows with the format of (ϕ_P, ϕ_T) where ϕ_P includes the features of a proof state, and ϕ_T characterizes a tactic related to the proof state. We transform each proof state to a sparse feature vector ϕ_P containing the features' occurrence counts. Since there may be a large number of features in a given Coq development environment, which may hinder the efficiency of training and prediction, it is reasonable to decrease the dimension of the vectors. We hash the features to $20,000$ buckets by using the modulo of the feature's index. As above, we also remap the tactic hashes to a $20,000$-dimensional space separated from the state features.

The training examples get labels 1 or 0 based on the tactics being useful or not for the proof state. A tactic for a certain proof state is labeled as positive if it is exactly the one applied to this state in the library. In contrast, negative tactics are elements in the tactic space that differ from the positive instance. We obtain negative data by two approaches: *strong* negatives and *random* negatives. Strong negative instances are obtained by arbitrarily selecting a subset from the best-100 k-NN predictions for this state. In the other approach, negative instances are arbitrarily chosen from the entire tactic space.

With a trained gradient boosted trees model, we can predict the scores of the tactics for an unseen proof state P. First, the top-100 k-NN predictions are preselected. Then, for each tactic, we input (ϕ_P, ϕ_T) to the model to obtain the score of T. The tactics are then sorted according to their scores.

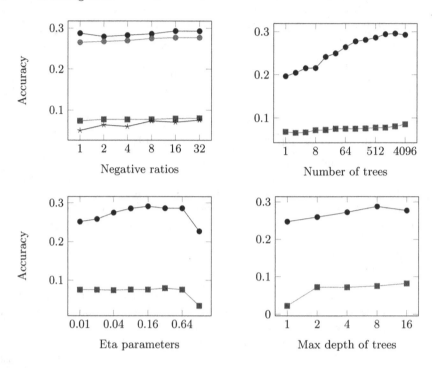

Fig. 2. Results of hyperparameter tuning for gradient boosted trees. In consistence with Fig. 1, the blue circle (red square) corresponds to top-10 (top-1) accuracy, respectively. The graph of negative ratios contains two additional curves of random negative examples. The brown circle relates to top-10 accuracy, whereas the black star presents the results of top-1 accuracy. (Color figure online)

Tuning Hyperparameters. Similarly as for the random forest model (Sect. 3.2), we optimize the most important hyperparameters of the XGBoost training algorithm on the data coming from the non-sink nodes in the dependency graph of Coq's standard library (see Sect. 4.1). One essential parameter is the *ratio* of negative examples. Ratio n indicates that we generate n negative instances for each recorded proof state. Other influential parameters that we tune are: *eta* (learning-rate), *number of trees*, and *max depth*. Due to the limitations of computing resources, we assume a set of default parameters: *ratio* = 8, *eta* = 0.2, *number of trees* = 500, *max depth* = 10, and then separately modify each of these parameters to observe the influence caused by the change, which is depicted in Fig. 2. Both strong and random negatives are evaluated. Obviously, strong negatives perform better than random negatives, and increasing the negative ratios will certainly lead to higher success rates. The figure also shows that a higher number of trees results in better performance. Learning rates are between 0.08 and 0.64 give good results. It is also apparent that deeper trees (at least 8) increase the accuracy.

Table 1. Performance of the three tested machine learning models in two types of evaluation: using a split of the dataset and a chronological evaluation through the dataset. top-n refers to the frequency of the correct tactic being present in the first n predictions from a machine learning model.

| | Machine learning system | | | | | |
| | k-NN | | Random Forest | | XGBoost | |
Evaluation type	top-1	top-10	top-1	top-10	top-1	top-10
Split	18.8%	34.2%	32.1%	41.2%	18.2%	38.2%
Chronological	17.3%	43.7%	29.9%	58.9%	18.2%	43.4%

Experimental Setup. The XGBoost model is evaluated on the task of tactic prediction both in the split setting and the chronological setting (illustrated in Sect. 4). We use the strong negative examples and determine the final parameters—*ratio* = 16, *eta* = 0.2, *number of trees* = 1024, *max depth* = 10—for generating a model from non-sink nodes and use that to predict for sink nodes.

Since the entire dataset contains approximately 250,000 proof states, and it is time-consuming to generate a unique XGBoost model for each test case, we propose several ways to speed up the chronological evaluation. Instead of training on the data from all preceding states, we merely provide 1,000 instances occurring previously as the training data. According to the results of parameter tuning depicted in Fig. 2, we decide on the hyperparameters—*ratio* = 4, *eta* = 0.2, *number of trees* = 256, *max depth* = 10—to balance the accuracy and efficiency.

4 Experimental Evaluation

To compare the performance of the described machine learning models, we perform three kinds of experiments: *split* evaluation, *chronological* evaluation, and evaluation in Tactician. Achieving good performance in the last type of evaluation is the main goal. All three machine learning models are evaluated in the first two kinds of experiments, while in Tactician we only evaluate k-NN and online random forest. This is because the XGBoost system, while being potentially the strongest machine learner among tested, may not be easily turned into an online learner and integrated into Tactician. We adopt the original features—term and term pairs—for evaluation outside Tactician, whereas both the original features and the new are tested on Tactician's benchmark. To determine the relative importance of the feature classes described in Sect. 2, we benchmark the addition of each class separately in Tactician. All evaluations are performed on data extracted from the standard library of Coq 8.11.

4.1 Split Evaluation

In the directed acyclic graph of dependencies of the Coq modules, there are 545 nodes. 104 of them are *sink nodes*, i.e., these are the modules that do not appear among dependencies of any other module. We used these modules as final testing data for evaluation outside Tactician. The rest of the data was randomly split into training and validation parts and was used for parameter tuning of random forest and gradient boosted trees. The models with tuned hyperparameters were evaluated on the testing data. The results of the evaluation of the three tested models are shown in the first row of Table 1.

4.2 Chronological Evaluation

Although the split evaluation from the previous experiment is interesting, it does not correspond entirely to the Tactician's internal mode of operation. To simulate the real-world scenario in an offline setting, we create an individual model for each proof state by learning from all the previous states—data from dependent files and preceding lines in the local file. The second row of Table 1 presents the results of the evaluation in chronological order.

4.3 Evaluation in Tactician

Table 2 shows the results of the evaluation of two online learners—the k-NN and the random forest—within Tactician. The hyperparameters of the random forest model were chosen based on the grid search in Sect. 3.2. We run the proof search for every lemma in the library with a 40-s time limit on both the original and the improved features.

The random forest performed marginally better than k-NN on both kinds of features. With old features the k-NN proved 3831 lemmas (being 33.7% out of all 11370), whereas the random forest proved 4011 lemmas (35.3% of all). With the new features, both models performed better, and again, the random forest proved more lemmas (4117, 36.2% of all) than k-NN (3945, 34.7% of all).

It is somewhat surprising that the random forest, which performed much better than k-NN on the split in the offline evaluation, is only better by a small margin in Tactician. This may be related to the time and memory consumption of random forest, which may be higher than for k-NN on certain kinds of data.[2]

It is worth noting that k-NN and random forest resulted in quite different sets of proofs. The columns marked as *union* show that the size of the union of proofs constructed by the two models is significantly larger than the number of proofs found by each model separately. In total, both models resulted in 4503 (39.6%) proofs using old features and 4597 (40.4%) proofs using the new features.

---

[2] Doing the splits in the leaves has quadratic time complexity with respect to the number of examples stored in the leaf; sometimes it happens, that leaves of the trees store large number of examples.

Table 2. Proving performance of two online learners integrated with Tactician, k-NN and random forest, in the Coq Standard Library. The percentages in the table correspond to the fraction of lemmas proved in a given Coq module. The columns *union* show what fraction of the lemmas was proved by at least one of the learners. RF is an abbreviation of random forest.

Coq module	#Lemmas	Features type					
		Original			New		
		k-NN	RF	*union*	k-NN	RF	*union*
All	1137	33.7%	35.3%	39.6%	34.7%	36.2%	40.4%
Arith	293	52%	59%	65%	56%	59%	66%
Bool	130	93%	87%	93%	92%	88%	92%
Classes	191	80%	76%	81%	79%	79%	83%
FSets	1137	32%	34%	37%	32%	35%	39%
Floats	5	20%	20%	20%	40%	19%	40%
Init	164	73%	51%	73%	73%	56%	73%
Lists	388	38%	43%	47%	38%	44%	49%
Logic	341	31%	27%	34%	32%	31%	35%
MSets	830	38%	40%	43%	36%	40%	43%
NArith	288	37%	43%	44%	35%	42%	47%
Numbers	2198	23%	22%	27%	24%	23%	27%
PArith	280	31%	40%	44%	35%	39%	45%
Program	28	75%	64%	75%	78%	66%	78%
QArith	295	33%	40%	43%	31%	39%	45%
Reals	1756	19%	23%	25%	21%	24%	26%
Relations	37	29%	24%	40%	27%	26%	29%
Setoids	4	1.00	1.00	1.00	1.00	97%	1.00
Sets	222	43%	42%	49%	49%	47%	53%
Sorting	136	26%	29%	33%	25%	30%	33%
Strings	74	22%	22%	27%	17%	14%	20%
Structures	390	45%	49%	54%	51%	51%	56%
Vectors	37	37%	29%	40%	21%	23%	27%
Wellfounded	36	19%	05%	19%	16%	13%	16%
ZArith	953	41%	46%	49%	40%	43%	46%
btauto	44	11%	20%	20%	20%	17%	22%
funind	4	75%	50%	75%	50%	73%	75%
micromega	339	21%	27%	29%	27%	25%	30%
nsatz	27	33%	33%	37%	40%	26%	40%
omega	37	40%	67%	67%	48%	63%	64%
rtauto	33	30%	39%	48%	33%	44%	51%
setoid_ring	362	21%	23%	26%	27%	27%	30%
ssr	311	68%	55%	69%	70%	57%	71%

4.4 Feature Evaluation

Table 3 depicts the influence of adding the new classes of features described in Sect. 2 to the previous baseline.[3] All of the newly produced features improve the success rates. However, the top-down oriented AST walks contribute little, probably due to Tactician having already included term tree walks up to length 2.

---

[3] The results here are not directly comparable to those in Table 2 mainly due to the usage of a non-indexed version of k-NN in contrast to the algorithm presented in 1.

Table 3. Proving performance of each feature modification. $\mathcal{O}, \mathcal{W}, \mathcal{V}, \mathcal{T}, \mathcal{S}, \mathcal{C}$ denote original features, top-down oriented AST walks, vertical abstract walks, top-level structures, premise and goal separation, and adding feature occurrence, respectively. The symbol $\oplus$ denotes that we combine the original features and a new modification during the experiments.

Features	$\mathcal{O}$	$\mathcal{O} \oplus \mathcal{W}$	$\mathcal{O} \oplus \mathcal{V}$	$\mathcal{O} \oplus \mathcal{T}$	$\mathcal{O} \oplus \mathcal{S}$	$\mathcal{O} \oplus \mathcal{C}$
Success rates (%)	32.75	32.82	34.16	33.65	34.42	34.97

Every other modification obtains a reasonable improvement, which confirms the intuitions described in Sect. 2.

5   Related Work

Random forests were first used in the context of theorem proving by Färber [12], where multi-path querying of a random forest would improve on k-NN results for premise selection. Nagashima and He [22] proposed a proof method recommendation system for Isabelle/HOL based on decision trees on top of precisely engineered features. A small number of trees and features allowed for explainable recommendations. Frameworks based on random boosted trees (XGBoost, LightGBM) have also been used in automated reasoning, in the context of guiding tableaux connection proof search [19] and the superposition calculus proof search [9], as well as for handling negative examples in premise selection [24].

Machine learning to predict tactics was first considered by Gauthier et al. [14] in the context of the HOL4 theorem prover. His later improvements [15] added Monte-Carlo tree search, tactic orthogonalization, and integration of both Metis and a hammer [13]. A similar system for HOL Light was developed by Bansal et al. [1]. Nagashima and Kumar developed the proof search component [23] of such a system for Isabelle/HOL. This work builds upon Tactician [4,5], adapting and improving these works for dependent type theory and the Coq proof assistant.

6   Conclusion

We have implemented several new methods for learning tactical guidance of Coq proofs in the Tactician system. This includes better proof state features and an improved version of approximate k-nearest neighbor based on locality sensitive hashing forests. A completely new addition is our online implementation of random forest in Coq, which can now be used instead of or together with the k-nearest neighbor. We have also started to experiment with strong state-of-the-art learners based on gradient boosted trees, so far in an offline setting using binary learning with negative examples.

Our random forest improves very significantly on the k-nearest neighbor in an offline accuracy-based evaluation. In an online theorem-proving evaluation, the improvement is not as big, possibly due to the speed of the two methods and the importance of backtracking during the proof search. The methods are, however, quite complementary and running both of them in parallel increases the overall performance of Tactician from 33.7% (k-NN with the old features) to 40.4% in 40s. Our best new method (RF with the new features) now solves 36.2% of the problems in 40s.

The offline experiments with gradient boosted trees are so far inconclusive. They outperform k-nearest neighbor in top-10 accuracy, but the difference is small, and the random forest performs much better in this metric. Since the random forest learns only from positive examples, this likely shows that learning in the binary setting with negative examples is challenging on our Tactician data. In particular, we likely need good semantic feature characterizations of the tactics, obtained e.g., by computing the difference between the features of the proof states before and after the tactic application. The experiments, however, already confirm the importance of choosing good negative data to learn from in the binary setting.

References

1. Bansal, K., Loos, S.M., Rabe, M.N., Szegedy, C., Wilcox, S.: HOList: an environment for machine learning of higher order logic theorem proving. In: Chaudhuri, K., Salakhutdinov, R. (eds.) Proceedings of the 36th International Conference on Machine Learning, ICML 2019, Long Beach, California, USA, 9–15 June 2019. Proceedings of Machine Learning Research, vol. 97, pp. 454–463. PMLR (2019)
2. Bawa, M., Condie, T., Ganesan, P.: LSH forest: Self-tuning indexes for similarity search. In: Ellis, A., Hagino, T. (eds.) Proceedings of the 14th International Conference on World Wide Web, WWW 2005, Chiba, Japan, 10–14 May 2005, pp. 651–660. ACM (2005)
3. Bentley, J.L.: Multidimensional binary search trees used for associative searching. Commun. ACM 18(9), 509–517 (1975)
4. Blaauwbroek, L., Urban, J., Geuvers, H.: Tactic learning and proving for the Coq proof assistant. In: Albert, E., Kovács, L. (eds.) Proceedings of the 23rd International Conference on Logic for Programming, Artificial Intelligence and Reasoning, LPAR 2020. EPiC Series in Computing, vol. 73, pp. 138–150. EasyChair (2020)
5. Blaauwbroek, L., Urban, J., Geuvers, H.: The tactician. In: Benzmüller, C., Miller, B. (eds.) CICM 2020. LNCS (LNAI), vol. 12236, pp. 271–277. Springer, Cham (2020). https://doi.org/10.1007/978-3-030-53518-6_17
6. Breiman, L.: Random forests. Mach. Learn. 45(1), 5–32 (2001)
7. Broder, A.Z.: On the resemblance and containment of documents. In: Carpentieri, B., Santis, A.D., Vaccaro, U., Storer, J.A. (eds.) Compression and Complexity of SEQUENCES 1997, Positano, Amalfitan Coast, Salerno, Italy, 11–13 June 1997, Proceedings, pp. 21–29. IEEE (1997)
8. Chen, T., Guestrin, C.: XGBoost: a scalable tree boosting system. In: Proceedings of the 22nd ACM SIGKDD International Conference on Knowledge Discovery and Data Mining, pp. 785–794 (2016)

9. Chvalovský, K., Jakubův, J., Suda, M., Urban, J.: ENIGMA-NG: efficient neural and gradient-boosted inference guidance for E. In: Fontaine, P. (ed.) CADE 2019. LNCS (LNAI), vol. 11716, pp. 197–215. Springer, Cham (2019). https://doi.org/10.1007/978-3-030-29436-6_12

10. Domingos, P.M., Hulten, G.: Mining high-speed data streams. In: Ramakrishnan, R., Stolfo, S.J., Bayardo, R.J., Parsa, I. (eds.) Proceedings of the sixth ACM SIGKDD International Conference on Knowledge Discovery and Data Mining, pp. 71–80. ACM (2000)

11. Driscoll, J.R., Sarnak, N., Sleator, D.D., Tarjan, R.E.: Making data structures persistent. J. Comput. Syst. Sci. **38**(1), 86–124 (1989)

12. Färber, M., Kaliszyk, C.: Random forests for premise selection. In: Lutz, C., Ranise, S. (eds.) FroCoS 2015. LNCS (LNAI), vol. 9322, pp. 325–340. Springer, Cham (2015). https://doi.org/10.1007/978-3-319-24246-0_20

13. Gauthier, T., Kaliszyk, C.: Premise selection and external provers for HOL4. In: Leroy, X., Tiu, A. (eds.) Proceedings of the 4th Conference on Certified Programs and Proofs (CPP 2015), pp. 49–57. ACM (2015)

14. Gauthier, T., Kaliszyk, C., Urban, J.: TacticToe: learning to reason with HOL4 tactics. In: Eiter, T., Sands, D. (eds.) Proceedings of the 21st International Conference on Logic for Programming, Artificial Intelligence and Reasoning, LPAR-21. EPiC Series in Computing, vol. 46, pp. 125–143. EasyChair (2017)

15. Gauthier, T., Kaliszyk, C., Urban, J., Kumar, R., Norrish, M.: TacticToe: learning to prove with tactics. J. Autom. Reason. **65**(2), 257–286 (2021)

16. Gionis, A., Indyk, P., Motwani, R.: Similarity search in high dimensions via hashing. In: Atkinson, M.P., Orlowska, M.E., Valduriez, P., Zdonik, S.B., Brodie, M.L. (eds.) Proceedings of 25th International Conference on Very Large Data Bases, VLDB 1999, Edinburgh, Scotland, UK, 7–10 September 1999, pp. 518–529. Morgan Kaufmann (1999)

17. Har-Peled, S., Indyk, P., Motwani, R.: Approximate nearest neighbor: towards removing the curse of dimensionality. Theory Comput. **8**(1), 321–350 (2012)

18. Jones, K.S.: A statistical interpretation of term specificity and its application in retrieval. J. Documentation **60**(5), 493–502 (2004)

19. Kaliszyk, C., Urban, J., Michalewski, H., Olšák, M.: Reinforcement learning of theorem proving. In: Bengio, S., Wallach, H., Larochelle, H., Grauman, K., Cesa-Bianchi, N., Garnett, R. (eds.) Advances in Neural Information Processing Systems 31, pp. 8836–8847. Curran Associates, Inc. (2018)

20. Kaliszyk, C., Urban, J., Vyskočil, J.: Efficient semantic features for automated reasoning over large theories. In: Yang, Q., Wooldridge, M. (eds.) Proceedings of the 24th International Joint Conference on Artificial Intelligence, (IJCAI 2015), pp. 3084–3090. AAAI Press (2015)

21. Mitchell, T.M.: Machine Learning, International Edition. McGraw-Hill Series in Computer Science. McGraw-Hill (1997)

22. Nagashima, Y., He, Y.: PaMpeR: proof method recommendation system for Isabelle/HOL. In: Huchard, M., Kästner, C., Fraser, G. (eds.) Proceedings of the 33rd ACM/IEEE International Conference on Automated Software Engineering, ASE 2018, Montpellier, France, 3–7 September 2018, pp. 362–372. ACM (2018)

23. Nagashima, Y., Kumar, R.: A proof strategy language and proof script generation for Isabelle/HOL. In: de Moura, L. (ed.) CADE 2017. LNCS (LNAI), vol. 10395, pp. 528–545. Springer, Cham (2017). https://doi.org/10.1007/978-3-319-63046-5_32

24. Piotrowski, B., Urban, J.: ATPBOOST: learning premise selection in binary setting with ATP feedback. In: Galmiche, D., Schulz, S., Sebastiani, R. (eds.) IJCAR 2018. LNCS (LNAI), vol. 10900, pp. 566–574. Springer, Cham (2018). https://doi.org/10.1007/978-3-319-94205-6_37

25. Saffari, A., Leistner, C., Santner, J., Godec, M., Bischof, H.: On-line random forests. In: 12th IEEE International Conference on Computer Vision Workshops, ICCV Workshops 2009, Kyoto, Japan, 27 September–4 October 2009, pp. 1393–1400. IEEE Computer Society (2009)

26. The Coq Development Team: The Coq proof assistant, version 8.11.0, October 2019

27. Zhang, C., Zhang, Y., Shi, X., Almpanidis, G., Fan, G., Shen, X.: On incremental learning for gradient boosting decision trees. Neural Process. Lett. **50**(1), 957–987 (2019)

Improving Stateful Premise Selection
with Transformers

Krsto Proroković$^{(\boxtimes)}$, Michael Wand, and Jürgen Schmidhuber

Instituto Dalle Molle di Studi sull'Intelligenza Artificiale (IDSIA), USI & SUPSI,
Lugano, Switzerland
{krsto,michael,juergen}@idsia.ch

Abstract. Premise selection is a fundamental task for automated reasoning in large theories. A recently proposed approach formulates premise selection as a sequence-to-sequence problem, called stateful premise selection. Given a theorem statement, the goal of a stateful premise selection method is to predict the set of premises that would be useful in proving it. In this work we use the Transformer architecture for learning the stateful premise selection method. We outperform the existing recurrent neural network baseline and improve upon the state of the art on a recently proposed dataset.

Keywords: Premise selection · Machine learning · Neural networks

1 Introduction

When proving new theorems we usually rely on already proven facts as intermediate steps. The task of choosing useful facts is called premise selection. The input to the premise selection method is the statement of the theorem we are trying to prove (in some computer-friendly format [6]) and the output is a list of premises that should be useful in proving it. Early work on premise selection includes handcrafted methods such as SiNe [4] and MePo [14]. Lately, different machine learning algorithms have been used to learn a premise selection medthods; these include: naïve Bayes [27], kernel methods [26], k-nearest neighbors [7,8], gradient boosted trees [18], and neural networks [5,11]. Recently, [19] used the fact that premises are not independent between themselves and formulated premise selection as a sequence-to-sequence problem [25], called stateful premise selection. They used recurrent neural networks (RNNs) to map a theorem statement to a *set* of premises. RNNs process the input sequence in a sequential order (i.e. symbol by symbol), encode it into a real-valued vector, then decode from it the output sequence. The Transformer architecture [28], unlike RNNs, relies on the attention mechanism to process the entire input sequence in parallel.

This work was supported by the ERC Advanced grant no. 742870. We would like to thank Kazuki Irie for constructive feedback on the manuscript as well as Róbert Csordás and Dieuwke Hupkes for useful advice about the Transformer architecture.

F. Kamareddine and C. Sacerdoti Coen (Eds.): CICM 2021, LNAI 12833, pp. 84–89, 2021.
https://doi.org/10.1007/978-3-030-81097-9_6

Given the success of Transformers on sequence tasks such as machine translation and language modeling, it is natural to ask whether the same holds for automated theorem proving. In [20] Transformer was used for theorem proving in the Metamath environment [13]. In this work, we study the performance of different sequence-to-sequence models such as Long-Short Term Memory (LSTM) neural networks [3] and Transformers for stateful premise selection. We show that Transformer models perform substantially better, making them more suitable for this task. While here we use quadratic Transformers, we remark that linear Transformers have been shown to be equivalent [21] to fast weight programmers - feedforward neural networks where one network programs the changes of the fast weights of another network [22].

2 Data

We use the corpus introduced in [19]. The data is taken from the Mizar Mathematical Library [2] translated into the TPTP language [24]. More precisely, the MPTP2078 benchmark consisting of 2078 Mizar theorems is used. From those 2078 theorems, 1469 are proved using ATPBoost [18] (using XGBoost [1] and the E theorem prover [23]) yielding 24087 different proofs (between 1 and 265 per theorem, 16.4 on average). This corpus is split into the train set containing 18361 proofs of 1100 theorems and the test set containing 298 different theorems.

As in [19], we consider two ways of representing the theorem statements. The first, called *standard* is just tokenized statements in standard TPTP syntax. The length of theorems in this format ranges between 6 and 536, 81.23 on average. The other is using *prefix* (also called Polish) notation. The length of theorems in this format ranges between 5 and 224, 34.03 on average. For an example, see Table 1.

Table 1. An example of theorem statement in different formats.

Format	Statement
Mizar	`for A being set st A is empty holds A is finite`
TPTP	`![A] : (v1 xboole 0(A) => v1 finset 1(A))`
Standard	`! [ A ] : ( v1 xboole 0 ( A ) => v1 finset 1 ( A ) )`
Prefix	`! A => v1 xboole 0 A v1 finset 1 A`

3 Experiments

In this section we experiment with several different neural network architectures. To perform model selection, we take 98 theorems from the training set together with their proofs and use them as a validation set. We make sure that every premise that appears in the validation set also appears in the training set. Following [19], to evaluate the performance of our models we use Jaccard index and coverage defined as:

$$\text{Jaccard}(A, B) = \frac{|A \cap B|}{|A \cup B|} \qquad \text{Coverage}(A, B) = \frac{|A \cap B|}{|B|}.$$

For every theorem in the dataset, we take the union of premises over all of its available proofs. Using the above defined metrics, we compare that set (B in equations above) to the union of premises taken from the output of the beam search with our models (A in the equations above). In other words, every hypothesis in a beam corresponds to a set of premises to be used in a possible proof of a theorem. Here, we use beam search with a beam of width 10.

For training LSTM based encoder-decoder attention models, we use the OpenNMT tookit [9]. We vary the number of layers, hidden units, and training steps and use a batch size of 64. We use Luong attention variant [12] and observe that removing it dramatically reduces the performance. The top-performing architecture is a 2-layer, 500 units LSTM encoder and decoder trained with 100K steps. This happens to be the same architecture used in [19]. For training Transformers we use our own implementation in PyTorch [17]. Similarly, we vary the number of layers, hidden units, and the number of training epochs and use a batch size of 128. We observe that removing the positional encoding from the premise embeddings slightly improves the performance. The best performing model is a 3-layer Transformer with state size of 512, 8 attention heads, and feedforward dimension of 2048, trained for 500 epochs.

After finishing the model selection we train the best performing architectures on the entire training set and evaluate on the test set. On the test set we also evaluate the predictions of our models using the E theorem prover [23] and count the number of theorems proved. The results are displayed in Table 2.

Table 2. Performance of neural models on the test set.

	Format					
	Standard			Prefix		
Model	Jaccard	Coverage	Proved	Jaccard	Coverage	Proved
LSTM	0.22	0.46	0.29	0.22	0.43	0.27
Transformer	0.27	0.56	0.42	0.29	0.60	0.45

We see that Transformer model substantially outperforms LSTMs, both in set-theoretic metrics and the amount of theorems proved.

We continue by augmenting the training dataset with subproofs. We do this by taking the statements of intermediate lemmas and the premises from the corresponding proofs. This yields additional 46094 lemma-premises pairs. Again, we train the best performing models on the augmented training set and evaluate on the test set as before. The results are displayed in Table 3.

Table 3. Performance of neural models on the test set after training on augmented dataset.

Model	Jaccard	Coverage	Proved
LSTM	0.27	0.51	0.40
Transformer	0.27	0.58	0.48

It is interesting to see that the value of the Jaccard index and the coverage for the Transformer model is lower compared to the training on the non-augmented dataset. However, the number of theorems proved is higher, again substantially outperforming LSTMs and improving upon the state of the art for this dataset[1].

4 Conclusion and Future Work

In this paper we investigated the performance of LSTM and Transformer models for stateful premise selection and have shown that the Transformer architecture works better than the existing recurrent neural network baseline. Depending on the theorem prover used, the output of the model might need to be a *set* (and not a sequence) of premises. Therefore, it would be worthwhile to investigate whether incorporating permutation invariance in the models helps. This might be achieved, for instance, using the Hungarian matching algorithm [10]. Another possibility is using reinforcement learning to improve the performance of the model by interacting with the theorem prover. This could be useful even when the proofs of the theorems are not available. Also, all the methods presented here are syntactic; the premises are just tokens and the models and have to learn their semantics. Integrating the meaning of premises might further improve the results and seems as a promising future direction [15, 16].

References

1. Chen, T., Guestrin, C.: XGBoost: a scalable tree boosting system. In: Proceedings of the 22nd ACM SIGKDD International Conference on Knowledge Discovery and Data Mining, pp. 785–794 (2016)
2. Grabowski, A., Kornilowicz, A., Naumowicz, A.: Mizar in a nutshell. J. Formaliz. Reason. **3**(2), 153–245 (2010)
3. Hochreiter, S., Schmidhuber, J.: Long short-term memory. Neural Comput. **9**(8), 1735–1780 (1997)
4. Hoder, K., Voronkov, A.: Sine qua non for large theory reasoning. In: Bjørner, N., Sofronie-Stokkermans, V. (eds.) CADE 2011. LNCS (LNAI), vol. 6803, pp. 299–314. Springer, Heidelberg (2011). https://doi.org/10.1007/978-3-642-22438-6_23

---

[1] The code for reproducing the results displayed here is available at https://github.com/krstopro/stateful-premise-selection-with-transformers.

5. Irving, G., Szegedy, C., Alemi, A.A., Een, N., Chollet, F., Urban, J.: Deepmath - deep sequence models for premise selection. In: Lee, D., Sugiyama, M., Luxburg, U., Guyon, I., Garnett, R. (eds.) Advances in Neural Information Processing Systems, vol. 29. Curran Associates, Inc. (2016). https://proceedings.neurips.cc/paper/2016/file/f197002b9a0853eca5e046d9ca4663d5-Paper.pdf

6. Kaliszyk, C., Rabe, F.: A survey of languages for formalizing mathematics. In: Benzmüller, C., Miller, B. (eds.) CICM 2020. LNCS (LNAI), vol. 12236, pp. 138–156. Springer, Cham (2020). https://doi.org/10.1007/978-3-030-53518-6_9

7. Kaliszyk, C., Urban, J.: Learning-assisted automated reasoning with Flyspeck. J. Autom. Reason. **53**(2), 173–213 (2014)

8. Kaliszyk, C., Urban, J.: Mizar 40 for Mizar 40. J. Autom. Reason. **55**(3), 245–256 (2015)

9. Klein, G., Kim, Y., Deng, Y., Senellart, J., Rush, A.: OpenNMT: open-source toolkit for neural machine translation. In: Proceedings of ACL 2017, System Demonstrations, pp. 67–72. Association for Computational Linguistics, Vancouver, Canada (Jul 2017). https://www.aclweb.org/anthology/P17-4012

10. Kuhn, H.W.: The Hungarian method for the assignment problem. Naval Res. Logist. Q. **2**(1–2), 83–97 (1955)

11. Loos, S., Irving, G., Szegedy, C., Kaliszyk, C.: Deep network guided proof search. In: LPAR-21, 21st International Conference on Logic for Programming, Artificial Intelligence and Reasoning, pp. 85–105 (2017). http://arxiv.org/pdf/1701.06972.pdf. ISSN 2398–7340

12. Luong, M.T., Pham, H., Manning, C.D.: Effective approaches to attention-based neural machine translation. In: Proceedings of the 2015 Conference on Empirical Methods in Natural Language Processing, pp. 1412–1421 (2015)

13. Megill, N., Wheeler, D.A.: Metamath: A Computer Language for Mathematical Proofs (2019). http://us.metamath.org/downloads/metamath.pdf

14. Meng, J., Paulson, L.C.: Lightweight relevance filtering for machine-generated resolution problems. J. Appl. Log. **7**(1), 41–57 (2009)

15. Olšák, M., Kaliszyk, C., Urban, J.: Property invariant embedding for automated reasoning. In: Giacomo, G.D., et al. (eds.) ECAI 2020–24th European Conference on Artificial Intelligence, 29 Aug – 8 Sept 2020, Santiago de Compostela, Spain, Aug 29 – Sept 8, 2020 - Including 10th Conference on Prestigious Applications of Artificial Intelligence (PAIS 2020). Frontiers in Artificial Intelligence and Applications, vol. 325, pp. 1395–1402. IOS Press (2020). https://doi.org/10.3233/FAIA200244

16. Paliwal, A., Loos, S., Rabe, M., Bansal, K., Szegedy, C.: Graph representations for higher-order logic and theorem proving. In: Proceedings of the AAAI Conference on Artificial Intelligence, vol. 34, pp. 2967–2974 (2020)

17. Paszke, A., et al.: Pytorch: an imperative style, high-performance deep learning library. In: Wallach, H., Larochelle, H., Beygelzimer, A., d'Alché-Buc, F., Fox, E., Garnett, R. (eds.) Advances in Neural Information Processing Systems 32, pp. 8024–8035. Curran Associates, Inc. (2019). http://papers.neurips.cc/paper/9015-pytorch-an-imperative-style-high-performance-deep-learning-library.pdf

18. Piotrowski, B., Urban, J.: ATPBOOST: learning premise selection in binary setting with ATP feedback. In: Galmiche, D., Schulz, S., Sebastiani, R. (eds.) IJCAR 2018. LNCS (LNAI), vol. 10900, pp. 566–574. Springer, Cham (2018). https://doi.org/10.1007/978-3-319-94205-6_37

19. Piotrowski, B., Urban, J.: Stateful premise selection by recurrent neural networks. In: Albert, E., Kovacs, L. (eds.) LPAR23, LPAR-23: 23rd International Conference on Logic for Programming, Artificial Intelligence and Reasoning. EPiC Series in Computing, vol. 73, pp. 409–422. EasyChair (2020). 0). https://doi.org/10.29007/j5hd. https://easychair.org/publications/paper/g38n

20. Polu, S., Sutskever, I.: Generative language modeling for automated theorem proving. CoRR abs/2009.03393 (2020). https://arxiv.org/abs/2009.03393

21. Schlag, I., Irie, K., Schmidhuber, J.: Linear transformers are secretly fast weight memory systems. CoRR abs/2102.11174 (2021). https://arxiv.org/abs/2102.11174

22. Schmidhuber, J.: Reducing the ratio between learning complexity and number of time varying variables in fully recurrent nets. In: Gielen, S., Kappen, B. (eds.) ICANN 1993, pp. 460–463. Springer, London (1993). https://doi.org/10.1007/978-1-4471-2063-6_110

23. Fermüller, C.G., Voronkov, A. (eds.): LPAR 2010. LNCS, vol. 6397. Springer, Heidelberg (2010). https://doi.org/10.1007/978-3-642-16242-8

24. Sutcliffe, G.: The TPTP world – infrastructure for automated reasoning. In: Clarke, E.M., Voronkov, A. (eds.) LPAR 2010. LNCS (LNAI), vol. 6355, pp. 1–12. Springer, Heidelberg (2010). https://doi.org/10.1007/978-3-642-17511-4_1

25. Sutskever, I., Vinyals, O., Le, Q.V.: Sequence to sequence learning with neural networks. Adv. Neural Inf. Process. Syst. **27**, 3104–3112 (2014)

26. Tsivtsivadze, E., Urban, J., Geuvers, H., Heskes, T.: Semantic graph kernels for automated reasoning. In: Proceedings of the 2011 SIAM International Conference on Data Mining, pp. 795–803. SIAM (2011)

27. Urban, J.: MPTP 0.2: design, implementation, and initial experiments. J. Autom. Reason. **37**(1–2), 21–43 (2006)

28. Vaswani, A., et al.: Attention is all you need. Adv. Neural Inf. Process. Syst. **30**, 5998–6008 (2017)

Towards Math Terms Disambiguation
Using Machine Learning

Ruocheng Shan$^{(\boxtimes)}$ and Abdou Youssef

The George Washington University, Washington, DC, USA
{shanruocheng,ayoussef}@gwu.edu

Abstract. Word disambiguation has been an important task in natural language processing. However, the problem of disambiguation is still less explored in mathematical text. Similar to natural languages, some math terms are not assigned a unique interpretation. As math text is an important part of the scientific literature, an accurate and efficient way of performing disambiguation of math terms will be a significant contribution. In this paper, we present some investigations on math-term disambiguation using machine learning. All experimental data are selected from the DLMF dataset. Our experiments consist of 3 steps: (1) create a labeled dataset of math equations (from the DLMF) where the instances are (math token, token meaning) pairs, grouped by equation; (2) build machine learning models and train them using our labeled dataset, and (3) evaluate and compare the performance of our models using different evaluation metrics. Our results show that machine learning is an effective approach to math-term disambiguation. The accuracy of our models ranges from 70% to 85%. There is potential for considerable improvements once we have much larger labeled datasets with more balanced classes.

Keywords: Math-term · LaTeX · Disambiguation · Mathematical equations · Machine Learning

1 Introduction

In natural languages, a specific word can have different meanings depending on the context in which it appears. Identifying the proper sense of the word is crucial in many NLP tasks. The task of Word Sense Disambiguation (WSD) is to determine the intended sense of an ambiguous word based on the context. This is a basic problem in NLP and has a variety of solutions [1]. Machine Learning (ML) and Natural Language Processing (NLP) have started to be applied to math language processing and math knowledge discovery. In this research, we study the ambiguities of math terms in the context of math equations, where we mark terms that have different meanings in different equations and assign a sense to the term using machine learning models. Table 1 shows, as an example, two possible meanings of the math term "prime" ($'$).

© Springer Nature Switzerland AG 2021
F. Kamareddine and C. Sacerdoti Coen (Eds.): CICM 2021, LNAI 12833, pp. 90–106, 2021.
https://doi.org/10.1007/978-3-030-81097-9_7

Table 1. Examples of ambiguities of "prime"

Explanation	Example equation
Derivative	$f'(z) = \frac{df}{dz} = \lim_{h \to 0} \frac{f(z+h)-f(z)}{h}$
Part of symbol name	$a' = -a + \sum_{j=1}^{n} b_j$

While most of the "prime" tokens used in equations in many math manuscripts (e.g., the DLMF [2]) represent the derivative of a function, primes can have different meanings. For example, it can signify complementation (in logic, Boolean algebra, and set theory), or it can be an integral part (a glyph) of a symbol name. Table 2 shows other forms of possible ambiguities that were identified by Youssef and Miller [3].

Table 2. Examples of ambiguities of math terms, identified in [3]

Ambiguity	Explanation
Superscript	Can indicate a power, an index, the order of differentiation, a postfix unary operator, etc.
Prime	Can denote the derivative of y, or the logical complement of y, or a morphological glyph
Juxtaposition	Can signify multiplication, concatenation, or function application
Scope	Typically occurring when delimiters are omitted. E.g., "$\sin 2\pi x + 5$" is likely intended to mean "$\sin(2\pi x) + 5$"
Data type	Necessary to completely resolve semantics; conversely, can help disambiguate other ambiguities, e.g., Superscript

Math content processing presents some of the same challenges faced in natural language processing (NLP), such as math disambiguation and math semantics determination. These challenges must be surmounted to enable more effective math knowledge management, math knowledge discovery, automated presentation-to-computation (P2C) conversion, and automated math reasoning [4].

While purely linguistic approaches can work well for disambiguation in certain contexts, we believe that machine learning approaches (e.g., classifiers), alone or combined with linguistic approaches, have much more potential for more accurate disambiguation, especially for math terms where often the set of possible senses of a term is not fully known *a priori*.

In this paper, we carry out some investigations of math term disambiguation using machine learning. The ultimate goal is to build a (nearly) universal math-term disambiguator, that is, a model that can determine the intended sense of (nearly) every math term in (nearly) every input STEM manuscript. However, such a lofty goal is inachievable at this time for two reasons. First, it requires considerably large, labeled math datasets, which are still sorely lacking, and second, the task of building such a disambiguator is a multi-year incremental effort. Therefore, in this paper, we aim for a scaled-down realistic goal of disambiguating a small subset of math terms, using the relatively small DLMF dataset[1], to test and evaluate the promise of machine learning in math disambiguation, and to learn lessons for bigger-scope disambiguation and for creating bigger and better-labeled math datasets for the disambiguation task.

To that end, we limit our disambiguation investigation to three items/groups in the DLMF [2]: (1) the Gamma (Γ) symbol in its several variants, (2) the prime ($'$), and (3) superscripts. To train and test machine learning models for this limited disambiguation task, we looked into the labeled DLMF dataset that was recently developed by Youssef and Miller [5]. Although the labeling in that dataset is fairly rich and multi-faceted, it was not adequate for our task. Therefore, we had to manually create new labels targeted to our three disambiguation groups, for a small subset of the DLMF (due to the lack of time and resources). Afterwards, we trained and tested classical machine learning models as well as one deep learning (DL) model. Our experiments show that the classical ML models perform quite well on our scaled-down disambiguation task, boding well for much broader disambiguation of math terms. Our results also show that our deep learning model under-performed the classical ones, which was not too surprising because deep learning models require much larger datasets than currently available. This paper will present our studies and experiments, draw some conclusions and lessons learned, and identify directions for future work in this important area of math language processing.

2   Related Works

2.1   The DLMF Dataset

Much of the mathematical literature is mostly in LaTeX. In this study, we utilized the Digital Library of Mathematical Functions (DLMF) of NIST. The dataset is structured and labeled in a specific way. For each math equation and expression in the DLMF, there is a record that provides annotation and contextual elements. The whole dataset has 20,040 sentences; 25,930 math elements; and 8,494 numbered equations [5].

We extracted equations from the DLMF and divided them into smaller groups by identifying whether an equation contains the terms that need to be disambiguated.

---

[1] https://github.com/abdouyoussef/math-dlmf-dataset/.

2.2   Part-of-Math Tagger

In preparation for labeling the math terms, we use the Part-of-Math (POM) Tagger provided by Youssef to tokenize equations [4].

The tagger takes as input a math equation or expression, and tags each math term and some sub-expressions with two kinds of tags. The first kind consists of definite tags (such as operation, relation, numerator, etc.) that the tagger is certain of. The second kind consists of alternative, tentative features (including alternative roles and meanings) drawn from a knowledge base that was developed for the POM tagger. Using the tagger and some manual post-processing and labeling, we created the labeled a set of equations that have one or more of our target list of ambiguous math terms.

2.3   Word Sense Disambiguation in NLP

Word Sense Disambiguation is a technique to find the exact sense of an ambiguous word in a particular context [6–8]. WSD typically involves two main tasks: (1) determining the different possible senses (or meanings) of each word, and (2) tagging each word of a text with its most likely intended sense in context.

For the former task, in NLP, the precise definition of a sense is still under discussion and remains an open problem. At the moment, the most used Sense Repository is WordNet [9]. However, when it comes to Math-Terms, no such agreed-upon resource exists, and often the list of possible senses of a math term varies from area to area within mathematics, making the problem domain-specific. Furthermore, the intended sense of a math term can be totally new (specified by the authors) and defined somewhere within the manuscript; in such cases, the problem shifts to that of definition harvesting, which is an entirely different task than the one under consideration in this paper.

The second task has mainly two approaches: knowledge-based and corpus-based methods. The knowledge-based method in WSD depends on external knowledge sources, such as Machine Readable Dictionaries, which exist prior to the disambiguation process. In the corpus-based methods, the information is gathered from contexts of previously annotated examples of a word. These methods extract the knowledge from examples by applying Statistical or Machine Learning Methods.

Disambiguation of word sense and disambiguation of math terms share much in common: (1) the sources are all in text format, and should be processed within a context that is a sequence of tokens; (2) they both have a set of classes or labels for each element (word senses and math term definitions); and (3) the corpus-based approaches are identical in terms of computation.

However, the lack of pre-existing semantic relations between math terms makes it impossible to apply some knowledge-based algorithms that proved so effective in WSD.

2.4   Machine Learning Models

WSD, as well as math-term disambiguation, can be viewed as a classification task: math definitions are the classes, and an automatic classification method (i.e., a classifier) is used to assign each occurrence of a math term to one of the classes based on the evidence from the context and from external knowledge sources.

Machine learning models/classifiers have proved effective in WSD. In 2014, Singh et al. achieved 71.75% accuracy in Manipuri language with 400 test words and 1600 training words [10]. In 2018, Faisal, Nurifan and Sarno used Support Vector Machine with TF-IDF as feature extraction method and achieved 87.7% accuracy in Bahasa Indonesia language [11].

Deep learning has been applied on NLP tasks, including WSD, with considerable success. With enough training data and computing resources, deep learning can be effective because: (1) it uses sequence processing and considers the word order; (2) neural networks do not require any previous hand crafted feature engineering. In 2017 Raganato et al. used DL with SemCor 3.0 [12] as training corpus and tested on SemEval2007 [13]. Their Bi-LSTM model reached 83.1% F-score while another Seq2Seq model of theirs reached 82.3% F-score. In 2019, Nithyanandan and C.Raseek used Bi-LSTM and achieved 93% accuracy [1] on the One-Million Sense Tagged Corpus(OMSTC) [14].

Compared with Deep Learning, which is now the state-of-the-art approach to perform WSD, classical machine learning models can provide relatively good results using only small training datasets. Given that our dataset is quite small, we decided to investigate the possibilities of performing math-term disambiguation using primarily classical machine learning model.

However, to get some sense of how well deep learning can do in math-term disambiguation using only a small dataset, we examine in this paper one deep learning model. The Sequence-to-Sequence approach in deep learning is especially suitable for math disambiguation. Besides the benefits of deep learning we discussed before, a Sequence-to-Sequence model can produce a sequence of classes corresponding to the input tokens of an equation. In this paper, we train and test a sequence-to-sequence model using Long Short Term Memory (LSTM) neural network [15], and compare its performance with those of classical machine learning models.

2.5   Math Language Processing

While machine learning and natural language processing are being applied to math language processing (MLP) and math knowledge discovery, many related studies are carried out to solve certain MLP tasks.

In 2018, Youssef and Miller applied different deep learning models to math semantics extraction and processing and conducted comparative performance evaluations of the models [3]. They also presented exploratory investigations of math embedding by testing it on MLP tasks, such as math-term similarity, analogy, math search and so on [16]. In 2018, Schubotz, et al. introduced a Gold

Standard MathMLben to facilitate the conversion between different mathematical formats such as LaTeX variations and Computer Algebra Systems (CAS) [17]. In 2021, Scharpf, Schubotz and Gipp presented an approach to structure and speed up the annotation and linking process between mathematical formulae and semantic concepts [18].

3   The Dataset

As indicated earlier, we had to carve out a subset of the DLMF dataset, and label it manually for the Gamma symbols, the prime, and superscripts. In this section, we describe the dataset and provide some statistics about it.

Tabel 3 shows an example of a labeled equation:

$$a' = -a + \sum_{j=1}^{n} b_j.$$

The LaTeX format of this equation is:

```
a\^{\prime}=-a+\sum\_{j=1}\xhat{n}b\_{j}
```

Table 3. A labeled equation as tokens and labels. The equation is: $a' = -a + \sum_{j=1}^{n} b_j$. The label "O" means that a token belongs to no class

Token	a	superscript	{	prime	}	=	-	a	+	Σ	-	{	j
Label	O	part_of_name	O	part_of_name	O	O	O	O	O	O	O	O	O

Token	=	1	}	superscript	{	n	}	b	_	{	j	}
Label	O	O	O	summation_upper_bound	O	O	O	O	O	O	O	O

Tables 4, 5, 6 show the number of samples for each of our three groups, the classes per group, and their labels and sizes.

Table 4. Data distribution of Gamma

Label	Explanation	Samples
multivariate_gamma_function	The multivariate Gamma function	50
q_gamma_function	The q-gamma function	21
incomplete_gamma_function	The incomplete gamma function	57
gamma_function	The gamma function	1577
Total size	1705	

Table 5. Data distribution of superscript

Label	Explanation	Samples
integral_upper_bound	Indicates the upper bound of integration	864
summation_upper_bound	Indicates the upper bound of summation	86
part_of_name	The part of name of a variable or function	923
power	The power of a variable or function	7014
Total size	8887	

Table 6. Data distribution of Prime

Label	Explanation	Samples
derivative	Derivative of a function	352
part_of_name	The part of name of a variable or function	35
Total size	387	

4   Machine Learning Approach

Figure 1 shows the basic architecture of our approach to Math Term Disambiguation. The main stages of this project are: Data Prepossessing, Feature Engineering, Training the Models, and Evaluation. The Data Prepossessing stage performs the pre-processing of the dataset which makes it easier for computation, where we tokenize the equations, apply a placeholder to duplicate tokens in an equation (as will be explained shortly), and perform under-sampling to balance the different classes. The Feature Engineering stage computes the feature vector of every equation (explained later). The Training stage performs the training of our machine learning models and the tuning of the hyperparameters. The Evaluation stage gives the test results in different performance metrics.

4.1   Data Prepossessing

4.1.1   Place Holding
In some equations, the target math term appears more than once. In this paper, we only select one of the duplicate terms as target, and replace all the other occurrences of the same term with a placeholder. In future work, our models will label all occurrences, but in this paper, we limit the classifier scope to just one occurrence of a term, on the assumption that all occurrences of the same term in the same equation have the same sense. Figure 2 shows an example of the place-holding process.

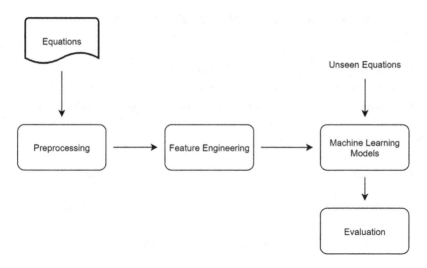

Fig. 1. Basic architecture of the system

4.1.2 Data Under-Sampling

In Sect. 3, the data distributions were presented, where the class imbalance is obvious. The imbalance would wrongly lean the models towards the majority classes, that is, the trained classifiers would more likely predict the class of a test data instance as the majority class.

We perform random under-sampling on the data set to reduce the number of samples of certain classes and yet keep its majority position, to a mitigated extent.

Tables 7, 8, 9 show the statistics for each of the 3 groups after under-sampling.

Table 7. Data distribution of Gamma after under-sampling

Label	Explanation	Samples
multivariate_gamma_function	The multivariate Gamma function	50
q_gamma_function	The q-gamma function	21
incomplete_gamma_function	The incomplete gamma function	57
gamma_function	The gamma function	200
Total size	328	

Table 8. Data distribution of superscript after under-sampling

Label	Explanation	Samples
integral_upper_bound	Indicates the upper bound of integration	864
summation_upper_bound	Indicates the upper bound of summation	86
part_of_name	The part of name of a variable or function	923
power	The power of a variable or function	1500
Total size	3373	

Table 9. Data distribution of prime after under-sampling

Label	Explanation	Samples
derivative	Derivative of a function	100
part_of_name	The part of name of a variable or function	35
Total size	135	

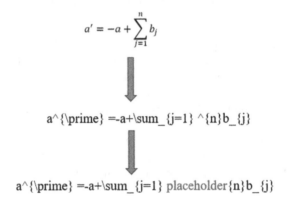

$$a' = -a + \sum_{j=1}^{n} b_j$$

a^{\prime} =-a+\sum_{j=1} ^{n}b_{j}

a^{\prime} =-a+\sum_{j=1} placeholder{n}b_{j}

Fig. 2. An example of place holding

4.2   Feature Engineering

First we use the CountVectorizer function provided by scikit learn[2] on the tokenized sequence of math terms to form the feature space. An encoded vector is returned with a length of the entire vocabulary and an integer count for the number of times each word appeared in the document.

After obtaining the count-vector representations, we then apply the TF-IDF (Term Frequency - Inverse Document Frequency) algorithm to further enhance the features. TF-IDF is a statistical measure that evaluates how relevant a word is to a document in a collection of documents. It is the product of: how many

---

[2] https://scikit-learn.org/stable/modules/generated/sklearn.feature_extraction.text. \penalty-\@MCountVectorizer.html.

times a word appears in a document, and the log of the inverse document frequency of the word across a set of documents.

The TF-IDF is calculated via this formula:

$$tfidf\,(t, d, D) = tf\,(t, d) \times idf\,(t, D)$$

Where:

$$tf\,(t, d) = log\,(1 + freq\,(t, d))$$

$$idf\,(t, D) = log\left(\frac{N}{count\,(d \in D \mid t \in d)}\right)$$

Here, t stands for a math term; d is a document, which in this paper is an equation; D is the equation corpus; N is the total number of equations; $freq\,(t, d)$ is the term frequency of a term t in a document (*i.e.*, equation) d; $count\,(d \in D \mid t \in d)$ is the number of documents that contain the term t.

4.3   Training the Models

4.3.1   Models

We train and test 4 different machine learning models for math term disambiguation. The first three are from classical machine learning, and the fourth is from deep learning. The four models are described next.

Decision tree (DT) [19] is used to denote classification rules in a tree structure that recursively divides the training data set. Each internal node of the decision tree denotes a test which is applied on a feature value, and each branch denotes an output of the test. When a leaf node is reached, the sense of the word is represented (if possible).

Random forest (RF) [20] is an ensemble of decision trees, usually trained with the "bagging" method. The general idea of the bagging method is that a combination of learning models increases the accuracy of the overall result.

Support Vector Machine (SVM) [21] depends on the idea of learning a hyperplane using a training dataset. The hyperplane separates positive and negative examples. It maximizes the distance between the closest positive and negative examples (called support vectors). The Support Vector Machine implements optimization to find a hyperplane that separates training examples.

Deep Learning (LSTM) We used the LSTM neural network [15] to perform Sequence-to-Sequence disambiguation. The network structure is shown in Fig. 3. One of the biggest benefits of this approach is that we do not need any feature engineering; all we need is the sentences (or equations) and their labeled words (or math terms); the rest of the work is carried in by the embedding layer. For this specific task, the output shape of the Dense layer equals the length of the label sequence, for each token has a corresponding label.

4.3.2 Tuning

When data sets are small, K-fold cross-validation is the method of choice for training, tuning, and testing of a model. In K-fold cross-validation, the data is divided into K subsets. Now the holdout method is repeated K times. Each time, one of the K subsets is used as the test-set, the other $K - 1$ subsets are put together to form a training set; after the training is completed, the test accuracy is computed on the holdout dataset, and recorded. The overall test accuracy of the model is taken (i.e. approximated) to be the average of the K test accuracies so computed.

Tuning of the hyperparameters refers to finding the best combination of hyperparameyter values, i.e., the combination that yields the highest test accuracy. This is done by trying all possible combinations of hyperparameter values. For each combination, the K-fold cross-validation method is performed on the dataset, and the average test accuracy is computed. The combination that yields the highest test accuracy is taken to be the best combination of hyperparameter values, and those values are adopted for the model.

In this research, because our datasets are small in each of the three disambiguation problems, we used 10-fold cross-validation for training+tuning+testing of each of our models. Again, we emphasize that this is standard practice when datasets are quite small, i.e., when the dataset is not large enough to be split into separate disjoint training set, validation set and testing set.

For SVM, we tuned the C value (with candidates 0.5, 0.75, 1.0, 1.25 and 1.5) and the kernel type (where the candidate values are: candidates linear, poly, rbf and sigmoid). For DT, we tuned the max depth (where the candidate values are auto, sqrt and log2) and max features (where the candidate values are "all features", 10 and 100). For RF, we tuned the number of estimators, which is the number of decision trees inside the forest (with candidate values 50, 75, 100, 125, 150, 175 and 200)

Table 10 shows the optimal hyperparameters of each model for each classification problem.

Note that, for lack of adequate training data, we did not tune the LSTM model. Instead, we took the hyperparameter values that have been optimized in the literature for similar tasks.

Figure 4 shows the learning curve of SVM on the Gamma problem using the optimal hyperparameters. Similar learning curves are obtained for all the models and all three classification tasks, but are not included for lack of space.

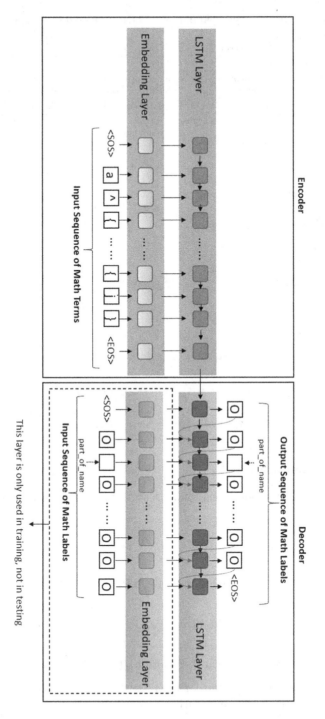

Fig. 3. Structure of The Neural Network. Using example of $a' = -a + \sum_{j=1}^{n} b_j$. Here SOS and EOS are the placeholders for the start and end of the equation sequence

Table 10. Optimal hyperparamters selected by K-fold cross validation

Model	Math Term		
	Gamma	Prime	Superscript
Decision Tree	max_depth = all #features = sqrt	max_depth = 100 #features = sqrt	max_depth = 10 #features = sqrt
Random Forest	#estimators = 125	#estimators = 100	#estimators = 200
SVM	C = 1.5 kernel = poly	C = 1.25 kernel = poly	C = 1.5 kernel = poly

Fig. 4. SVM learning curve for Gamma

4.4 Evaluation Metric

We use accuracy, precision, recall and F1 score to evaluate the performance of models.

$$Accuracy = TP+TN/TP+FP+FN+TN$$

$$Precision = TP/TP+FP$$

$$Recall = TP/TP+FN$$

$$F1\ Score = 2*(Recall * Precision)/(Recall + Precision)$$

where TP, TN, FP, FN stand for the numbers of True Positives, True Negatives, False Positive and False Negative, respectively.

5   Results

5.1   Gamma

Table 11 shows the performance of our models for the disambiguation of the term Γ.

All the three classical ML models gave very good and comparable performance, especially in terms of accuracy and F1 score. In terms of Precision, the Decision Tree model (follows closely by SVM) gave much better performance than RF; while in Recall the situation is reversed. The fact that the Decision Tree model reaches the highest precision can be attributed to its ability to find better (than other models) the patterns that characterize each class/label, when the dataset size is fairly small.

Table 11. Evaluation of Gamma Γ

Model	Accuracy	Precision	Recall	F1 score
Decision Tree	0.82	**0.92**	0.76	0.83
Random Forest	**0.83**	0.83	**0.79**	0.81
SVM	0.82	0.91	0.76	0.82
LSTM	0.45	0.55	0.4	0.46

The LSTM model performance was predictably much lower, due to the lack of adequate training data.

Actually, even the classical ML models can benefit from somewhat larger training datasets. With our current dataset size, we found that those models experienced some over-fitting, and we believe that with more training data, their performance will increase to some extent.

5.2   Prime

Table 12 shows the performance of models for the disambiguation of the math term prime $\prime$. The Decision Tree model is a clear winner, and by a significant amount, for nearly all the metrics. Here again, we attribute that to DTs' ability to learn better the patterns that characterize each class when the dataset is small, whereas the other models need larger datasets. Also, one can observe the low performance of LSTM here as well.

5.3   Superscript

Table 13 shows the performance of models for the disambiguation of the superscript. Here, SVM delivers the best performance, while the DT gave the least performance among the 3 classical ML models. We believe that this is due to the much larger dataset for this particular classification problem. The LSTM model is the least performing here too, but it performs better than in the other two disambiguation problems due to the larger size of the dataset for superscripts.

Table 12. Evaluation of Prime /

Model	Accuracy	Precision	Recall	F1 score
Decision Tree	**0.84**	**0.92**	**0.78**	**0.83**
Random Forest	0.78	0.8	0.78	0.79
SVM	0.78	0.87	0.7	0.78
LSTM	0.56	0.57	0.51	0.54

Table 13. Evaluation of superscript

Model	Accuracy	Precision	Recall	F1 score
Decision Tree	0.72	0.75	0.66	0.7
Random Forest	**0.83**	0.86	0.83	0.85
SVM	**0.83**	**0.92**	**0.86**	**0.87**
LSTM	0.65	0.68	0.59	0.63

6   Conclusion and Future Work

In this paper, we examined the machine learning approach towards math term disambiguation. The performance of different models was presented. While our studies need extensive future experimentation, the results show the promise of (classical) machine learning models in math-term labeling and disambiguation.

Also, we found that when the dataset size is fairly small, Decision Trees were able to learn the differentiating patterns better than any other model we tried, and as the datasets become larger (and cover more cases), the other models (especially SVM) outperformed DTs.

As predicted, the deep learning model (LSTM) resulted in a much lower and rather inadequate performance, as this approach needs a much larger dataset.

This is a stage-one study of applying machine learning and testing deep learning on math disambiguation. In our future work, we plan to expand the labeled dataset in size and coverage to (1) achieve more disambiguation functionality, and (2) exploit the great potential of deep learning models for this task. We will also explore different deep learning models and different embedding techniques, including contextualized embedding, to obtain higher disambiguation performance.

References

1. Nithyanandan, S., Raseek, C.: Deep learning models for word sense disambiguation: A comparative study (2019)
2. Olver, F.W.J., et al. (eds.): NIST Digital Library of Mathematical Functions. https://dlmf.nist.gov/. Release 1.0.20 of 2018-09-1

3. Youssef, A., Miller, B.R.: Deep learning for math knowledge processing. In: Rabe, F., Farmer, W.M., Passmore, G.O., Youssef, A. (eds.) CICM 2018. LNCS (LNAI), vol. 11006, pp. 271–286. Springer, Cham (2018). https://doi.org/10.1007/978-3-319-96812-4_23

4. Youssef, A.: Part-of-math tagging and applications. In: Geuvers, H., England, M., Hasan, O., Rabe, F., Teschke, O. (eds.) CICM 2017. LNCS (LNAI), vol. 10383, pp. 356–374. Springer, Cham (2017). https://doi.org/10.1007/978-3-319-62075-6_25

5. Youssef, A., Miller, B.R.: A contextual and labeled math-dataset derived from NIST's DLMF. In: Benzmüller, C., Miller, B. (eds.) CICM 2020. LNCS (LNAI), vol. 12236, pp. 324–330. Springer, Cham (2020). https://doi.org/10.1007/978-3-030-53518-6_25

6. Pal, A.R., Saha, D.: Word sense disambiguation: a survey. arXiv preprint, arXiv: 1508.01346 (2015)

7. Navigli, R.: Word sense disambiguation: a survey. ACM Comput. Surv. (CSUR) **41**(2), 1–69 (2009)

8. Nameh, M., Fakhrahmad, S., Jahromi, M.Z.: A new approach to word sense disambiguation based on context similarity. In: Proceedings of the World Congress on Engineering, vol. 1, pp. 6–8 (2011)

9. Miller, G.A.: Wordnet: a lexical database for English. Commun. ACM **38**(11), 39–41 (1995)

10. Singh, R.L., Ghosh, K., Nongmeikapam, K., Bandyopadhyay, S.: A decision tree based word sense disambiguation system in Manipuri language. Adv. Comput. **5**(4), 17 (2014)

11. Faisal, E., Nurifan, F., Sarno, R.: Word sense disambiguation in Bahasa Indonesia using SVM. In: 2018 International Seminar on Application for Technology of Information and Communication, pp. 239–243. IEEE (2018)

12. Miller, G.A., Leacock, C., Tengi, R., Bunker, R.T.: A semantic concordance. In: HUMAN LANGUAGE TECHNOLOGY: Proceedings of a Workshop Held at Plainsboro, New Jersey, 21–24 March 1993 (1993)

13. Pradhan, S., Loper, E., Dligach, D., Palmer, M.: SemEval-2007 task-17: English lexical sample, SRL and all words. In: Proceedings of the Fourth International Workshop on Semantic Evaluations (SemEval 2007), pp. 87–92 (2007)

14. Taghipour, K., Ng, H.T.: One million sense-tagged instances for word sense disambiguation and induction. In: Proceedings of the Nineteenth Conference on Computational Natural Language Learning, pp. 338–344 (2015)

15. Hochreiter, S., Schmidhuber, J.: Long short-term memory. Neural Comput. **9**(8), 1735–1780 (1997)

16. Youssef, A., Miller, B.R.: Explorations into the use of word embedding in math search and math semantics. In: Kaliszyk, C., Brady, E., Kohlhase, A., Sacerdoti Coen, C. (eds.) CICM 2019. LNCS (LNAI), vol. 11617, pp. 291–305. Springer, Cham (2019). https://doi.org/10.1007/978-3-030-23250-4_20

17. Schubotz, M., Greiner-Petter, A., Scharpf, P., Meuschke, N., Cohl, H., Gipp, B.: Improving the representation and conversion of mathematical formulae by considering their textual context. In: Proceedings of the 18th ACM/IEEE on Joint Conference on Digital Libraries (2018)

18. Scharpf, P., Schubotz, M., Gipp, B.: Fast linking of mathematical Wikidata entities in Wikipedia articles using annotation recommendation. arXiv preprint arXiv:2104.05111 (2021)

19. Breiman, L., Friedman, J., Stone, C.J., Olshen, R.A.: Classification and Regression Trees. CRC Press, Boca Raton (1984)
20. Breiman, L.: Random forests. Mach. Learn. **45**(1), 5–32 (2001)
21. Boser, B.E., Guyon, I.M., Vapnik, V.N.: A training algorithm for optimal margin classifiers. In: Proceedings of the Fifth Annual Workshop on Computational Learning Theory, pp. 144–152 (1992)

Heterogeneous Heuristic Optimisation and Scheduling for First-Order Theorem Proving

Edvard K. Holden$^{(\boxtimes)}$ and Konstantin Korovin

The University of Manchester, Manchester, UK
{edvard.holden,konstantin.korovin}@manchester.ac.uk

Abstract. Good heuristics are essential for successful proof search in first-order automated theorem proving. As a result, state-of-the-art theorem provers offer a range of options for tuning the proof search process to specific problems. However, the vast configuration space makes it exceedingly challenging to construct effective heuristics. In this paper we present a new approach called HOS-ML, for automatically discovering new heuristics and mapping problems into optimised local schedules comprising of these heuristics. Our approach is based on interleaving Bayesian hyper-parameter optimisation for discovering promising heuristics and dynamic clustering to make optimisation efficient on heterogeneous problems. HOS-ML also use constraint programming to devise locally optimal schedules and machine learning for mapping unseen problems into such schedules. We evaluated HOS-ML on the theorem prover iProver and demonstrated that it can discover new heuristics that considerably improve performance and can solve problems that have not been solved previously by any other system.

Keywords: Theorem proving · Machine learning · Heuristic optimisation · Heuristic selection · Dynamic clustering

1 Introduction

Automated Theorem Provers (ATPs) are tools for automatically proving mathematical theorems, and have a wide range of applications from verification of software and hardware to automating interactive theorem proving in systems such as Sledgehammer [14]. ATPs have also contributed to large mathematical formalisation projects such as the MML (Mizar Mathematical Library) through the MPTP (Mizar Problems for Theorem Proving) [20].

State-of-the-art ATPs such as iProver [9], Vampire [10], E [18] and SPASS [22] have large sets of parameters that can be used to guide the proof search. It is well known that slight changes in values of these parameters can render problems from being not solved to being instantly solved and vise versa. Unfortunately, there is no general recipe for good parameters values or *heuristics*. While heuristics are essential for success, finding good heuristics is a major challenge due to the vast number of possible parameter combinations and values. Manually discovering good heuristics is time-consuming and in most cases not feasible even for system experts. For example, iProver has over 100

© Springer Nature Switzerland AG 2021
F. Kamareddine and C. Sacerdoti Coen (Eds.): CICM 2021, LNAI 12833, pp. 107–123, 2021.
https://doi.org/10.1007/978-3-030-81097-9_8

parameters with parameter types in the domain of reals, integers, Boolean, categorical and lists. These parameters govern a wide range of simplifications, clause and literal selection strategies in a combination of instantiation, resolution and superposition calculi.

In this paper we develop a new approach, called HOS-ML, for automatically discovering new heuristics and mapping problems into optimised local schedules comprising of these heuristics. One of the key ingredients in our approach is Bayesian hyper-parameter optimisation. Hyper-parameter optimisation works well when applied to a homogeneous set of problems where it tries to find heuristics that optimise some performance metric over the whole set of problems. However, in practice problem sets are largely heterogeneous where vastly different heuristics are required to solve different problems. One way of dealing with this issue is to cluster similar problems and apply hyper-parameter optimisation individually to each cluster. A major challenge is that there is no obvious way of grouping problems into homogeneous clusters of similar problems based solely on syntactic properties. This is because even slight syntactic changes in a problem can result in a completely different problem which requires different heuristics to solve. In this paper, we solve this challenge by interleaving Bayesian hyper-parameter optimisation with dynamic clustering based on evaluation features. In this approach hyper-parameter optimisation and clustering incrementally refine each other: Bayesian hyper-parameter optimisation generates new heuristics that are used for clustering similar problems and in turn clustering similar problems helps Bayesian hyper-parameter optimisation to find diverse heuristics with good performance on each cluster. Other ingredients of HOS-ML include: i) training an embedding model for expanding clusters with similar unsolved problems using machine learning, ii) computing optimal local schedules for clusters using constraint programming, and iii) mapping unseen problems into local schedules using machine learning models.

We implemented HOS-ML and applied it to a theorem prover iProver. Experimental results show that HOS-ML can discover new heuristics that considerably increase the number of solved problems, including problems that have not been solved so far by any other system. Finally, we remark that the HOS-ML approach is rather general and can be applied to other domains for heuristics optimisation over heterogeneous problems.

Related Work. Although parameter optimisation for first-order theorem proving received considerable attention [6, 7, 16, 21], it is primarily based on the assumption that problems are homogeneous and optimisation is performed uniformly over the whole problem set. In other domains, heuristic optimisation for heterougenous instances has been approached with one-off static feature clustering [8, 12, 17]. One of the major differences with our approach is that in HOS-ML hyper-parameter optimisation and clustering are dynamically interleaved which strengthen both optimisation and clustering during the run of the algorithm.

Heuristic selection is often approached by predicting the optimal heuristic for a given problem [1, 11, 23]. The main drawback of this approach is that it is unclear how to proceed when there are multiple good heuristics. A different approach was carried out in [15], where the internal prover state was used to predict the heuristic to run in the next time-slice. This is a promising approach but does not utilise predictive power of Bayesian hyper-parameter optimisation nor clustering. In our approach, we leverage the power of discovered heuristics by constructing schedules for each homogeneous cluster and build an embedding model for mapping unseen problems into schedules.

2 Hyper-Parameter Optimisation

Let $\mathcal{A}$ be a target algorithm, Θ a parameter space, $\mathcal{C}_\mathcal{A}$ a performance cost function, I a set of problem instances. If p is a problem in I, then $\mathcal{C}_\mathcal{A}(\theta, p) \in \mathbb{R}$ defines the performance cost associated with the run of the algorithm $\mathcal{A}$ with parameters (*heuristic*) θ on a problem p. Performance cost can be running time but can be a more sophisticated function that, e.g., increases cost if the problem was not solved within the given time limit and reduces cost if the problem was solved with this heuristic but was not solved by previously found heuristics. In Sect. 4.2 we discuss this in more detail.

Hyper-parameter optimisation for $\mathcal{A}$ over a problem set I is the problem of finding parameters $\theta_{\min}$ that minimize the cost function over all problem instances in I:

$$\theta_{\min}^I = \arg\min_{\theta \in \Theta} \Sigma_{p \in I} \mathcal{C}_\mathcal{A}(\theta, p).$$

Hyper-parameter optimisation [4] is well suited for homogeneous problem collections where we can assume that $\theta_{\min}^I$ is optimal or near optimal for all instances $p \in I$.

However, in our setting we are dealing with large collections of heterogeneous problems where there is no uniform best heuristic but rather different heuristics perform better on different classes of problems. Unfortunately, there is no simple criteria for grouping problems into homogeneous clusters that allow for single (or just few) near optimal heuristic(s) per cluster. We can observe that the search for optimal heuristics and clustering are interrelated problems. This observation is at the core of our HOS-ML approach where we interleave search for optimal heuristics with dynamic clustering based on the performance of these heuristics on individual problems.

3 Heterogeneous Heuristic Optimisation and Scheduling

Our approach for heterogeneous heuristic optimisation and scheduling (HOS-ML) is shown in Fig. 1. Let us first overview HOS-ML at a high-level and in later sections we elaborate on each component. HOS-ML consists of three phases described below.

Phase 1: Heuristic Optimisation for Heterogeneous Instances. This phase is applied to a set of training problems. The goal of this phase is to discover new heuristics that i) solve problems which could not be solved by heuristics discovered in previous iterations, and ii) improve the performance of problems that were previously solved. These conditions can be represented by a cost function for hyper-parameter optimisation.

One of the main challenges is that problems in our setting are heterogeneous, this prevents hyper-parameter optimisation to discover diverse heuristics which solve different types of problems. To address this challenge we cluster problems based on *dynamic evaluation features*. Dynamic evaluation features are problem features based on the evaluation of all heuristics discovered in previous iterations. These features reflect problem similarity based on the performance of different heuristics, and they are dynamic due to the growing number of discovered heuristics (see, Sect. 4).

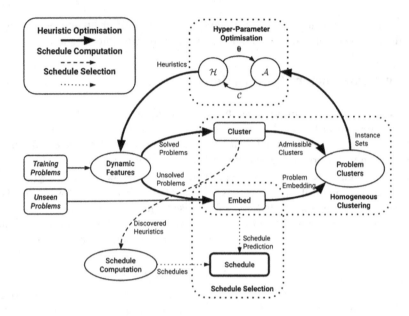

Fig. 1. HOS-ML: heuristic optimisation and selection for heterogeneous problems.

The *heterogeneous heuristic optimisation loop* outlined by thick arrows in Fig. 1, interleaves re-clustering based on dynamic evaluation features and hyper-parameter optimisation over each cluster.

Clustering based on dynamic features is suitable for problems that can be solved by some of the available heuristics but is not applicable to unseen or unsolved problems. We address this problem by training a machine learning model for embedding static problem features into dynamic features. This *admissible embedding model* is re-trained after each loop iteration.

By combining problem clustering and embedding, we acquire homogeneous problem clusters. Next, we perform hyper-parameter optimisation over each problem cluster separately. This results in a set of well-performing heuristics for each cluster which we evaluate globally on all training problems. The heuristics evaluation is used to update the dynamic feature representation for each problem. Subsequently, we re-cluster problems based on the new evaluation features, increasing homogeneity of clusters and re-train the admissible embedding model. This loop is repeated until the global time limit or some other termination criterion is reached.

Phase 2: Local Schedule Computation. After Phase 1 is completed we compute schedules for the final clusters. We use constraint programming to create a schedule for each problem cluster based on discovered heuristics and their evaluation over the training set (Sect. 5).

Phase 3: Schedule Selection. The final phase is the deployment of HOS-ML on unseen problems. This is done by first mapping the problem into a cluster using the admissible embedding model and then extracting the schedule associated with the corresponding cluster computed in Phase 2. This phase is computationally cheap as the model and schedules have been computed in Phases 1 and 2, respectively.

In the following sections we will detail each part of HOS-ML.

4 Heuristic Optimisation for Heterogeneous Instances

In this section we describe in detail Phase 1, which is heuristic discovery and optimisation on heterogeneous problems. This phase is applied to a set of training problems.

The heuristic discovery and optimisation loop is detailed in Algorithm 1, it takes two inputs: *initial_heuristics* and *problems*. The goal of the algorithm is to discover new *global_heuristics* which improve the performance over *problems* in local clusters, with the *initial_heuristics* serving as starting points. This is achieved through interleaving homogeneous clustering and heuristic optimisation with the use of the inner and outer loops.

The algorithm first clusters solved problems based on the current dynamic heuristic evaluation features (detailed in Subsect. 4.1). Then, the algorithm trains a machine learning model for embedding problems into clusters based on static problem features (detailed in Subsect. 4.3). In this phase, this *admissible embedding model* is used to embed unsolved problems into clusters to achieve a balance between solved and unsolved problems in each cluster.

Next, the algorithm enters the inner loop to perform *local heuristic optimisation* over each problem cluster to discover good heuristics for each cluster which are added to *local_heuristics*. Then, *local_heuristics* are evaluated globally on the whole problem set to obtain new dynamic evaluation features for each problem. In the next iteration of the outer loop the problems are re-clustered based on these new dynamic evaluation features. With each iteration, problem clusters become increasingly more homogeneous with respect to accumulated heuristics performance. In the initial iterations, when there are only few heuristics we randomly sub-sample large clusters into smaller clusters.

In the following, we describe the key parts of Algorithm 1 which are: dynamic evaluation clustering, local heuristic optimisation, and the admissible embedding model.

4.1 Dynamic Evaluation Clustering

One way of clustering similar problems is using syntactic features such as the number of formulas, number of equalities, number of Horn or EPR formulas, etc. Such clustering is suitable when problems fall into well-behaved fragments, e.g., Horn or EPR. However, most problems are mixtures of formulas with different properties and do not fall into such classes. For such problems syntactic features poorly reflect similarity as e.g., adding a single non-Horn formula to a Horn problem can drastically change the behaviour of the problem and similar for other types of formulas.

In this work, we propose to use dynamic evaluation features which are based on solver performance under different heuristics. Such features directly link problem similarity with the solver performance, moreover these features are dynamically extended during the run of Algorithm 1 due to newly discovered heuristics by local heuristic optimisation.

Algorithm 1. Heterogeneous Heuristic Optimisation

Input: *initial_heuristics, problems*
Output: Learnt heuristics (*global_heuristics*)
1: *global_heuristics ← evaluate_heuristics(initial_heuristics, problems)*
2: **repeat**
3:     *evaluation ← get_evaluation(global_heuristics)*
4:     *solved, unsolved ← split(problems, evaluation)*
5:     *problem_clusters ← compute_clusters(solved, evaluation)*
6:     *cluster_model ← train_model(problem_clusters, solved)*
7:     *problem_clusters ← problem_clusters ∪ embed(cluster_model, unsolved)*
8:     *local_heuristics ← ∅*
9:     **for** *cluster ∈ problem_clusters* **do**
10:         *incumbent ← select_best_heuristic(cluster, global_heuristics)*
11:         *local_heuristics ← local_heuristics ∪ optimise(incumbent, cluster)*
12:     **end for**
13:     *global_heuristics ← global_heuristics ∪ evaluate(local_heuristics, problems)*
14: **until** Timeout
15: **return** *global_heuristics*

Given a problem p, a heuristic θ, and a time limit β, the function $time_\beta$ gives the solving time t of θ executed on p with the time limit β, if a solution is found and ∞ otherwise. Given a set of heuristics $H \subset \Theta$, we can obtain the problem's heuristic evaluation vector $\mathbf{e_p}$ by computing $time_\beta$ for each problem-heuristic pair. The *evaluation vector* $\mathbf{e_p}$ represents the relationship between p and H. By computing the evaluation vector for the set of problems I, we obtain the heuristic evaluation matrix $\mathbf{E_{IxH}}$.

Admissible Features. The evaluation vector represents solving times of the successful solving attempts. However, similar problems can have different solving times, e.g., problems may differ by size but not structure. We want to cluster problems so local heuristic optimisation can transfer learning from simpler problems to more complex problems of the same type. This is achieved using clustering based on admissible features. First, we define when a heuristic is admissible for a problem. Assume we have problem p and a set of heuristics $H = \{\theta_1, \cdots, \theta_n\}$, where at least one of the heuristics solves p within the time limit β. Further, $t_H^*(p)$ is the fastest solution of p in H. Then, θ is *admissible in H* for p if $time_\beta(\theta, p)$ is approximate to $t_H^*(p)$, where the tolerance is defined by additive and multiplicative constants ϵ_k and ϵ_p, respectively.

$$Admissible_{(H,\beta)}(\theta, p) = \begin{cases} 1 & \text{if } time_\beta(\theta, p) \leqslant t_H^*(p) \cdot (1 + \epsilon_p) + \epsilon_k, \\ 0 & \text{otherwise.} \end{cases}$$

In particular, a heuristic is admissible for a problem, if it yields either the fastest or close to the fastest known solving time, and is not admissible if its performance is considerably worse or does not solve the problem at all. We can compute admissible heuristics based on the problem evaluation vector $\mathbf{e_p}$ and obtain its *admissible heuristic vector* $\mathbf{a_p}$.

Admissible Distance. Admissible heuristic vectors create a performance-based feature representation based in the known heuristic evaluations. Next, we need a distance function that can be used to group problems with similar behavioural properties. Let us note that Euclidean distance is poorly suited for this purpose, instead we considered Jaccard similarity distance and Sørensen-Dice distance, the latter lead to better clustering in our experiments. Let $|\cdot|$ be the L_1 norm over binary vectors, which is equal to the sum of all 1s in the vector. The Sørensen-Dice semi-metric distance can be defined as follows (Fig. 2).

$$d(\mathbf{a_p}, \mathbf{a_{p'}}) = 1 - \frac{2 * (\mathbf{a_p} \cdot \mathbf{a_{p'}})}{|\mathbf{a_p}| + |\mathbf{a_{p'}}|}$$

Fig. 2. Sørensen-Dice distance between two admissible vectors $\mathbf{a_p}$ and $\mathbf{a_{p'}}$.

The Sørensen-Dice distance ranges between 0 and 1, 0 if the admissible vectors are equal and 1 if they have no admissible heuristics in common.

Admissible Clustering. We use the K-medoids algorithm (see, e.g., [13]) to cluster problems based on their admissible heuristic vectors and Sørensen-Dice similarity distance. K-medoids clustering partitions the problems into K clusters by minimising the sum of distances between each data point and the medoid of their cluster. The medoids act as a cluster centre and must be a data point, making it more robust towards outliers. K-medoid clustering tries to minimise the K-medoids cost function (Fig. 3).

$$cost = \sum_{i=1}^{K} \sum_{p \in k_i} d(\mathbf{a_p}, \mathbf{m_i})$$

Fig. 3. The K-medoids cost function is the sum over all clusters of dissimilarities between the medoid of the cluster and members of the cluster.

The optimal number of clusters K can be computed using the elbow method. This is done by analysing the function representing dependency between cluster distortions and the number of clusters. The optimal number of clusters is reached at the elbow point, which is roughly defined as the point of maximum curvature of this function. This means that at this point, increasing the number of clusters does not result in any significant increase in cluster quality.

4.2 Local Heuristic Optimisation

After acquiring *problem_clusters*, we iterate local heuristic optimisation over each homogeneous *cluster* to discover new heuristics. The heuristic optimisation searches for heuristics which minimise the following cost function.

Heuristic Cost Function. A new heuristic improves the performance of *global_heuristics*, if either it solves problems that were previously not solved or improves solving times of previously solved problems.

To accommodate these requirements we define the cost function as follows. Let H be the set of *global_heuristics*, β the time limit, $t_H^*(p)$ the fastest solution of p by heuristics in H. Consider a problem cluster I. Then we define the *heuristic cost function* for cluster I wrt H as:

$$C_H^I(\theta, p) = \begin{cases} time_\beta(\theta, p) & \text{if } time_\beta(\theta, p) < \infty \text{ and } t_H^*(p) < \infty \\ -\beta|I| & \text{if } time_\beta(\theta, p) < \infty \text{ and } t_H^*(p) = \infty \\ \beta & \text{if } time_\beta(\theta, p) = \infty \end{cases}$$

Heuristic Optimisation. For each cluster, we first compute the *incumbent*, which acts as a baseline and a starting point in the heuristic space. The *incumbent* is computed as the heuristic in *global_heuristics* with the smallest cost in the *cluster*. Next, we use Bayesian hyper-parameter optimisation to discover efficient heuristics for each *cluster*, as shown in Fig. 4. The Bayesian optimiser builds a statistical model for predicting the cost of running a heuristic on the problem cluster and uses this model to find promising heuristics. The most promising heuristics are evaluated on the problem cluster. Associated costs are used to update the model belief, which improves the prediction of heuristics costs. Continuously updating the model and evaluating the most promising heuristics is crucial as each evaluation demands considerable computation resources. In this work, we use the hyper-parameter optimiser SMAC (Sequential Model-based Algorithm Configuration) [5].

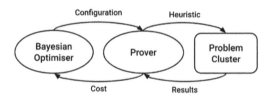

Fig. 4. The Bayesian optimiser creates heuristics which are evaluated over the cluster. The performance is scored and returned to the optimiser as the cost.

Global Evaluation. After performing hyper-parameter optimisation, we select a subset of locally evaluated heuristics to evaluate globally. For this we greedily compute a set cover of the solved problems by the most effective heuristics and add them to the set of *local_heuristics*. Next, the *local_heuristics* are evaluated on the global problem set, and added to the *global_heuristics*. Evaluations of new heuristics are used to extend dynamic evaluation features and re-cluster problems as described in Subsect. 4.1. Discovering new heuristics by local heuristics optimisation and re-clustering continues for each iteration of Algorithm 1 until it reaches the termination condition.

4.3 Embedding Unsolved Problems

Admissible heuristic vectors are suitable for clustering problems that are solved by at least one heuristic. However, if a problem has no solutions by *global_heuristics* within the time limit β, admissible heuristics can not be determined. Nevertheless, unsolved problems should be clustered with similar solved problems, which would help heuristic optimisation to discover heuristics that can solve these problems. We observe that, in most cases, for some sufficiently large time limit β^* each unsolved problem will have at least one admissible heuristic in *global_heuristics*. This is the case in our application due to completeness of the underling calculi for first-order logic. Unfortunately, such time limits could be arbitrary large and infeasible to compute in practice. Instead, we propose to build a machine learning model to predict admissible heuristic vectors using static problem features. This *admissible embedding model* is trained on solved problems and is applied to unsolved problems to predict admissible heuristic vectors. Using this model we can assign each unsolved problems to a nearest cluster of solved problems. As a result, we acquire homogeneous problem clusters consisting of both solved and unsolved problems, as shown in Fig. 5.

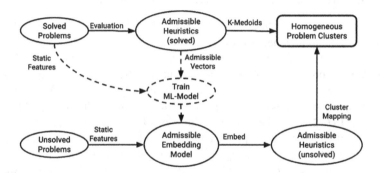

Fig. 5. Computing homogeneous clusters consisting of both solved and unsolved problems.

Static Problem Features. We consider two types of static features: syntactic features and solver state features. Syntactic features include properties such as the number of equational, Horn, EPR formulas, etc. As we noted before, such features do not always reflect algorithmic properties of formulas. To mitigate this we consider *solver state features*. During a run, the solver executes numerous function calls and applies various simplification techniques. Solver state features include solver statistics on key function calls, successful simplifications and corresponding timing statistics. We compute the solver state features by attempting a problem with single heuristic for a low-timelimit and extracting the solver statistics after termination.

Admissible Embedding Model. For a problem p, we denote its static feature vector as $\mathbf{s_p}$. Let H be the set of *global_heuristics*. The *admissible embedding model* $\mathcal{E}$ learns the mapping between problems static features and their admissible heuristics vectors.

As admissible heuristics vectors are binary vectors, we use a multi-label machine learning model as the embedding function. We separate the multi-label classification task into $|H|$ binary classification tasks, where a separate binary classification model $\mathcal{M}_\theta$ is trained for each heuristic θ in H. We considered different machine learning methods for building binary classification models: random forests, tree models and neural networks. In our experiments the decision tree algorithm XGBoost [2] yielded the best performance. Once binary models are trained for each heuristic, the admissible embedding model is then defined as $\mathcal{E}(\mathbf{s_p}) = (\mathcal{M}_{\theta_1}(\mathbf{s_p}), \cdots, \mathcal{M}_{\theta_{|H|}}(\mathbf{s_p}))$. The admissible embedding model can then be used to predict the admissible heuristics vector of any given problem.

Mapping Unsolved Problems to Clusters. The embedding model is trained on the solved problems and used to predict the unsolved problems' admissible heuristics vector. Next, we need to map problems into discovered homogeneous clusters. This is achieved by first computing the admissible distance between each predicted admissible vector and each cluster medoid. Second we add the n closest unsolved problems to each cluster. This results in homogeneous clusters consisting of both solved and unsolved problems.

5 Local Schedules for Heterogeneous Instances

In this section we describe Phase 2 of HOS-ML, which is the computation of heuristic schedules for each homogeneous problem clusters.

The scheduled running time t of heuristic θ is described by the pair (θ, t). A *heuristic schedule* is an ordered set of heuristic-time pairs $[(\theta_1, t_1), \cdots, (\theta_n, t_n)]$ where the total running time does not exceed the global time limit $\sum_{i=1}^{n} t_i \leq \beta$. We describe the task of creating a schedule as the *heuristic scheduling problem*. Given the problem set I, the heuristic set $H \subset \Theta$ and the heuristic evaluations $\mathbf{E_{I \times H}}$, find the heuristic run-times $[t_1, \ldots, t_n]$, which maximise the performance on I subject to the global time-limit β.

We solve the heuristic scheduling problem using constraint programming with the following encoding. Let $|H| = n$ and $|I| = m$. First we create the run-time variables $t_1, \ldots, t_n$ which represent the running time of each heuristic in H. Next, we ensure that the total running time of the schedule does not exceed β with the constraint $\sum_{i=1}^{n} t_i \leq \beta$. Using known evaluations $\mathbf{E_{I \times H}}$ we represent that heuristic h_i solves problem p_j in allocated time t_i as $E_{ji} \leq t_i$. A problem p_j is solved by the schedule if $E_{j1} \leq t_1 \vee \ldots \vee E_{jn} \leq t_n$ holds. We denote this condition as s_j.

The objective is to maximise the number of problems solved by the schedule. Hence, the task of the constraint solver is to find the heuristic runtimes $t_1, \ldots, t_n$ which maximise $\sum_{i=1}^{m} s_i$.

After acquiring the solution, we discard all heuristics θ_i for which $t_i = 0$ and order the remaining heuristics in ascending order according to their run-times. The result is a heuristic schedule that maximises the number of solved problems over the problem set based on the known heuristic performance.

6 Schedule Selection

Phase 2 of HOS-ML computes schedules for each homogeneous problem cluster. This results in a set of optimal local schedules.

In Phase 3, we create a mapping between unseen problems and local schedules based on the embedding function, as shown in Fig. 6. First, we extract the static features of the problems and predict their admissible heuristic vectors. Next, we use the predicted admissible heuristics to map the problems to their appropriate clusters. Finally, we attempt the problems with the schedule of their assigned cluster.

Fig. 6. Mapping a problem to a local schedule.

This concludes the description of all phases of HOS-ML. In the next section we discuss implementation and evaluation results.

7   Experimental Evaluation

HOS-ML is implemented in Python 3. Pandas and scikit-learn were used for data handling and processing. The heuristic discovery phase[1] uses SMAC [5] as the hyperparameter optimiser, while CP-SAT[2] is used as the constraint solver for computing the schedules[3]. To perform clustering, we use the sklearn_extra implementation of K-medoids. Kneed[4] is used to compute the optimal value of K. The binary base predictor in the embedding function is implemented using XGBoost [2].

The base prover for HOS-ML is iProver [3,9] a high performance theorem prover for first-order logic which is based on a combination of instantiation, resolution and superposition calculi. iProver heuristics are made up of 120 different parameters with diverse parameter values consisting of boolean, real, ordinal, priority lists and categorical values. The extensive range of values and parameters yield a vast and complex heuristic space. Our system supports optimisation over all of iProver parameters. However, in this experimental evaluation, we restrict optimisation to the parameters related to the newly developed superposition functionality [3]. We also use iProver to compute the prover state features, which comprise of 170 individual statistics covering both the problem properties and the prover behaviour. The experiments were run on a cluster of 33 machines, each with 4 Intel(R) Xeon(R) CPU L5410 @ 2.33 GHz.

7.1   Discovering New Heuristics

Our first experiment evaluated the heterogeneous heuristic optimisation phase on the TPTP library (v7.4.0) [19]. The library contains problems with varying difficulty from

---

[1] Heuristic discovery is available at: https://gitlab.com/korovin/iprover-smac.

[2] CP-SAT is available at: https://github.com/google/or-tools.

[3] Schedule computation is available at: https://gitlab.com/edvardholden/scpeduler.

[4] kneed is available at: https://github.com/arvkevi/kneed.

different domains ranging from verifying authentication protocols to MPTP problems from the Mizar mathematical library. The training set was created by randomly sampling 4000 of the 17053 FOF and CNF problems.

We ran five iterations of the outer loop of HOS-ML, with iProver's default heuristic as the initial heuristic. For each iteration, we optimised iProver's superposition options on three sampled problem clusters. The hyper-parameter optimiser evaluated 1000 candidate heuristics, each with a time limit of 20 s. The algorithm ran for approximately 61 h and discovered a total of 53 new heuristics. The discovered heuristics where evaluated on a testing set consisting of the remaining TPTP problems (13053) with a time-limit of 20 s.

Next, we compared the performance difference between the default iProver heuristic and the set of heuristics discovered by heterogeneous heuristic optimisation. The results are shown in Table 1. We can observe that the new heuristics considerably increase the number of solved problems in both problem sets. The discovered heuristics also decrease the average solving time of the problems solved in the intersection of both approaches.

Table 1. The performance of the default and the global heuristics (20 s).

	Training		Testing		Total	
	Solved	Avg time	Solved	Avg time	Solved	Avg time
Default	1975	1.81	6774	1.53	8749	1.60
Discovered	2272	0.98	7771	0.66	10043	0.73

7.2 Revealing Homogeneity with Admissible Evaluation Clustering

One of the key ideas of HOS-ML is to discover homogeneous problem clusters by clustering on admissible heuristic features. To verify this claim, we compute admissible clusters and apply the best local heuristic of each cluster to its members. Further, we compute the intersection between problems solved by the best global heuristic and the set of problems solved by the best local heuristics. Next, we compute the average solving time of the problems in the intersection. If the performance of the global and local approaches is the same, the clusters are equivalent to random sampling. However, if the local heuristics perform better, the clusters are more homogeneous.

The global heuristics sampled at each iteration of the outer loop forms the five heuristic sets A, B, C, D and E applied to the 4000 training problems. Next, we compute the performance of both approaches as shown in Table 2. We can observe that the local heuristics offer a considerable performance increase. Hence, we acquire homogeneous problem clusters through admissible clustering.

Table 2. Performance of the best global heuristic versus the best local heuristics.

Heuristic set	A	B	C	D	E
Number of heuristics	18	32	41	51	54
Number of clusters	12	18	98	119	124
Solved global	1975	1975	1975	1975	1975
Solved local	2106	2159	2254	2269	2271
Solved intersection	1958	1960	1975	1975	1975
Avg time global	1.76	1.76	1.81	1.81	1.81
Avg time local	1.45	1.35	1.29	1.22	1.22
Performance increase	17.32%	22.89%	28.60%	32.47%	32.51%

7.3 Embedding Evaluation Features

HOS-ML embeds problems into admissible heuristic features during heuristic optimisation and selection. To evaluate the embedding performance we create a model for embedding the selected 4000 TPTP problems into the evaluation data from experiment 7.1, as follows. First, we compute static problem features by collecting prover statistics of the problems with a 1-s time-limit. The prover statistics are transformed into features through log-scaling and standardisation. Next, we remove all problems that were either solved during processing or failed to parse within the time-limit. Further, we remove unsolved problems and problems with solutions below five seconds. This results in a challenging yet solvable problem set which is further divided into training and validation sets with a 70–30% split. The multi-label model comprises of binary classification models for each heuristic, trained using XGBoost [2].

In Table 3 we see that a single binary model is able to capture whether a heuristic is admissible for a problem. In Table 4 we can observe that the embedding model is able to predict admissible heuristic vectors of problems with good accuracy.

- **Admissible Similarity:** The Sørensen-Dice similarity between two admissible vectors $\mathbf{a}$ and $\mathbf{a}'$, which is equal to $1 - d(\mathbf{a}, \mathbf{a}')$.
- **Geometric Accuracy:** The sensitivity is the true positive rate, and the specificity is the true negative rate of the model predictions. The geometric accuracy is defined as $\sqrt{sensitivity * specificity}$, and by computing the average of each binary model geometric accuracy, we obtain the average geometric accuracy.

7.4 Optimal Scheduling of Heuristics

After discovering a set of strong heuristics, we devise a strategy for applying the heuristics to new problems. In this section, we evaluate three different heuristic strategies, each with a time limit of 20 s per problem:

- **Best Heuristic:** The heuristic which solves the most training problems.
- **Global Schedule:** The global heuristic schedule computed over the problem set.

Table 3. One of the binary XGBoost models.

Actual	Predicted 1	Predicted 0
1	157	21
0	41	112

Metric	Score
Accuracy	0.81
F1-Score	0.78
Geometric	0.80

Table 4. The multi-label model.

Heuristic set	Geometric	Similarity
A	0.72	0.71
B	0.71	0.68
C	0.72	0.68
D	0.72	0.68
E	0.72	0.67

- **Admissible Schedule:** A set of local schedules computed for each problem cluster.

We constructed schedules on the training problems and evaluated their performance on the testing problems. The results of each approach are shown in Table 5, and Fig. 7. The best heuristic and the global schedule perform similarly on the training set in terms of the number of solved problems. However, on the testing set it becomes apparent that attempting a problem with multiple heuristics is advantageous. Still, to utilise the full potential of a heuristic set, it is essential to create schedules for problems with similar performance. This is illustrated by the admissible schedule solving nearly one thousand problems more than the global schedule on the test set.

Table 5. The number of solved problems of each scheduling approach (20 s).

Approach	Training	Testing	Total
Best heuristic	1975	6774	8749
Global schedule	1976	6794	8770
Admissible schedule	2258	7637	9895

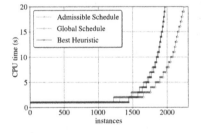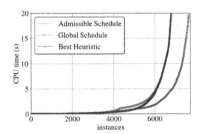

Fig. 7. The performance on the training set (left) and testing set (right).

7.5   Overall Performance Contribution

TPTP problems are rated based on their difficulty on a scale from zero to one. A problem solved by almost all state-of-the-art ATP systems has a rating of zero, while a problem with no recorded solutions has a rating of one. There are 3984 TPTP problems with a rating of 0.9 or higher, and we characterise these problems as "highly challenging".

When run with a 20 s time limit, the 54 global heuristics discovered by HOS-ML solved 47 highly challenging problems. Nevertheless, challenging problems are likely to require more time. While the conventional time limit in ATP is 300 s, this would carry a substantial computational cost for 54 heuristics. Instead, we reduce the heuristic set by computing the set cover of solved problems and select the ten most contributing heuristics. Next, we evaluated the selected ten heuristics over all TPTP problems with a time limit of 300 s.

The ten heuristics solved a total of 10696 problems, of which 130 problems have a rating of 0.9 or above. These include 54 MPTP problems from the Mizar mathematical library. When combining these results with the 20-s evaluations, the number of highly challenging solved problems increases to 136 problems. Thirteen of these problems have the rating one, including four MPTP problems. As a result, the new heuristics solve MML problems with no previously recorded ATP solutions.

8   Conclusion

In this paper, we presented HOS-ML, a new method for heuristic optimisation and scheduling over heterogeneous problem sets. HOS-ML interleaves dynamic clustering with hyper-parameter optimisation and uses machine learning for embedding problems into clusters and local schedules. We applied HOS-ML to iProver and demonstrated that HOS-ML can discover new heuristics that can considerably improve prover performance over heterogeneous instances. Our evaluation showed that HOS-ML discovered heuristics that increase the number of solved TPTP problems by 14.8%, including problems with the rating 1, that have not been previously solved by any other system. These heuristics also decrease the solving time of previously solved problems by 54.4%. As a future work we will investigate applications of HOS-ML to different domains.

References

1. Bridge, J.P., Holden, S.B., Paulson, L.C.: Machine learning for first-order theorem proving - learning to select a good heuristic. J. Autom. Reason. **53**(2), 141–172 (2014)
2. Chen, T., Guestrin, C.: XGBoost. In: Proceedings of the 22nd ACM SIGKDD International Conference on Knowledge Discovery and Data Mining (2016)
3. Duarte, A., Korovin, K.: Implementing superposition in iProver (system description). In: Peltier, N., Sofronie-Stokkermans, V. (eds.) IJCAR 2020. LNCS (LNAI), vol. 12167, pp. 388–397. Springer, Cham (2020). https://doi.org/10.1007/978-3-030-51054-1_24
4. Feurer, M., Hutter, F.: Hyperparameter optimization. In: Hutter, F., Kotthoff, L., Vanschoren, J. (eds.) Automated Machine Learning. TSSCML, pp. 3–33. Springer, Cham (2019). https://doi.org/10.1007/978-3-030-05318-5_1

5. Hutter, F., Hoos, H.H., Leyton-Brown, K.: Parallel algorithm configuration. In: Hamadi, Y., Schoenauer, M. (eds.) LION 2012. LNCS, pp. 55–70. Springer, Heidelberg (2012). https://doi.org/10.1007/978-3-642-34413-8_5

6. Jakubuv, J., Suda, M., Urban, J.: Automated invention of strategies and term orderings for vampire. In: Benzmüller, C., Lisetti, C.L., Theobald, M. (eds.) 3rd Global Conference on Artificial Intelligence, GCAI 2017. EPiC Series in Computer, vol. 50, pp. 121–133. Easy-Chair (2017)

7. Jakubuv, J., Urban, J.: Blistrtune: hierarchical invention of theorem proving strategies. In: Bertot, Y., Vafeiadis, V. (eds.) Proceedings of the 6th ACM SIGPLAN Conference on Certified Programs and Proofs, CPP, pp. 43–52. ACM (2017)

8. Kadioglu, S., Malitsky, Y., Sellmann, M., Tierney, K.: ISAC - instance-specific algorithm configuration. In: Coelho, H., Studer, R., Wooldridge, M.J. (eds.) 19th European Conference on Artificial Intelligence, ECAI 2010. Frontiers in Artificial Intelligence and Applications, vol. 215, pp. 751–756. IOS Press (2010)

9. Korovin, K.: iProver – an instantiation-based theorem prover for first-order logic (system description). In: Armando, A., Baumgartner, P., Dowek, G. (eds.) IJCAR 2008. LNCS (LNAI), vol. 5195, pp. 292–298. Springer, Heidelberg (2008). https://doi.org/10.1007/978-3-540-71070-7_24

10. Kovács, L., Voronkov, A.: First-order theorem proving and VAMPIRE. In: Sharygina, N., Veith, H. (eds.) CAV 2013. LNCS, vol. 8044, pp. 1–35. Springer, Heidelberg (2013). https://doi.org/10.1007/978-3-642-39799-8_1

11. Kühlwein, D., Schulz, S., Urban, J.: E-MaLeS 1.1. In: Bonacina, M.P. (ed.) CADE 2013. LNCS (LNAI), vol. 7898, pp. 407–413. Springer, Heidelberg (2013). https://doi.org/10.1007/978-3-642-38574-2_28

12. Lindawati, L.H.C., Lo, D.: Instance-based parameter tuning via search trajectory similarity clustering. In: Coello, C.A.C. (ed.) 5th International Conference on Learning and Intelligent Optimization, LION 5. Selected Papers. LNCS, vol. 6683, pp. 131–145. Springer, Heidelberg (2011). https://doi.org/10.1007/978-3-642-25566-3_10

13. Park, H., Jun, C.: A simple and fast algorithm for k-medoids clustering. Expert Syst. Appl. **36**(2), 3336–3341 (2009)

14. Paulson, L.C.: Three years of experience with sledgehammer, a practical link between automatic and interactive theorem provers. In: Schmidt, R.A., Schulz, S., Konev, B. (eds.) Proceedings of the 2nd Workshop on Practical Aspects of Automated Reasoning, PAAR-2010. EPiC Series in Computer, vol. 9, pp. 1–10. EasyChair (2010)

15. Rawson, M., Reger, G.: Dynamic strategy priority: empower the strong and abandon the weak. In: Konev, B., Urban, J., Rümmer, P. (eds.) Proceedings of the 6th Workshop on Practical Aspects of Automated Reasoning co-located with Federated Logic Conference 2018, FLoC 2018. CEUR Workshop Proceedings, vol. 2162, pp. 58–71. CEUR-WS.org (2018)

16. Schäfer, S., Schulz, S.: Breeding theorem proving heuristics with genetic algorithms. In: Gottlob, G., Sutcliffe, G., Voronkov, A. (eds.) Global Conference on Artificial Intelligence, GCAI. EPiC Series in Computer, vol. 36, pp. 263–274. EasyChair (2015)

17. Schneider, M., Hoos, H.H.: Quantifying homogeneity of instance sets for algorithm configuration. In: Hamadi, Y., Schoenauer, M. (eds.) LION 2012. LNCS, pp. 190–204. Springer, Heidelberg (2012). https://doi.org/10.1007/978-3-642-34413-8_14

18. Schulz, S.: System description: E 1.8. In: McMillan, K., Middeldorp, A., Voronkov, A. (eds.) LPAR 2013. LNCS, vol. 8312, pp. 735–743. Springer, Heidelberg (2013). https://doi.org/10.1007/978-3-642-45221-5_49

19. Sutcliffe, G.: The TPTP Problem Library and Associated Infrastructure. From CNF to TH0, TPTP v6.4.0. J. Autom. Reason. **59**(4), 483–502 (2017)

20. Urban, J.: MPTP 0.2: Design, implementation, and initial experiments. J. Autom. Reason. **37**(1–2), 21–43 (2006)

21. Urban, J.: Blistr: the blind strategymaker. In: Gottlob, G., Sutcliffe, G., Voronkov, A. (eds.) Global Conference on Artificial Intelligence, GCAI 2015. EPiC Series in Computer, vol. 36, pp. 312–319. EasyChair (2015)

22. Weidenbach, C., Dimova, D., Fietzke, A., Kumar, R., Suda, M., Wischnewski, P.: SPASS version 3.5. In: Schmidt, R.A. (ed.) CADE 2009. LNCS (LNAI), vol. 5663, pp. 140–145. Springer, Heidelberg (2009). https://doi.org/10.1007/978-3-642-02959-2_10

23. Xu, L., Hutter, F., Hoos, H.H., Leyton-Brown, K.: Satzilla: portfolio-based algorithm selection for SAT. J. Artif. Intell. Res. **32**, 565–606 (2008)

Inductive Benchmarks for Automated Reasoning

Márton Hajdu[1] , Petra Hozzová[1(✉)] , Laura Kovács[1] ,
Johannes Schoisswohl[1,2] , and Andrei Voronkov[2,3]

[1] TU Wien, Vienna, Austria
{marton.hajdu,petra.hozzova,laura.kovacs}@tuwien.ac.at,
johannes.schoisswohl@manchester.ac.uk
[2] University of Manchester, Manchester, UK
[3] EasyChair, London, UK
andrei@voronkov.com

Abstract. We present a large set of benchmarks for automated theorem provers that require inductive reasoning. Motivated by the need to compare first-order theorem provers, SMT solvers and inductive theorem provers, the setting of our examples follows the SMT-LIB standard. Our benchmark set contains problems with inductive data types as well as integers. In addition to SMT-LIB encodings, we provide translations to some other less common input formats.

1 Introduction

Recently, automated reasoning approaches have been extended with inductive reasoning capabilities, for example in the context of superposition theorem proving [5,6,12] and SMT solving [13]. Evaluation of these developments prompts comparison not only among first-order theorem provers and/or SMT solvers but also with inductive provers (e.g., ACL2 [3], Zeno [15] or Imandra [11]). As a part of our work on automating induction in the first-order theorem prover Vampire [6], we created a benchmark set of 3516 benchmarks based on variations of properties of inductive data types as well as integers. To facilitate comparison of different solvers and provers, we translated our benchmarks into the input formats of other state-of-the-art inductive reasoners, supporting for example the SMT-LIB input format [2] and functional program encodings.

Our dataset is comparable to the TIP repository of inductive benchmarks [4], with which it shares 9 benchmarks. We note however that TIP focuses on classic problems with inductive data types, while our dataset contains variants of problems of increasing sizes for both inductive data types and integers. Furhter, TIP uses a non-standard variant of SMT-LIB, and offers tools for translating the benchmarks into standard SMT-LIB. Our dataset employs the current standard SMT-LIB 2.6 syntax, allowing us to potentially integrate our examples in any repository using the SMT-LIB standard. Our benchmark set is available at:

https://github.com/vprover/inductive_benchmarks

© Springer Nature Switzerland AG 2021
F. Kamareddine and C. Sacerdoti Coen (Eds.): CICM 2021, LNAI 12833, pp. 124–129, 2021.
https://doi.org/10.1007/978-3-030-81097-9_9

2   Benchmark Format

We provide all benchmarks in the standard SMT-LIB 2.6 syntax. We chose SMT-LIB as the main format for our benchmarks, since it is the most common format used by automated reasoners (SMT solvers and first-order provers, e.g., CVC4 [1] or Vampire [8]) and verification tools (e.g., CBMC [9], Dafny [10], or eThor [14]). In our examples, we use the SMT-LIB construct `declare-fun` to declare functions and `assert` to axiomatize functions (see the example benchmarks in Sect. 3). In addition to the SMT-LIB syntax, we also translated our examples to other formats depending on the data types used in these examples: three subsets of our benchmark set use inductively defined data types, and one subset uses integers (see Sect. 3). For the benchmarks with inductively defined data types, we also provide SMT-LIB encoding using the `define-fun-rec` construct for recursive function definitions.

Besides the SMT-LIB format, we also provide our benchmarks translated into other, less common input formats supported by state-of-the-art solvers for automating induction. Namely, for our benchmarks with inductively defined data types, we provide two encodings for Zipperposition [5] (using Zipperposition's native input format `.zf` with/without function definitions encoded as rewrite rules), and when possible[1] functional program encodings for ACL2 [3] (in Lisp), Imandra [11] (in OCaml) and Zeno [15] (in Haskell). For our inductive benchmarks over integers, we only provide translation into Lisp for ACL2. To the best of our knowledge, in addition to Vampire [7] and CVC4 [13], ACL2 is the only prover supporting inductive reasoning with integers.

3   Benchmark Categories

Our benchmark set consists of two categories, requiring different kinds of inductive reasoning, as follows. The benchmark category `dty` uses structural induction over inductively defined data types, whereas our `int` benchmark suite exploits integer induction. Further, our benchmark set `dty` is organized within three categories `nat`, `list` and `tree`, respectively collecting inductive properties over naturals, lists and trees.

3.1   `dty` - Benchmarks with Inductively Defined Data Types

The 3396 problems within the category `dty` involve three different inductively defined data types: natural numbers, lists of natural numbers, and binary trees of natural numbers. These data types are defined as follows:

```
(declare-datatypes ((nat 0) (list 0) (tree 0))
  (((zero) (s (s0 nat)))
   ((nil) (cons (head nat) (tail list)))
   ((Nil) (node (lc tree) (val nat) (rc tree)))))
```

---

[1] Some concepts, like conjectures that contain existential quantification, or some uninterpreted functions used to model out of bounds access for list indexing, are not straightforwardly translatable into these formats.

The benchmark category `dty` collects results of [6]. It is split into three subcategories `nat`, `list`, and `tree`, depending on the algebraic data types used in the examples. The category `nat` uses natural numbers only, `list` uses lists and natural numbers, and `tree` uses all three of the data types. Each of these categories within `dty` contains examples defining functions and predicates on the respective data type and a conjecture/goal to prove about these functions and predicates, as described next. To avoid repetition in the displayed examples, we use short descriptions of repeated content beginning with the comment sign `;-`.

`nat` *Examples.* The category `nat` contains a set of hand-crafted benchmarks encoding basic properties like commutativity of addition and multiplication. Additionally, `nat` contains three groups of generated benchmarks. In group `add_<m>var_<n>occ`, the conjecture of each benchmark consists of an equality of two sums of variables, with arbitrary bracketing, and n variables on each sides of the equality, where m distinct variables occur in the conjecture. In group `add_<n>sym`, the conjectures are equalities with an arbitrary combination of the successor function, zero, addition, and variables, on both hand sides. Each side of the equality in these benchmarks contains n symbols in total. The group `leq_<m>var_<n>_<o>occ` has a less-or-equal inequality as conjecture. It contains m distinct variables, with a total of n variables on the left-hand side arbitrarily added up, and a total of o variables occurring on the right-hand side, where each variable on the left-hand side is contained on the right-hand side at least as often as on the left one in order to ensure that the conjecture is indeed valid.

Inductive `nat` example from the set `add_2var_4occ`
```
(set-logic UFDT)

(declare-datatypes ((nat 0)) (((zero) (s (s0 nat)))))

(declare-fun add (nat nat) nat)
(assert (forall ((y nat)          ) (= (add zero y) y              )))
(assert (forall ((x nat) (y nat)) (= (add (s x) y) (s (add x y)))))

(assert (not (forall ((v0 nat) (v1 nat))
   (= (add (add v0 (add v1 v1)) v1) (add (add (add v1 v1) v1) v0)))))

(check-sat)
```

The conjecture is a combination of associativity and commutativity of addition of natural numbers for two variables with four occurrences in total.

`list` *Examples.* These examples describe basic properties about lists, such as relating concatenation of lists to the resulting list length. Similarly to `nat`, the category `list` also contains two generated example sets: `concat_<m>var_<n>occ` contains examples as in `add_<m>var_<n>` occurrences, but using list concatenation instead of list addition, while `pref_<m>var_<n>_<o>occ` is defined in the same way as `leq_<m>var_<n>_<o>occ`, but replacing the less-or-equal order with the prefix relation and using list concatenation instead of natural addition.

Inductive `list` example from the set **crafted** ────────────

```
(set-logic UFDT)

;- nat and list declaration, as shown at the beginning of this Section
;- add function declaration and axiomatization, as in the example above

(declare-fun app (list list) list)
(assert (forall ((r list) ) (= (app nil r) r)))
(assert (forall ((a nat) (l list) (r list))
    (= (app (cons a l) r) (cons a (app l r)))))
(declare-fun len (list) nat)
(assert                          (= (len nil      ) zero       ))
(assert (forall ((e nat) (l list)) (= (len (cons e l)) (s (len l)))))

(assert (not (forall ((x list) (y list))
    (= (add (len x) (len y)) (len (app x y))))))

(check-sat)
```
- -

The conjecture asserts that addition of lengths of two lists is equal to the length of the two lists concatenated.

tree *Examples.* This category has two main subcategories: one problem set relates binary trees indirectly by flattening them to lists, the other relates them directly to each other. The defined functions are two in-order flattening variants, two functions that recursively rotate a tree completely to the left and to the right at its root, one counting the number of non-leaf nodes in a tree and one checking if two trees are mirror images of each other. Occurrences of the flattenning and rotating functions are varied to get variants for each problem.

Inductive `tree` example from the set **flatten0_rotate_5var** ────────

```
(set-logic UFDT)

;- data types declaration, as shown at the beginning of this Section
;- app function declaration and axiomatization, as in the example above

(declare-fun flat0 (tree) list)
(assert (= (flat0 Nil) nil))
(assert (forall ((p tree) (x nat) (q tree))
    (= (flat0 (node p x q)) (app (flat0 p) (cons x (flat0 q))))))

(assert (not (forall ((p tree) (q tree) (r tree) (x nat) (y nat))
    (= (flat0 (node (node p x q) y r)) (flat0 (node p x (node q y r)))))
)))

(check-sat)
```
- -

The conjecture asserts that the result of a tree flattening does not depend on the rotation in the root.

3.2 int - Benchmarks with Integers

The int category of our benchmark set contains 120 problems for inductive reasoning with integers. It is inspired by software verification problems [7] for three programs: power, computing powers of integers, sum, computing sums of integer intervals, and val, using integers as array indices to encode array properties. These benchmarks were used for evaluating the work from [7]. A sample problem from power expressing that the recursively defined power function on integers for positive exponents is distributive over multiplication, is:

Inductive int example from the set power ————————————————

```
(set-logic UFNIA)

(declare-fun pow (Int Int) Int)
(assert (forall ((x Int)) (= (pow x 1) x)))
(assert (forall ((x Int) (e Int))
    (=> (<= 2 e) (= (pow x e) (* x (pow x (- e 1)))))))

(assert (not (forall ((x Int) (y Int) (e Int))
    (=> (<= 1 e) (= (pow (* x y) e) (* (pow x e) (pow y e)))))))

(check-sat)
```

The conjecture asserts that for positive exponents, the power function distributes over multiplication of integers.

All variations of the int benchmarks were created by varying the constraints and constants in the definitions and goals. For example, variations of the sample problem above use the function pow defined starting from 0 instead of 1, or introduce additional constraints on variables x, y and e in the goal.

4 Conclusions

We describe our benchmark set for evaluating inductive capabilities of automated reasoners. Although we primarily provide our problems in the standard SMT-LIB syntax, we also translated them to other input formats of state-of-the-art reasoners.

Future work includes extending our benchmark set with further examples coming from application domains of security and safety verification, as well as formalization of mathematics. Another task for future work is a possible integration of our dataset with the TIP benchmark set or with the SMT-LIB repository. One possibility for incorporating our benchmark set into SMT-LIB would be to add a new subset or an annotation for inductive problems in SMT-LIB, since SMT-LIB does not currently distinguish benchmarks focused on induction from those which can be easily solved without induction. Another possibility is to introduce subsets of the DT (data types) set from SMT-LIB for each notable algebraic data type (natural numbers, lists, trees).

Acknowledgements. This work has been partially funded by the ERC CoG ARTIST 101002685, the ERC StG 2014 SYMCAR 639270, the EPSRC grant EP/P03408X/1 and the Austrian FWF research project LogiCS W1255-N23.

References

1. Barrett, C., et al.: CVC4. In: Gopalakrishnan, G., Qadeer, S. (eds.) CAV 2011. LNCS, vol. 6806, pp. 171–177. Springer, Heidelberg (2011). https://doi.org/10.1007/978-3-642-22110-1_14
2. Barrett, C., Fontaine, P., Tinelli, C.: The Satisfiability Modulo Theories Library (SMT-LIB). www.SMT-LIB.org (2016)
3. Boyer, R.S., Moore, J.S.: A Computational Logic Handbook, Perspectives in computing, vol. 23. Academic Press (1979)
4. Claessen, K., Johansson, M., Rosén, D., Smallbone, N.: TIP: tons of inductive problems. In: Kerber, M., Carette, J., Kaliszyk, C., Rabe, F., Sorge, V. (eds.) CICM 2015. LNCS (LNAI), vol. 9150, pp. 333–337. Springer, Cham (2015). https://doi.org/10.1007/978-3-319-20615-8_23
5. Cruanes, S.: Superposition with structural induction. In: Proceedings of FRoCoS, pp. 172–188 (2017)
6. Hajdú, M., Hozzová, P., Kovács, L., Schoisswohl, J., Voronkov, A.: Induction with generalization in superposition reasoning. In: Benzmüller, C., Miller, B. (eds.) CICM 2020. LNCS (LNAI), vol. 12236, pp. 123–137. Springer, Cham (2020). https://doi.org/10.1007/978-3-030-53518-6_8
7. Hozzová, P., Kovács, L., Voronkov, A.: Integer induction in saturation. EasyChair Preprint no. 5176 (EasyChair, 2021)
8. Kovács, L., Voronkov, A.: First-order theorem proving and vampire. In: Proceedings of CAV, pp. 1–35 (2013)
9. Kroening, D., Tautschnig, M.: CBMC – C bounded model checker. In: Ábrahám, E., Havelund, K. (eds.) TACAS 2014. LNCS, vol. 8413, pp. 389–391. Springer, Heidelberg (2014). https://doi.org/10.1007/978-3-642-54862-8_26
10. Leino, K.R.M.: Dafny: an automatic program verifier for functional correctness. In: Clarke, E.M., Voronkov, A. (eds.) LPAR 2010. LNCS (LNAI), vol. 6355, pp. 348–370. Springer, Heidelberg (2010). https://doi.org/10.1007/978-3-642-17511-4_20
11. Passmore, G., et al.: The imandra automated reasoning system (system description). In: Peltier, N., Sofronie-Stokkermans, V. (eds.) IJCAR 2020. LNCS (LNAI), vol. 12167, pp. 464–471. Springer, Cham (2020). https://doi.org/10.1007/978-3-030-51054-1_30
12. Reger, G., Voronkov, A.: Induction in saturation-based proof search. In: Proceedings of CADE, pp. 477–494 (2019)
13. Reynolds, A., Kuncak, V.: Induction for SMT solvers. In: Proceedings of VMCAI, pp. 80–98 (2015)
14. Schneidewind, C., Grishchenko, I., Scherer, M., Maffei, M.: ethor: Practical and provably sound static analysis of ethereum smart contracts, pp. 621–640 (2020). https://doi.org/10.1145/3372297.3417250, https://doi.org/10.1145/3372297.3417250
15. Sonnex, W., Drossopoulou, S., Eisenbach, S.: Zeno: an automated prover for properties of recursive data structures. In: Proceedings of TACAS, pp. 407–421 (2012)

A Heuristic Prover for Elementary Analysis in *Theorema*

Tudor Jebelean[✉]

RISC–Linz, JKU, Linz, Austria
Tudor.Jebelean@jku.at
https://www.risc.jku.at

Abstract. We present a plug-in to the *Theorema* system, which generates proofs similar to those produced by humans for theorems in elementary analysis and is based on heuristic techniques combining methods from automated reasoning and computer algebra. The prover is able to construct automatically natural-style proofs for various examples related to convergence of sequences as well as to limits, continuity, and uniform continuity of functions. Additionally to general inference rules for predicate logic, the techniques used are: the S-decomposition method for formulae with alternating quantifiers, use of Quantifier Elimination by Cylindrical Algebraic Decomposition, analysis of terms behavior in zero, bounding the ϵ-bounds, semantic simplification of expressions involving absolute value, polynomial arithmetic, usage of equal arguments to arbitrary functions, and automatic reordering of proof steps in order to check the admissibility of solutions to the metavariables. The problem of proving such theorems directly without using refutation and clausification is logically equivalent to the problem of satisfiability modulo the theory of real numbers, thus these techniques are relevant for SMT solving also.

Keywords: Satisfiability checking · Natural-style proofs · Computer algebra · Symbolic computation · Satisfiability Modulo Theories

1 Introduction

In this paper we present our results on a class of proof problems which arise in elementary analysis, namely those involving formulae with alternating quantifiers. We implement the following heuristic techniques, which extend our previous work [5,6,9]: the S-decomposition method for formulae with alternating quantifiers [8], use of Quantifier Elimination by Cylindrical Algebraic Decomposition [4], analysis of terms behavior in zero, bounding the ϵ-bounds, semantic simplification of expressions involving absolute value, polynomial arithmetic, usage of equal arguments under unknown functions, and automatic reordering of proof steps in order to check the admissibility of solutions to the metavariables.

Our prover, implemented in the frame of the *Theorema* system [3], aims at producing natural-style proofs for simple theorems involving convergence of

© Springer Nature Switzerland AG 2021
F. Kamareddine and C. Sacerdoti Coen (Eds.): CICM 2021, LNAI 12833, pp. 130–134, 2021.
https://doi.org/10.1007/978-3-030-81097-9_10

sequences and of functions, continuity, uniform continuity, etc. The prover does not need to access a large collection of formulae (expressing the properties of the domains involved). Rather, the prover uses techniques from computer algebra in order to discover relevant terms and to check necessary conditions, and only needs as starting knowledge the definitions of the main notions involved. The size of this short paper does not allow an overview of the relevant literature, so we only mention [2], which in contrast to our prover is based mostly on rewriting of logical terms and does not handle alternating quantifiers.

2   Application of Special Techniques

Example: Product of Convergent Sequences. We illustrate the heuristics by the proof of the theorem *"The product of two convergent sequences is convergent"*, which is presented in detail together with other examples and explanations of the techniques in [7]. The proof starts from the definitions of product of two functions and of convergence of a function $f : \mathbb{N} \longrightarrow \mathbb{R}$:

$$\underset{a\in\mathbb{R}}{\exists} \ \underset{\substack{e\in\mathbb{R}\\ e>0}}{\forall} \ \underset{M\in\mathbb{N}}{\exists} \ \underset{\substack{n\in\mathbb{N}\\ n\geq M}}{\forall} \ |f[n] - a| < e$$

After introducing Skolem constants f_1, f_2 for the arbitrary convergent sequences and expansion of the goal and of the assumptions by the definitions of convergence and of product of functions, the prover is left with two main assumptions and one goal (instances of the formula above), which have parallel alternating quantifiers.

The S-decomposition Method. The main structure of the proof (see [8]) is as follows: the quantifiers are removed from the 3 statements in parallel, using a combination of inference steps which decompose the proof into several branches. When the 3 formulae are existential, first introduce the Skolem constants for the assumptions, and then introduce a witness for the goal. The proof branches into: a main branch with the new goal, and secondary branches for proving the sub-goals stating that the type and the condition of the existential variable hold for the witness. When the 3 formulae are universal, first introduce Skolem constants for the goal, and then introduce the instantiation terms for the assumptions. Similarly to above, separate secondary branches are created for the type and condition checking of the instantiation terms.

Thus in this proof the prover produces, in order: Skolem constants a_1, a_2, witness $a_1 + a_2$; Skolem constant e_0, instantiation term $\text{Min}\left[1, \frac{e_0}{|a_2|+|a_1|+1}\right]$; Skolem constants M_1, M_2, witness $\text{Max}[M_1, M_2]$; Skolem constant n_0, instantiation term n_0. (The names are similar to the corresponding variables in the definition.)

At every iteration of the proof cycle one needs a witness for the existential goal and an one or more instantiation terms for the universal assumptions: these are the difficult steps in the proof, for which we use special proof techniques based on computer algebra.

Reasoning About Terms Behavior in Zero: by polynomial arithmetic the prover infers the value of the witness for a by equating all the expressions under the absolute value to zero.

Use of Metavariables: the existential variable in the goal (or the universal variable in an assumption) is replaced by a new symbol (metavariable), which is a name for the term (solution of the metavariable) which we need to find. This term is determined later in the proof, and the subgoals stating the type and the condition are checked on the secondary branches. Also, one must ensure that the solution to the metavariable does not contain Skolem constants which are introduced later in the proof. If this condition is not fulfilled, the prover tries to reorder the steps of the proof.

Quantifier Elimination is used in order to find the solution of the metavariable in relatively simple situations – as for instance in this proof for $Max[M_1, M_2]$, as described in [1].

Identification of Equal Terms Under Unknown Functions. This is used for finding the instantiation term n_0.

Since f_1 and f_2 are arbitrary, we do not know anything about their behaviour. In the goal f_1 and f_2 have argument n_0, therefore the prover uses the same argument in the assumptions, otherwise it would be impossible us the assumptions in the proof of the goal.

Algebraic Manipulations. The most challenging part in this proof is the automatic generation of the instantiation term $Min\left[1, \frac{e_0}{|a_2|+|a_1|+1}\right]$, which is performed by a heuristic combination of solving, substitution, and simplifying, as well as rewriting of expressions under the absolute value function, and it is realized at the end of the proof. The goal in this moment is:

$$|(f_1[n_0] * f_2[n_0]) - (a_1 * a_2)| < e_0 \tag{1}$$

and the main assumptions are:

$$|f_1[n_0] - a_1| < e \tag{2}$$

$$|f_2[n_0] - a_2| < e \tag{3}$$

Internally the prover replaces $f_1[n_0]$ and $f_2[n_0]$ by x_1 and x_2, respectively, both in the goal and in the assumptions. The argument of the absolute value in the transformed goal is $E_0 = x_1 * x_2 - a_1 * a_2$ and in the transformed assumptions $E_1 = x_1 - a_1$ and $E_2 = x_2 - a_2$.

First we use the following heuristic principle: transform the goal expression E_0 such that it uses as much as possible E_1 and E_2, because about those we know that they are small. In order to do this we take new variables y_1, y_2, we solve the equations $y_1 = E_1$ and $y_2 = E_2$ for x_1, x_2, we substitute the solutions in E_0 and the result simplifies to: $a_1 * y_2 + a_2 * y_1 + y_1 * y_2$. This is the internal representation of the absolute value argument in the goal (4).

$$|a_1 * (f_2[n_0] - a_2) + a_2 * (f_1[n_0] - a_1) + (f_1[n_0] - a_1) * (f_2[n_0] - a_2)| < e_0 \tag{4}$$

Note that the transformation from (1) to (4) is relatively challenging even for a human prover.

$$|a_1 * (f_2[n_0] - a_2) + a_2 * (f_1[n_0] - a_1) + (f_1[n_0] - a_1) * (f_2[n_0] - a_2)| \quad (5)$$
$$\leq |a_1 * (f_2[n_0] - a_2)| + |a_2 * (f_1[n_0] - a_1)| + |(f_1[n_0] - a_1) * (f_2[n_0] - a_2)|$$
$$= |a_1| * |f_2[n_0] - a_2| + |a_2| * |f_1[n_0] - a_1| + |f_1[n_0] - a_1| * |f_2[n_0] - a_2|$$
$$< |a_1| * e + |a_2| * e + e * e \leq |a_1| * e + |a_2| * e + e = e * (|a_1| + |a_2| + 1)$$
$$= \frac{e_0}{|a_2| + |a_1| + 1} * (|a_1| + |a_2| + 1) = e_0$$

The formula (5) is realized by *rewriting of the absolute value expressions*. Namely, we apply certain rewrite rules to expressions of the form $|E|$ and their combination, as well as to the metavariable e. Every rewrite rule transforms a (sub)term into one which is not smaller, so we are sure to obtain a greater or equal term. The final purpose of these transformations is to obtain a strictly positive ground term t multiplied by the target metavariable (here e). Since we need a value for e which fullfils $t * e \leq e_0$, we can set e to e_0/t. The rewrite rules come from the elementary properties of the absolute value function: (e.g. $|u + v| \leq |u| + |v|$)) and from the principle of *bounding the ϵ-bounds*: Since we are interested in the behaviour of the expressions in the immediate vicinity of zero, the bound e can be bound from above by any positive value. In the case of product (presented here), we also use the rule: $e * e \leq e$, that is we bound e to 1. This is why the final expression of e is the minimum between 1 and the term t found as above.

Proving Simple Conditions. At certain places in the proof, the conditions upon certain quantified variables have to be proven. The prover does not display a proof of these simple statements, but just declares them to be consequences of "elementary properties of $\mathbb{R}$". (Such elementary properties are also invoked when developing formulae (4) and (5)). In the background, however, the prover uses *Mathematica* functions in order to check that these statements are correct. This happens for instance for the subgoal $\forall_{e_0} (e_0 > 0 \Rightarrow e > 0)$ and will be treated after the instatiation term for e is found, by using QE on this formula (where e has the found value $\text{Min}[\ldots]$), which returns *True* in *Mathematica*.

3   Conclusion and Further Work

When applied to problems over reals, *Satisfiability Modulo Theories (SMT)* solving combines techniques from automated reasoning and from computer algebra. From the point of view of automated reasoning, proving unsatisfiability of a set of clauses appears to be quite different from producing natural-style proofs. Indeed the proof systems are different (resolution on clauses vs. some version of sequent calculus), but they are essentially equivalent, relaying on equivalent transformations of formulae. Moreover, the most important steps in first order proving, namely the instantiations of universally quantified formulae (which in natural-style proofs is also present as the equivalent operation of finding witnesses for existentially quantified goals), are actually the same or very similar.

The full automation of proofs in elementary analysis constitutes a very interesting application for the combination of logic and algebraic techniques, which is essentially equivalent to SMT solving (combining satisfiability checking and symbolic computation). Our experiments show that complete and efficient automation is possible by using certain heuristics in combination with complex algebraic algorithms.

Further work includes a systematic treatment of various formulae which appear in textbooks, and extension of the heuristics to more general types of formulae. In this way we hope to address the class of problems which are usually subject to SMT solving.

References

1. Abraham, E., Jebelean, T.: Adapting cylindrical algebraic decomposition for proof specific tasks. In: Kusper, G. (ed.) ICAI 2017: 10th International Conference on Applied Informatics (2017) (in print)
2. Bauer, A., Clarke, E., Zhao, X.: Analytica - an experiment in combining theorem proving and symbolic computation. J. Autom. Reasoning **21**(3), 295–325 (1998). https://doi.org/10.1023/A:1006079212546
3. Buchberger, B., Jebelean, T., Kutsia, T., Maletzky, A., Windsteiger, W.: Theorema 2.0: computer-assisted natural-style mathematics. JFR **9**(1), 149–185 (2016)
4. Collins, G.E.: Quantier elimination for real closed fields by cylindrical algebraic decomposition. In: Automata Theory and Formal Languages. LNCS, vol. 33, pp. 134–183. Springer (1975)
5. Jebelean, T.: Techniques for natural-style proofs in elementary analysis. ACM Commun. Comput. Algebra **52**(3), 92–95 (2019)
6. Jebelean, T.: Techniques for natural-style proofs in elementary analysis (extended abstract). In: Bigatti, A.M., Brain, M. (eds.) Third International Workshop on Satisfiability Checking and Symbolic Computation (2018)
7. Jebelean, T.: A heuristic prover for elementary analysis in Theorema. Tech. Rep. 21–07, Research Institute for Symbolic Computation (RISC), Johannes Kepler University Linz (2021)
8. Jebelean, T., Buchberger, B., Kutsia, T., Popov, N., Schreiner, W., Windsteiger, W.: Automated reasoning. In: Buchberger, B., et al. (eds.) Hagenberg Research, pp. 63–101. Springer (2009). https://doi.org/10.1007/978-3-642-02127-5_2
9. Vajda, R., Jebelean, T., Buchberger, B.: Combining logical and algebraic techniques for natural style proving in elementary analysis. Math. Comput. Simul. **79**(8), 2310–2316 (2009)

Search and Classification

Searching for Mathematical Formulas Based on Graph Representation Learning

Yujin Song and Xiaoyu Chen[✉]

LMIB-SKLSDE-BDBC, School of Mathematical Sciences,
Beihang University, Beijing 100191, China
chenxiaoyu@buaa.edu.cn

Abstract. Significant advances have been witnessed in the area of representation learning. Recently, there have been some attempts of applying representation learning methods on mathematical formula retrieval. We introduce a new formula embedding model based on a kind of graph representation generated from hierarchical representation for mathematical formula. Such a representation characterizes structural features in a compact form by merging the same part of a mathematical formula. Following the approach of graph self-supervised learning, we pre-train Graph Neural Networks at the level of individual nodes to learn local representations and then produce a global representation for the entire graph. In this way, formulas can be embedded into a low-dimensional vector space, which allows efficient nearest neighbor search using cosine similarity. We use 579,628 formulas extracted from Wikipedia Corpus provided by NTCIR-12 Wikipedia Formula Browsing Task to train our model, leading to competitive results for full relevance on the task. Experiments with a preliminary implementation of the embedding model illustrate the feasibility and capability of graph representation learning in capturing structural similarities of mathematical formulas.

Keywords: Math formula search · Graph representation learning · Self-supervised learning · Formula embedding

1 Introduction

Representation learning, also known as feature learning, has been demonstrated to be effective and powerful in various application fields including computer vision, audio, and natural language processing [3]. Its main objective is to represent data with low-dimensional dense vectors that are able to capture useful features of data through appropriate learning models other than artificial feature engineering. While such kind of distributed representations, taking advantages of excellent robustness and extensibility than symbolic representations of data, have been well studied on words and paragraphs, the question of how to learn continuous vector representations for mathematical formulas which play an important role in dissemination and communication of scientific information has become a compelling line of inquiry.

© Springer Nature Switzerland AG 2021
F. Kamareddine and C. Sacerdoti Coen (Eds.): CICM 2021, LNAI 12833, pp. 137–152, 2021.
https://doi.org/10.1007/978-3-030-81097-9_11

As for the task of information retrieval involving mathematical formulas, the goal is to learn appropriate formula embedding capable of capturing formula similarity. Considering the measures of formula similarity may vary in different scenarios which heavily affects the performance and evaluation of embedding, in this work we focus on structural similarity in isolated formula search task without using surrounding text, the same setting as in [15]. As formulas are inherently hierarchical and symbols therein have semantic relationships between each other which would be implicit in sequential representations, we wonder whether graph representation learning could enhance the embedding performance since significant advances have been achieved by Graph Neural Networks (GNNs). To this end, we introduce a new formula embedding model based on a kind of graph representation generated from hierarchical representation for mathematical formula. Such a representation characterizes structural features in a compact form by merging the same part of a mathematical formula. Given isolated formulas without meta-information, we leverage the self-supervised learning strategies at node level proposed in [11] to produce node embeddings and then average them to obtain a vector representation for the entire graph of a formula which allows efficient nearest neighbor search using cosine similarity. We explore the effects of different factors on embedding performance, including node feature initialization, the scale of node labels and different graph neural network architectures. Our model[1] achieves competitive results on NTCIR-12 Wikipedia Formula Browsing Task [26].

The remainder of this paper is structured as follows. We first review related work on mathematical formula representations, similarity measures in traditional mathematical information retrieval (MIR) and the new trend of mathematical formula embedding in Sect. 2. In Sect. 3, we present the design of graph representation for mathematical formulas and then briefly introduce self-supervised learning tasks and our embedding model based on GNNs in Sect. 4. We evaluate our model using two metrics for information retrieval in Sect. 5. Finally, we conclude the paper and prospect the future work in Sect. 6.

2   Related Work

Math Formula Representation. There are two choices for representing math formula abstractly [27]: one is Symbol Layout Tree (SLT) indicating formula appearance, i.e., symbols' spatial arrangement towards a writing baseline; the other is Operator Tree (OPT) indicating formula semantics such as argument types, operator syntax, and their logical relations. These two abstract representations have their own specific file formats. Those for SLTs include LaTeX, a well-known markup language for typesetting, and Presentation MathML, a markup language based on XML for displaying math on the web. SLT representations may be ambiguous as the same symbol may be of different mathematical types in different contexts. To reduce the ambiguity, sTeX [12] and content LaTeX [17] provided semantic annotations for LaTeX documents. Those for

---

[1] PyTorch implementation: https://github.com/Franknewchen/MathEmb.

OPTs include Content MathML and OpenMath [5,7], both standard XML languages, which could provide semantics to Computer Algebra Systems (CAS) like Maple and Mathematica to perform computations. Various tools allow for conversions between different formats. Schubotz et al. [22] presented nine tools and performed a quantitative evaluation of them on a benchmark dataset. Greiner-Petter et al. [9] introduced the first translation tool for special functions between LaTeX and CAS.

Similarity Measure. The matching between a query formula and indexed formulas is essential in MIR systems, so how to measure similarity between formulas is a key question. Approaches fall into two main categories, text-based and tree-based [28]. Text-based approaches linearize expression trees to text strings with normalization, such as using canonical orderings for commutative and associative operators, and replacing symbols by their mathematical types, while the hierarchical information of formulas may be lost to some extent due to the linearization. And then text retrieval methods can be applied, such as using term frequency-inverse document frequency (TF-IDF) [17,23]. Kumar et al. [19] proposed an approach to retrieve LaTeX string by matching the largest common substring, which could capture more structural information but required a quadratic algorithm. Tree-based approaches use expression trees directly, aiming at matching complete trees, subtrees or paths traversed in some order [4,6,13,31]. The more common substructures are matched, the more similar two formulas are considered. These approaches are more effective than the text-based according to the results of NTCIR [1,26], but often time-consuming because of the complexity of structure matching. Zhong et al. [30] proposed a rank-safe dynamic pruning algorithm for faster substructure retrieval.

Math Formula Embedding. At an early stage, Thanda et al. [24] explored math formula embedding by using the distributed bag of words (PV-DBOW) model, a variant of doc2vec algorithm. Gao et al. [8] followed the continuous bags-of-words (CBOW), one architecture of the word2vec [16] model with negative sampling and distributed memory model of paragraph vectors (PV-DM) to learn vector representations for math symbols and formulas respectively. Krstovski and Blei [14] proposed a model to embed both equations and their surrounding text based on word embedding by treating an equation appearing in the context of different words as a "singleton word". The joint embedding of text and equation is also adopted by Yasunaga and Lafferty [25]. They applied a Recurrent Neural Network (RNN) to model each equation as a sequence of LaTeX tokens. Pathak et al. [18] conducted symbol-level embedding as in [8], and then created a Formula Entailment (LFE) module based on Long Short Term Memory (LSTM) neural network to recognize entailment between formula pairs. Mansouri et al. [15] created tuples to represent depth-first paths between pairs of symbols and then embedded tuples using the fastText n-gram embedding model derived from the word2vec model. The above approaches are almost based on word embedding techniques in natural language processing tasks. Their use and effectiveness were explored by Greiner-Petter et al. in five different mathematical scenarios. The results show that math embedding holds much promise for similarity, analogy, and search tasks [10]. To the best of our knowledge, Pfahler et al. [20] fed tree-structured MathML formulas to GNNs for the first time. Aiming at retrieving formulas appearing in the paragraphs or articles related to query formulas rather than exact matches, they designed node-level masking and graph-level contextual similarity self-supervised learning tasks to embed mathematical expressions.

Benchmark for MIR. As Aizawa and Kohlhase presented in [2], a major obstacle to MIR research is the lack of readily available large-scale datasets with structured mathematical formulas, carefully designed tasks, and established evaluation methods. Benchmarks published by NTCIR [1,26] and the latest released benchmark ARQMath [29] have promoted the development of MIR.

3   Graph Representation for Mathematical Formula

The formula dataset we work on is obtained from Wikipedia Corpus for NTCIR-12 Wikipedia Formula Browsing Task. The corpus contains 31,839 HTML articles in MathTagArticles directory and 287,850 HTML articles in TextArticles directory. Each formula therein is encoded in three formats: LaTeX, Presentation MathML and Content MathML. As the amount of formulas existing in TextArticles directory only account for 2% of the total number and those formulas are mainly in the form of isolated symbols, we construct a formula dataset by extracting a total number of 579,628 formulas from the articles in MathTagArticles directory and converting each formula from Content MathML into OPT representation by using tools developed in [6].

In order to make full use of the advances of GNNs, we propose a labeled directed acyclic graph (DAG) representation based on the OPT representation by sharing the recurring substructures therein. Such a representation characterizes structural features in a compact form. For example, as shown in Fig. 1, the number "1" and the part "$a - b$", which occur twice in tree representation while only occur once in graph representation respectively. In order to prevent the emergence of multiple edges, especially in the representation of matrices, we do not merge substructures if their parent nodes are the same. Considering the matrix $\begin{bmatrix} x & x \\ y & z \end{bmatrix}$ shown in Fig. 2(a), the node "x" cannot be merged otherwise a multiple edge between node "R" and node "x" will occur in the graph. In the case of its transposed matrix $\begin{bmatrix} x & y \\ x & z \end{bmatrix}$ (Fig. 2(b)), the sharing of node "x" can be conducted and the resulting graph is shown in Fig. 2(c).

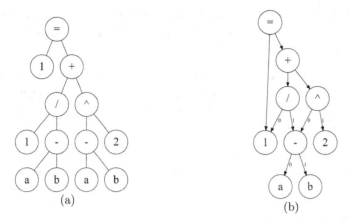

Fig. 1. Comparison of two representations for $\frac{1}{a-b}+(a-b)^2=1$. (a) OPT representation; (b) Graph representation with "1" and "$a-b$" shared (where edge labels are used to declare the argument positions).

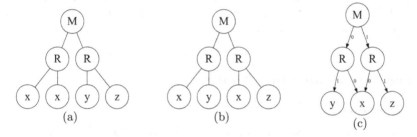

Fig. 2. Representations for matrices. "M" and "R" are abbreviations for "Matrix" and "Row" respectively.

Node Labels. We label nodes in the form of "Type!Value" as proposed in [6]. There are 12 types extracted from Content MathML tags in total, including number (denoted as N!), constant (denoted as C!), variable (denoted as V!), function (denoted as F!), object with group structure (denoted as M!) like matrix, text (denoted as T!) like "lim" and "max", commutative operator (denoted as U!), non-commutative operator (denoted as O!), compound operator (denoted as +!) using a subtree to define an operation, whitespace (denoted as W!), unknown type (denoted as -!) and error (denoted as E!), while the value of a node is its corresponding symbols occurring in the formula. For example, the node labels of "a" and "1" in Fig. 1 are represented as "V!a" and "N!1" respectively. In the constructed formula dataset, there are 24,567 labels in the form of "Type!Value" totally, among which about 50% labels only occur once and 41% occur less than fifteen times. Since the amount of labels is so large and 91% of them only occur a few times, we discard the labels whose occurrence frequencies are less than a certain number δ (called *discarding threshold*) and the nodes with these labels are relabeled with a unified artificial symbol "[unif]" in our current setting. We compare the embedding performance when $\delta = 0, 5, 15$ and report the results in Sect. 5.

Edge Labels. Edge labels are used to declare argument positions as in OPT representation [6]. For a commutative operator like "+" whose argument order does not affect the calculation result, argument edges are all labeled with "0". For a non-commutative operator, argument edges are labeled with indices in the argument order starting from 0.

For a mathematical formula, we implement an algorithm of converting its OPT representation into the above graph representation, denoted as a quadruple (V, E, L_V, L_E), where V is the set of nodes, E is the set of directed edges, L_V and L_E are the sets of node labels and edge labels respectively. Accordingly, the formula dataset in graph representation can be denoted as $\mathcal{G} = \{G_1, G_2, \ldots, G_{579628}\}$, where the whole set of node labels is denoted as $\mathcal{L}_\mathcal{V} = L_{V_{G_1}} \cup L_{V_{G_2}} \cup \cdots \cup L_{V_{G_{579628}}}$ and $|\mathcal{L}_\mathcal{V}| = 24,567$. As for the whole set of edge labels $\mathcal{L}_\mathcal{E}$, elements are numbers indicating argument positions, where the minimum element is 0 and the maximum element is less than 68, the maximum degree of the nodes in $\mathcal{G}$. The node with the maximum degree appears in a polynomial with respect to "x" which has 69 terms and the degree of the polynomial is 71.

4 Formula Embedding Model

4.1 Self-supervised Learning Tasks

Since we focus on the isolated formula search task without meta-information, self-supervised learning would suit the task. In this work, we follow the strategies for pre-training GNNs presented in [11] which have enhanced the performances of downstream classification tasks in biology and chemistry fields. We adopt two self-supervised learning tasks therein at node level: (1) Context Prediction is a binary classification task of whether a particular subgraph and a particular context graph belong to the same node. The subgraph is a k-hop neighborhood around a randomly selected center node and the context graph is the surrounding graph structure that is between r_1-hop and r_2-hop ($r_1 < r_2$) from the center node. The neighborhood-context pair to be predicted is obtained using a negative sampling ratio of 1. (2) Attribute Masking is a task of predicting a set of randomly masked node labels using a linear model applied on top of GNNs, aiming to capture the regularities of node labels distributed over different graph structures. The masked nodes are labeled with "[mask]" during the process of training. We train GNNs by adding the losses for both two self-supervised learning tasks.

4.2 Graph Neural Networks

We adopt three architectures, Graph Convolution Network (GCN), Graph SAmple and aggreGatE (GraphSAGE) and Graph Isomorphism Network (GIN), to learn node representations and then produce the entire graph embedding by averaging its node representations. As input features of GNNs, each node and each edge with raw labels are respectively embedded by

$$h_v^{(0)} = \text{EmbNode}\,(i_v) \tag{1}$$

$$h_e^{(0)} = \text{EmbEdge}\,(j_e) \tag{2}$$

where i_v and j_e denote the index of node v's raw label in $\mathcal{L}_\mathcal{V}$ and the index of edge e's raw label in $\mathcal{L}_\mathcal{E}$ respectively. EmbNode($\cdot$) and EmbEdge($\cdot$) can be viewed as an initial layer for node features and edge features, mapping indices to randomly generated d-dimensional real vectors. In general, for each node v, GNNs update its representation at the k-th layer by

$$h_v^{(k)} = \text{Combine}^{(k)}\left(h_v^{(k-1)}, \text{Aggregate}^{(k)}\left(\left\{\left(h_v^{(k-1)}, h_u^{(k-1)}, e_{uv}\right) : u \in \mathcal{N}(v)\right\}\right)\right)$$

where e_{uv} is the feature vector of edge between node u and v, and $\mathcal{N}(v)$ is a set neighbors of node v. The representation of node v is iteratively updated by combining its last representation with aggregated information from its neighboring nodes and edges. Combine and Aggregate approaches are different in different network architectures, for details of which refer to [11].

Considering the inherited relationships between labels exiting in formula dataset, we also apply word2vec on the sequentialized form of formulas to extract initial features for nodes and construct the following embedding operation:

$$h_v^{(0)} = \text{W2vNode}\,(l_v) \tag{3}$$

where $l_v \in \mathcal{L}_\mathcal{V}$ denotes the raw label of node v. W2vNode($\cdot$) first maps each label in $\mathcal{L}_\mathcal{V}$ to a $(d-1)$-dimensional real vector using word2vec. Then each vector is expanded to a d-dimensional vector by filling with 0 at the d-th dimension. For the label "[mask]", the first $d-1$ dimensions are all set to be 0, and the last dimension is set to be 1. For the artificial symbol "[unif]", the initial representation is generated randomly in each training batch to reduce manual bias caused by unifying the discarded labels. In a word, W2vNode($\cdot$) performs as a dictionary, providing initial features of fixed d-dimensional vectors for nodes that will be fed to GNNs.

4.3   Hyperparameter Choices

We train the presented model for 100 epochs with Adam optimization, embedding dimension of 300, batch size of 256, learning rate of 0.001, the number of GNN layers of 5, mask rate of 0.15 in Attribute Masking task, and $k = 5$, $r_1 = 2$ and $r_2 = 5$ in Context Prediction task.

5   Experiments and Evaluation

In this section, we evaluate our formula embedding model in different settings relying on 20 concrete queries provided by NTCIR-12 MathIR Wikipedia Formula Browsing Task.

5.1 Evaluation Metric

During the task, each hit from participating systems was evaluated by two human assessors recruited by organizers of NTCIR-12. Each assessor scores a hit with 0, 1 or 2, indicating the degree of relevance from low to high. The agreement between evaluators for this task has the lowest agreement value among all MathIR tasks since some evaluators were very concerned with formula semantics, while others seemed to consider primarily visual similarity when rating hits [26]. The final relevance rating is a score between 0 and 4, i.e. the sum of the two assessor scores. Scores of 3 or 4 are considered fully relevant while scores of 1 or 2 are considered partially relevant and a score of 0 is considered nonrelevant.

We use bpref on top-1000 results and precision@k for $k = 5, 10, 15, 20$ as evaluation metrics. For a query with R judged relevant documents and N judged nonrelevant documents, let r be a relevant document and n be a member of the first R judged nonrelevant documents as retrieved by the system, then

$$\text{bpref} = \frac{1}{R} \sum_r 1 - \frac{|n \text{ ranked higher than } r|}{\min(R, N)},$$

which is designed to evaluate IR systems only using judged documents [21]. Precision@$k = \frac{s}{k}$, where s is the number of relevant documents in the top k retrieval results, is an effective evaluation metric to indicate whether the top retrieval results are helpful to users.

5.2 Evaluation Results

We explore the impact of different graph neural network architectures, different initializations for node features and different scales of node labels as shown in Table 1. Firstly, we discard node labels with discarding threshold $\delta = 15$, so that the scale of node labels are reduced from 24,567 to 2,157. Then we initialize node features using EmbNode in which setting GCN performs the best. As a comparison, we adopt W2vNode to initialize node features. This setting only slightly improves the performance of GIN and GCN but impairs the performance of GraphSage by 2%. When the node labels are discarded with $\delta = 5$, the scale node labels is increased from 2,157 to 5,000. Then GCN achieves higher partial and full bpref scores, while both GraphSAGE and GIN perform inconsistent improvements on partial and full bpref scores. In both settings with different discarding thresholds, GCN performs the best, 1% to 5% better than the other two network architectures. This demonstrates that the classic GCN may be a more suitable encoder for formula embedding in characterizing structural features. Finally, to compare the effects of different discarding thresholds and initialization methods, we use GCN to conduct another round of experiment which shows that discarding threshold $\delta = 5$ helps improve the performance of GCN both in partial and full relevance, while using W2vNode does not help.

Table 1. Avg. bpref@1000 of NTCIR-12 results in different settings

Network architecture	Size of label set	Initialization method	Partial bpref	Full bpref
GCN	2,157	EmbNode	**0.5349**	**0.6167**
GraphSAGE	2,157	EmbNode	0.5244	0.5970
GIN	2,157	EmbNode	0.4845	0.5926
GCN	2,157	W2vNode	0.5256	**0.6195**
GraphSAGE	2,157	W2vNode	0.5058	0.5779
GIN	2,157	W2vNode	0.4982	0.6069
GCN	5,000	W2vNode	**0.5408**	**0.6250**
GraphSAGE	5,000	W2vNode	0.4937	0.5814
GIN	5,000	W2vNode	0.5185	0.5822
GCN	5,000	EmbNode	**0.5568**	0.6070
GCN	24,567	EmbNode	0.5278	0.5829
GCN	24,567	W2vNode	0.5309	0.5865

Next we compare our formula embedding model with other models, among which Tangent-CFT [15] is an embedding model, Approach0 [31] is a tree-based model and TanApp, the combination of Tangent-CFT and Approach0, achieves state-of-the-art performance. As Table 2 illustrates, our model achieves a competitive full bpref score. The reason for low partial bpref scores is that the top-1000 results retrieved by our model only hit a few judged formulas for some queries. An example is query #18, for which there are 71 judged formulas, but we only retrieve 14 of them. Another example is query #17 which had the highest harmonic mean bpref score (0.931) over all queries in Tangent-CFT retrieval results. The top-5 results retrieved by our model and Tangent-CFT are shown in Table 3. The three formulas ranked from the second to the fourth in our retrieval results are from the same article as the query is and seem more relevant than those in Tangent-CFT retrieval results. However, they were not judged during the task, leading to a low bpref score. In spite of this, our model can retrieve the exact match as the top-1 formula for each query except for query #1 (ranked the third in the retrieval results). The use of tokenizing formula tuples makes Tangent-CFT easier to retrieve formulas containing more same symbols as queries, which may be judged to be partially relevant, while our model focuses more on relationships between symbols and tends to retrieve formulas with similar structures as queries, which may be judged to be fully relevant (Fig. 3).

The precision@k score is just a lower bound as some retrieved results may be not judged. We mainly compare our model with Approach0 considering that all or partly results of other models were judged during NTCIR-12 task and the precision@k score of Tangent-CFT was not provided in [15]. As shown in Table 4, our model achieves competitive scores compared to Approach0 in both full and partial relevances. The reason why the score for query "β" (query #2) is zero is that there are so many unjudged "β" existing in the dataset that our model only takes the unjudged ones as top-5 results. And the zero score for query #13

Table 2. Avg. bpref@1000 of NTCIR-12 results of different models

Model	Partial bpref	Full bpref
Our model	0.54	0.63
Tangent-CFT	0.71	0.60
Approach0	0.59	0.67
TanApp	0.73	0.70
Tangent-s [6]	0.59	0.64
MCAT [13]	0.57	0.57

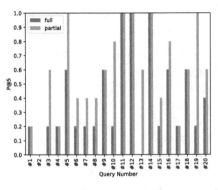

Fig. 3. P@5 for each query of our model

Table 3. Top-5 results for query $x - 1 - \frac{1}{2} - \frac{1}{4} - \frac{1}{5} - \frac{1}{6} - \frac{1}{9} - \cdots = 1$

Model	Rank	Retrieved results
Our model	1	$x - 1 - \frac{1}{2} - \frac{1}{4} - \frac{1}{5} - \frac{1}{6} - \frac{1}{9} - \cdots = 1$
	2	$x - 1 = 1 + \frac{1}{2} + \frac{1}{4} + \frac{1}{5} + \frac{1}{6} + \frac{1}{9} + \cdots$
	3	$x - 1 - \frac{1}{2} = 1 + \frac{1}{5} + \frac{1}{6} + \frac{1}{7} + \frac{1}{10} + \frac{1}{11} + \frac{1}{12} + \cdots$
	4	$x - 1 = 1 + \frac{1}{3} + \frac{1}{5} + \frac{1}{6} + \frac{1}{7} + \frac{1}{9} + \frac{1}{10} + \frac{1}{11} + \cdots$
	5	$\frac{1}{1} + \frac{1}{1} + \frac{1}{2} + \frac{1}{3} + \frac{1}{5} + \frac{1}{8} + \cdots = \psi$
Tangent-CFT	1	$x - 1 - \frac{1}{2} - \frac{1}{4} - \frac{1}{5} - \frac{1}{6} - \frac{1}{9} - \cdots = 1$
	2	$1 - \frac{1}{2} - \frac{1}{4} + \frac{1}{3} - \frac{1}{6} - \frac{1}{8} + \frac{1}{5} - \frac{1}{10} - \frac{1}{12} + \cdots$
	3	$1 - \frac{1}{2} - \frac{1}{4} + \frac{1}{8} - \frac{1}{16} + \cdots = \frac{1}{3}$
	4	$\frac{1}{18} = \frac{1}{2} - \frac{1}{3} - \frac{1}{3^2}$
	5	$\frac{\pi}{4} = 1 - \frac{1}{3} + \frac{1}{5} - \frac{1}{7} + \cdots$

in full relevance is caused by an error in the public assessment scores.[2] It is worth noting that the ideal precision@k score of full relevance is not 1 for every query, because if there is only one formula judged to be fully relevant among all judged formulas for some query, the ideal score is 0.2. Our model achieves ideal scores for 8 queries in full relevance and 5 queries in partial relevance and additionally outperforms the average P@5 score of Approach0 for 7 queries in partial relevance.

---

[2] When we carry out experiments, we find an error score in "NTCIR12-MathWiki-13 xxx Mathematical_morphology:24 2.0", a line in the document that contains all judged formulas with relevance scores. The query formula with name "NTCIR12-MathWiki-13" is exactly the 24-th formula in the article "Mathematical_morphology". Therefore, the score should be 4.0 indicating full relevance.

Remark. Because queries #1 and #2 are both isolated symbols represented as single nodes in our graph representation which contain no structural information to learn, we evaluate our model on the other 18 queries and achieve a partial bpref score 0.57 and a full bpref score 0.65 respectively, and higher P@k scores.

Table 4. Avg. P@k of NTCIR-12 results of our model and Approach0

Model	Partially relevant				Fully relevant			
	P@5	P@10	P@15	P@20	P@5	P@10	P@15	P@20
Our model	0.5900	0.4450	0.4100	0.3800	0.3900	0.2500	0.2200	0.1875
Approach0	0.5300	0.4650	0.4100	0.3850	0.4000	0.2900	0.2233	0.1950

In order to intuitively compare our model with other models, we illustrate some specific queries. Our model achieves ideal P@5 score in full relevance for the following queries:

$$O(mn \log m). \qquad \qquad \text{(query \#12)}$$

$$\cos \alpha = - \cos \beta \cos \gamma + \sin \beta \sin \gamma \cosh \frac{a}{k}. \qquad \text{(query \#14)}.$$

For query #12, the top-5 results retrieved by our model, Tangent-CFT and Approach0 are shown in Table 5. It is obvious that the retrieval results by our model are highly consistent with those by Approach0, i.e., after substituting some single symbols, the retrieval results become the same as the query. As for query #14, in the top-10 results Tangent-CFT missed 4 fully relevant formulas found in that range by Approach0, including $\cos A = - \cos B \cos C + \sin B \sin C \cosh a$ and $\cos C = - \cos A \cos B + \sin A \sin B \cosh c$. Our model not only hits the two formulas, but also hits the query itself as the first one in the top-10 results.

Table 5. Top-5 results for query $O(mn \log m)$

Rank	Our model	Tangent-CFT	Approach0
1	$O(mn \log m)$	$O(mn \log m)$	$O(mn \log m)$
2	$O(nk \log k)$	$O(m \log n)$	$O(nk \log k)$
3	$O(nk \log(n))$	$O(n \log m)$	$O(KN \log N)$
4	$O(KN \log N)$	$O(n \log m)$	$O(VE \log V)$
5	$O(VE \log V)$	$O(nm)$	$O(n \log n \log \log n)$

Another example is $0 \to G^\wedge \xrightarrow{\pi^\wedge} X^\wedge \xrightarrow{\imath^\wedge} H^\wedge \to 0$ (query #7), for which Tangent-CFT performed better in both partial and full bpref than Approach0.

Among the top-1000 results, Tangent-CFT was able to retrieve formulas such as $1 \to K \xrightarrow{i} G \xrightarrow{\pi} H \to 1$ and $W \to X \xrightarrow{f} Y \xrightarrow{g} Z \xrightarrow{h} 1$ which Approach0 failed to retrieve. Our model performs better than them. The following four formulas

$$0 \to G^\wedge \xrightarrow{\pi^\wedge} X^\wedge \xrightarrow{i^\wedge} H^\wedge \to 0,$$

$$0 \to H \xrightarrow{i'} X' \xrightarrow{\pi'} G \to 0,$$

$$1 \to K \xrightarrow{i'} G' \xrightarrow{\pi'} H \to 1,$$

$$0 \to H \xrightarrow{i_H} H \times G \xrightarrow{\pi_G} G \to 0,$$

are in the top-5 results. The second and the fourth formula were not judged, which is the reason why the P@5 scores in full and partial relevances are only 0.2 and 0.4 respectively, but they are actually from the same article as the query is.

Consider the following three queries:

$$\tau_{rms} = \sqrt{\frac{\int_0^\infty (\tau - \overline{\tau})^2 A_c(\tau) d\tau}{\int_0^\infty A_c(\tau) d\tau}} \qquad \text{(query \#16)}$$

$$P_i^x = \frac{N!}{n_x!(N - n_x)!} p_x^{n_x} (1 - p_x)^{N - n_x} \qquad \text{(query \#18)}$$

$$r_{xy} = \frac{\sum_{i=1}^n (x_i - \overline{x})(y_i - \overline{y})}{(n-1)s_x s_y} = \frac{\sum_{i=1}^n (x_i - \overline{x})(y_i - \overline{y})}{\sqrt{\sum_{i=1}^n (x_i - \overline{x})^2 \sum_{i=1}^n (y_i - \overline{y})^2}}. \qquad \text{(query \#20)}$$

The three queries have complicated structures containing more operators and symbols. For query #16, our model can retrieve

$$\alpha_{sun} = \frac{\int_0^\infty \alpha_\lambda I_{\lambda sun}(\lambda) \, d\lambda}{\int_0^\infty I_{\lambda sun}(\lambda) \, d\lambda}$$

as Tangent-CFT did, which is ranked the sixth in our results. In addition, formulas such as

$$\frac{1}{\kappa} = \frac{\int_0^\infty (\kappa_{\nu,es} + \kappa_{\nu,ff})^{-1} u(\nu, T) d\nu}{\int_0^\infty u(\nu, T) d\nu},$$

$$(\Delta k)^2 = \frac{\int_{-\infty}^\infty (k - k_0)^2 F(k) F^*(k) \, dk}{\int_{-\infty}^\infty F(k) F^*(k) \, dk},$$

which are also judged to be fully relevant, are ranked in top-5 in our results. For query #18, Approach0 could retrieve two formulas judged partially relevant while Tangent-CFT was not able to do so. In our top-5 results, the following two fully relevant formulas can be retrieved.

$$f(p) = \frac{(n+1)!}{s!(n-s)!}p^s(1-p)^{n-s}$$

$$p_n(k) = \frac{n!}{(n-k)!k!}p^k(1-p)^{n-k}$$

For query #20, the formula with the largest number of nodes and the deepest depth, Tangent-CFT could not retrieve the second formula below based on OPT representation, while our model could retrieve it and rank it in top-15. Besides, the first formula below is ranked the second in our results. They are both fully relevant.

$$\text{sim}(d_j, q) = \frac{\mathbf{d_j} \cdot \mathbf{q}}{\|\mathbf{d_j}\|\,\|\mathbf{q}\|} = \frac{\sum_{i=1}^{N} w_{i,j}w_{i,q}}{\sqrt{\sum_{i=1}^{N} w_{i,j}^2}\sqrt{\sum_{i=1}^{N} w_{i,q}^2}}$$

$$\text{similarity} = \cos(\theta) = \frac{\mathbf{A} \cdot \mathbf{B}}{\|\mathbf{A}\|\|\mathbf{B}\|} = \frac{\sum_{i=1}^{n} A_i \times B_i}{\sqrt{\sum_{i=1}^{n} (A_i)^2} \times \sqrt{\sum_{i=1}^{n} (B_i)^2}}$$

Our model also performs well on continued fractions and matrices, such as queries #5, #9 and #19. For query #5, the partial bpref score is 1.00, which means that all 35 formulas judged as relevant during the task can be retrieved by our model and no nonrelevant formulas rank above them. Queries #9 and #19 demonstrate the strength of our model in terms of matrix formulas. For example, for query #9

$$\begin{bmatrix} V_1 \\ I_2 \end{bmatrix} = \begin{bmatrix} h_{11} & h_{12} \\ h_{21} & h_{22} \end{bmatrix} \begin{bmatrix} I_1 \\ V_2 \end{bmatrix},$$

formulas equivalent to the query after substituting variable names could be retrieved in top-10 results, such as

$$\begin{bmatrix} I_1 \\ V_2 \end{bmatrix} = \begin{bmatrix} g_{11} & g_{12} \\ g_{21} & g_{22} \end{bmatrix} \begin{bmatrix} V_1 \\ I_2 \end{bmatrix},$$

$$\begin{bmatrix} a_1 \\ b_1 \end{bmatrix} = \begin{bmatrix} T_{11} & T_{12} \\ T_{21} & T_{22} \end{bmatrix} \begin{bmatrix} b_2 \\ a_2 \end{bmatrix}.$$

Remark. For the proposed DAG representation, merging the same substructures would not change the linkage between these substructures and their parent nodes. In other words, for each node in such a DAG, its "children nodes" and "parent nodes" are the same as those in the OPT representation. The first reason why we use DAG rather than OPT is the amount of computation of GNNs can be reduced. For the same subexpressions, the same node embedding will be computed repeatedly in OPT while only once in DAG. If the occurrence times or size of the same subexpression is large in an expression, then DAG will demonstrate its advantage in computing efficiency. The second reason is that the presented self-supervised learning tasks would benefit from such a compact form of representation as recurring substructures are ignored.

The DAG representation preserves structural differences of formulas but only children nodes' messages are aggregated when using GNNs to learn node embeddings. This is the main reason that our model performs more similarly to tree-based models, like Approach0 and Tangent-s. If we use undirected graphs (i.e., add the reverse edges) to train the model, a higher partial bpref score would be achieved. The reason is that node embedding with an undirected graph will aggregate messages not only from children nodes but also from parent nodes. Undirected graphs weaken the "order" information of operations in math expressions and are not capable of preserving the structural differences but have more capabilities in capturing local structures.

6   Conclusion and Future Work

We propose a new mathematical formula embedding model based on graph neural networks in this paper. A kind of graph representation is designed to be generated from hierarchical representation for mathematical formula by merging the same part in the formula. Following the approach of graph self-supervised learning, we represent formulas in distributed dense vectors. The embedding model can be applied in the task of searching for mathematical formulas and achieve competitive full bpref and precision@k scores. The good performance in full relevance indicates a great potential of feature-based graph representation learning in capturing structural information of mathematical formulas. Moreover, our experiments also show that GCN may be a more suitable architecture for this task.

For future work, optimal self-supervised learning strategies at the level of entire graph and evaluation on ARQMath benchmark will be investigated. Considering the embedding effect of undirected graph representation, whether an ensemble of undirected and directed graph embeddings will produce better results is worth studying at a later stage.

Acknowledgements. This work has been supported by National Natural Science Foundation of China (Grant No. 61702025) and State Key Laboratory of Software Development Environment.

References

1. Aizawa, A., Kohlhase, M., Ounis, I., Schubotz, M.: NTCIR-11 Math-2 task overview. In: Proceedings of the 11th NTCIR Conference on Evaluation of Information Access Technologies, pp. 88–98. National Institute of Informatics (2014)
2. Aizawa, A., Kohlhase, M.: Mathematical information retrieval. In: Sakai, T., Oard, D.W., Kando, N. (eds.) Evaluating Information Retrieval and Access Tasks. TIRS, vol. 43, pp. 169–185. Springer, Singapore (2021). https://doi.org/10.1007/978-981-15-5554-1_12

3. Bengio, Y., Courville, A., Vincent, P.: Representation learning: a review and new perspectives. IEEE Trans. Pattern Anal. Mach. Intell. **35**(8), 1798–1828 (2013)
4. Chen, H.: Mathematical formula similarity comparing based on tree structure. In: Proceedings of the 12th International Conference on Natural Computation, Fuzzy Systems and Knowledge Discovery. IEEE (2016)
5. Davenport, J.H., Kohlhase, M.: Unifying math ontologies: a tale of two standards. In: Carette, J., Dixon, L., Coen, C.S., Watt, S.M. (eds.) CICM 2009. LNCS (LNAI), vol. 5625, pp. 263–278. Springer, Heidelberg (2009). https://doi.org/10.1007/978-3-642-02614-0_23
6. Davila, K., Zanibbi, R.: Layout and semantics: combining representations for mathematical formula search. In: Proceedings of the 40th International ACM SIGIR Conference on Research and Development in Information Retrieval, pp. 1165–1168. Association for Computing Machinery (2017)
7. Dewar, M.: OpenMath: an overview. SIGSAM Bull. **34**(2), 2–5 (2000)
8. Gao, L., Jiang, Z., Yin, Y., Yuan, K., Yan, Z., Tang, Z.: Preliminary exploration of formula embedding for mathematical information retrieval: Can mathematical formulae be embedded like a natural language? ArXiv abs/1707.05154 (2017)
9. Greiner-Petter, A., Schubotz, M., Cohl, H.S., Gipp, B.: Semantic preserving bijective mappings for expressions involving special functions between computer algebra systems and document preparation systems. Aslib J. Inf. Manag **71**(3), 415–439 (2019)
10. Greiner-Petter, A., et al.: Math-word embedding in math search and semantic extraction. Scientometrics **125**(3), 3017–3046 (2020). https://doi.org/10.1007/s11192-020-03502-9
11. Hu, W., et al.: Strategies for pre-training graph neural networks. In: Proceedings of the 8th International Conference on Learning Representations (2020)
12. Kohlhase, M.: Using LaTex as a semantic markup format. Math. Comput. Sci. **2**(2), 279–304 (2008)
13. Kristianto, G.Y., Topic, G., Aizawa, A.: MCAT math retrieval system for NTCIR-12 mathir task. In: Proceedings of the 12th NTCIR Conference on Evaluation of Information Access Technologies, pp. 323–330. National Institute of Informatics (2016)
14. Krstovski, K., Blei, D.: Equation embeddings. ArXiv abs/1803.09123 (2018)
15. Mansouri, B., Rohatgi, S., Oard, D.W., Wu, J., Giles, C.L., Zanibbi, R.: Tangent-CFT: an embedding model for mathematical formulas. In: Proceedings of the 2019 ACM SIGIR International Conference on Theory of Information Retrieval, pp. 11–18. Association for Computing Machinery (2019)
16. Mikolov, T., Chen, K., Corrado, G., Dean, J.: Efficient estimation of word representations in vector space. In: Proceedings of the 1st International Conference on Learning Representations, pp. 1–12 (2013)
17. Miller, B.R., Youssef, A.: Technical aspects of the digital library of mathematical functions. Ann. Math. Artif. Intell. **38**(1), 121–136 (2003)
18. Pathak, A., Pakray, P., Das, R.: LSTM neural network based math information retrieval. In: Proceedings of the 2nd International Conference on Advanced Computational and Communication Paradigms, pp. 1–6 (2019)
19. Pavan Kumar, P., Agarwal, A., Bhagvati, C.: A structure based approach for mathematical expression retrieval. In: Sombattheera, C., Loi, N.K., Wankar, R., Quan, T. (eds.) MIWAI 2012. LNCS (LNAI), vol. 7694, pp. 23–34. Springer, Heidelberg (2012). https://doi.org/10.1007/978-3-642-35455-7_3

20. Pfahler, L., Morik, K.: Semantic search in millions of equations. In: Proceedings of the 26th ACM SIGKDD International Conference on Knowledge Discovery & Data Mining, pp. 135–143. Association for Computing Machinery (2020)
21. Sakai, T.: Alternatives to bpref. In: Proceedings of the 30th International ACM SIGIR Conference on Research and Development in Information Retrieval, pp. 71–78. Association for Computing Machinery (2007)
22. Schubotz, M., Greiner-Petter, A., Scharpf, P., Meuschke, N., Cohl, H.S., Gipp, B.: Improving the representation and conversion of mathematical formulae by considering their textual context. In: Proceedings of the 18th ACM/IEEE on Joint Conference on Digital Libraries, pp. 233–242. Association for Computing Machinery (2018)
23. Sojka, P., Líška, M.: The art of mathematics retrieval. In: Proceedings of the 11th ACM Symposium on Document Engineering, pp. 57–60. Association for Computing Machinery (2011)
24. Thanda, A., Agarwal, A., Singla, K., Prakash, A., Gupta, A.: A document retrieval system for math queries. In: Proceedings of the 12th NTCIR Conference on Evaluation of Information Access Technologies, pp. 346–353. National Institute of Informatics (2016)
25. Yasunaga, M., Lafferty, J.D.: TopicEq: a joint topic and mathematical equation model for scientific texts. Proc. AAAI Conf. Artif. Intell. **33**, 7394–7401 (2019)
26. Zanibbi, R., Aizawa, A., Kohlhase, M., Ounis, I., Topic, G., Davila, K.: NTCIR-12 MathIR task overview. In: Proceedings of the 12th NTCIR Conference on Evaluation of Information Access Technologies, pp. 299–308. National Institute of Informatics (2016)
27. Zanibbi, R., Blostein, D.: Recognition and retrieval of mathematical expressions. Int. J. Doc. Anal. Recogn. **15**(4), 331–357 (2011)
28. Zanibbi, R., Davila, K., Kane, A., Tompa, F.W.: Multi-stage math formula search: using appearance-based similarity metrics at scale. In: Proceedings of the 39th International ACM SIGIR Conference on Research and Development in Information Retrieval, pp. 145–154. Association for Computing Machinery (2016)
29. Zanibbi, R., Oard, D.W., Agarwal, A., Mansouri, B.: Overview of ARQMath 2020: CLEF lab on answer retrieval for questions on math. In: Arampatzis, A., et al. (eds.) CLEF 2020. LNCS, vol. 12260, pp. 169–193. Springer, Cham (2020). https://doi.org/10.1007/978-3-030-58219-7_15
30. Zhong, W., Rohatgi, S., Wu, J., Giles, C.L., Zanibbi, R.: Accelerating substructure similarity search for formula retrieval. In: Jose, J.M., et al. (eds.) ECIR 2020. LNCS, vol. 12035, pp. 714–727. Springer, Cham (2020). https://doi.org/10.1007/978-3-030-45439-5_47
31. Zhong, W., Zanibbi, R.: Structural similarity search for formulas using leaf-root paths in operator subtrees. In: Azzopardi, L., Stein, B., Fuhr, N., Mayr, P., Hauff, C., Hiemstra, D. (eds.) ECIR 2019. LNCS, vol. 11437, pp. 116–129. Springer, Cham (2019). https://doi.org/10.1007/978-3-030-15712-8_8

10 Years Later: The Mathematics Subject Classification and Linked Open Data

Susanne Arndt[1], Patrick Ion[1,2,3], Mila Runnwerth[1], Moritz Schubotz[1,2,3(✉)], and Olaf Teschke[3]

[1] TIB Leibniz Information Centre for Science and Technology, Hanover, Germany
{susanne.arndt,mila.runnwerth}@tib.eu
[2] University of Michigan, Ann Arbor, MI, USA
[3] zbMATH, FIZ Karlsruhe, Karlsruhe, Germany
{moritz.schubotz,olaf.teschke}@fiz-karlsruhe.de

Abstract. Ten years ago, the Mathematics Subject Classification MSC 2010 was released, and a corresponding machine-readable Linked Open Data collection was published using the Simple Knowledge Organization System (SKOS). Now, the new MSC 2020 is out.

This paper recaps the last ten years of working on machine-readable MSC data and presents the new machine-readable MSC 2020. We describe the processing required to convert the version of record, as agreed by the editors of zbMATH and Mathematical Reviews, into the Linked Open Data form we call MSC2020-SKOS. The new form includes explicit marking of the changes from 2010 to 2020, some translations of English code descriptions into Chinese, Italian, and Russian, and extra material relating MSC to other mathematics classification efforts. We also outline future potential uses for MSC2020-SKOS in semantic indexing and sketch its embedding in a larger vision of scientific research data.

Keywords: Mathematics Subject Classification (MSC) · Linked Open Data (LOD) · Simple Knowledge Organisation System (SKOS)

1 Introduction

The Mathematics Subject Classification (MSC) is a subject-specific indexing schema for mathematics. Like universal library classifications such as the Dewey Decimal Classification[1], the MSC can be used to assign to mathematical knowledge, whether in a printed book, electronic journal article, or conference recording, codes representing topics (categories or classes of mathematical items) covered within the discipline of mathematics or closely related research areas. The MSC is well established in the community and used by scientists, publishers, and librarians. Beyond indexing mathematical research resources, it is also employed

---

S. Arndt, P. Ion, M. Runnwerth, M. Schubotz and O. Teschke—All authors contributed equally.

[1] https://www.loc.gov/aba/dewey/.

© Springer Nature Switzerland AG 2021
F. Kamareddine and C. Sacerdoti Coen (Eds.): CICM 2021, LNAI 12833, pp. 153–158, 2021.
https://doi.org/10.1007/978-3-030-81097-9_12

to describe specialties desired for academic positions or content of conference talks. It plays a very useful role in matching papers to suitable reviewers, especially at the two major post-publication reviewing services in mathematics who are responsible for the MSC.

In 2020, the fourth official major release was published by the executive editors of Mathematical Reviews (MR) and zbMATH [2]. Although minor modifications are implemented as needed by MR and zbMATH, major revisions are released each decade. The editorial process is governed by MR and zbMATH in collaboration. Suggestions from mathematicians or knowledge engineers are submitted, both by mail and at the msc2020.org website, and their adoption is discussed subsequently. As of last Friday, 7 May 2021, all open issues resulting from the feedback on the MSC2020 revision have been resolved by MR and zbMATH, and MSC 2020 has its final form at last; a definitive SKOS form can now be made.

The MSC is organised into three hierarchical levels: The 63 top levels list all major mathematical fields as topics. They range from the foundations of mathematics to algebra, analysis, geometry and topology, and also include a wide array of topics concerning mathematics in its applications. The MSC is fundamentally a simple three-level tree; it can be thought of as rooted in a node for all mathematics of which the top-level classes are children, and is actually a rooted labelled planar tree in mathematical terms. The 1.037 s-level classes represent sub-fields of each speciality. The 5.503 third-level classes reflect the intricacies of sub-fields, for instance, the subtleties of different views on real or complex functions. In addition there are cross-references from one topic to another of various types.

Each class is assigned a code in a notation with five characters, e.g., 68-XX or 03B25. The first two digits indicate the top level classes numbered from 00 to 97 with gaps that leave room for future developments; the remaining three characters of top level codes are '-XX'. For instance classes 19, 37 and 74 have all been added since 1980. In practice, MR and zbMATH editors, and others, often omit these last three characters, e.g., one uses '68' as a short form for '68-XX' to refer to Computer Science, or 11 for Number Theory.(categories or classes)

The second level classes are of two kinds (we are using the digits 99 as placeholders to. illustrate the formats):

99-99 Second-level classes with codes that begin with the two digits of a top-level class, then a hyphen "-", and are followed by two digits; these are used for formal meta descriptions providing special categories for such items as textbooks, historical works, e. g., 11-03 for history of number theory or 11-06 for conference proceedings in number theory. MSC 2020 extended these facet classes in accordance with the needs of the community, and standardized their relation with subject classes, by the introduction of further numerical codes, e. g, '-10' classes for mathematical modeling and simulation, and '-11' for research data across the top level classes (e. g., 11-11 for research data in number theory).

99Axx Classes whose codes have the structure of two digits, an uppercase letter, followed by two lowercase x's; these indicate specific mathematical areas within a top-level class. For example, 11Axx is the second-level category for 'Elementary number theory'.

Brid finally, the third-level classes are the narrowest and most specialised categories for annotating mathematical information. Their codes can be recognised from an uppercase letter in third position followed by two decimal digits, e. g., 03B25 for "Decidability of theories and sets of sentences [See also 11U05, 12L05, 20F10]".

Figure 1 shows the inner hierarchical structure of four selected MSC classes 00, 11, 31 and 45; one sees the subtrees rooted on the major classes displayed, and that Number Theory has been much more finely coded than the other three subjects.[2]

While no top-level class has been changed in the MSC2020 version, several second-level classes have been added and reorganized, as have many third-level classes. One may note the large variation in the granularity of the classifications provided, which reflects the different needs of the respective mathematical commu-

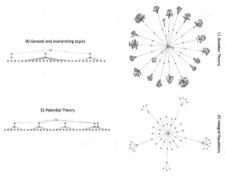

Fig. 1. Example visualisations of the hierarchical distribution within four MSC (2010) classes provided by [8].

nities. Accordingly, the number of documents assigned particular third-level classes varies a lot and is influenced by the different publication cultures within mathematics. Hence, one must be very careful when performing quantitative scientometric analysis using MSC classes – pure comparison of numbers will often be very misleading.

Apart from the reorganization of the second-level facet classes mentioned above, another significant feature of MSC2020 has been a complete overhaul of the descriptive texts with the aim of more precise disambiguations. The experience from the SKOSification of MSC2010 has been extremely helpful in this regard. Now, every single description of a third-level class is unique regardless of its top level or second level components; this used not to be so as descriptive text was reused. The relations between MSC classes have been standardized accordingly.

Class name changes are subject to careful editorial review by zbMATH and MR and not made lightly. The problem of shifting meaning, and community attention, within mathematics is one of those that management of this branch of knowledge has to deal with.

---

[2] That this is so reflects that the AMS published three ever larger collections of Reviews in Number Theory, edited by William J. Leveque and Richard K.Guy. As these thousands of reviews were collected together it became possible to distinguish nuances in sub-sub-topics, and an extension of the codes beyond 5 characters was suggested; that is the 3-level tree was to be extended with more levels.

The first conversion of the MSC to RDF Linked Data was published in 2012 as a Turtle serialisation [4,5]. The motivation was to encourage reuse, maintenance, and versatile access with a low-threshold according to the best practices of the time [5]. The modeling decisions made then have been comprehensively documented in [4]. SKOS Core was chosen as a point of departure and gradually extended to represent the MSC's semantic subtleties. This resulted in an extension *mscvocab* defining inter alia: *related part of*, *see also*, and *see mainly*. Another subject specific characteristic is the use of the Mathematical Markup Language (MathML)[3] within a SKOS vocabulary.

The data required to represent the complete model for MSC 2010 are publicly available[4].

This approach inspired other projects tackling semantification of mathematics according to LOD principles, for example *OntoMathPRO* [6] or *coli-conc* [1]. The *Encyclopedia of mathematics* used to annotate its records with the SKOSified MSC 2010 via SPARQL query [7].

2   MSC 2020 SKOSification

The latest release gives us an opportunity to revisit and improve the Linked Open Data forrn of the MSC. We challenge, and largely, confirm the concept modeling decisions made before. Moreover, we add state-of-the-art metadata to describe the different SKOS versions of each release, and license information to legally describe and verify its open access use. Finally, we justify our approach with specific use cases which rely on an RDF Linked Data representation of the MSC 2020 (including back-links to its history).

2.1   Reasons for a New Version

The first SKOS model showed a level of sophistication that we would like to adhere to, i. e. there will be no unnecessary modifications.

An obvious reason for a new SKOS version are the MSC modifications made between the two releases MSC 2010 and 2020. In addition, particularly for further reuse in German speaking countries, we are adding German labels.

Specifically for reuse in web applications we complement the literals in LaTeX syntax with consistent HTML (including MathML) syntax. We do not, however, additionally provide plain text literals, instead for these we refer to conversion tools like the *html-to-text npm package*[5].

Significant reasons for a revised SKOS formalisation of the MSC are three specific use cases in libraries:

1. Automated subject indexing of mathematical library inventories with the toolkit annif [9]. The optimal input format for classifications and vocabularies is a Turtle serialisation.

---

[3] https://www.w3.org/TR/MathML3/.

[4] http://msc2010.org/resources/MSC/2010/info/.

[5] https://www.npmjs.com/package/html-to-text.

2. Providing a SKOS version compatible with the MSC2010s for the extensive mapping project *coli-conc*, including its mapping editor *Cocoda* [1]. The project already records the Dewey Decimal Classification, the MSC 2010, and Wikidata and includes several mappings between classifications.

3. The *Open Research Knowledge Graph* (ORKG) aims at providing machine interpretable semantic graphs for research questions and individual papers in order to make them comparable using standardised queries [3]. The quality of such a graph depends on the authority files or thesauri upon which it is built. Since the ORKG follows the LOD principles a SKOS formalisation of the MSC would be compatible and could be applied to graphs derived from mathematical scholarly knowledge.

However, those reasons do not touch upon the structural requirements for a sustainable MSC 2020 in the Semantic Web. In a first step, we tidied up minor bugs, e. g. spaces in URIs to guarantee a valid and consistent serialisation. Then, we made well-founded conceptual adjustments as shown in the following subsection. One long-term goal is to reduce the effort of moving from one MSC release to another.

We provide a *GitHub*[6] repository containing the Turtle file itself and its extensions, but also with the appropriate automation scripts.

The final public version of MSC 2020 is expected offer a number of alternate formats for the collected data, as the MSC 2010 did on http://ms2010.org, such as its MediaWiki form, various printable PDFs, KWIC indices, and even the TiddlyWiki tool (done at MR but not yet public).

3 Conclusion and Future Work

Our main objective was to provide a consistent, valid, complete MSC 2020 SKOS version for use-cases in knowledge organisation mainly motivated by uses in libraries. The SKOS version is largely similar from its predecessor but features some improvements with respect to the quality of the data itself and the modeling. It does mean that MSC information available as LOD will be up to date.

Of course, there are still short-term requirements:

As for the MSC 2010, an infrastructure for the MSC 2020 SKOS version needs to be provided: URIs must resolve correctly and meaningfully, an official website must be provided with the data itself, its documentation, and a SPARQL endpoint. This landing page should be linked to a development repository where the SKOS model can be further refined. These are ongoing aspects fo the project which have not been finished yet. As mentioned above, the editorial aspects of MSC 2020 have only just been finalized.

The small number of actual changes to MSC (on the order of hundreds) means that some of the pending additions planned, such as the descriptive text from other languages will and relationships to DDC and UDC will carry over relatively simply from MSC 2010. For instance, not many new translations are

---

[6] https://github.com/runnwerth/MSC2020_SKOS.

needed. They additions have not yet been made public as of this text's writing, but the project continues.

In the future, we would also like to address the following desiderata:

Establish an editorial process that allows for supervised additions (e. g., more languages or discussions) based on the SKOS model representation.

Provide a broad agreement on the modeling decisions and appropriate documentation to facilitate the transition from MSC 2020 to 2030.

References

1. Balakrishnan, U., Voss, J., Soergel, D.: Towards integrated systems for kos management, mapping, and access: Coli-conc and its collaborative computer-assisted kos mapping tool cocoda. In: Proceedings of the Fifteenth International ISKO Conference, Advances in Knowledge Organization, Porto, Portugal, 9–11 July 2018, pp. 693–701 (2018). ISBN 978-3-95650-421-1, https://doi.org/10.5771/9783956504211-693

2. Dunne, E., Hulek, K.: Mathematics subject classification 2020. Not. Am. Math. Soc. **67**(3) (2020). https://www.ams.org/journals/notices/202003/rnoti-p410.pdf

3. Jaradeh, M.Y., et al.: Open research knowledge graph: Next generation infrastructure for semantic scholarly knowledge. In: Proceedings of the 10th International Conference on Knowledge Capture, K-CAP '19, pp. 243–246. Association for Computing Machinery (2019). ISBN 9781450370080, https://doi.org/10.1145/3360901.3364435

4. Lange, C., et al.: Bringing mathematics to the web of data: the case of the mathematics subject classification. In: Simperl, E., Cimiano, P., Polleres, A., Corcho, O., Presutti, V. (eds.) ESWC 2012. LNCS, vol. 7295, pp. 763–777. Springer, Heidelberg (2012). https://doi.org/10.1007/978-3-642-30284-8_58

5. Lange, C., et al.: Reimplementing the mathematics subject classification (MSC) as a linked open dataset. In: Jeuring, J., et al. (eds.) CICM 2012. LNCS (LNAI), vol. 7362, pp. 458–462. Springer, Heidelberg (2012). https://doi.org/10.1007/978-3-642-31374-5_36

6. Nevzorova, O.A., Zhiltsov, N., Kirillovich, A., Lipachev, E.: OntoMathPRO ontology: a linked data hub for mathematics. In: Klinov, P., Mouromtsev, D. (eds.) KESW 2014. CCIS, vol. 468, pp. 105–119. Springer, Cham (2014). https://doi.org/10.1007/978-3-319-11716-4_9

7. Rehmann, U.: Encyclopedia of mathematics - now enhanced by StatProb: another invitation for cooperation. Eur. Math. Soc. Newsl. **100**, 5–6 (2016). ISSN 1027–488X, https://www.ems-ph.org/journals/newsletter/pdf/2016-06-100.pdf

8. Schreiber, M.: Mathematics subject classification graphs (2011). https://purl.org/zb/12, Accessed 23 Mar 2021

9. Suominen, O.: Annif: diy automated subject indexing using multiple algorithms. Liber Q. (2019). https://doi.org/10.18352/lq.10285

WebMIaS on Docker
Deploying Math-Aware Search in a Single Line of Code

Dávid Lupták$^{(\boxtimes)}$ ⓘ, Vít Novotný ⓘ, Michal Štefánik ⓘ,
and Petr Sojka ⓘ

Faculty of Informatics, Masaryk University, Brno, Czech Republic
{dluptak,witiko,stefanik.m}@mail.muni.cz, sojka@fi.muni.cz
https://mir.fi.muni.cz/

Abstract. Math informational retrieval (MIR) search engines are absent in the wide-spread production use, even though documents in the STEM fields contain many mathematical formulae, which are sometimes more important than text for understanding. We have developed and open-sourced the WebMIaS MIR search engine that has been successfully deployed in the European Digital Mathematics Library (EuDML). However, its deployment is difficult to automate due to the complexity of this task. Moreover, the solutions developed so far to tackle this challenge are imperfect in terms of speed, maintenance, and robustness. In this paper, we will describe the virtualization of WebMIaS using Docker that solves all three problems and allows anyone to deploy containerized WebMIaS in a single line of code. The publicly available Docker image will also help the community push the development of math-aware search engines in the ARQMath workshop series.

Keywords: Math information retrieval · WebMIaS · MIaS · Docker virtualization · Digital mathematical libraries · Math web search · EuDML · ARQMath

1 Introduction

Searching for math formulae does not appear as a task for search engines at first glance. Text retrieval is dominant among search engines, while math-awareness is a specialized area in the field of information retrieval: Springer's LaTeX Search, the MathWebSearch of zbMATH Open (formerly known as Zentralblatt MATH), and the Math Indexer and Searcher (MIaS) of the European Digital Mathematics Library (EuDML) are all examples of systems with math-aware search deployed in production. Our MIaS search engine [9] runs on the industry-grade, robust, and highly-scalable full-text search engine Apache Lucene with our own preprocessing of mathematical formulae. The text is tokenized and stemmed to unify inflected word forms whereas math is expected

The second author's work was graciously funded by the South Moravian Centre for International Mobility as a part of the Brno Ph.D. Talent project.

© Springer Nature Switzerland AG 2021
F. Kamareddine and C. Sacerdoti Coen (Eds.): CICM 2021, LNAI 12833, pp. 159–164, 2021.
https://doi.org/10.1007/978-3-030-81097-9_13

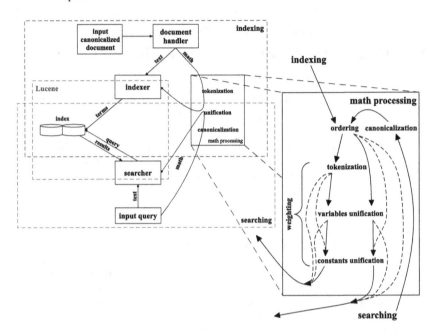

Fig. 1. The architecture of MIaS with indexing and searching phases overlapping over Lucene index. Besides standard text processing, the math input from indexing (a document) and searching (a query) stage is canonicalized, ordered, tokenized, and unified, afterward returned back to the indexer and searcher module, respectively.

to be in the MathML format, which is then canonicalized, ordered, tokenized, and unified, see Fig. 1.

To provide a web user interface for MIaS, we have developed and opensourced the WebMIaS [6,9] search engine. In WebMIaS, users can input their mixed queries in a combination of text and math with a native support for LaTeX and MathML. Matches are conveniently highlighted in the search results. The user interface of WebMIaS is shown in Fig. 2.

Although the (Web)MIaS system has been deployed in the European Digital Mathematics Library (EuDML) already, the complicated deployment process might be an obstacle for a more wide-spread deployment to other digital mathematics libraries that avail of or can extend to the MathML markup. To solve this problem, we will describe the virtualization of WebMIaS using Docker [3] that allows anyone to deploy WebMIaS in a single line of code. Whether you have an open-access repository such as DSpace, or just a number of mathematical documents, you can benefit from the math-aware search provided by WebMIaS. For testing, we also provide the MREC dataset [4].

In the rest of our paper, we will describe our deployment process in Sect. 2, evaluate the speed and quality of WebMIaS in Sect. 3, and conclude in Sect. 4.

Match [all ▼] of the following rules

[Any field   ▼] [Einstein   ]
[Any field   ▼] [vortex density   ] remove
Add clause

Contains the following formula:

[k/H_0^2]

Rendered: k/H_0^2 Search using: [presentation and content ▼]

                                                         Search in: [NTCIR-0 ▼]
[Search]   Verbose output: ☐

Total hits: 16, showing 1-16 . Core searching time: 246 ms Total searching time: 745 ms

<u>Exact solutions of embedding the 4D Universe in a 5D Einstein manifold</u>

... where $\Omega_k = k/H_0^2$ and ... , $\Omega_m = C/H_0^2$, and ... Exact solutions of embedding the 4D Universe in a 5D Einstein manifold ... Provided that the induced matter is described by a perfect fluid with density score = 1.171408
f085122.xhtml - cached XHTML

Fig. 2. Searching text and formulae with a single mixed query in WebMIaS.

2   Deployment Process Description

All modules of the MIaS system are Java projects, so users first need to 1) install the Java environment prerequisites and then 2) build the respective system modules. The next step in the process is to 3) index a dataset of mathematical documents using the command-line interface of MIaS. Finally, the users can 4) run Apache Tomcat with the WebMIaS servlet as a user interface.

Over the years, we have attempted to automate the above steps into running a single Makefile or Jupyter Notebook. However, these solutions were slow, fragile, and hard to maintain. We propose a better solution using lightweight virtualization via Docker with instant deployment, a short but powerful Dockerfile configuration, and a complete workflow that automates all the steps of the deployment process. Moreover, GitHub Actions provide continuous integration and automate the publishing of Docker images to Docker Hub.

Both MIaS and WebMIaS are containerized into separate Docker images named miratmu/mias and miratmu/webmias, respectively. This allows users to run both the indexing and the retrieval without a specific configuration of the environment. Resolving the dependencies and building all modules is up to the continuous integration workflow (see Fig. 3), and users receive Docker images with everything prebuilt. After downloading a dataset to the working directory,

Fig. 3. The continuous integration of *WebMIaS* and the build times of the respective packages: *MathMLCan* canonicalizes different MathML encodings of equivalent formulae. *MathMLUnificator* generalizes distinct mathematical formulae so that they can be structurally unified. *MIaSMath* adds math processing capabilities to Lucene or Solr. *MIaS* indexes text with math in Lucene/Solr-based full-text search engines. Finally, *WebMIaS* provides a web interface for *MIaS*.

users can index the `dataset` directory into the `index` directory using MIaS, see Listing 1.

```
1  $ wget https://mir.fi.muni.cz/MREC/MREC2011.4.439.tar.bz2
2  $ mkdir dataset ; tar xj -f MREC2011.4.439.tar.bz2 -C dataset
3  $ docker run -v "$PWD"/dataset:/dataset:ro -v "$PWD"/index:/index:rw --rm
   ↪  miratmu/mias
4  $ docker run -v "$PWD"/dataset:/dataset:ro -v "$PWD"/index:/index:ro --rm
   ↪  --name webmias -d -p 127.0.0.1:8888:8080 miratmu/webmias
```

Finally, the users can deploy WebMIaS in a single line of code with the `dataset` and `index` directories in a container named `webmias` running at the TCP port 8888 on the `localhost`. The WebMIaS system will be running at https://www.localhost:8888/WebMIaS/.

3   Evaluation

We performed a speed evaluation of MIaS on the MREC dataset [4] (see Table 1), and a quality evaluation on the NTCIR-10 Math [1,5], NTCIR-11 Math-2 [2,9] (see Table 2), NTCIR-12 MathIR [8,10], and ARQMath 2020 [7,11] datasets. We also measured the time to deploy WebMIaS without Docker (see Fig. 3).

The speed evaluation shows that the indexing time of our system is linear in the number of indexed documents and that the average query time is 469 ms. Additionally, the dockerization of WebMIaS reduces the deployment time from

Table 1. The linear indexing speed on the MREC dataset using 448G of RAM, and eight Intel Xeon^{TM} X7560 2.26 GHz CPUs.

	Mathematical (sub) formulae		Indexing time (min)	
Documents	Input	Indexed	Real (Wall clock)	CPU
10,000 (2.28%)	3,406,068	64,008,762	35.75 (2.05%)	35.05
100,000 (22.76%)	36,328,126	670,335,243	384.44 (22.00%)	366.54
439,423 (100%)	158,106,118	2,910,314,146	1,747.16 (100%)	1,623.22

Table 2. Quality evaluation results on the NTCIR-11 Math-2 dataset. The mean average precision (MAP), and precisions at ten (P@10) and five (P@5) are reported for queries formulated using Presentation (PMath), and Content MathML (CMath), a combination of both (PCMath), and LaTeX. Two different relevance judgement levels of ≥ 1 (partially relevant), and ≥ 3 (relevant) were used to compute the measures. Number between slashes (/·/) is our rank among all teams of NTCIR-11 Math-2 Task.

Measure	Level	PMath	CMath	PCMath	LaTeX
MAP	3	0.3073	**0.3630** /1/	0.3594	0.3357
P@10	3	0.3040	**0.3520** /1/	0.3480	0.3380
P@5	3	0.5120	**0.5680** /1/	0.5560	0.5400
P@10	1	0.5020	0.5440	**0.5520** /1/	0.5400

about 10 min to a matter of seconds. With respect to quality evaluation, MIaS has notably won the NTCIR-11 Math-2 task.

4   Conclusion

An open-source environment brings reproducibility and the possibility of trying out the projects of one's interest without limitations. However, the installation instructions are often hard to follow with many prerequisites and possible conflicts with the running operating environment on the go. Automation tools, continuous integration, and package virtualization ease the development process. With this motivation and in the hope of helping the math community, we have dockerized our math-aware web search engine WebMIaS. As a result, anyone can now deploy WebMIaS in a single line of code. The software is accessible and at the fingertips of the math community, see https://github.com/MIR-MU/WebMIaS.

References

1. Aizawa, A., Kohlhase, M., Ounis, I.: NTCIR-10 math pilot task overview. In: Proceedings of the 10th NTCIR Conference, pp. 654–661. NII, Tokyo (2013)
2. Aizawa, A., Kohlhase, M., Ounis, I., Schubotz, M.: NTCIR-11 math-2 task overview. In: Proceedings of the 11th NTCIR Conference, pp. 88–98. NII, Tokyo (2014). http://research.nii.ac.jp/ntcir/workshop/OnlineProceedings11/pdf/NTCIR/OVERVIEW/01-NTCIR11-OV-MATH-AizawaA.pdf
3. Boettiger, C.: An introduction to Docker for reproducible research. ACM SIGOPS Oper. Syst. Rev. **49**(1), 71–79 (2015)
4. Líška, M., Sojka, P., Růžička, M., Mravec, P.: Web interface and collection for mathematical retrieval: WebMIaS and MREC. In: Proceedings of DML 2011 Workshop, pp. 77–84. Masaryk University (2011). https://hdl.handle.net/10338.dmlcz/702604

5. Líška, M., Sojka, P., Růžička, M.: Similarity search for mathematics: masaryk university team at the NTCIR-10 math task. In: Proceedings of the 10th NTCIR Conference, pp. 686–691. NII Tokyo, Tokyo (2013). https://research.nii.ac.jp/ntcir/workshop/OnlineProceedings10/pdf/NTCIR/MATH/06-NTCIR10-MATH-LiskaM.pdf

6. Líška, M., Sojka, P., Růžička, M.: Math indexer and searcher web interface. In: Watt, S.M., Davenport, J.H., Sexton, A.P., Sojka, P., Urban, J. (eds.) CICM 2014. LNCS (LNAI), vol. 8543, pp. 444–448. Springer, Cham (2014). https://doi.org/10.1007/978-3-319-08434-3_36

7. Novotný, V., Sojka, P., Štefánik, M., Lupták, D.: Three is better than one. In: CEUR Workshop Proceedings, Thessaloniki, Greece, pp. 1–30 (2020). http://ceur-ws.org/Vol-2696/paper_235.pdf

8. Růžička, M., Sojka, P., Líška, M.: Math indexer and searcher under the hood: fine-tuning query expansion and unification strategies. In: Proceedings of the 12th NTCIR Conference, pp. 331–337. NII Tokyo (2016). https://research.nii.ac.jp/ntcir/workshop/OnlineProceedings12/pdf/ntcir/MathIR/05-NTCIR12-MathIR-RuzickaM.pdf

9. Růžička, M., Sojka, P., Líška, M.: Math indexer and searcher under the hood: history and development of a winning strategy. In: Proceedings of the 11th NTCIR Conference, pp. 127–134 (2014) https://is.muni.cz/auth/publication/1201956/en

10. Zanibbi, R., Aizawa, A., Kohlhase, M., Ounis, I., Topic, G., Davila, K.: NTCIR-12 MathIR task overview. In: Proceedings of the 12th NTCIR, pp. 299–308. NII Tokyo (2016)

11. Zanibbi, R., Oard, D.W., Agarwal, A., Mansouri, B.: Overview of ARQMath 2020: CLEF lab on answer retrieval for questions on math. In: Arampatzis, A., et al. (eds.) CLEF 2020. LNCS, vol. 12260, pp. 169–193. Springer, Cham (2020). https://doi.org/10.1007/978-3-030-58219-7_15

Teaching and Geometric Reasoning

Learning to Solve Geometric Construction Problems from Images

Jaroslav Macke[1,2] , Jiri Sedlar[2(✉)] , Miroslav Olsak[3] , Josef Urban[2] , and Josef Sivic[2]

[1] Charles University, Prague, Czech Republic
[2] Czech Technical University, Prague, Czech Republic
jiri.sedlar@cvut.cz
[3] University of Innsbruck, Innsbruck, Austria

Abstract. We describe a purely image-based method for finding geometric constructions with a ruler and compass in the Euclidea geometric game. The method is based on adapting the Mask R-CNN state-of-the-art visual recognition neural architecture and adding a tree-based search procedure to it. In a supervised setting, the method learns to solve all 68 kinds of geometric construction problems from the first six level packs of Euclidea with an average 92% accuracy. When evaluated on new kinds of problems, the method can solve 31 of the 68 kinds of Euclidea problems. We believe that this is the first time that purely image-based learning has been trained to solve geometric construction problems of this difficulty.

Keywords: Computer vision · Visual recognition · Automatic geometric reasoning · Solving geometric construction problems

1 Introduction

In this work, we aim to create a purely image-based method for solving geometric construction problems with a ruler, compass, and related tools, such as a perpendicular bisector. Our main objective is to develop suitable machine learning models based on convolutional neural architectures to predict the next steps in the geometric constructions represented as images.

In more detail, the input to our neural model is an image of the scene consisting of the parts that are already constructed (red) and the goal parts that remain to be drawn (green). The output of the neural model is the next step of the construction. An example of the problem setup is shown in Fig. 1.

Our first objective is to solve as many geometric construction problems as possible when the method is used in a *supervised setting*. This means solving

This work was partly supported by the European Regional Development Fund under the projects IMPACT and AI&Reasoning (reg. no. CZ.02.1.01/0.0/0.0/15_003/0000468 and CZ.02.1.01/0.0/0.0/15_003/0000466) and the ERC Consolidator grant *SMART* no. 714034.

F. Kamareddine and C. Sacerdoti Coen (Eds.): CICM 2021, LNAI 12833, pp. 167–184, 2021.
https://doi.org/10.1007/978-3-030-81097-9_14

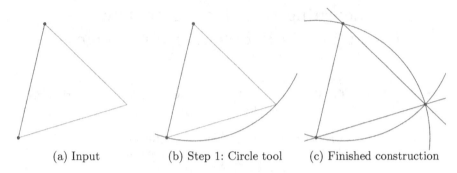

(a) Input   (b) Step 1: Circle tool   (c) Finished construction

Fig. 1. Example solution of Euclidea level *Alpha-05* (construct an equilateral triangle with the given side). In all examples, the red channel contains the current state of the construction and the green channel the remaining goal. (a) Initial state: one side is given and the goal is to construct the remaining two sides. (b) State after the first step: construction of a circle. (c) State after the last step: finished construction. (Color figure online)

construction problems that may look very different from images in the training problems, but are solved by the same abstract sequences of construction steps. This setting is still hard because the neural model needs to decide where and how to draw the next construction step in a new image. Our second objective is to solve problems unseen during the training. This means finding sequences of construction steps that were never seen in the training examples. We evaluate our method in both these settings.

Table 1. Euclidea tools and their argument types. The asterisk denotes interchangeable arguments. For a detailed description of the tools and their arguments see the supplementary material available at the project webpage [1].

Tool	Arguments
Point	(coordinates)
Line	(point*, point*)
Circle	(point, point)
Perpendicular Bisector	(point*, point*)
Angle Bisector	(point*, point, point*)
Perpendicular	(line, point)
Parallel	(line, point)
Compass	(point*, point*, point)

We train and test our models on instances of geometric problems from the Euclidea [2] game. Euclidea is an online construction game where each level represents one kind of geometric problem. Table 1 lists the construction tools available in Euclidea. Each level specifies which of the tools can be used. Euclidea construction problems vary across a wide spectrum of difficulty. While lower levels are relatively simple or designed specifically to introduce a new tool, more advanced levels quickly grow in difficulty. These advanced problems are not trivial even for reasonably trained mathematicians, including participants of the International Mathematics Olympiad (IMO). Our high-level research objective is to explore the question whether computers can learn to solve geometric problems similarly to humans, who may come up with solutions without knowing any algebraic and analytic methods. Solving formally stated IMO problems has already been considered as a grand reasoning challenge[1].

Solving construction problems from input images poses several challenges. First, the same geometric problem can have an infinite amount of different variants with a different scale, rotation or different relative position of individual geometric primitives. The visual solver has to deal with this variability. Second, the search space of all possible geometric constructions is very large. For example, a construction with ten steps and (for simplicity) ten different possible construction choices at each step would require searching 10^{10} possible constructions. To address these challenges we adapt a state-of-the-art convolutional neural network visual recognizer that can deal with the large variability of the visual input and combine it with a tree-search procedure to search the space of possible constructions. We namely build on the Mask R-CNN object detector [3] that has demonstrated excellent performance in localizing objects (e.g. cars, pedestrians or chairs) in images and adapt it to predict next steps in geometric constructions, for example, to draw a circle passing through a point in the construction, as shown in Fig. 1b. Despite the success on real images, the off-the-shelf "Vanilla" Mask R-CNN approach can solve only the very basic level packs of the Euclidea game and adapting Mask R-CNN to our task is non-trivial. In this work we investigate: (i) how to train the network from synthetically generated data, (ii) how to convert the network outputs into meaningful construction steps, (iii) how to incorporate the construction history, (iv) how to deal with degenerate constructions and (v) how to incorporate the Mask R-CNN outputs in a tree-based search strategy.

Contributions. In summary, the contributions of this work are three-fold. First, we describe an approach to solving geometric construction problems directly from images by learning from example constructions. This is achieved by adapting a state-of-the-art Mask R-CNN visual recognizer and combining it with a tree search procedure to explore the space of construction hypotheses. Second, we demonstrate that our approach can solve the first 68 levels (which cover all available construction tools) of the geometric construction game Euclidea with 92% accuracy. Finally, we show that our approach can also solve new problems, unseen at training. The system as well as our modified Euclidia environment are available online.[2]

---

[1] https://imo-grand-challenge.github.io/.

[2] https://github.com/mackej/Learning-to-solve-geometric-construction-problems-from-images, https://github.com/mirefek/py_euclidea/.

The rest of the paper is structured as follows. Section 2 gives a brief overview of related work. Section 3 presents our Euclidea environment. Section 4 describes the methods we developed to solve problems in the supervised setting. This includes a description of the neural image recognition methods and their modifications for our tasks. Section 5 describes our methods for solving new problems, unseen during the training. This includes generating sets of proposed steps and searching the tree of possible constructions. Section 6 evaluates the methods on levels seen and unseen during the training.

2 Related Work

Visual recognition techniques can be used for interpreting a geometrical question given by a diagram. Such a geometry solver was proposed in [4,5]. The input problem is specified by a diagram and a short text. This input is first decoded into a formal specification describing the input entities and their relations using visual recognition and natural language processing tools. The formal specification is then passed to an optimizer based on basin hopping. In contrast, we do not attempt to convert the input problem into a formal specification but instead use a visual recognizer to directly guide the solution steps with only images as input.

The most studied geometry problems are those where the objective is to find a proof [6]. This contrasts with our work, where we tackle construction problems. An algebraic approach to a specific type of construction problem is used by Argotrics [7]. This is a Prolog-based method for finding constructions that satisfy given axiomatically proven propositions.

Automated provers for geometry problems are mostly of two categories. They are either synthetic [8,9], i.e., they mimic the classical human geometrical reasoning, and prove the problems by applying predefined sets of rules/axioms (similar triangles, inscribed angle theorem, etc.). The other type of solvers are based on algebraic methods such as Wu's method [10] or the Gröbner basis method [11]. These have better performance than the synthetic ones but do not provide a human readable solution. There are also methods combining the two approaches. They may for example use some algebra but keep the computations simple (the Full angle method or the Area method [12]). We cannot compare directly with such provers because of the constructional nature of the problems we study. However, our approach is complementary to the above methods and can be used, for example, to suggest possible next construction steps based on the visual configuration of the current scene.

Automated theorem provers (ATPs) such as Otter [13] and Prover9 [14] have been used for solving geometric problems, e.g., in Tarskian geometry [15–17]. Proof checking in interactive theorem provers (ITPs) such as HOL Light and Coq has been used to verify geometric proofs formally [18]. Both ATPs and ITPs have been in recent years improved by using machine learning and neural guidance [19,20]. ATPs and ITPs however assume that a formalization of the problem is available, which typically includes advanced mathematical education and nontrivial cognitive effort. The formal representations are also closer to text, which informs the choice of neural architectures successfully used in ATPs and ITPs (GNNs, TNNs, Transformers). In contrast, we try to skip the formalization step and learn solving geometric construction problems directly from images. This also means that our methods could be used on arbitrary informal images, such as human geometry drawings, creating their own internal representations.

3   Our Euclidea Geometric Construction Environment

Euclidea is an online geometric construction game in 2-dimensional Euclidean space. The main goal is to find a sequence of construction steps leading from an initial configuration of objects to a given goal configuration. The construction steps utilize a set of straightedge and compass-based tools (see Table 1). Every tool takes up to 3 arguments with values specified by the coordinates of clicks on the image of the scene, e.g., circle(A, B), where A, B are points in the image. Euclidea is divided into 15 level packs (Alpha, Beta, Gamma, ..., Omicron) with increasing difficulty; each level pack contains around 10 levels with a similar focus. In Euclidea, each level has its analytical model, which is projected onto an image and the player does not have access to this model, only to the image. Each construction is validated with the analytical model to prevent cheating by drawing lines or circles only similar to the desired goal.

   In addition, our Euclidea environment can also generate new instances of the levels. A new instance is generated by randomly choosing initial parameters of the level inside Euclidea. However, some of these instances can be "degenerate", i.e., unsolvable based on the image data. To prevent such degenerate configurations, we enforce multiple constraints, e.g., that different points cannot be too close to each other in the image or that a circle radius cannot be too small. We use this process of generating new problem instances for collecting examples to train our model.

4   Supervised Visual Learning Approach

This section describes our method for learning to solve geometric problems. We build on Mask R-CNN [3], a convolutional neural network for the detection and segmentation of objects in images and videos. Given an image, Mask R-CNN outputs bounding boxes, segmentation masks, class labels and confidence scores of objects detected in the input image.

   Mask R-CNN is a convolutional neural network architecture composed of two modules. The first module is a region proposal network that proposes candidate regions in the image that may contain the target object (e.g. a "car"). The second module then, given a proposed candidate region, outputs its class (e.g. "car", "pedestrian" or "background"), bounding box, segmentation mask and confidence score.

   We adapt the Mask R-CNN model for the task of solving geometric construction problems. Figure 2 shows the diagram of our approach. The main idea is to train Mask R-CNN to predict the tool that should be used at a given step, including its arguments. For example, as shown in Fig. 2, the input is the image depicting the current state of the construction in the red channel of the image (three points in red) and the goal in the green channel (the three sides of the triangle). Mask R-CNN predicts here to execute the Line tool. The predicted bounding box of the line is shown in magenta. For this purpose, Mask R-CNN network has to recognize the two points in the input image and predict their location, represented by the rectangular masks. The output masks are then transformed to coordinates of the two points that need to be "clicked" to execute the Line tool in the Euclidea environment.

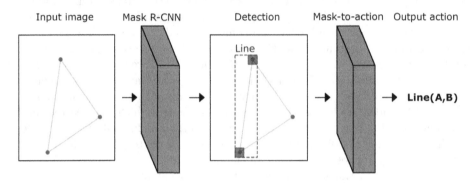

Fig. 2. Diagram of our approach. The goal is to construct a triangle given three points. The input is an RGB image with the current state of the construction in the red channel (the three points) and the goal is given in the green channel (the three sides of the triangle). The Mask R-CNN predicts a line between two of the three points. The dashed rectangle denotes the bounding box of the line and the small square magenta masks denote the two points on the line. This Mask R-CNN line detection is then converted into a Euclidea tool action, $Line(A, B)$, represented by the tool name and its arguments (the locations of the two points). The process that converts the Mask R-CNN output masks into actions in the Euclidea environment is described in Sect. 4.2. (Color figure online)

To train Mask R-CNN to solve geometric construction problems, we have to create training data that represent applications of the Euclidea tools and adjust the network outputs to work with our Euclidea environment. To generate training data for a given Euclidea level, we follow a predefined construction of the level and transform it to match the specific generated level instances (see Sect. 3). Each use of a Euclidea tool corresponds to one example in the training data. We call each application of a tool in our environment an *action*, represented by the tool name and the corresponding click coordinates. For example, the Line tool needs two action clicks, representing two points on the constructed line.

The following sections show the generation of training data for Mask R-CNN (Sect. 4.1), describe how we derive Euclidea actions from the detected masks at test time (Sect. 4.2), present our algorithm for solving construction problems

(Sect. 4.3), and introduce additional components that improve the performance of our method (Sect. 4.4).

4.1   Action to Mask: Generating Training Data

Here we explain how we generate the training data for training Mask R-CNN to predict the next construction step. In contrast to detecting objects in images where object detections typically do not have any pre-defined ordering, some of the geometric tools have non-interchangeable arguments and we will have to modify the output of Mask R-CNN to handle such tools.

We represent the Mask R-CNN input as a 256×256 RGB image of the scene with the current state in the red channel and the remaining goal in the green channel; the blue channel contains zeros. Note that for visualization purposes, we render the black background as white. Each training example consists of an input image capturing the current state of the construction together with the action specifying the application of a particular tool. The action is specified by a mask and a class, where the class identifies the tool (or its arguments, see below) and the mask encodes the location of each point click needed for application of the tool in the image, represented as a small square around each click location. The Perpendicular tool and Parallel tool have a line as their argument (see Table 1), passed as a mask of either the whole line or one click on the line.

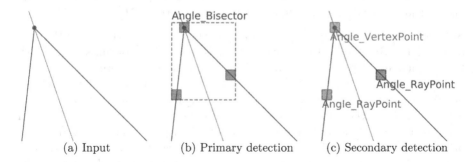

(a) Input   (b) Primary detection   (c) Secondary detection

Fig. 3. An example from training data for Euclidea level *Beta-02* (construct the line that bisects the given angle). The current state is in red and the remaining goal in green. (a) Input for the Mask R-CNN model. (b) Primary detection of the Mask R-CNN model identifying the tool type: Angle Bisector tool (purple). (c) Three secondary detections identifying the arguments of the tool: one angle vertex point (yellow) and two angle ray points (purple and turquoise). (Color figure online)

Primary and Secondary Detections. Encoding clicks as in the previous paragraph is not sufficient for tools with non-interchangeable parameters. For example, the Circle tool has two non-interchangeable parameters: 1) the center and 2) a point on the circle, defining the radius. To distinguish such points, we add a secondary output of the Mask R-CNN model. For example, for the Circle tool, we detect not just the circle itself but also the circle center and the radius point. We denote the detection of the tool (Line tool, Circle tool, ...) as the *primary detection*, and the detection of its parameters as the *secondary detections*. Figure 3 shows an example of primary and secondary detections for the Angle Bisector tool, including the corresponding classes: Angle_Bisector (primary detection), Angle_VertexPoint, and Angle_RayPoint (secondary detections).

4.2   Mask to Action: Converting Output Masks to Euclidea Actions

To solve Euclidea levels, we have to transform the Mask R-CNN output to fit the input of the Euclidea environment. We refer to this step as "mask-to-action" as it converts the output of Mask R-CNN, which is in the form of image masks specifying the primary and secondary detections (see Sect. 4.1), into tool actions in the Euclidea environment. The mask-to-action conversion consists of two stages. The first stage obtains locations of individual "point clicks" from the primary detections for the predicted tool and the second stage determines the order of parameters using the secondary detections.

First Stage: To localize individual points, we use the heat map produced by the final Mask R-CNN layer. The heat map assigns each pixel the probability of being a part of the mask and can be transformed into a binary mask by thresholding. Instead, we use the heat map directly to localize the detected points more accurately. We select points with the highest probability in the masks using a greedy non-maximum-suppression method [21].

Second Stage: We will explain this stage on the example of the Angle Bisector tool (see Fig. 3). A detection of this tool has 4 detection outputs from Mask R-CNN, namely, 1 primary and 3 secondary detections. The primary detection corresponds to the whole tool and the secondary detections to the individual points, i.e., one angle vertex point and two angle ray points (see Fig. 3). To use the Angle Bisector tool, we have to determine the correspondence between the primary and secondary detections. We obtain 3 point coordinates from the primary detection in the first stage, as described above. We can also get 3 points from the 3 secondary detections, one point per detection. Each point in the primary detection should correspond to one point in the secondary detection, but these points may not exactly overlap. The point correspondence is determined by finding a matching between the primary and secondary points that minimizes the sum of distances between the primary and secondary points such that each point is used exactly once.

4.3   Solving Construction Problems by Sequences of Actions

Next, we can create an agent capable of solving Euclidea construction problems. In the previous section, we have described how to get a Euclidea action from Mask R-CNN outputs. However, Mask R-CNN can predict multiple candidate detections (that correspond to different actions) for one input image. Mask R-CNN returns for each detection also its score, representing the confidence of the prediction. To select the next action from the set of candidate actions (derived from Mask R-CNN detections) in each step, the agent follows Algorithm 1, which chooses the action with the highest confidence score at each state.

> **Result:** Test level inference: True if level completed, False otherwise.
> Initialize a level;
> **while** *level not complete* **do**
> > $s \leftarrow$ current state of the level;
> > $p \leftarrow model.predict(s)$;
> > **if** *predictions p are empty* **then**
> > > **return** False;
> >
> > $a \leftarrow$ action from p with highest score;
> > execute a
>
> **return** True;

Algorithm 1: Solving construction problems by choosing the action with the highest score.

4.4 Additional Components of the Approach

Here we introduce several additional extensions to the approach described above and later demonstrate their importance in Sect. 6.

Automatic Point Detection. Our Euclidea environment requires that each point important for the solution is identified using the Point tool. For example, when we have to find the third vertex of the triangle in Fig. 1, we have to use the Point tool to localize the intersections of the circles. The Automatic point detection modification automatically adds points to the intersections of objects.

History Channel. To better recognize which construction steps have already been done and which still need to be constructed, we add a third, history channel (blue) to the input of Mask R-CNN, containing the construction state from the previous step.

4+ Stage Training. Mask R-CNN is typically trained in 2 stages: first, only the head layers are trained, followed by training of the whole network, including the 5-block convolutional backbone. The 4+ Stage training modification splits the training into 3 stages: first, the head layers are trained, then also the fourth and fifth backbone blocks, and finally, the whole network.

Intersection Degeneration Rules. To decide whether a generated level can be solved using only the image information, we apply the following rules to identify degenerate configurations: a) the radius of a circle cannot be too small, b) the distance between points, lines, or their combinations cannot be too small. In this modification, we add a third rule: c) any intersection of geometric primitives cannot be too close to points that are necessary for the construction. This prevents possible alternative solutions from being too close to each other and the auxiliary intersections created during the construction from being too close to points from the initial state and the goal.

On-the-fly Data Generation. Generating training data on-the-fly allows us to (potentially infinitely) expand the training set and thus train better models.

5 Solving Unseen Geometric Problems via Hypothesis Tree Search

In the previous section, we have shown how to train a visual recognition model to predict the next step of a given construction from a large number of examples of the same construction with different geometric configurations of the primitives. In this section, we investigate how to solve new problems, which we have not seen at training time. This is achieved by (i) using models trained for different construction problems (see Sect. 4) to generate *a set of hypotheses* for each construction step of the new problem and then (ii) searching the tree of possible constructions. These two parts are described next.

5.1 Generating Action Hypotheses

Each primary detection from the Mask R-CNN model (see Sect. 4.1) can be transformed into an action. We denote each action, its arguments, and results as a *hypothesis*. The result of an action contains a geometric primitive, constructed during the action execution, and a reward, indicating whether the output primitive is a part of the remaining goal or not. If an action constructs a part of the goal, the reward is $1/n$, where n is the total number of primitives in the initial goal, otherwise it is equal to zero. Figure 4b shows a hypothesis that successfully constructs one of the four lines in the goal and its reward thus equals 0.25.

We can extract multiple actions from the Mask R-CNN model output by considering multiple output candidate detections, transform them into multiple hypotheses, and explore their construction space. We can also utilize hypotheses from models trained for different tasks. However, the Mask R-CNN scores are not comparable across hypotheses from different models, so in a setup with multiple models we have to search even hypotheses with lower scores.

5.2 Tree Search for Exploring Construction Hypotheses

We use tree search to explore the hypothesis space given by the predictions from one or more Mask R-CNN models. The tree search has to render the input image and obtain predictions from all considered Mask R-CNN models in each node of the tree, which increases the time spent in one node. However, as a result, we search only within the space of hypotheses output by the Mask R-CNN models, which is much smaller than the space of all possible constructions. We use iterative deepening, which is an iterated depth-limited search over increasing depth (see Algorithm 2).

Hypotheses produced by different Mask R-CNN models increase the branching factor and thus also the search time. To speed up the tree search, we group all mutually similar hypotheses and explore only one of them. For this purpose, we consider two hypotheses as similar if their output geometric primitive is the same; note that such hypotheses can have different arguments, including different tools.

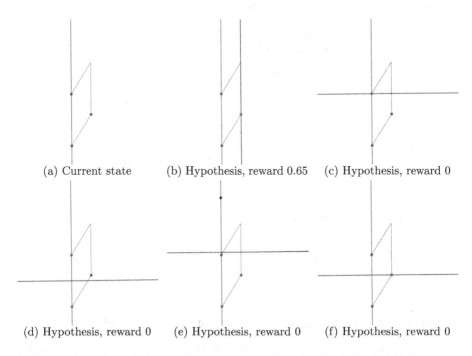

(a) Current state   (b) Hypothesis, reward 0.65   (c) Hypothesis, reward 0

(d) Hypothesis, reward 0   (e) Hypothesis, reward 0   (f) Hypothesis, reward 0

Fig. 4. Multiple hypotheses for the next step in Euclidea level *Epsilon-03* (construct a parallelogram whose three of four vertices are given). (a) Current state. (b) Hypothesis with reward 0.25 that constructs one of the four lines in the goal (green). (c–f) Hypotheses with reward 0. Each image contains the current state (red), remaining goal (green), hypothesis produced by Mask R-CNN (blue), and parameters of the tool (purple). For example, hypothesis (b) selects the Parallel tool to construct the blue line as parallel to the purple line and intersecting the purple point. A positive reward indicates contribution to the goal, so we select the hypothesis (b), which has the highest reward. (Color figure online)

6   Experiments

This section shows the performance of our method for both the *supervised setting*, where we see examples of the specific level in both training and test time, and the *unseen setting*, where we are testing on new levels, not seen during training. We will compare the benefits of the different components of our approach and show an example solution produced by our method.

Result: Solve level with Iterative Deepening.

Function IterativeDeepening-DFS(*InitialState*):

> SolutionMaxLength ⟵ 0;
>
> Solution ⟵ **null**;
>
> **while** *(Solution = **null**) and (SolutionMaxLength < MaxIterationDepth)*
> **do**
>
> > *SolutionMaxLength* ⟵ *SolutionMaxLength* + 1;
> >
> > Solution ⟵ FindSolution(*InitialConfig*, SolutionMaxLength);
>
> **return** Solution

Function FindSolution(*CurrentState, Depth*):

> **if** *CurrentState.IsTheGoal* **then**
> > **return** success // collect solution on the backtracking
>
> **if** *Depth* = 0 **then**
> > **return** null // e.g., solution not found.
>
> *Hypotheses* ⟵ *Models.GetAllHypotheses*(*CurrentState*);
>
> // Hypotheses sorted in the order: Reward, Confidence score
>
> **foreach** *h* ∈ *Hypotheses* **do**
> > *NewState* ⟵ *Apply*(*h, CurrentState*);
> >
> > *Solution* = *FindSolution*(*NewState, Depth* − 1);
> >
> > **if** *Solution* ≠ ***null*** **then**
> > > **return** Solution
>
> **return** null

Algorithm 2: Tree search for exploring construction hypotheses using Iterative Deepening Depth-First Search algorithm.

6.1 Benefits of Different Components of Our Approach

As the base method we use the off-the-shelf Mask R-CNN approach ("Vanilla Mask R-CNN"), which has a low accuracy even on simple Alpha levels. To improve over this baseline, we have introduced several additional components, namely, "Automatic point detection", "History channel", "4+ Stage training", "Intersection degeneration rules", and "On-the-fly data generation" (see Sect. 4.4). Table 2 compares their cumulative benefits. These components are crucial for solving levels in advanced level packs, e.g., the Gamma level pack, which could not be solved without the Intersection degeneration rules.

6.2 Evaluation of the Supervised Learning Approach

We evaluated our method on the first six level packs of Euclidea with various training setups. The results (see Fig. 5) show that models specialized to individual level packs ("one model per level pack") or even levels ("one model per level") have better accuracy than a single, more general model for multiple levels/packs ("one model for all levels"). We also investigate the benefits of using our tree search procedure (see Sect. 5.2) instead of using only the most confident hypothesis, as in the supervised setting. We find the tree search improves the accuracy, especially on Alpha and Gamma level packs, by searching the space of possible candidate solutions for each step of the construction.

Table 2. Performance of the base method (Vanilla Mask R-CNN) together with the additional components of our approach. The Performance is evaluated on Euclidea level packs with increasing difficulty (from Alpha to Zeta). We trained a separate model for every level in each level pack and evaluated the model on 500 new instances of that level. The table presents the accuracy averaged across all levels in each level pack. The components are applied to the base method (Vanilla Mask R-CNN) in an additive manner. For example, the 4+ Stage training includes all previous components, i.e., Automatic point detection and History channel. A description of the different components is given in Sect. 4.4.

Component/Level pack	Alpha	Beta	Gamma	Delta	Epsilon	Zeta
Vanilla Mask R-CNN [3]	71.0	-	-	-	-	-
+ Automatic point detection	95.1	-	-	-	-	-
+ History channel	98.1	69.3	-	-	-	-
+ 4+ Stage training	91.7	82.3	-	-	-	-
+ Intersection degeneration rules	91.7	82.3	79.9	73.5	-	-
+ On-the-fly data generation	**98.7**	**96.2**	**97.8**	**99.1**	**92.8**	**95.7**

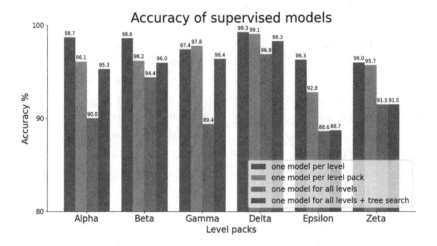

Fig. 5. Accuracy of our approach on Euclidea level packs Alpha to Zeta. The model uses all components from Table 2. We compare four approaches: one model per level (blue), one model per level pack (orange), one model for all levels (green), and one model for all levels with hypothesis tree search (red). All were evaluated on 500 instances of each level and the accuracy was averaged across all levels in each level pack. (Color figure online)

6.3   Evaluation on Unseen Problems

To evaluate performance on unseen levels, we use the leave-one-out (LOO) evaluation. In our setup, *LOO levels* evaluates, e.g., level *Alpha-01* using models trained on each of the other Alpha levels, whereas *LOO packs* evaluates, e.g., each

Alpha level using models trained on level packs Beta, Gamma, Delta, Epsilon, and Zeta. Table 3 compares the LOO evaluation and the supervised approach, both with the hypothesis tree search, for level pack Alpha. We ran a similar evaluation for all 6 levels packs and were able to solve 30 out of 68 levels using *LOO levels* and 31 out of 68 levels using *LOO packs*. The results show that our method can solve many levels unseen during the training, although some levels remain difficult to solve.

Table 3. Leave-one-out evaluation on the Alpha levels. Completion accuracy of the leave-one-out evaluation across levels within a level pack (LOO levels), across level packs (LOO packs), and, for comparison, our best supervised model trained to solve the first six Euclidea level packs (Alpha-Zeta); the tree search was used in all three cases. The leave-one-out evaluation was performed on 20 instances of each level, while the supervised model was evaluated on 500 instances of each level. Using models from all level packs except Alpha (LOO packs) works better than using models trained only on other levels of the Alpha level pack (LOO levels). This is likely because models in the "LOO packs" set-up have seen a larger set of different constructions.

Alpha levels	LOO levels	LOO packs	Supervised
01 T1 Line	40.0	10.0	85.0
02 T2 Circle	5.0	45.0	100.0
03 T3 Point	100.0	90.0	100.0
04 TIntersect	100.0	100.0	99.0
05 TEquilateral	50.0	70.0	100.0
06 Angle60	55.0	100.0	94.0
07 PerpBisector	35.0	100.0	99.0
08 TPerpBisector	0.0	100.0	75.0
09 MidPoint	5.0	60.0	100.0
10 CircleInSquare	0.0	100.0	87.0
11 RhombusInRect	25.0	40.0	99.0
12 CircleCenter	10.0	0.0	100.0
13 SquareInCircle	0.0	10.0	100.0
Average	42.5	63.4	95.3

6.4   Qualitative Example

Figure 6 shows a step-by-step walk-through construction of an advanced Euclidea level.

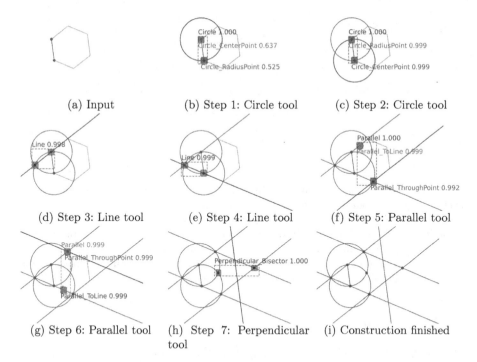

(a) Input

(b) Step 1: Circle tool

(c) Step 2: Circle tool

(d) Step 3: Line tool

(e) Step 4: Line tool

(f) Step 5: Parallel tool

(g) Step 6: Parallel tool

(h) Step 7: Perpendicular tool

(i) Construction finished

Fig. 6. Example construction of Euclidea level *Epsilon-12* (construct a regular hexagon by the side). (a) Initial configuration of the problem. (b-h) Seven construction steps, including Mask R-CNN detections, and an object proposed to construct in each step. (i) Final construction step, level solved. Red denotes the current state of the construction, green the remaining goal, blue the geometric primitive proposed by the detection, and other colors the prediction masks, bounding boxes, class names, and scores for the next predicted action. More examples can be found in the y material available at the project webpage [1]. (Color figure online)

Connections Between Levels. From the leave-one-out evaluation, we can also observe which levels are similar. We denote that level X is *connected* to level Y if a model trained for Y contributes with a hypothesis to a successful construction during the inference for level X. Note that this relation is not symmetric, e.g., when X is connected to Y, then Y is not necessarily connected to X. We run the hypothesis tree search during the leave-one-out evaluation and obtain connections in the following way: If the search is successful, we collect all models that contributed to the solution in the final backtracking of the search. The connections for all levels in the level pack Alpha are shown in Fig. 7.

Fig. 7. Connection graph created during the leave-one-out evaluation of the Alpha level pack using models for individual levels. Models trained on more difficult levels (indicated by higher numbers) often help construct easier levels (lower numbers). For example, level 13 could not be solved (has no incoming connections), but its predictions were used for solution of levels 1, 4, 5, 7, 9, 11, 12. Our method can often construct simpler tasks based on more complex constructions. However, combining multiple simple tasks into a complex construction remains a challenge.

7   Conclusion

We have developed an image-based method for solving geometric construction problems. The method builds on the Mask R-CNN visual recognizer, which is adapted to predict the next step of a geometric construction given the current state of the construction, and further combined with a tree search mechanism to explore the space of possible constructions. To train and test the method, we have used Euclidea, a construction game with geometric problems with an increasing difficulty. To train the model, we have created a data generator that generates new configurations of the Euclidea constructions.

In a supervised setting, the method learns to solve all 68 kinds of geometric construction problems from the first six level packs of Euclidea with an average 92% accuracy. When evaluated on new kinds of problems unseen at training, which is a significantly more challenging set-up, our method solves 31 of the 68 kinds of Euclidea problems. To solve the unseen problems our model currently relies on having seen a similar (or more complex) problem at training time. Solving unseen problems that are more complex than those seen at training remains an open challenge. Addressing this challenge is likely going to require developing new techniques to efficiently explore the space of constructions as well as mechanisms to learn from successfully completed constructions, a set-up similar to reinforcement learning.

Although in this paper we focus on synthetically generated data, our results open up the possibility to solve even hand-drawn geometric problems if corresponding training data is provided. In real-world settings, descriptions and discussions of problems in math, physics and other sciences often contain an image or a drawing component. Diagrams and illustrations are also an essential part of real-world technical documentation (e.g. patents). The ability to automatically identify and combine visually defined geometrical primitives into more complex patterns, as done in our work, is a step towards automatic systems that can identify compositions of geometric patterns in technical documentation. Think, for example, of an "automatic patent lawyer assistant".

References

1. Project webpage. https://data.ciirc.cvut.cz/public/projects/2021Geometry Reasoning
2. Euclidea. https://www.euclidea.xyz
3. He K., Gkioxari G., Dollár P., Girshick, R.: Mask R-CNN. In: 2017 IEEE International Conference on Computer Vision (ICCV) (2017)
4. Seo, M.J., Hajishirzi, H., Farhadi, A., Etzioni, O.: Diagram understanding in geometry questions. In: American Association for Artificial Intelligence (2014)
5. Seo, M., Hajishirzi, H., Farhadi, A., Etzioni, O., Malcolm, C.: Solving geometry problems: combining text and diagram interpretation. Association for Computational Linguistics (2015)
6. Quaresma, P.: Thousands of Geometric Problems for Geometric Theorem Provers (TGTP). Springer, Heidelberg (2011)
7. Vesna, M.: ArgoTriCS – automated triangle construction solver. J. Exper. Theor. Artif. Intell. **29**(2), 247–271 (2017)
8. Balbiani, P., Cerro, L.F.: Affine Geometry of Collinearity and Conditional Term Rewriting. Springer, Heidelberg (1995)
9. Chou, S.C., Gao, X.S., Zhang, J.Z.: A deductive database approach to automated geometry theorem proving and discovering. J. Autom. Reasoning **25**, 219–246 (2000)
10. Gao, X.: Transcendental functions and mechanical theorem proving in elementary geometries. J. Autom. Reasoning **6**, 403–417 (1990)
11. Deepak, K.: Using Gröbner bases to reason about geometry problems. J. Symbolic Comput. **2**(4), 399–408 (1986)
12. Chou, S.C., Gao, X.S., Zhang, J.: Machine Proofs in Geometry: Automated Production of Readable Proofs for Geometry Theorems (1994)
13. McCune, W., Wos, L.: Otter: the CADE-13 competition incarnations. J. Autom. Reasoning **18**(2), 211–220 (1997)
14. McCune, W.: Prover9 and Mace4. http://www.cs.unm.edu/~mccune/prover9/
15. Beeson, M., Wos, L.: Finding proofs in Tarskian geometry. J. Autom. Reasoning **58**(1), 201–207 (2017)
16. Durdevic, S.S., Narboux, J., Janicic, P.: Automated generation of machine verifiable and readable proofs: a case study of Tarski's geometry. Ann. Math. Artif. Intell. **74**(3–4), 249–269 (2015)
17. Quaife, A.: Automated Development of Fundamental Mathematical Theories. Kluwer Academic Publishers, Dordrecht (1992)
18. Beeson, M., Narboux, J., Wiedijk, F.: Proof-checking Euclid. Ann. Math. Artif. Intell. **85**, 213–257 (2019). https://doi.org/10.1007/s10472-018-9606-x
19. Jakubův, J., Chvalovský, K., Olšák, M., Piotrowski, B., Suda, M., Urban, J.: ENIGMA anonymous: symbol-independent inference guiding machine (System Description). In: Peltier, N., Sofronie-Stokkermans, V. (eds.) IJCAR 2020. LNCS (LNAI), vol. 12167, pp. 448–463. Springer, Cham (2020). https://doi.org/10.1007/978-3-030-51054-1_29

20. Gauthier, T., Kaliszyk, C., Urban, J., Kumar, R., Norrish, M.: TacticToe: learning to prove with tactics. J. Autom. Reasoning **65**(2), 257–286 (2021)
21. Hosang, J., Benenson, R., Schiele, B.: Learning non-maximum suppression. In: Conference on Computer Vision and Pattern Recognition (CVPR) (2017)

Automated Generation of Exam Sheets for Automated Deduction

Petra Hozzová$^{(\boxtimes)}$ ⓘ, Laura Kovács ⓘ, and Jakob Rath ⓘ

TU Wien, Vienna, Austria
{petra.hozzova,laura.kovacs,jakob.rath}@tuwien.ac.at

Abstract. Amid the COVID-19 pandemic, distance teaching became default in higher education, urging teachers and researchers to revise course materials into an accessible online content for a diverse audience. Probably one of the hardest challenges came with online assessments of course performance, for example by organizing online written exams. In this teaching-related project paper we survey the setting we organized for our master's level course "Automated Deduction" in logic and computation at TU Wien. The algorithmic and rigorous reasoning developed within our course called for individual exam sheets focused on problem solving and deductive proofs; as such exam sheets using test grids were not a viable solution for written exams within our course. We believe the toolchain of automated reasoning tools we have developed for holding online written exams could be beneficial not only for other distance learning platforms, but also to researchers in automated reasoning, by providing our community with a large set of randomly generated benchmarks in SAT/SMT solving and first-order theorem proving.

1 Motivation

Amid the COVID-19 pandemic, higher education has moved to distance teaching. While online lecturing was relatively fast to implement via webinars, recordings, streaming and online communication channels, coming up with best practices to assess course performance was far from trivial. Even with very sophisticated technical infrastructure (use of which, on the other hand, would be unethical to require from course participants), avoiding collusion in the virtual environment is very hard to achieve, if possible at all. While work on online feedback generation has already been initiated, see e.g. [7,15], not much work on online examinations has emerged so far.

In this paper we survey our teaching-related project work in organizing online written exams, where the exam solutions require rigorous logical reasoning and proofs rather than using mechanized test grids. In particular, we are faced with the challenge of organizing online written exams for our master's level course "Automated Deduction" in logic and computation at TU Wien[1]. This course

---

[1] https://tiss.tuwien.ac.at/course/courseDetails.xhtml?dswid=2002&dsrid=601&courseNr=184774&semester=2020S.

© Springer Nature Switzerland AG 2021
F. Kamareddine and C. Sacerdoti Coen (Eds.): CICM 2021, LNAI 12833, pp. 185–196, 2021.
https://doi.org/10.1007/978-3-030-81097-9_15

introduces algorithmic techniques and fundamental results in automated reasoning, by focusing on specialised algorithms for reasoning in various fragments of first-order logics, such as propositional logic, combinations of ground theories, and full first-order logic with equality. As such, topics of the course cover theoretical and practical aspects of SAT/SMT solving [4,5,13] and first-order theorem proving using superposition reasoning [9,12].

By no means are we claiming that the framework we developed for online examination is optimal. Given the time constraints of examination periods, we aimed for an online exam setting that (i) reduces collusion among students and (ii) requires the same workload on each participant. Note that there is a trade-off between (i) and (ii) – very similar problems require comparable effort to be solved, while solving very different problems requires unequal effort. Therefore our goal was to strike a balance between (i) and (ii).

The algorithmic reasoning developed within our course called for exam sheets focused on problem solving and deductive proofs; hence, exam sheets using test grids were not a viable solution for written exams within our course. We have therefore used and adapted the automated reasoning approaches introduced in our course to automate the generation of individual exam sheets for students enrolled in our course, by making sure that the exam tasks remain essentially the same in each generated exam sheet. As such, we have randomly generated individual exam problems on

- SAT solving, by imposing (mostly) syntactical constraints on randomly generated SAT formulas (Sect. 2.1);
- Satisfiability modulo theory (SMT) reasoning, by exploiting reasoning in a combination of theories and varying patterns of SMT problem templates (Sect. 3.1);
- First-order theorem proving, by adjusting simplification orderings in superposition reasoning and using redundancy elimination in first-order proving, both in the ground/quantifier-free and non-ground/quantified setting (Sects. 2.2 and 3.2).

For each of the SMT and first-order problems we generated, we used respective SMT and first-order solvers to perform an additional sanity check (Sect. 4). Our toolchain and the generated benchmarks/exams are available at https://github.com/AutomatedDeductionTUW/exagen.

We believe our framework is beneficial not only for other distance learning platforms, but also to researchers in automated reasoning as we provide a large set of randomly generated benchmarks in SAT/SMT solving and first-order theorem proving to our scientific community. While our teaching-related project delivery is specific to formal aspects of automated reasoning, we note that our work can be extended with further constraints to scale it to other courses in formal methods.

This paper is structured as follows. In Sects. 2 and 3 we discuss the high-level approach to generating the exam problems. Section 4 surveys the main implementation principles supporting our solution. Finally, in Sect. 5 we compare the teaching outcomes of our online written exam with those coming from previous in-class examinations. Based on these outcomes, we believe our online examination maintained the overall course quality in the study curricula.

2   Random Problem Generation

We first describe our solution for generating automated reasoning benchmarks in a fully automated and random manner. We used this setting to generate exam problems on SAT solving and first-order theorem proving by filtering out problem instances that are either too hard or too easy. Throughout this paper, we assume basic familiarity with standard first-order logic and refer to the literature [2,9] for further details.

2.1   Boolean Satisfiability (SAT)

In our exam problem on SAT solving (Problem 1 of Fig. 1), students were asked to (a) determine which atoms are of pure polarity in the formula, (b) compute a polarity-optimized clausal normal form (CNF) [14], and (c) decide satisfiability of the computed CNF formula by applying the DPLL algorithm.

Randomly generating propositional formulas in a naive setting would lead to a huge variety of formulas, spanning both formulas for which the above questions are trivial to answer (e.g., clauses as propositional tautologies) and others requiring much more effort (e.g., arbitrary formulas using only "$\leftrightarrow$"). More work was thus needed to ensure comparable workload for solving exam sheets.

To this end, we identified several syntactical characteristics that the exam problems on SAT solving should exhibit, and filtered the generated formulas by these, as summarized partially below.

(i) The SAT formula contains exactly seven logical connectives and exactly three different propositional variables.

(ii) There is at least one atom that appears with a pure polarity.

(iii) The connectives "$\leftrightarrow$", "$\rightarrow$", and "$\neg$" appear at least once, with "$\leftrightarrow$" appearing at most twice. At least one of "$\wedge$" and "$\vee$" appears.

(iv) Recall that the polarity-optimized clausal normal form involves a set of definitions, each of which is of the form $n \circ \varphi$ with $\circ \in \{\rightarrow, \leftarrow, \leftrightarrow\}$, a fresh propositional variable n, and a formula φ. We restrict the SAT formula such that at least two of the choices for $\circ$ appear in its CNF.

(v) The SAT formula has at most six models.

Our aim was to create problems of similar difficulty as in previous iterations of the course, which is why we used exams from previous years as a reference point. Some of the criteria, such as the number of connectives and variables, come from this previous experience. Other criteria, such as the restrictions on connectives and atom polarity, have been refined iteratively by checking the output for trivial or too complicated instances.

Automated Deduction – SS 2020
Final Exam – June 17, 2020   *Version 2020-06-17 / 36*

Problem 1. (25 points) Consider the formula:

$$(r \wedge \neg(q \rightarrow p)) \vee (q \leftrightarrow \neg(p \rightarrow q))$$

(a) Which atoms are pure in the above formula?

(b) Compute a clausal normal form C of the above formula by applying the CNF transformation algorithm with naming and optimization based on polarities of subformulas;

(c) Decide the satisfiability of the computed CNF formula C by applying the DPLL method to C. If C is satisfiable, give an interpretation which satisfies it.

Problem 2. (25 points) Consider the formula:

$$b = c \wedge f(b+1) \neq b+2 \wedge read(A, f(c+1)) = c$$
$$\wedge\, (read(A, f(b+1)) = b+3 \vee read(write(A, b+2, f(c)), f(c+1)) = c+2)$$

where b, c are constants, f is a unary function symbol, A is an array constant, *read, write* are interpreted in the array theory, and $+, -, 1, 2, 3, \ldots$ are interpreted in the standard way over the integers.

Use the Nelson-Oppen decision procedure in conjunction with DPLL-based reasoning in the combination of the theories of arrays, uninterpreted functions, and linear integer arithmetic. Use the decision procedures for the theory of arrays and the theory of uninterpreted functions and use simple mathematical reasoning for deriving new equalities among the constants in the theory of linear integer arithmetic. If the formula is satisfiable, give an interpretation that satisfies the formula.

Problem 3. (25 points) Consider the KBO ordering $\succ$ generated by the precedence $f \gg a \gg b \gg g$ and the weight function w with $w(f) = 0, w(b) = 1, w(g) = 1, w(a) = 3$. Let σ be a well-behaved selection function wrt $\succ$. Consider the set S of ground formulas:

$$f(g(b)) = a \vee f(g(a)) = a$$
$$g(b) = a$$
$$g(a) = a$$
$$g(b) \neq g(b) \vee f(a) \neq a$$

Show that S is unsatisfiable by applying saturation on S using an inference process based on the ground superposition calculus $\text{Sup}_{\succ,\sigma}$ (with the inference rules of binary resolution BR_σ included). Give details on what literals are selected and which terms are maximal.

Problem 4. (25 points) Consider the following inference:

$$\frac{P(h(g(g(d,d),b))) \vee \neg P(h(f(d))) \vee f(d) \neq h(g(a,a)) \quad \neg P(h(g(x,b))) \vee f(d) \neq h(g(y,y))}{\neg P(h(f(d))) \vee f(d) \neq h(g(a,a))}$$

in the non-ground superposition inference system Sup (including the rules of the non-ground binary resolution inference system BR), where P is a predicate symbol, f, g, h are function symbols, a, b, d are constants, and x, y are variables.

(a) Prove that the above inference is a sound inference of Sup.

(b) Is the above inference a simplifying inference of Sup? Justify your answer based on conditions of clauses being redundant.

Fig. 1. An example of a randomly generated exam sheet of automated deduction.

Although the combination of the above conditions (i)–(v) might seem very restrictive, we note that there are 20 390 076 different SAT formulas satisfying the above criteria. Further, if we do not want to distinguish formulas that differ only by a permutation of atoms, 3 398 346 formulas remain. We are thus able to generate a large number of unique SAT formulas to be used in online examinations and beyond. Problem 1 of Fig. 1 showcases one SAT reasoning challenge we automatically generated for one online examination sheet.

We finally note that, while experimenting with the different constraints (i)–(v) above, we encountered the following issues that may arise if the restrictions on the randomly generated formula are too strict:

- The sample space might be empty or very sparse. In practice, it seems to the user as if the problem generator got stuck, usually resulting in the process being killed by the user. For example, consider the restriction on polarities of propositional variables. Combined with the other restrictions, it is impossible to get a formula that contains atomic propositions of purely positive and purely negative polarity at the same time.
- The second issue manifests less drastically but is perhaps more problematic: the sample space may be too uniform, leading to the generation of trivial and/or very similar formulas. In particular, we encountered this problem when we restricted the number of models to exactly one, or zero. We note that there simply are not that many ways to rule out eight interpretations using only seven connectives.

2.2 Non-ground Superposition with Redundancy

Moving beyond Boolean satisfiability, we developed a random problem generator for first-order formulas with equality, in the setting of superposition-based first-order theorem proving with redundancy elimination [9,12]. In this problem, a concrete inference[2] was given to the students, and their task was to (a) prove that the inference is sound and (b) that the inference is a simplification inference (Problem 4 of Fig. 1).

We recall that a simplification inference is an inference that removes clauses from the proof search space, whereas a generating inference adds new clauses to the search space [9]. In our work, we considered the simplification inference of *subsumption resolution*

$$\frac{A \vee C \quad \neg B \vee D}{D} \qquad \text{or} \qquad \frac{\neg A \vee C \quad B \vee D}{D} \qquad (1)$$

where A, B are atoms and C, D are clauses such that A and B are unifiable with the most general unifier θ, and we have $A\theta \vee C\theta \subseteq B \vee D$. Due to the last condition, the second premise $\neg B \vee D$ (or $B \vee D$) of (1) is redundant and can be deleted from the search space after applying (1) within proof search.

We randomly generated first-order instances of the inference rule (1), as discussed next. Our setting could however be easily extended to other simplification inferences, such as subsumption demodulation [6], and even generating inferences.

---

[2] I.e., an instance of an inference rule as opposed to the rule itself.

(i) To randomly generate first-order terms and literals, we fixed a first-order signature consisting of predicate and function symbols and specified a set of logical variables. We controlled the shape of the generated terms by giving bounds on the *depth* of the term, that is the maximal nesting level of function calls (e.g., a constant symbol b has depth 0, while the term $g(f(x), d)$ has depth 2).

(ii) To obtain random instances of (1), we first generated non-ground clauses $C_1 := L_1 \lor L_2$ corresponding to an instance of the first premise of (1). To this end, we generated a random uninterpreted literal L_1 containing exactly one variable occurrence, and a random equality literal L_2 containing at least two occurrences of a different variable.

(iii) We next generated the clause $C_2 := \overline{L_1\theta} \lor L_2\theta \lor L_3$ as an instance of the second premise of (1) where θ is a randomly generated grounding substitution, L_3 is a randomly generated ground literal, and $\overline{L}$ is the complementary[3] literal to L.

(iv) We set $C_3 := L_3 \lor L_2\theta$ as an instance of the conclusion of (1), yielding thus the inference $\dfrac{C_1 \quad C_2}{C_3}$ as an instance of (1).

We found that with the concrete signature used for our exam, based on the above steps (i)–(iv), our approach can generate more than 10^{11} different instances of the inference (1). Problem 4 of Fig. 1 lists one such an instance.

3   Random Variation of Problem Templates

We now describe our framework for generating random quantifier-free first-order formulas with and without theories, that was used in the SMT reasoning and ground superposition proving tasks of our exam. For both of these tasks, we used quantifier-free first-order formula templates and implemented randomization over these templates by considering theory reasoning and simplification orderings.

Using this approach we achieved highly controlled output: exam problems which did not require any additional filtering. However, we note that the number of generated problems was limited, and to obtain additional problems, we would have to modify the templates.

3.1   Satisfiability Modulo Theories (SMT)

We considered first-order formula templates in the combined, quantifier-free theories of equality, arrays and linear integer arithmetic, corresponding to the logic AUFLIA of SMT-LIB [1]. We aimed at generating SMT formulas over which reasoning in all three theories was needed, by exploiting the DPLL(T) framework [13] in combination with the Nelson-Oppen decision procedure [11] (Problem 2 of Fig. 1).

---

[3] I.e., $\overline{L} = \neg L$ and $\overline{\neg L} = L$.

With naive random generation, it might however happen that, for example, array reasoning is actually not needed to derive (un)satisfiability of the generated SMT formula. We therefore constructed an SMT formula template and randomly introduced small perturbations in this template, so that the theory-specific reasoning in all generated SMT instances is different while reasoning in all theories is necessary. For doing so, we considered an SMT template with two constants of integer sort and replaced an integer-sorted constant symbol c by integer-sorted terms $c + i$, where $i \in \{-3, -2, \ldots, 3\}$ is chosen randomly. We flattened nested arithmetic terms such as $(c + i) + j$ to $c + k$, where i, j, k are integers and $k = i + j$. As a result, we generated 49 different SMT problems; we show one such formula, together with the corresponding reasoning tasks, in Problem 2 of Fig. 1.

3.2   Ground Superposition

For generating quantifier-free first-order formulas with equalities, over which ground and ordered superposition reasoning had to be employed (Problem 3 of Fig. 1), we aimed at (i) generating unsatisfiable sets S of ground formulas with uninterpreted functions symbols, such that (ii) refutation proofs of S had similar lengths and complexities. Similarly to Sect. 3.1, we fixed a template for S and only varied its instantiation and the Knuth-Bendix ordering (KBO) [8] $\succ$ to be used for refuting S within the superposition calculus. To this end, we considered variations of weight function w and symbol precedence $\gg$ over S, yielding thus different KBOs $\succ$ to be used for refuting S. The main steps of our approach are summarized below.

Table 1. Weights and precedences for the ground superposition problem.

Weight of:	f	g	a	b	Precedence	Weight of:	f	g	a	b	Precedence
$w_{1,f}$:	1	3	2	1	$p_{1,f} : a \gg b \gg f \gg g$	$w_{1,g}$:	3	1	2	1	$p_{1,g} : a \gg b \gg g \gg f$
$w_{2,f}$:	0	3	2	1	$p_{2,f} : f \gg a \gg g \gg b$	$w_{2,g}$:	3	0	2	1	$p_{2,g} : g \gg a \gg f \gg b$
$w_{3,f}$:	0	1	3	1	$p_{3,f} : f \gg a \gg b \gg g$	$w_{3,g}$:	1	0	3	1	$p_{3,g} : g \gg a \gg b \gg f$
$w_{4,f}$:	1	2	3	1	$p_{4,f} : g \gg f \gg a \gg b$	$w_{4,g}$:	2	1	3	1	$p_{4,g} : f \gg g \gg a \gg b$

(i) We fixed the template for S to be the following set of four clauses

$$E(F(X)) = a \vee E(G(Y)) = a \tag{2}$$
$$F(X) = a \,[\vee H(b) \neq H(b)] \tag{3}$$
$$G(Y) = a \,[\vee H(b) \neq H(b)] \tag{4}$$
$$E(a) \neq a \,[\vee H(b) \neq H(b)], \tag{5}$$

where $E, F, G, H \in \{f, g\}$, $X, Y \in \{a, b\}$, and the literal in [ ] is added to the clauses optionally.

(ii) We created instances of S of this template ensuring that no clause in S is redundant, by considering the following constraints.
- $E \neq H$ and $F(X) \neq G(Y)$;
- Either X or Y is not a. Similarly, either F or G is not E;
- The literal $H(b) \neq H(b)$ is in exactly one of the clauses (3), (4), (5).

As a result, we produced 12 instances of S satisfying the above properties.

Table 2. Assignment of KBOs to instances of the ground superposition problem.

Condition	i_1, I_1	i_2, I_2	i_3, I_3
$F \neq G$ and $X \neq Y$	$1, E$	$2, E$	$3, E$
$F \neq G$ and $X = Y$	$1, H$	$2, E$	$4, H$
$F = G$ and $X \neq Y$	$1, H$	$2, H$	$3, E$

(iii) We considered the term algebras induced by the generated instances of S and designed KBOs $\succ$ such that refuting the respective instances of S using $\succ$ requires ordering terms both using weight w and precedence $\gg$. In addition, we imposed that either $F(X) \succ a \succ G(Y)$ or $G(Y) \succ a \succ F(X)$ holds. With such orderings $\succ$, the shortest refutations of instances of S are of the same length, and in at least one application of superposition, a is replaced by either $F(X)$ or $G(Y)$ in the resulting clause. We generated eight different KBOs $\succ$ fulfilling these conditions. The weights and precedences used to generate the KBOs are displayed in Table 1. The table shows all weight and precedence combinations, denoted as $w_{i,I}, p_{i,I}$ for $i \in \{1, 2, 3, 4\}$ and $I \in \{f, g\}$.[4] Each instance of S was combined with three different KBOs, generated by pairs $(w_{i_1,I_1}, p_{i_1,I_1}), (w_{i_2,I_2}, p_{i_2,I_2}), (w_{i_3,I_3}, p_{i_3,I_3})$. The values of $i_1, I_1, i_2, I_2, i_3, I_3$ are chosen based on the values of F, G, X, Y, as expressed by the conditions in Table 2.

Ultimately, we obtained 36 different problems (combinations of instances of S and $\succ$) for the ground superposition reasoning task of our exam. Problem 3 of Fig. 1 shows such an instance.

4   Implementation

We implemented our approach to randomly generating SAT, SMT, and non-ground first-order problems in Haskell, whereas our ground superposition problem generator was implemented in Python. All together, our toolchain involved

---

[4] Note that for all values of i, $w_{i,f}(f) = w_{i,g}(g)$ and $w_{i,f}(g) = w_{i,g}(f)$, and the precedences $p_{i,f}, p_{i,g}$ are the same except for the precedence of f, g. However, for convenience, the table contains both $w_{i,f}$ and $w_{i,g}$, as well as $p_{i,f}$ and $p_{i,g}$ for all values of i.

about 2 300 lines of code, including additional scripts for putting parts together. We encoded each randomly generated SMT and first-order formula into the SMT-LIB input format [1] and, for sanity checks, ran the SMT solver Z3 [10] and the first-order theorem prover Vampire [9] for proving the respective formulas. In addition, each formula has been converted to LaTeX, yielding randomly generated exam sheets – one such exam sheet is given in Fig. 1.

Regarding the filtering of generated formulas using the constraints discussed in Sect. 2, we implemented restrictions on the shape of formulas (items (i) and (iii) in Sect. 2.1) as constraints during formula generation, while other criteria were realized as post-generation filters. Regarding post-generation filtering, we did not require very efficient algorithms since the formulas under consideration are very small. For example, for the restriction on the number of models we used a naive satisfiability test based on evaluating the formula under each possible interpretation. Thanks to this approach it is easy to add new filters/constraints.

For the random problem generation setting of Sect. 2, we applied design principles of the Haskell library QuickCheck [3]. With QuickCheck, randomly generated data can easily be defined in an embedded generator language. However, because of our many filtering criteria, we wanted the generator to additionally support backtracking. We were also interested in determining the size of the filtered sample space. To this end, we created a simple typeclass `MonadChoose` in the style of the monad transformer library (mtl), with a single primitive operation `choose` for choosing an element from a list of possible choices:

```
class MonadPlus m => MonadChoose m where
  choose :: [a] -> m a
```

Our generator implementations are generic over the monad, constrained by `MonadChoose`. The following listing shows (a slightly simplified) part of the inference generator discussed in Sect. 2.2.

```
genExamInference :: MonadChoose m => m Inference
genExamInference = do
  -- Define signature (partially omitted)
  let vars = ["x", "y", "z"]
  let opts = GenOptions{ vars = vars, ... }

  -- Choose variables to appear in l1 and l2
  v1 <- choose vars
  v2 <- choose (filter (/= v1) vars)

  -- Generate literals
  -- l1: exactly one occurrence of v1
  l1 <- mfilter ((==1) . length . toListOf variables)
        $ genUninterpretedLiteral opts{ vars = [v1] }
  -- l2: at least two occurrences of v2
  l2 <- mfilter ((>=2) . length . toListOf variables)
        $ genEqualityLiteral opts{ vars = [v2] }
```

```
-- l3: ground literal
l3 <- genUninterpretedLiteral opts{ vars = [] }

-- (rest omitted)
return inference

genEqualityLiteral, genUninterpretedLiteral
  :: MonadChoose m => GenOptions -> m Literal
-- (literal generators omitted)
```

We used two concrete implementations to evaluate generators:

1. `RandomChoice`, a monad that implements `choose` as uniform random choice with backtracking support. Conceptually, this is like the standard list monad where `choose` works like the regular monadic bind for lists except that it first shuffles the list with a random permutation. This evaluation method is used to generate random exams.
2. The standard list monad to enumerate the sample space. This second evaluation method helps verifying that the sample space is sufficiently large.

5   Evaluation of Online Exam Outcomes

In Summer 2020, all together 31 students took the online written exam in "Automated Deduction". We note that in Summer 2018 and Summer 2019, there have been 17 and respectively 31 students taking the in-class exam of the course. We believe that the online lecturing and examination in Summer 2020 did not have negative impact on the students' course performance.

In the online written examination of Summer 2020, the students solved their respective unique exam assignments on paper and submitted scanned versions of their solutions online. The types of exam problems from Summer 2020 were the same as in previous editions of the course. However, contrary to previous years, different students had different exam assignments, to minimise opportunity for collusion between students.

While building the pipeline described in this paper required much more work than creating just one exam sheet, our approach was more efficient than it would be to create 31 different exam sheets manually. Additionally, our approach guaranteed that the exam problems were unique, yet required comparable effort to solve. Also, reusing our pipeline in the future requires only minimal changes.

Further, the types of the problems in our exam are not trivial to grade, since the solutions require applying complicated reasoning algorithms on paper, and the grade has to take into account the whole process, not just the result. However, the use of templates of Sect. 3 made the grading fairly similar to grading multiple solutions of the same problem by providing a clear pattern to follow. This observation extends to the problem on non-ground superposition (Subsect. 2.2), because the argument required in the solution does not depend majorly on the generated parts, even though we did not use an explicit template. The situation is different for the problem on boolean satisfiability (Subsect. 2.1). There, the solution varies greatly with the input formula, and grading a different instance requires mentally stepping through the problem again. One might suggest to also generate fully worked solutions to this problem, however it is not immediately clear that this would be helpful: at various points, the students may choose among multiple correct possibilities, each of which leads to differences in subsequent parts of the solution.

The average exam score was 79.9%, compared to 80% in 2019 and 76% in 2018. Based on the comparable exam averages, we believe our online written examination from Summer 2020 did not bring any significant change in the overall course performances of students enrolled in the course.

Finally, eight students filled out a feedback survey for the course in Summer 2020. All of them reported high levels of satisfaction with the course, with one student explicitly praising the online exam format. Our course in Summer 2020 has been also nominated for the *Best Distance Learning Award 2020* of the TU Wien.

6   Conclusion

We describe a randomized approach and toolchain for generating exam problems in automated reasoning, in particular in the setting of SAT, SMT, and first-order theorem proving. Our approach was used to generate individual exam sheets focused on problem solving within automated deduction, and could be adapted to other constraints and course frameworks.

Acknowledgments. We acknowledge funding supporting this work, in particular the ERC CoG ARTIST 101002685, the ERC StG 2014 SYMCAR 639270 and the Austrian FWF research project LogiCS W1255-N23.

References

1. Barrett, C., Fontaine, P., Tinelli, C.: The SMT-LIB standard: Version 2.6. Technical report, Department of Computer Science, The University of Iowa (2017). www.SMT-LIB.org
2. Biere, A., Heule, M., van Maaren, H., Walsh, T. (eds.): Handbook of Satisfiability, Frontiers in Artificial Intelligence and Applications, vol. 185. IOS Press, Amsterdam (2009)
3. Claessen, K., Hughes, J.: Quickcheck: a lightweight tool for random testing of Haskell programs. In: Proceedings of ICFP, pp. 268–279 (2000)
4. Davis, M., Logemann, G., Loveland, D.W.: A machine program for theorem-proving. Commun. ACM **5**(7), 394–397 (1962)
5. Ganzinger, H., Hagen, G., Nieuwenhuis, R., Oliveras, A., Tinelli, C.: DPLL(T): fast decision procedures. In: Alur, R., Peled, D.A. (eds.) CAV 2004. LNCS, vol. 3114, pp. 175–188. Springer, Heidelberg (2004). https://doi.org/10.1007/978-3-540-27813-9_14

6. Gleiss, B., Kovács, L., Rath, J.: Subsumption demodulation in first-order theorem proving. In: Peltier, N., Sofronie-Stokkermans, V. (eds.) Proceedings of IJCAR, pp. 297–315. Springer, Cham (2020)

7. Gulwani, S., Radicek, I., Zuleger, F.: Automated clustering and program repair for introductory programming assignments. In: Proceedings of PLDI, pp. 465–480 (2018)

8. Knuth, D.E., Bendix, P.B.: Simple word problems in universal algebras. In: Computational Problems in Abstract Algebra, pp. 263–297. Pergamon Press (1970)

9. Kovács, L., Voronkov, A.: First-order theorem proving and VAMPIRE. In: Sharygina, N., Veith, H. (eds.) CAV 2013. LNCS, vol. 8044, pp. 1–35. Springer, Heidelberg (2013). https://doi.org/10.1007/978-3-642-39799-8_1

10. de Moura, L., Bjørner, N.: Z3: an efficient SMT solver. In: Ramakrishnan, C.R., Rehof, J. (eds.) TACAS 2008. LNCS, vol. 4963, pp. 337–340. Springer, Heidelberg (2008). https://doi.org/10.1007/978-3-540-78800-3_24

11. Nelson, G., Oppen, D.C.: Simplification by cooperating decision procedures. ACM Trans. Program. Lang. Syst. 1(2), 245–257 (1979)

12. Nieuwenhuis, R., Rubio, A.: Paramodulation-based theorem proving. In: Handbook of Automated Reasoning, pp. 371–443 (2001)

13. Tinelli, C.: A DPLL-based calculus for ground satisfiability modulo theories. In: Proceedings of JELIA, pp. 308–319 (2002)

14. Tseytin, G.S.: On the complexity of derivation in propositional calculus. In: Studies in Constructive Mathematics and Mathematical Logic, pp. 115–1125. Steklov Mathematical Institute (1970)

15. Wang, K., Singh, R., Su, Z.: Search, align, and repair: data-driven feedback generation for introductory programming exercises. In: Proceedings of PLDI, pp. 481–495 (2018)

Gauss-Lintel, an Algorithm Suite for Exploring Chord Diagrams

Abdullah Khan[1]📙, Alexei Lisitsa[2](✉)📙, and Alexei Vernitski[1]📙

[1] Department of Mathematical Sciences, University of Essex, Essex, UK
{ak20749,asvern}@essex.ac.uk
[2] Department of Computer Science, University of Liverpool, Liverpool, UK
a.lisitsa@liverpool.ac.uk

Abstract. Gauss diagrams, or more generally chord diagrams are a well-established tool in the study of topology of knots and of planar curves. In this paper we present a system description of Gauss-lintel, our implementation in SWI-Prolog of a suite of algorithms for exploring chord diagrams. Gauss-lintel employs a datatype which we call "lintel", which is a list representation of an odd-even matching for the set of integers $[0,...,2n-1]$, for efficiently generating Gauss diagrams and testing their properties, including one important property called realizability. We report on extensive experiments in generation and enumeration of various classes of Gauss diagrams, as well as on experimental testing of several published descriptions of realizability.

1 Gauss Diagrams and Their Properties

Gauss diagrams are a mathematical construction used for expressing some properties of closed planar curves (or of projections of knots on a plane). Let us think about a closed planar curve as the image of a (suitably smooth) mapping $\gamma : S^1 \rightarrow R^2$, where S^1 is the circumference of a circle and R^2 is the plane. Figure 1a) presents an example of a closed planar curve. The Gauss diagram of the curve, shown in Fig. 1b), is the circle S^1 together with all chords inside the circle which connect the two pre-images of each intersection of the curve; in other words, a chord connects two points x and y on the circumference of the circle if $\gamma(x) = \gamma(y)$.

As one studies *chord diagrams*, that is, circles with chords, like in Fig. 1b), it is possible to prove that not every chord diagram correspond to a closed planar curve; those that do are called *realizable*.

A classical question of computational topology asked by Gauss [7] is which of the chords diagrams are realizable. Gauss himself found a necessary (but not sufficient) condition - *in a realizable diagram every chord intersects an even number of other chords*. This is why a slight distinction is made between the concepts of a chord diagram and a Gauss diagram; namely, a Gauss diagram is a chord diagram in which every chord intersects an even number of other chords. The first description of realizable Gauss diagrams was discovered in the

F. Kamareddine and C. Sacerdoti Coen (Eds.): CICM 2021, LNAI 12833, pp. 197–202, 2021.
https://doi.org/10.1007/978-3-030-81097-9_16

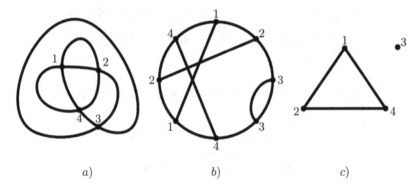

Fig. 1. Example of a) a planar curve; b) its Gauss diagram and c) its interlacement graph.

1930's by Dehn [6], and since then many descriptions of realizability and efficient algorithms for checking the realizability of a Gauss diagram have been developed; an incomplete list of references includes [3,5,12,14]. One of the most interesting discoveries in this research [5,14,15] is that the realizability of a Gauss diagram can be decided just using its interlacement graph, that is, a record of which chords intersect within the circle. An *interlacement graph* of a chord diagram is an undirected graph whose vertices are the chords of the diagram, and in which there is an edge between two vertices, if the chords corresponding to these vertices intersect. See Fig. 1c) for example; this is the interlacement graph of the Gauss diagram in Fig. 1b). We will refer to a graph representing a diagram itself, like that in Fig. 1b), as the *diagram* graph. We will say that two chord diagrams are *equivalent* if their diagram graphs are isomorphic.

A chord diagram is called *prime* if its interlacement graph is connected (if a diagram is not prime, it is called *composite*). For example the diagram from Fig. 1 is composite.

Some recent studies [2,8] proposed very simple descriptions of realiziability, expressible over interlacement graphs in terms of first-order logic extended by parity quantifiers $\exists^{even} x$ (meaning "there exists an even number of x such that"). None of the previously published variants of realiziability criteria were known to be expressible so simply, without using the second order quantification or variants of transitive closure operators. The simple and declarative form of these conditions opens an opportunity for experimental investigation of Gauss diagrams using constraint satisfaction and related computational techniques. We took this opportunity as a starting point of our research in experimental mathematics with the primary aim to enumerate various classes of Gauss diagrams [10].

2   Even-Odd Matchings and Lintels

In our implementation, we use a convenient representation of Gauss diagrams.

Let n be a positive integer. A *lintel* is an n-tuple of pairs of numbers $((a_1^1, a_1^2), \ldots, (a_n^1, a_n^2))$ such that **1)** the set of numbers in the lintel $\{a_i^1, a_i^2, \ldots, a_n^1, a_n^2\}$ is equal to the set $\{0, 1, \ldots, 2n - 1\}$, and **2)** in each pair (a_i^1, a_i^2) the difference $a_i^1 - a_i^2$ is odd. The number n will be called the size of the lintel. Each pair (a_i^1, a_i^2) will be called a chord of the lintel.

Two lintels are *strongly equivalent* if they can be transformed into one another by steps of the following two types: **1)** swapping the positions of two numbers in a chord; **2)** swapping the positions of chords in the list. Two lintels are *equivalent* if they can be transformed into one another by steps of the following types: 1) and 2) as above; 3) shifting the value of each entry of the lintel cyclically modulo $2n$; 4) inverting the value of each entry of the lintel modulo $2n$.

A lintel is a *sorted lintel* if each pair in it is sorted, and first elements of pairs are sorted, that is, for each i we have $a_i^1 < a_i^2$, and for all $i < j$ we have $a_i^1 < a_j^1$. In each class of strongly equivalent lintels there is exactly one sorted lintel. In each class of equivalent lintels the sorted lintel which is the first in the lexicographic order of lintels (we call such lintels *Lyndon lintels*, by analogy with Lyndon words [13]) can serve as the canonical representative of the class, and there is a one-to-one correspondence between Lyndon lintels and Gauss diagrams.

For a given lintel L, we can produce the corresponding Lyndon lintel as follows.

Algorithm 1. *1. Produce the sorted lintel M corresponding to L.*

2. Applying cyclic shifts to M for all values $s = 1, \ldots, 2n - 1$, produce lintels L_s.

3. Produce the sorted lintels M_s corresponding to L_s.

4. Applying the inverting step to L, produce the lintel L'.

5. Produce the sorted lintel M' corresponding to L'.

6. Applying cyclic shifts to M' for all values $s = 1, \ldots, 2n - 1$, produce lintels L'_s.

7. Produce the sorted lintels M'_s corresponding to L_s^-.

8. Among the sorted lintels M, M', L_s, L'_s, choose the least one relative to a lexicographic order on lintels.

For efficient lintels generation we use the the following simple bijective map from the symmetric group S_n to the set P_{2n} of all even-odd matchings on $V_{2n} = \{0, \ldots, 2n-1\}$. For $\sigma \in S_n$, $\sigma : [1..n] \to [1..n]$, $\beta(\sigma) = \{\{2*i-1, 2*\sigma(i)-2\} | i \in [1..n]\}$.

3   Implementation

We have implemented the algorithms suite `Gauss-Lintel` for Gauss diagram generation, equivalence checking, canonization, and realizability conditions using the concept of lintels. The prototype implementation in the logic programming language SWI-Prolog [17] is available at [11]. The choice of Prolog is justified by the fact that it is very efficient in implementation of combinatorial search using built-in backtracking and unification mechanisms. As we use the lintel concept/data structure, all generated chord diagrams in our implementation satisfy necessary condition for Gauss diagrams. We utilise a list of lists representation of lintels in Prolog. We use dynamic facts[1] to store intermediate and final results of computations. E.g. a dynamic fact "lintel(Size,L)" stores a generated canonical lintel satisfying some conditions (depending on the user's choice).

3.1 Lintel Generation and Canonization

The canonical lintel generation is based on efficient built-in Prolog predicate `permutation(X,Y)` for the generation of all permutations of a given list (assigned to) X and the use of bijection $\beta : S_n \rightarrow P_{2n}$. The generic generation process proceeds as follows. Once a permutation σ is generated, the bijection β is applied to it, and then Algorithm 1 is applied to $\beta(\sigma)$. The resulting canonical lintel then checked on

- whether it satisfies a chosen combination of conditions, for example, a lintel which represents 1) prime Gauss diagram, 2) satisfying B conditions from [2], 3) not realizable;
- whether it has not been stored yet as a dynamic fact.

If both conditions are satisfied then the lintel is added as a dynamic fact, and the process is backtracked to the generation of the new permutation. When no new permutations are left, the database of dynamic facts provides a list of all canonical non-equivalent lintels of a given size satisfying a chosen combination of properties. In the implementation of Algorithm 1 we used an efficient built-in Prolog predicate `sort/4` for sorting lintels.

3.2 Properties/Conditions Checking

We have implemented a number of properties, including, most importantly, the following ones: primality, a classical algorithm (CA) for realiziability checking from [6,9], realizability conditions B, GL and STZ suggested in [2,8] and [15], respectively.

- STZ conditions state that a prime Gauss diagram is realizable iff for the adjacency matrix M_g of its interlacement graph there is a diagonal matrix Λ_g such that $M_g + \Lambda_g$ is an idempotent matrix (all matrices are considered over $GF(2)$, the finite field of two elements).
- GL conditions specify realizabilty of an interlacement graph g as 1) each pair of non-neighbouring vertices has an *even* number of common neighbours (possibly, zero); and 2) the same holds true for the reduced graph g/v [8] for each vertex v of g.
- B conditions include first GL condition and further require that in the interlacement graph any three pairwise connected vertices $a, b, c \in V$ the sum of the number of vertices adjacent to a, but not adjacent to b nor c, and the number of vertices adjacent to b and c, but not adjacent to a, is even.

---

[1] A dynamic fact is a Prolog fact (atomic formula) which can be added or removed during run time. Using dynamic facts goes outside of the pure Prolog paradigm, but it is very useful for keeping information about the global state.

The implementation is extensible. In `Gauss-lintel` we provide many auxiliary predicates for manipulating lintels and checking their properties which makes it easy to extend with further realizability criteria and other properties.

4 Experiments and Results

Using `Gauss-lintel` we have conducted various experiments and enumerated the classes of non-equivalent Gauss diagrams, satisfying various combinations of properties. Selected results are shown in Table 1. The Comments column reports on cross-validation of the calculated sequences with the sequences found in either OEIS (The Online Encyclopedia of Integer Sequences), or in other publications. In the case a sequence is not found anywhere it is labelled as "new".

Table 1. The number of non equivalent Gauss diagrams of sizes $= 3, \ldots, 11$, satisfying various realizability conditions

	3	4	5	6	7	8	9	10	11	Comments
CA [6,9]	1	1	2	3	10	27	101	364	1610	OEIS A264759
STZ [15]	1	1	2	3	10	27	101	364	1610	OEIS A264759
B [2]	1	1	2	3	10	27	**102**	**370**	**1646**	new
GL [8]	1	1	2	3	10	27	**102**	**370**	**1646**	new
PRIME	1	1	4	8	40	183	1354	11079	...	new
ALL	3	5	17	53	260	1466	10915	93196	...	[16] (up to n=7)

The first two lines, found also in the OEIS article A264759 [1], together with the fact that generated corresponding lists of Gauss diagrams are the same, verify that STZ conditions [15] are correct and complete realizability conditions up to the size 11. Next two lines show that despite the claims in [2,8] the corresponding B and GL conditions are incomplete. Indeed, the numbers in bold, which are different from the corresponding numbers in CA and STZ rows, demonstrate that there Gauss diagrams satisfying B and GL conditions which are not realizable. Explicit counterexamples can be found in [10,11]. Next line demonstrates the numbers of non-equivalent prime Gauss diagrams (realizable and non-realizable). The last line shows the number of *all* non-equivalent Gauss diagrams (not necessarily prime or realizable), which expands on the results of [16].

5 Related Work

Alternative implementations for chord diagrams generation include TaiteCurves program[2] by J. Betrema and GAP code presented in [4]. Unlike `Gauss-lintel`

---

[2] TaitCurves.

both implementations deal with realiziable and prime diagrams only, each using fixed realizability conditions. On comparable tasks of the generation of realizable diagrams, TaiteCurves and GAP code are more, and respectively, less efficient than `Gauss-lintel`.

Acknowledgements. This work was supported by the Leverhulme Trust Research Project Grant RPG-2019-313.

References

1. The On-Line Encyclopedia of Integer Sequences. http://oeis.org/A264759
2. Biryukov, O.N.: Parity conditions for realizability of Gauss diagrams. J. Knot Theor. Ramifications **28**(1), 1950015 (2019)
3. Cairns, G., Elton, D.M.: The planarity porblem II. J. Knot Theor. Ramification **5**(2), 137–144 (1996)
4. Chmutov, M., Hulse, T., Lum, A., Rowell, P.: Plane and spherical curves: an investigation of their invariants. In: Summer Mathematics Research Institute, REU 2006 Proceedings, Oregon State University (2006)
5. de Fraysseix, H., Ossona de Mendez, P.: A short proof of a Gauss problem. In: DiBattista, G. (ed.) GD 1997. LNCS, vol. 1353, pp. 230–235. Springer, Heidelberg (1997). https://doi.org/10.1007/3-540-63938-1_65
6. Dehn, M.: Über Kombinatorische Topologie. Acta Math. **67**, 123–168 (1936)
7. Gauss, C.F.: Werke, vol. VII. Tuebner, Leipzig (1900)
8. Grinblat, A., Lopatkin, V.: On realizabilty of Gauss diagrams and constructions of meanders. J. Knot Theor. Ramifications **29**(5), 2050031 (2020)
9. Kauffman, L.H.: Virtual knot theory. Eur. J. Comb. **20**(7), 663–691 (1999)
10. Khan, A., Lisitsa, A., Vernitski, A.: Experimental mathematics approach to Gauss diagrams realizability. arxiv:2103.02102 (2021)
11. Khan, A., Lisitsa, A., Vernitski, A.: Gauss-lint algorithms suite for Gauss diagrams generation and analysis. Zenodo (2021). https://doi.org/10.5281/zenodo.4574590
12. Lovász, L., Marx, M.L.: A forbidden substructure characterization of Gauss codes. Bull. Am. Math. Soc. **82**(1), 121–122 (1976)
13. Lyndon, R.C.: On Burnside's problem. Trans. Am. Math. Soc. **77**, 202–215 (1954)
14. Rosenstiehl, P.: Solution algébrique du problème de Gauss sur la permutation des points d'intersection d'une ou plusieurs courbes fermées du plan. C.R. Acad. Sci. **283**(série A), 551–553 (1976)
15. Shtylla, B., Traldi, L., Zulli, L.: On the realization of double occurrence words. Discrete Math. **309**(6), 1769–1773 (2009)
16. Valette, G.: A classification of spherical curves based on Gauss diagrams. Arnold Math. J. **2**(3), 383–405 (2016). https://doi.org/10.1007/s40598-016-0049-3
17. Wielemaker, J., Schrijvers, T., Triska, M., Lager, T.: SWI-prolog. Theor. Pract. Logic Program. **12**(1–2), 67–96 (2012)

Logic and Systems

A New Export of the Mizar Mathematical Library

Colin Rothgang[1]([⊠])(iD), Artur Korniłowicz[2](iD), and Florian Rabe[3](iD)

[1] Mathematics, TU Berlin, Berlin, Germany
colin.rothgang@posteo.net
[2] Institute of Computer Science, Bialystok, Poland
[3] Computer Science, FAU Erlangen-Nürnberg, Erlangen, Germany

Abstract. The Mizar Mathematical Library (MML) is a prime target of library exports, i.e., translations of proof assistant libraries that make the libraries available to knowledge management systems or other deduction systems. The MML has been exported multiple times in the past, including our own export from Mizar to OMDoc done in 2011. But the exporters tend to be very difficult and expensive to maintain.

We present a complete reimplementation of our previous export. It incorporates many lessons learned and leverages improvements made both on the Mizar and the OMDoc side.

1 Introduction

The interoperability of proof assistants and the integration of their libraries is a long-standing goal in theorem proving. One of the biggest prizes here is the Mizar Mathematical Library (MML) [BBG+18]. It has been exported multiple times [Urb03,IKRU13] and other efforts are ongoing [KP19]. Mizar stores all kernel data structures in externally readable XML files [Urb05] so that exports are reduced to interpreting the XML files. However, Mizar generates about a dozen XML files per MML article, and these use ad-hoc, under-documented, and evolving XML schemas that are as complex as Mizar's feature-rich language and contain many parts that are only needed internally.

This was a major difficulty in our first translation of the MML to OMDoc [IKRU13], an XML-based representation format for mathematical knowledge and made the translation, while successful, prohibitively difficult to maintain. In the ten years since then, two things have changed. The Mizar XML data structures have been heavily improved, both for internal reasons and in response to the woes of translation developers. And we have developed much better routines for prover library translations [KR20]. The present system description redoes the export from scratch.

Like [IKRU13], we manually formalize the Mizar logic as a theory M in a logical framework of the LF family, which is realized in MMT [RK13]. Then we generate one MMT theory relative to M for every article in the MML. All these MMT theories are stored in OMDoc format [Koh06] and are available online. During the export, we aim at both preserving all Mizar features exactly as they are (as opposed to implementing logically complex feature eliminations) and simplifying the language by reducing features to the primitives provided by the MMT framework.

ⓒ Springer Nature Switzerland AG 2021
F. Kamareddine and C. Sacerdoti Coen (Eds.): CICM 2021, LNAI 12833, pp. 205–210, 2021.
https://doi.org/10.1007/978-3-030-81097-9_17

Besides rejuvenating the export, we go beyond [IKRU13] in multiple ways: (i) We implement the relevant parts of Mizar's XML schema as a set of Scala data types, from which the parser is automatically generated, thus massively simplifying the maintenance of the translation. (ii) Our translation is almost entirely context-free (every file can be exported without processing its dependencies), which is critical for scalability of the export, and we identify the last remaining context-sensitivity issues in the XML schemas. (iii) We represent Mizar's rich set of declarations as MMT patterns in the sense of [HR15] and Mizar's structures (akin to record types) as an MMT structural feature in the sense of [MRRK20]. (iv) We cover many recondite Mizar features that were not handled well in [IKRU13] such as redefinitions.

2 Design

2.1 Formalizing the Mizar Logic

At the object-level, we formalize Mizar's softly-typed set theory in a logical framework in MMT. We omit technical details that are already part of [IKRU13] and only point out that we use LF-style HOAS with $\{\_\}\_$ and $[\_]\_$ representing Π and λ. At the declaration-level, we represent Mizar's many conservative extension principles such as definitions and registrations as MMT patterns [HKR12] and structural features [MRRK20]. The formalization is available at https://gl.mathhub.info/MMT/LATIN2/.

For example, Mizar's direct partial predicate definitions are formalized as the MMT pattern below. Its header takes natural numbers n (the arity of the new predicate pred) and m (the number of cases in its definition), a list argTps of n argument types (each potentially depending on the other arguments), m cases (each consisting of a condition $cases_i$ on the n arguments and the resulting predicate $caseRes_i$), a default result defRes if no case applies, and a proof cons that the results of cases agree when their conditions overlap (we omit the definition of consDirectPredDef). These are the argument given in Mizar and exported in the XML files. The body of the pattern contains the elaboration performed by Mizar: the n-ary predicate pred and its defining axiom means. Typical for all pattern is the heavy use of MMT's support for flexary operators such as conjunction and mapping over argument sequences.

> pattern directPartPredDef(n : NAT, m : NAT, argTps : $(\text{term}^n \to \text{tp})^n$,
>   cases : $(\text{term}^n \to \text{prop})^m$, caseRes : $(\text{term}^n \to \text{prop})^m$, defRes : $\text{term}^n \to \text{prop}$
>   cons : consDirectPredDef n argTps m cases caseRes)   =
> pred : $\text{term}^n \to \text{prop}$
> consistency = cons
> means : $\{x : \text{term}^n\} \langle \vdash x.i \text{ : } (\text{argTps.i}) \ x \mid i : n \rangle \to$
> $\vdash \text{nary\_and } m \langle (\text{cases.j}) \ x \Rightarrow (\text{pred } x) \Leftrightarrow (\text{caseRes.j}) \ x \mid j : m \rangle$
> $\land \text{nary\_and } m \langle \neg (\text{cases.k}) \ x \mid k : m \rangle \Rightarrow \text{pred } x \Leftrightarrow \text{defRes } x$

2.2 Exporting the MML as XML

The Mizar verifier creates several XML files per source file that store information of the various processing phases. The most important are Weakly Strict Mizar (WSM, .wsx files) [BA12,NP16], which contain the syntax trees of statically analyzed articles and More Strict Mizar (MSM, .msx files), which extends WSM with the resolution of variables, constants, and labels. To additionally keep the original syntax, Even more Strict Mizar (EMSM, .msx files) is being developed, which adds semantic information about used *constructors* and Mizar *patterns* (which store the used format, constructor, argument types, and positions of visible arguments for a definition).

For example, the definition of subset below contains the formula x in Y, which results in EMSM in the XML fragment underneath. Here the attribute spelling gives the original syntax. The other blue-highlighted attributes are what we can use to form identifiers in OMDOC for the three different kinds of references: the constant in defined in the MML, and the kinds of bound variables Y (bound by the declaration) and x (bound by a quantifier). The other attributes (nr, formatnr, etc.) represent internally used numbers that we ignore. The decision which attributes to use/ignore requires a Mizar expert but is now documented in our export.

definition let X,Y; pred X c= Y means for x being object holds x in X implies x in Y; reflexivity; end;

```
<Relation−Formula nr="3" formatnr="6" patternnr="3" absolutepatternMMLId=
    "HIDDEN:3" leftargscount="1" spelling="in" sort="Relation-Formula"
    constrnr="2" absoluteconstrMMLId="HIDDEN:2" originalnr="0" position="72\47">
<Arguments>
<Simple−Term idnr="2" spelling="x" position="72\44" origin="BoundVar"
    sort="BoundVar" serialnr="29" varnr="1"/>
<Simple−Term idnr="9" spelling="Y" position="72\49" origin="ReservedVar"
    sort="Constant" serialnr="8" varnr="2"/></Arguments></Relation-Formula>
```

2.3   Reading the XML into Scala Classes

Contrary to other parser generators, which generate the source code of the classes and the parser from a grammar, we directly implement the classes in Scala and then generate the parser. For example, the (heavily simplified) classes below are used to pick out the relevant attributes from the Simple_ −Term element visible above. Expression is the abstract class of all Mizar expressions, and LocalConstAttr is an auxiliary class that groups XML attributes that often occur together.

```
abstract class MizTerm extends Expression
case class Simple_Term(serialnr: Int, spelling:String, sort:String) extends MizTerm
case class Arguments(_children:List[MizTerm])
```

This is sufficient to generate the XML parser using Scala reflection. This has the advantage that the Scala classes, which are what the translation developer interacts with primarily in the next step, are much more easily maintainable, can be better documented than generated code, and can be manually tweaked better to be practical.

These classes are available at https://github.com/UniFormal/MMT/ in the package info.kwarc.mmt.mizar. Note that this XML parsing step is independent of MMT. Thus, other developers can easily reuse these classes and our XML parser as a starting point for translations into other target languages.

2.4   Translating the Scala Classes to MMT

The logical heart of the translation is now isolated in an inductive function that traverses the Scala classes holding the MML XML and producing corresponding MMT classes. This happens in memory, and MMT's existing emitters for OMDoc and MMT source syntax can be used out of the box. Critically, it requires handling all idiosyncrasies of the Mizar language. The resulting export of the MML is available at https://gl.mathhub.info/Mizar/MML.

We translate each Mizar **article** to an MMT theory (relative to those from Sect. 2.1) that contains *include* declarations for all Mizar articles it depends on. Each **theorems** is translated to a single MMT declaration whose type gives the claim and whose definiens the proof. Each scheme, functor/predicate/mode, and attribute **definitions** as well as **synonyms/antonyms** and **registrations** are translated into instances of the corresponding patterns mentioned in Sect. 2.1. Where applicable, they are followed by declarations stating and proving the specially treated properties such as reflexivity for binary predicates. **Redefinitions** are translated into fresh constants with a new definition; if only the type is changed and no new definiens is provided, we synthesize a definition by applying the original constant to the corresponding arguments (this works, as the new types are required to be subtypes). **Structure** definitions (record types) are translated using an MMT structural feature in the style of [MRRK20] that reimplements in MMT Mizar's conservative extension principle for adding named record types. Mizar's forgetful functors between structures become record subtyping.

Proofs, which Mizar does not store entirely anyway, are translated only partially by using a special constant for a proof oracle: it takes a claim and a number of references to used theorems and returns a proof of the claim. This way proof dependencies are preserved in the export.

Improving on [IKRU13], our translation covers correctness conditions and properties of definitions, all registrations ([IKRU13] covered only existential registrations), forgetful-functors between structures, and partial proofs.

For example, consider the definition of the subset predicate from Sect. 2.2, which uses $n = 2$ arguments, whose types are just set and do not depend on other arguments, $m = 0$ cases, and one default case for the actual definition. Its name $R1R1$ is build from a character characterizing the kind of declaration (R) and the article-scoped counters contained in the absolutepatternMMLId and absoluteconstrMMLId, which yields a unique identifier within the article. It is translated to the following instance of the MMT pattern directPartPredDef from Sect. 2.1 (the formula $true \land true \Rightarrow \_$ is deliberately not simplified, to emphasize how it is derived by elaborating the directPartPredDef pattern):

instance tarski:R1R1 ?MizarPatterns/directPartPredDef(2 0 ⟨([x : term²] set), ([x : term²] set)⟩
  ⟨⟩ ⟨⟩ ([x : term²] for term [x/BV/29 : term] x/BV/29 in x.0 ⇒ x/BV/29 in x.1)
  (proof omitted))
//elaborates to
pred : term² → prop
consistency = (proof omitted)
means : {x : term²} ⊢ x.0 ⸵ set →⊢ x.1 ⸵ set →⊢ true ∧ true
  ⇒ (tarski:R1R1/pred x) ⇔ (for term [x/BV/29 : term] x/BV/29 in x.0 ⇒ x/BV/29 in x.1)

The translation is **context-free** except for a few cases where the EMSM files do not quite contain enough information yet—in those cases some static analysis of Mizar must be reimplemented in MMT and therefore the depended-upon articles must have been processed already:

- Some functor redefinitions and functorial registrations require type inference of the return type
- The arity of the original declaration of a redefinition without definiens must be determined.

The Mizar developers plan to address this issue with a new set of files in a new extension of EMSM.

3 Conclusion and Future Work

We have presented a thorough overhaul of the 10-year old export of the MML into OMDoc, leveraging all lessons learned and improvements made since then. Our export covers the entire MML with the only exception being the partial translation of proofs. The

Format	Size	Gen. time
MML	100 MB	-
XML	4.7 GB	15 min
MMT (zipped OMDoc)	18 MB	2 h
MMT (text syntax)	200 MB	30 h

table on the right gives an overview of the sizes and generation times of the digital artifacts, all of which are available online as referenced throughout the paper. The export has so far been run only on simple hardware, and we expect shorter times when parallelizing on a server as soon as all issues of context-sensitivity have been removed. The generation time of the Mizar XML is so short because it is parallelized and Mizar only needs to resolve identifiers, which does not require verifying the proofs. The generation time of the MMT text syntax is excessive due to a scalability issue in MMT that was uncovered by the present export; it is unrelated to the Mizar export and will be fixed in a future release. The sizes of the Mizar and the MMT text are not directly comparable: the latter lacks full proofs, but includes some longer generated variable names, includes instances with their elaborations, and uses a less optimized syntax for conciseness and readability.

The XML produced by Mizar has much higher quality, the representation uses modern MMT feature for declaratively mimicking Mizars's highly idiosyncratic language, and the export implementation is substantially more maintainable, easier to use, and scalable. This provides promising evidence that investments into proof assistant library export workflows (albeit costly ones at glacial pace) are putting library translations and the thus-enabled system integrations ever more feasible.

References

BA12.   Bylinski, C., Alama, J.: New developments in parsing Mizar. In: Jeuring, J., Campbell, J.A., Carette, J., Dos Reis, G., Sojka, P., Wenzel, M., Sorge, V. (eds.) CICM 2012. LNCS (LNAI), vol. 7362, pp. 427–431. Springer, Heidelberg (2012). https://doi.org/10.1007/978-3-642-31374-5_30

BBG+18.   Bancerek, G., et al.: The role of the Mizar Mathematical Library for interactive proof development in Mizar. J. Autom. Reason. **61**(1), 9–32 (2018). https://doi.org/10.1007/s10817-017-9440-6

HKR12.   Horozal, F., Kohlhase, M., Rabe, F.: Extending MKM formats at the statement level. In: Jeuring, J., et al. (eds.) CICM 2012. LNCS (LNAI), vol. 7362, pp. 65–80. Springer, Heidelberg (2012). https://doi.org/10.1007/978-3-642-31374-5_5

HR15.   Horozal, F., Rabe, F.: Formal logic definitions for interchange languages. In: Kerber, M., Carette, J., Kaliszyk, C., Rabe, F., Sorge, V. (eds.) CICM 2015. LNCS (LNAI), vol. 9150, pp. 171–186. Springer, Cham (2015). https://doi.org/10.1007/978-3-319-20615-8_11

IKRU13.   Iancu, M., Kohlhase, M., Rabe, F., Urban, J.: The Mizar Mathematical Library in OMDoc: translation and applications. J. Autom. Reason. **50**(2), 191–202 (2013). https://doi.org/10.1007/s10817-012-9271-4

Koh06.   Kohlhase, M.: OMDoc – An Open Markup Format for Mathematical Documents [version 1.2]. LNCS (LNAI), vol. 4180. Springer, Heidelberg (2006). https://doi.org/10.1007/11826095

KP19.   Kaliszyk, C., Pak, K.: Semantics of Mizar as an Isabelle object logic. J. Autom. Reason. **63**(3), 557–595 (2019). https://doi.org/10.1007/s10817-018-9479-z

KR20.   Kohlhase, M., Rabe, F.: Experiences from exporting major proof assistant libraries (2020). see https://kwarc.info/people/frabe/Research/KR_oafexp_20.pdf

MRRK20.   Müller, D., Rabe, F., Rothgang, C., Kohlhase, M.: Representing structural language features in formal meta-languages. In: Benzmüller, C., Miller, B. (eds.) CICM 2020. LNCS (LNAI), vol. 12236, pp. 206–221. Springer, Cham (2020). https://doi.org/10.1007/978-3-030-53518-6_13

NP16.   Naumowicz, A., Piliszek, R.: Accessing the Mizar library with a weakly strict Mizar parser. In: Kohlhase, M., Johansson, M., Miller, B., de Moura, L., Tompa, F. (eds.) CICM 2016. LNCS (LNAI), vol. 9791, pp. 77–82. Springer, Cham (2016). https://doi.org/10.1007/978-3-319-42547-4_6

RK13.   Rabe, F., Kohlhase, M.: A scalable module system. Inf. Comput. **230**(1), 1–54 (2013)

Urb03.   Urban, J.: Translating Mizar for first order theorem provers. In: Asperti, A., Buchberger, B., Davenport, J.H. (eds.) MKM 2003. LNCS, vol. 2594, pp. 203–215. Springer, Heidelberg (2003). https://doi.org/10.1007/3-540-36469-2_16

Urb05.   Urban, J.: XML-izing Mizar: making semantic processing and presentation of MML easy. In: Kohlhase, M. (ed.) MKM 2005. LNCS (LNAI), vol. 3863, pp. 346–360. Springer, Heidelberg (2006). https://doi.org/10.1007/11618027_23

A Language with Type-Dependent Equality

Florian Rabe[✉][iD]

Computer Science, FAU Erlangen-Nuremberg, Erlangen, Germany
florian.rabe@fau.de

Abstract. In soft type systems terms and types exist independently and
typing is a binary relation between them. That allows the same term to
have multiple types, which is in particular the case in the presence of
subtyping. Thus, a soft type system may define equality in such a way
that two terms can be equal at one type but unequal at another type.

We explore the design of soft type systems with such a type-dependent
equality. The most promising application is that it yields a more natural
treatment of quotient types: if two terms can be different at the base type
but equal at the quotient type, we can use the same representation in
both types without incurring the cost of using equivalence classes. That
can help formalize mathematics, where the official definition of quotients
uses equivalence classes but practical notations usually do not. The main
drawback of such a system is that the substitution of equals by equals
becomes more complex as it now depends on the type with which the
equal terms are used.

We analyze the general problem, show examples from major soft-typed
proof assistants, and then present a simple language that allows studying
type-dependent equality in a simple rigorous setting.

1 Introduction

To work with mathematical content in computer systems, it is necessary to
represent it in formal languages. So far combining the flexibility of informal
mathematical language with strong tool support has proved challenging. All
major proof assistants are at least partially motivated by this but must make
different trade-offs to obtain tool support. And despite massive progress, no
current system is even close to mimicking the flexibility of mathematical language [Wie07,KR20]. Arguably that is part of the reason why adoption of proof
assistants by mathematicians is much slower than hoped.

A fundamental issue is the decidability of typing and equality, which is not
a priority (arguable even a negative priority) in mathematics but often essential
in proof assistants. Therefore, features like subtyping via predicate types $\{x :
A|p(x)\}$ and equating objects via quotient types A/r are very difficult to design
in formal systems.

In **hard-typed** systems, every term has a unique type (possibly up to
some equality on types). Examples used in proof assistants are dependent

© Springer Nature Switzerland AG 2021
F. Kamareddine and C. Sacerdoti Coen (Eds.): CICM 2021, LNAI 12833, pp. 211–227, 2021.
https://doi.org/10.1007/978-3-030-81097-9_18

type theories such as the one in Coq [Coq15] and the higher-order logic family [Gor88]. Hard typing often yields better computational properties (in particular type inference, decidable equality) but requires formalization artifacts when mathematical operations on sets cannot be mapped direct to corresponding operations on types. For examples, quotients must usually be modeled via Setoids $\{A : \mathtt{type}, r : A \to A \to \mathtt{bool}\}$ and subtypes via dependent products $\Sigma x : A.P(x)$. Lean [dKA+15] uses an interesting compromise: it adds kernel-level proof automation for those artifacts even though they are library-level definitions and not part of the underlying logic.

Our focus here is on **soft-typed** systems, where terms exist independently of types and typing is giving by a binary predicate between terms and types. In particular, every term can have many different types, and types can be seen as unary predicates on terms. Proof assistants using soft typing include Nuprl [CAB+86, ABC+06] and Mizar [TB85]. These can accommodate predicate types (both) and quotient types (Nuprl) naturally at the cost of making typing and equality undecidable. A compromise solution is employed in PVS [ORS92]: it uses a hard type system with a lattice of soft predicate subtypes for each hard type.

In this paper we look at one particular feature in the design of soft type systems: type-dependent equality (TDE). With TDE, the equality operator is defined in such a way that the derivability of the formula $s =_A t$ depends on the type A—the same two terms might be equal at one type but unequal at a different type. Note that TDE is not a design option in hard type systems at all because there terms do not have multiple different types to begin with.

This paper is motivated by the observation that TDE, while used in some systems, has received disproportionately little systematic attention relative to its potential benefits and fundamental nature. In fact, the author coined the name "type-dependent equality" for the occasion of this paper. Even in proof assistants featuring (some variant of) TDE, it is not prominently advertised. This is all the more important as some of the TDE-related language design trade-offs in these systems are very subtle and little-known even to experts in the area of formalized mathematics.

We take a broad approach focusing on general ideas and presenting only a simple formal language with TDE. This is warranted because typing and equality are cross-cutting issues that affect virtually every other language feature and thus cannot be studied in isolation. Sect. 2 extensively discusses the benefits and dangers of TDE and how it interrelates with other language features. It also describes some of the subtleties of how TDE is or is not realized in current proof assistants. Then Sect. 3 introduces the syntax and semantics of a formal language with TDE. It serves as an example to better understand TDE and as a starting point to develop more advanced languages with TDE. Section 4 concludes.

2 Motivating Considerations and Related Work

2.1 Type-Dependent Equality

Benefits Equality is usually seen as a binary relation on objects. Even in typed languages, which often use a ternary equality relation $s =_A t$, equality is often absolute in the sense that the derivability of $s =_A t$ does not depend on A. The only effect of A in $=_A$ is to restrict s and t to be of type A—if s and t have both type A and B, then either both $s =_A t$ and $s =_B t$ hold or neither.

A type-*dependent* equality (TDE) relation is rare, and it is instructive to ponder why. In hard-typed languages such as HOL [Gor88] or the calculus of constructions underlying Coq [Coq15], all types are disjoint. Equality is ternary because it is a polymorphic family of binary relations, one for each type. The question of TDE does not come up because terms s and t never have two different types A and B.

Set theoretic languages are usually based on an axiomatization of set theory in first-order logic as in Mizar [TB85] or higher-order logic as in Isabelle/ZF [PC93]. In both cases, it is common to use a fixed base type U for the universe of sets, and binary equality on U is a primitive notion. In these languages, soft typing is an emergent feature: we can add the concept of types as unary predicates on U. But the binary equality on U both historically and foundationally precedes the introduction of soft types. Thus, TDE is usually not considered.

The only major system with systematic TDE that the author could find is Nuprl [CAB+86]. It uses TDE to handle quotients naturally by changing the equality at the quotient type. For example, it allows having both $0 \neq_{\mathbb{Z}} 2$ and $0 =_{\mathbb{Z}/\mathrm{mod}_2} 2$ without inconsistency. The key idea is to use a different equality relation at the quotient type than at the base type. This trick has the benefit that no fiddling with equivalence classes is needed: the term $2 : \mathbb{Z}$ can also be used as an element of $2 : \mathbb{Z}/\mathrm{mod}_2$. Thus, the canonical projection into the quotient is a no-op, which is far superior computationally and notationally to the standard approach of using equivalence classes.

Mizar [TB85] uses a light variant of TDE for record types, which we discuss in more detail in Sect. 2.4.

Arguably, TDE is how quotients are handled in practical mathematics as well. Even though mathematics officially defines the quotient as the set of equivalence classes, mathematical notation almost always reuses the terms of the original types as elements of the quotient—with the implicit understanding that related terms are equal when seen as elements of the quotient. However, this is considered a notational simplification, and the foundations of mathematics do not include a rigorous treatment of TDE.

Analogy to Typing. There is an elegant way to fit TDE into a general framework of formal systems if we think of typing as type-dependent definedness (TDD). Instead of thinking of $a : A$ as a binary predicate, we can think of it as a type-dependent unary predicate $:_A$ applied to a.

That yields a language with a unary and a binary type-dependent predicate: TDD $:_A$ and TDE $=_A$. TDD regulates which values are acceptable values at type A, and TDE regulates which of those are equal. The semantics of types can then be given by partial equivalence relations on objects [All87]: the denotational semantics of A is the universe U restricted to objects satisfying $:_A$ quotiented by $=_A$.

It is well-known that partial equivalence relations enjoy nice closure properties. In particular, TDE makes it easy to introduce

- predicate types $A|p$ for a unary predicate p on A: a copy of A with definedness restricted to p
- quotient types A/r for an equivalence relation r on A: a copy of A with equality broadened to r.

Dangers. Tweaking the equality relation at a type corresponds to changing the introduction rule of equality to make more things equal. Consequently, the elimination rule is applicable more often so that a naive version of TDE can easily be inconsistent. The elimination rule of equality varies between languages but is usually a substitution rule like

$$\frac{x : A \vdash F(x) : \texttt{bool} \qquad \vdash s =_A s' \qquad \vdash F(s)}{\vdash F(s')} \text{Sub}$$

This shows us how TDE can cause trouble: Assume in addition to the premises of Sub, we also have $x : B \vdash F(x)$ and $\vdash s : B$ and $\vdash s' : B$—a common situation in languages with subtyping. Then TDE+Sub is inconsistent if the plausible situation arises where $\vdash \neg s =_B s'$ and $\vdash F(s)$ and $\vdash \neg F(s')$. Intuitively, whenever terms can have multiple types, the equality relations at those types must be consistent with each other. At least if A is a subtype of B, then $s =_A s'$ should imply $s =_B s'$, i.e., the rule

$$\frac{\vdash s =_A s' \qquad \vdash A <: B}{\vdash s =_B s'}$$

should be present. Otherwise, we would no longer have a canonical embedding of A into B, which would be an unreasonably high price to pay.

But the details subtly depend on the specific language. To understand how Nuprl, which uses Sub, avoids inconsistency, the author had to resort to direct communication with the developers after exhausting the documentation and failing at reverse engineering: Nuprl prevents the above situation because $x : A \vdash F(x) : \texttt{bool}$ would not hold, thus making Sub not applicable. In fact and maybe surprisingly, it is possible in Nuprl to have $\vdash F(g) : \texttt{bool}$ for every closed term $g : A$ but still $x : A \nvdash F(x) : \texttt{bool}$. That is because the Nuprl proof system (of which well-formedness of propositions is a special case) privileges closed terms—there is even a type $Base$ of all closed terms. This unusual behavior is motivated also by other design considerations but is critical for the soundness of TDE+Sub in Nuprl.

2.2 Abstract Definitions and Quotient Types

Standard mathematics defines quotients via equivalence classes. It is instructive to ask whether there are alternative definitions.

Abstract vs. Concrete Definitions. We speak of an **abstract** definition of a language feature if the operations that form sets and their elements are axiomatized through their characteristic properties. We speak of a **concrete** definition if the operations are given as abbreviations of existing expressions.

A paradigmatic abstract definition is the Cartesian product, which is usually specified to have formation operator $\_ \times \_$, introduction form $(\_, \_)$, elimination forms $\_1$ and $\_2$, computation properties $(a, b)_1 = a$ and $(a, b)_2 = b$ (intuitively: elimination of introduction is identity), representation property $p = (p_1, p_2)$ (intuitively: introduction of elimination is identity; or introduction is surjective), and extensionality property $p = q$ iff $p_i = q_i$ for $i = 1, 2$ (intuitively: elimination is injective). To show the consistency, at least one concrete definition must be given, e.g., via Wiener pairs or Kuratowski pairs.

A paradigmatic concrete definition is the set of functions, which is usually defined by formation operator $A \to B = \{f \subseteq A \times B | \forall x : A.\exists^1 y : B.(x, y) \in f\}$, introduction form $\lambda x : A.t(x) = \{(a, t(a)) : a \in A\}$, elimination form $f\,a = $ **the** $b : B.(a, b) \in f$. For concrete constructions, the characteristic properties are the corresponding ones but must be proved instead of being axioms: computation $(\lambda x : A.t(x))\,a = t(a)$, representation $f = \lambda x : A.f\,x$, extensionality $f = g$ iff $f\,a = g\,a$ for $a : A$.

Abstract definitions allow for more scalable reasoning, can usually be done in simpler languages, allow defining language features orthogonally, and are more portable across systems. Thus, mathematics and computer science often prefer them, e.g., λ calculus is the abstract definition of function types obtained by abstracting from the concrete one used in mathematics.

Abstract Quotient Types. It is maybe surprising that quotient types are usually defined concretely by using equivalence classes:

$$A/r = \{[a]_r : a \in A\}, \quad [a]_r = \{a' : A | r\,a\,a'\} \quad (*)$$

Maybe this is because there is no natural competing concrete definition. Contrary to function sets, there is no commonly used abstract specification of quotient sets either. But we can systematically obtain an abstract specification by analogy to the ones above:

- formation operator A/r for a binary equivalence relation r on A
- introduction form $[a]_r$ for $a : A$
- elimination form $t(\rho q) : B$ for $q : A/r$ and $t(x) : A \xrightarrow{r} B$, where we write ρq for picking an arbitrary representative of class q and $t(x) : A \xrightarrow{r} B$ as a shorthand for $x : A \vdash t(x) : B$ and $r\,a\,a'$ implies $t(a) = t(a')$,
- computation property $t(\rho[a]_r) = t(a)$
- representation property $[\_]_r : A \xrightarrow{r} B$ and $q = [\rho q]_r$ whenever $q : A/r$
- extensionality property $p = q$ iff $t(\rho p) = t(\rho q)$ whenever $t(x) : A \xrightarrow{r} B$

Nuprl uses this abstract definition of quotient types that is a primitive part of the logic. An alternative definition of quotients equivalent to the one in Nuprl is given in [Nog02]. Introduction form $[\_]_r$ and elimination form ρ are no-ops, which is critical for performance and convenience. Mizar defines quotients concretely using $(*)$. Coq and Lean define quotients concretely via setoids, but that does not satisfy the above specification as equality is not redefined. However, Lean provides kernel-level support to eliminate that artifact.

2.3   Predicate and Quotient Types

Predicate Types. If p is a unary predicate on A, we write $A|p$ for the predicate subtype of A given by p. An abstract specification can be given by

- formation operator $A|p$
- introduction form $a|p : A|p$ if $a : A$ and $p\,a$
- elimination form $\iota s : A$ for $s : A|p$, and $p\,(\iota s)$
- computation property $\iota\,(a|p) = a$
- representation property $s = (\iota s)|p$ whenever $s : A|p$
- extensionality property $s = t$ iff $\iota s = \iota t$ for $s, t : A|p$

Mizar uses a concrete definition to introduce predicate types. Nuprl and PVS use abstract ones that are primitive parts of the logics. In all three systems, introduction form $a|p$ and elimination form ι are no-ops (i.e., the introduction form incurs a proof obligation that the system must try to discharge automatically). Hard-typed languages such as HOL or dependent type theory usually define set $A = A \to$ bool as the power type of A. Then p itself can be used instead of $A|p$. But this does not satisfy the above specification as p is a value and not a type. The HOL proof assistant family employ the conservative extension principle to turn the value p into a fresh type [Gor88]: essentially given p, it adds a fresh type S, a partial function $A \to^? S$ and the function $\iota : S \to A$ such that S becomes bijective to $A|p$. PVS uses HOL plus primitive operations corresponding to the above specification. Because it supports both $p :$ set A and the type $A|p$, conversions between the two are commonly used.

Duality. The abstract definitions of predicate and quotient types are dual in the following sense:

Property	Predicate type $A|p$	Quotient type A/r
Formation uses	unary predicate p	binary predicate r
Introduction	requires satisfaction of p	canonical projection $[\_]_r$
Elimination	canonical injection ι	requires preservation of r
Minimal predicate	$A|\lambda x.\mathtt{false} \cong$ void (initial)	$A/\lambda xy.\mathtt{false} \cong A$
Total predicate	$A|\lambda x.\mathtt{true} \cong A$	$A/\lambda xy.\mathtt{true} \cong$ unit (terminal)

Here, to enhance the duality, we do not require r to be an equivalence. Instead, we allow any binary relation and assume the semantics uses the generated equivalence relation. Nuprl and the setoid encoding require an equivalence relation.

The duality is weaker when using standard concrete definitions. Here concrete predicate types make it easy to use no-ops for introduction. But for concrete quotient types, the projection $[\_]_r$ is expensive. A guiding motivation for our work is to retain the duality and use no-ops in both cases.

This becomes particularly practical when chaining: Using no-ops, in $A|p|q$, we can use a predicate q on A as opposed to $A|p$. And we simply have $A|p|q = A|q|p = A|(\lambda x.p\,x \wedge q\,x)$. For quotient types, we desire the corresponding chain rule $A/r/s = A/s/r = A/(\lambda xy.r\,x\,y \vee s\,x\,y$ as opposed to awkwardly defining s on equivalence classes.

2.4   Records and Predicate/Quotient Types

Lax vs. Strict Records. For simplicity, we do not give formal rules for record types and instead consider them by example. We use record types like $R := \{x : A, y : B\}$ with introduction form $r := [x = a, y = b] : R$ and elimination forms $r.x : A$ and $r.y : B$. Specifically, we discuss the relation between R and $S := \{x : A\}$ as well as the forgetful functor $F : R \to S$. Using this example, we introduce a distinction between lax and strict records that is critical in the presence of soft typing and TDE.

If $\vdash r : S$, we speak of **lax records**. Intuitively, the elements of a lax record type are all records that have *at least* the fields prescribed by the type. Thus, larger record types have fewer record values. To check $r : S$, we only check $r.x : A$ and ignore the additional field $r.y$. Therefore, R is a subtype of S, and F is the subtype embedding and a no-op, and the empty record type $\{\}$ is the type of all records.

This is the case in most languages with primitive record types. In this situation, TDE (possibly only for record types) is a natural feature: for $s, t : R$, we can put $s =_R t$ if $s.x =_A t.x$ and $s.y =_B t.y$, but $s =_S t$ already if $s.x =_A t.x$. Thus, the subtype R has the stronger equality, and more terms may be equal at the supertype S. In particular, we might have $s =_S t$ but $s \neq_R t$.

This is how PVS records work. Mizar structures work almost the same way: However, the type argument of the equality relation is not explicit in Mizar. Instead, it is inferred to be the most specific type of the argument records, i.e. if $s, t : R$, then $s = t$ denotes $s =_R t$. In addition to R being a subtype of S, Mizar introduces explicit syntax for F to drop the additional fields, and then the equality $s =_S t$ can be stated as $F(s) = F(t)$. Nuprl does not have primitive records but derives lax record types as functions from some index set (representing the field labels) to types.

If $\nvdash r : S$, we speak of **strict records**. Intuitively, the elements of a strict record type are all records that have *exactly* the fields prescribed by the type. $F(r)$ explicitly removes the field y from r, and the empty record $\{\}$ is a unit type. This is common in languages that use derived record types (e.g., by generating an axiomatic specification, via product types $A \times B$, or via single-constructor inductive types $R = \mathtt{inductive}\,R(A, B)$). Examples are Coq and Isabelle. Here F can be an expensive operation, especially if many record fields must be copied or if the value of the field y must be re-inferred later on. TDE is not an option because no two records have both type R and type S.

There is no subtyping between strict record types R and S, and the relation between them can be better understood as a quotient. $\lambda r r' : R.\ r.x =_A r'.x$ is an equivalence relation on R, and F is the canonical projection. Contrary to general quotients, the equivalence relation always has canonical representatives: we can use the elements of S because S is isomorphic to the quotient.

Record Subtypes vs. Record Quotients. We can apply the quotient intuition also to lax records. As for strict records, we have the same equivalence relation on R, and F is also the canonical projection. However, the quotient type cannot be expressed: F is not surjective, and S is not isomorphic to the quotient—S is much bigger than the quotient (a supertype of R even). For that reason, Mizar introduces an additional operator that maps every record type S (which are lax by default) to the corresponding strict record type S^{strict} and provides syntax for the functor F that now maps $R \to S^{\mathrm{strict}}$.

Conversely, we can apply the subtype intuition to strict records. But F is not a no-op and thus not a proper subtype embedding. But languages that support implicit coercions can insert F automatically, thus creating the look and feel of subtyping for the user.

Thus, languages have substantial freedom in how to combine record types with subtyping and quotient typing as well as TDE.

Mathematical Records. In standard mathematics, records are not used explicitly. But effectively, they occur frequently, e.g., when using algebraic structures such as when S is Magma (tuple of a set and an operation) and R is Monoid (Magma with an additional unit). We can think of them as strict records derived via Cartesian products.

The cost of the explicit forgetful functor F is harmless here because the representation change from r to $F(r)$ is not done on paper and left to an implicit coercion in the reader's mind, i.e., we simply write r instead of $F(r)$. Therefore, mathematical language can flexibly switch between the subtype intuition (every monoid is a magma) and the quotient intuition (monoids can be projected to their magma).

3   Formal Language Definition

We develop a minimal formal language with systematic TDE.

3.1   Syntax and Inference System

Grammar. The grammar is given below. Types A are user-declared base types a, type variables k, built-in base type `bool`, predicate types $A|p$, quotient types A/r, and function types $A \to B$. Simple functions are needed to give the language practical expressivity and to form the unary/binary predicates p and r.

Dependent functions types or polymorphic type operators can be added easily but are not essential in the sequel. We add record types in Sect. 3.3.

Terms are user-declared constants c, bound variables x, the usual logical connectives and quantifiers on the type $\texttt{bool}$, and the usual λ-abstraction and application forms for $A \to B$. $A|p$ and A/r do not have associated term formation rules because they are populated by the same terms as A with introduction and elimination being no-ops. The distinction between A on the one hand and $A|p$ and A/r on the other hand is relegated to the judgments $t : A$ (TDD) and $s =_A t$ (TDE). In keeping with logical practice, the equality judgment is part of the term syntax as a $\texttt{bool}$-valued predicate. But the typing judgment must be a meta-level judgment because it defines which syntax is well-formed to begin with and because of subtle soundness issues discussed below.

$$
\begin{aligned}
A, B \quad &::= a \mid k \mid \texttt{bool} \mid A|p \mid A/r \mid A \to B \\
s, t, p, r &::= c \mid x \mid \texttt{true} \mid \texttt{false} \mid \texttt{if}(s)\,t\,\texttt{else}\,t' \mid \text{(logical operators)} \\
&\quad \mid \ \lambda x : A.t \mid t\,t \mid s =_A t \\
\Gamma \qquad &::= (x : \texttt{type} \mid x : A \mid t)^*
\end{aligned}
$$

User-declared theories Θ (omitted in the grammar) introduce global knowledge: base types $a : \texttt{type}$, constants $c : A$ for $A : \texttt{type}$, and axioms t for $t : \texttt{bool}$. Everything below should be understood as relative to a fixed theory, which we do not make explicit in the notation. Correspondingly, contexts Γ collect local (α-renamable) knowledge: type variables $k : \texttt{type}$, typed variables $x : A$ for $A : \texttt{type}$, and local assumptions t for $t : \texttt{bool}$.

Judgments. The judgments are given below. As usual for soft type theories, the rules for the typing and provability judgments are mutually recursive. A subtyping judgment is defined below as an abbreviation. Because types can contain terms, we also need a judgment for equality of types and a rule for substitution of equal types for each other, but we omit those here.

$\Gamma \vdash$	Γ is a well-formed context
$\Gamma \vdash A : \texttt{type}$	A is a well-formed type
$\Gamma \vdash t : A$	t is well-formed at type A
$\Gamma \vdash t$	boolean t is provable

$$\frac{\Gamma, x : A \vdash t(x) : B}{\Gamma \vdash \lambda x : A.t(x) : A \to B} \qquad \frac{\Gamma \vdash s : \mathtt{bool} \quad \Gamma, s \vdash t : A \quad \Gamma, \neg s \vdash t' : A}{\Gamma \vdash \mathtt{if}(s)t\,\mathtt{else}\,t' : A}$$

$$\frac{\Gamma \vdash s : A \quad \Gamma \vdash t : A}{\Gamma \vdash s =_A t : \mathtt{bool}} \qquad \frac{\Gamma \vdash s : \mathtt{bool} \quad \Gamma, s \vdash t : \mathtt{bool}}{\Gamma \vdash s \wedge t : \mathtt{bool}} \qquad \frac{\Gamma \vdash s \quad \Gamma, s \vdash t}{\Gamma \vdash s \wedge t}$$

$$\frac{\Gamma, x : A \vdash t(x) : \mathtt{bool}}{\Gamma \vdash (\forall x : A.t(x)) : \mathtt{bool}} \qquad \frac{\Gamma \vdash \forall x : A.t(x) \quad \Gamma \vdash s : A}{\Gamma \vdash t(s)}$$

Fig. 1. Selected rules for standard operators

Rules for Standard Operators. We omit most of the rules for context formation, logical operators, and functions and only give some selected rules in Fig. 1. We write $t(x)$ for a term with a distinguished free variable x and accordingly $t(s)$ for the substitution of s for x.

The rule for λ-abstraction is as usual. Because no constraints are put on $t(x)$, we later on incur the proof obligation that every term $t(x)$ respects $=_A$. The formation rule for equality shows that $s =_A t$ is only well-formed if s and t already have type A. The rule for if-then-else is interesting because a local assumption for the truth/falsity of the condition s is available to show the well-formedness of the expression t and t' in the then/else branch. Similarly, the rules for the quantifiers (here shown: $\forall$) and binary logical operators (here shown: $\wedge$) may use the truth of their first part to show the well-formedness of the second part; for the binary operators, that corresponds to lazy evaluation. That is important because the typing rules for predicate and quotient types are able to use those assumptions.

The proof rules for the binary operators (here shown: the introduction rule for $\wedge$) are similarly sequential. Contrary to both standard hard-typed higher-order logic and soft-typed Mizar, we allow empty types, which is the natural choice when working with predicate types. Therefore, some quantifier rules (here shown: the elimination rule of the universal) only allow terms whose free variables are from the current context; consequently, e.g., $\forall x : A.t(x) \Rightarrow \exists x : A.t(x)$ is only a theorem if A is known to be non-empty.

Type formation:

$$\frac{\Gamma \vdash A : \mathtt{type} \quad \Gamma \vdash p : A \to \mathtt{bool}}{\Gamma \vdash A|p : \mathtt{type}} \qquad \frac{\Gamma \vdash A : \mathtt{type} \quad \Gamma \vdash r : A \to A \to \mathtt{bool}}{\Gamma \vdash A/r : \mathtt{type}}$$

Introduction (TDD):

$$\frac{\Gamma \vdash t : A \quad \Gamma \vdash p\,t}{\Gamma \vdash t : A|p} \qquad \frac{\Gamma \vdash t : A}{\Gamma \vdash t : A/r}$$

Elimination:

$$\frac{\Gamma \vdash t : A|p}{\Gamma \vdash t : A} \qquad \frac{\Gamma \vdash t : A|p}{\Gamma \vdash p\,t}$$

$$\frac{\Gamma \vdash s : A/r \quad \Gamma, x : A \vdash t(x) : B \quad \Gamma, x : A, y : A, r\,x\,y \vdash t(x) =_B t(y)}{\Gamma \vdash t(s) : B}$$

Equality (TDE):

$$\frac{\Gamma \vdash s : A|p \quad \Gamma \vdash t : A|p \quad \Gamma \vdash s =_A t}{\Gamma \vdash s =_{A|p} t} \qquad \frac{\Gamma \vdash s : A \quad \Gamma \vdash t : A \quad \Gamma \vdash r\,s\,t}{\Gamma \vdash s =_{A/r} t}$$

Fig. 2. Rules for predicate and quotient types

Rules for Predicate and Quotient Types. Figure 2 gives all rules for predicate and quotient types. Together with the proof rules below, it is straightforward to show that these satisfy the abstract specifications described in Sect. 2: introduction and elimination forms are no-ops, and computation, representation, and extensionality are trivial.

Note that the equality rule for quotient types does not have to construct the equivalence closure of r. We only make all terms equal that satisfy $r\,s\,t$, at which point the usual rules for equality already induce the equivalence closure.

Equality introduction and elimination:

$$\frac{\Gamma \vdash t : A}{\Gamma \vdash t =_A t} \qquad \frac{\Gamma \vdash s =_A s' \quad \Gamma, x : A \vdash t(x) : \mathtt{bool} \quad \Gamma \vdash t(s)}{\Gamma \vdash t(s')}\,\mathrm{Sub}$$

Fig. 3. Rules for equality

Rules for Equality. Figure 3 gives the rules for equality. Reflexivity is the introduction rule. As usual, symmetry and transitivity can be derived.

The elimination rule Sub is the usual substitution rule. It is deceptively simple: its soundness is very sensitive to subtle variations in the language. The problem is that the type A may affect the derivability of the premise $s =_A s'$ but does not explicitly occur in the conclusion of the rule. Thus, whenever $t(s)$ and $\neg t(s')$, we can try to force an inconsistency by choosing some A at which s

and s' are equal, e.g., a suitable quotient of a sufficiently large type. The type system must prevent that by allowing $t(x)$ to use the variable $x : A$ only in ways that cannot distinguish A-equal terms.

For example, it may be unexpected that our syntax does not include bool-values terms $t \in A$. We could include that, say with a formation rule

$$\frac{\Gamma \vdash t : B \quad \Gamma \vdash A : \texttt{type}}{\Gamma \vdash t \in A : \texttt{bool}}$$

Here the first premise is necessary to ensure that only well-typed terms t may be used. But there is a deep problem: it would allow constructing terms that do not preserve equality. For example, assume a theory that declares the usual type $\mathbb{N}$ and constants for the natural numbers, and let $\texttt{mod}_m$ be equivalence modulo m and $\texttt{Prime}$ be the prime number property. Then for a variable $x : \mathbb{N}/\texttt{mod}_2$, the boolean $x \in \mathbb{N}|\texttt{Prime}$ would be well-formed and equivalent to $\texttt{Prime}(x)$. But that boolean would break the soundness of Sub as we have $2 =_{\mathbb{N}/\texttt{mod}_2} 4$ but $2 \in \mathbb{N}|\texttt{Prime}$ and $4 \notin \mathbb{N}|\texttt{Prime}$.

Remark 1. The author had originally included $t \in A : \texttt{bool}$ in the syntax but failed to obtain soundness even after trying multiple variants of the syntax and formation rule of $t \in A$.

However, without a bool-valued predicate $\in$, not much expressivity is lost: we can still express $x \in \mathbb{N}|p$ by simply putting $p\,x$. And we can easily add syntactic sugar to recover $\in$-based notations for that. Despite the similar expressivity, the inconsistency problem does not arise in that case: if $x : \mathbb{N}/\texttt{mod}_2$, the boolean $\texttt{Prime}\,x$ is ill-formed because $\texttt{Prime} : \mathbb{N} \to \texttt{bool}$ cannot be applied to $x : \mathbb{N}/\texttt{mod}_2$.

As a general language design principle, we must be careful what the syntax lets us do with terms of quotient types. In particular, given a variable $x : A/r$, it must not be allowed to inspect x via arbitrary predicates on A. The elimination rule of the quotient type already guarantees that only equality-preserving operations can be applied. But we must also check the interaction of quotient types with every other primitive operation in the language. This is formally established in the soundness theorem below.

Subtyping. In soft-typed systems, subtyping $A <: B$ is usually defined via

$$x : A \text{ implies } x : B \text{ for all } x \quad (a)$$

In the presence of TDE, the following stronger condition is more practical:

$$x : A, y : A, x =_A y \text{ implies } x =_B y \text{ for all } x, y \quad (b)$$

Note that (b) implies (a). (b) is only relevant in the presence of TDE: without TDE, it trivially follows from (a). Therefore, we use (b) to define the subtyping judgment $\vdash A <: B$.

We can now derive the usual contra/co-variance rules for $A \to B$ as well as $A|p <: A$ and $A <: A/r$. Maybe surprisingly, the quotient type becomes a super-type of the base type even though its semantics is a set with lower cardinality.

For every type A, we have the following subtype hierarchy from the void type to the unit type:

$$A|\lambda x.\texttt{false} <: A|p <: A|\lambda x.\texttt{true} = A = A/\lambda xy.\texttt{false} <: A/r \subseteq A/\lambda xy.\texttt{true}$$

On the left hand side, these capture the no-op canonical embeddings of predicate types via increasingly inclusive predicates, on the right hand side the no-op canonical projections of the quotient types via increasingly inclusive predicates.

3.2 Semantics

Partial Equivalence Relations. We recall the basic properties of partial equivalence relations (PERs). A PER S on set U is a symmetric and transitive binary relation on U. We write $\operatorname{dom} S = \{u \in U | (u, u) \in S\} = \{u \in U | \exists v \in U.(u, v) \in S\}$ for the set of elements touched by S, and $S|_V = S \cap V^2$ for the restriction of S to $V \subseteq U$, and $\operatorname{PER}(R)$ for the PER generated by the binary relation R on U. Then $S|_{\operatorname{dom} S}$ is an equivalence relation on $\operatorname{dom} S$, and we write $S^/$ for the corresponding quotient (in the usual set-theoretical sense).

Overview. We assume a set-theoretical universe U and interpret syntax according to the table below:

Syntax	Semantics	Intended meaning
type A	$[\![A]\!] \subseteq U \times U$	$\operatorname{PER}([\![A]\!])^/$
terms t	elements $[\![t]\!] \in U$	
typing $\vdash t : A$	$[\![t]\!] \in \operatorname{dom} [\![A]\!]$	equivalence class of $[\![t]\!]$ in $\operatorname{PER}([\![A]\!])^/$
equality $\vdash s =_A t$	$([\![s]\!], [\![t]\!]) \in \operatorname{PER}([\![A]\!])$	
subtyping $\vdash A <: B$	$[\![A]\!] \subseteq [\![B]\!]$	

Note that even though equality depends on the type, the interpretation of terms does not. Every term has an absolute meaning defined by induction on the language of terms, not by induction on typing derivations. The intended meaning of a type is a quotient of a subset of U. Terms can have multiple types, and the intended meaning of term t seen as an element of type A is the equivalence class of $[\![t]\!]$ in the intended meaning of A.

Interpretation of Identifiers. A *model* maps every part of the theory to its interpretation:

- a base type a to a PER $[\![a]\!] \subseteq U \times U$
- a constant $c : A$ to an element $[\![c]\!] \in \operatorname{dom} [\![A]\!]$
- an axiom t to a proof that t holds.

An *assignment* maps every part of a context to its interpretation accordingly. We write $\alpha, x \mapsto u$ for the extension of α with a case for x. The function $[\![-]\!]$ is actually relative to a model of the theory (which we omit from the notation) and an assignment α for the context. Note that the interpretation of types depends on the assignment even in the absence of type variables because terms can occur in types.

Interpretation Function. Given a fixed model (which we omit from the notation), we define the *interpretation function* $[\![-]\!]^\alpha$ for all types and terms in context Γ under an assignment α to Γ.

Constants a and c are interpreted according to the model, variables k and x according to the assignment. The remaining cases are:

$$[\![\texttt{bool}]\!]^\alpha = \{(0,0),(1,1)\} \quad \text{i.e.,} \quad \text{dom}\,[\![\texttt{bool}]\!]^\alpha = \{0,1\}$$

$$[\![\texttt{true}]\!]^\alpha = 1 \quad [\![\texttt{false}]\!]^\alpha = 0 \quad [\![\texttt{if}(s)t\,\texttt{else}\,t']\!]^\alpha = \begin{cases} [\![t]\!]^\alpha & \text{if } [\![s]\!]^\alpha = 1 \\ [\![t']\!]^\alpha & \text{otherwise} \end{cases}$$

$$[\![s =_A t]\!]^\alpha = \begin{cases} 1 & \text{if } ([\![s]\!]^\alpha, [\![t]\!]^\alpha) \in \text{PER}([\![A]\!]) \\ 0 & \text{otherwise} \end{cases}$$

$$[\![A \to B]\!]^\alpha = \\ \{(f,g) \in (\text{dom}\,[\![A]\!]^\alpha \to \text{dom}\,[\![B]\!]^\alpha)^2 \mid (u,v) \in [\![A]\!]^\alpha \text{ implies } (f(u),g(v)) \in [\![B]\!]^\alpha\}$$

$$[\![\lambda x : A.t(x)]\!]^\alpha = \{(u,[\![t(x)]\!]^{\alpha,x \mapsto u}) : u \in \text{dom}\,[\![A]\!]^\alpha\}$$

$$[\![f\,a]\!]^\alpha = [\![f]\!]^\alpha([\![a]\!]^\alpha)$$

$$[\![A|p]\!]^\alpha = [\![A]\!]^\alpha \cap \{u \in \text{dom}\,[\![A]\!]^\alpha \mid [\![p]\!]^\alpha(u) = 1\}^2$$

$$[\![A/r]\!]^\alpha = [\![A]\!]^\alpha \cup \{(u,v) \in \text{dom}\,[\![A]\!]^{\alpha^2} \mid [\![r]\!]^\alpha(u)(v) = 1\}$$

where we abbreviate $V^2 = V \times V$ as usual.

Soundness. The soundness theorem consists of multiple statements:

- the main theorem that provable booleans hold (3)
- the well-definedness of the interpretation function (1+2)
- the usual substitution lemma that interpretation commutes with substitution (4a)

– a lemma specific to the PER semantics that ensures that every term with free
variables preserves equality (4b)

Theorem 1. *For any theory and model, we have*

1. *if $\Gamma \vdash A : \textbf{type}$, then $[\![A]\!]^\alpha \subseteq U \times U$*
2. *if $\Gamma \vdash t : A$, then $[\![t]\!]^\alpha \in \text{dom}\,[\![A]\!]^\alpha$ for all α*
3. *if $\Gamma \vdash b$, then $[\![b]\!]^\alpha = 1$ for all α*
4. *for any $\Gamma, x : A \vdash t(x) : B$*
   (a) if $\Gamma \vdash s : A$, then $[\![t(s)]\!]^\alpha = [\![t(x)]\!]^{\alpha, x \mapsto [\![s]\!]}$ for all α
   (b) if $(u, v) \in [\![A]\!]^\alpha$, then $([\![t(x)]\!]^{\alpha, x \mapsto u}, [\![t(x)]\!]^{\alpha, x \mapsto v}) \in [\![B]\!]^\alpha$ for all α

Proof. All statements are proved in a joint induction on derivations. We only
mention a few critical cases. (4b) is needed to prove (2) for the case of λ-
abstraction. (4a) and (4b) are needed to prove (3) for the case of Sub.

We have so far not investigated any completeness properties. It is reasonable
to expect those are related to the completeness of HOL for Henkin models. But
it is non-obvious how to combine Henkin and PER semantics.

3.3 Lax Record Types

There are several ways to extend the language with record types. Lax records
are particularly attractive with TDE, and we sketch one way to add them.

Syntax and Semantics. We use contexts as record types and substitutions γ as
record values. That yields relatively powerful record types, which may contain
type fields, value fields, and axioms:

$$
\begin{aligned}
A &::= \{\Gamma\} \mid t.k \\
t &::= [\gamma] \mid t.x \\
\gamma &::= (k = A \mid x = t \mid P)^* \\
P &::= (\text{proof terms omitted})
\end{aligned}
$$

A substitution γ for context Γ maps every type/term/assumption declaration
in Γ to an appropriate type/term/proof. The last case of that requires extending
the syntax with a term language for proofs, which we omit.

We omit the typing and equality rules, which are complex but routine. For
example, the equality rule for an example record type is

$$
\frac{\Gamma \vdash r.k = s.k : \textbf{type} \qquad \Gamma \vdash r.x =_{r.k} s.x}{\Gamma \vdash r =_{\{k:\textbf{type}, x:k\}} s}
$$

where $r.k = s.k : \textbf{type}$ is an instance of the type equality judgment we omitted
above. The semantics is straightforward except for the usual problem of needing
some kind of universe hierarchy because record types containing type fields are
too big to be interpreted as a set in the universe. We gloss over that issue.

Mizar's strictness operator is not needed because lax records with TDE allows expressing equalities at different record types. Like with predicate and quotient typing, applying a forgetful functor is a no-op.

Subtyping and TDE. With the addition of lax records, we can form subtypes via record subtyping in addition to predicate subtyping. The main effect this has on the language design is that the argument of Remark 1 becomes less compelling: While a membership test $t \in A|p$ can be replaced with $p\,t$, a similar workaround does not exist for record subtyping.

Assume we added a `bool`-valued predicate $r \in S : \texttt{bool}$ for $r : R$ and record types $S <: R$. For example, this would allow inspecting an input $x : R$ to see if it provides more fields than guaranteed by R. A typical application would be to employ a more efficient semigroup algorithm if the input is a monoid. This can also be used if the additional fields are not uniquely determined, e.g., to check if a vector space comes with a distinguished base. Membership tests like this are routine in soft-typed computer algebra systems such as Gap [Lin07] or SageMath [S+13].

But attempts to add such tests to the syntax run into soundness issues. For example, assume record types $Monoid <: Semigroup$, a record $M : Semigroup$ that happens to satisfy the monoid axioms, and $M' : Monoid$ arising from M by adding the additional fields. Then $M =_{Semigroup} M'$ and $M \notin Monoid$ and $M' \in Monoid$, which makes Sub unsound if a naive membership test is added.

The author currently does not have a satisfactory solution for soundly testing record membership in the presence of TDE.

4   Conclusion

We coined the term "type-dependent equality" (TDE) for an existing but not widely known feature in soft-typed languages. We provided an overview of the advantages and pitfalls of designing formal systems with TDE and described their realizations in major proof assistants. We have used that to design a simple language with TDE that allows for an elegant treatment of predicate and quotient types. Importantly, many critical operations are no-ops, which is advantageous notationally and computationally.

Many aspects of the work are folklore such as the PER semantics for soft type systems or have been implemented before such as Nuprl's TDE and quotient types. The main contribution is to collect and analyze all these aspects in a simple formal language that exhibits the main characteristics while allowing a rigorous and clear presentation. Critically, the soundness theorem clarifies the consistency issues that must be taken care of when designing TDE-languages. And the syntax and semantics are simple enough to make the formal verification of the soundness theorem feasible.

Thus, the work provides an ideal starting point for designing more advanced TDE-languages that could allow for better formalizations of mathematical practices than supported by current proof assistants.

References

[ABC+06] Allen, S., et al.: Innovations in computational type theory using nuprl. J. Appl. Log. **4**(4), 428–469 (2006)

[All87] Allen, S.: A Non-type-theoretic Semantics for Type-theoretic Language. Ph.D. thesis, Cornell University (1987)

[CAB+86] Constable, R., et al.: Implementing Mathematics with the Nuprl Development System. Prentice-Hall (1986)

[Coq15] Coq Development Team: The Coq Proof Assistant: Reference Manual. Technical report, INRIA (2015)

[dKA+15] de Moura, L., Kong, S., Avigad, J., van Doorn, F., von Raumer, J.: The lean theorem prover (system description). In: Felty, A.P., Middeldorp, A. (eds.) CADE 2015. LNCS (LNAI), vol. 9195, pp. 378–388. Springer, Cham (2015). https://doi.org/10.1007/978-3-319-21401-6_26

[Gor88] Gordon, M.: HOL: a proof generating system for higher-order logic. In: Birtwistle, G., Subrahmanyam, P. (eds.) VLSI Specification, Verification and Synthesis, pp. 73–128. Kluwer-Academic Publishers (1988)

[KR20] Kaliszyk, C., Rabe, F.: A survey of languages for formalizing mathematics. In: Benzmüller, C., Miller, B. (eds.) CICM 2020. LNCS (LNAI), vol. 12236, pp. 138–156. Springer, Cham (2020). https://doi.org/10.1007/978-3-030-53518-6_9

[Lin07] Linton, S.: GAP: groups, algorithms, programming. ACM Commun. Comput. Algebra **41**(3), 108–109 (2007)

[Nog02] Nogin, A.: Quotient types: a modular approach. In: Carreño, V.A., Muñoz, C.A., Tahar, S. (eds.) TPHOLs 2002. LNCS, vol. 2410, pp. 263–280. Springer, Heidelberg (2002). https://doi.org/10.1007/3-540-45685-6_18

[ORS92] Owre, S., Rushby, J., Shankar. N.: PVS: a prototype verification system. In: Kapur, D. (eds.) 11th International Conference on Automated Deduction (CADE), pp. 748–752. Springer (1992)

[PC93] Paulson, L., Coen, M.: Zermelo-Fraenkel Set Theory, 1993. Isabelle distribution, ZF/ZF.thy

[S+13] Stein, W., et al.: Sage Mathematics Software. The Sage Development Team (2013). http://www.sagemath.org

[TB85] Trybulec, A., Blair, H.: Computer assisted reasoning with MIZAR. In: Joshi, A., (eds.) Proceedings of the 9th International Joint Conference on Artificial Intelligence, pp. 26–28. Morgan Kaufmann (1985)

[Wie07] Wiedijk, F.: The QED manifesto revisited. In: From Insight to Proof, Festschrift in Honour of Andrzej Trybulec, pp. 121–133 (2007)

Generating Custom Set Theories
with Non-set Structured Objects

Ciarán Dunne[✉], J. B. Wells, and Fairouz Kamareddine

Heriot-Watt University, Edinburgh, UK
cmd1@hw.ac.uk

Abstract. Set theory has long been viewed as a foundation of mathematics, is pervasive in mathematical culture, and is explicitly used by much written mathematics. Because arrangements of sets can represent a vast multitude of mathematical objects, in most set theories every object is a set. This causes confusion and adds difficulties to formalising mathematics in set theory. We wish to have set theory's features while also having many mathematical objects not be sets. A *generalized set theory* (GST) is a theory that has *pure sets* and may also have non-sets that can have internal structure and *impure sets* that mix sets and non-sets. This paper provides a GST-building framework. We show example GSTs that have sets and also (1) non-set ordered pairs, (2) non-set natural numbers, (3) a non-set exception object that can not be inside another object, and (4) modular combinations of these features. We show how to axiomatize GSTs and how to build models for GSTs in other GSTs.

1 Introduction

Set Theory as a Foundation of Mathematics. Set theories like Zermelo-Fraenkel (ZF), and closely related set theories like ZFC and Tarski-Grothendieck (TG), play many important roles in mathematics. ZF's axioms allow expressing a vast number of mathematical concepts. For most of the last century most mathematicians have accepted theories like ZF as suitable foundations of mathematics. ZF's axioms have been rigorously evaluated for roughly a century and have no known inconsistencies. Mathematical theories are often assessed against the standard of whether models can be constructed for them in theories like ZF (what Maddy [14] calls *risk assessment*). Much of mathematical notation and reasoning is rooted in set theory. A significant amount of mathematics has been formalised in set theory and computer-verified using proof assistants like Isabelle/ZF [9,18], Mizar [2], and Metamath [15].

Mathematics varies in the kind and degree of assumptions made of the underlying foundation. Some mathematics explicitly specifies a set-theoretic or type-theoretic foundation and some does not. Set theories like ZF are usually stated in first-order logic (FOL), but are sometimes stated in higher-order logic (HOL) or given as theories embedded in a dependent type system. In some mathematics, functions are sets of ordered pairs while in other mathematics functions are not

© Springer Nature Switzerland AG 2021
F. Kamareddine and C. Sacerdoti Coen (Eds.): CICM 2021, LNAI 12833, pp. 228–244, 2021.
https://doi.org/10.1007/978-3-030-81097-9_19

even sets. There is variation in how undefined terms are treated [6,19]. When viewing ZF as the underlying foundation, it is assumed that high-level mathematics has meaningful translations into ZF, or that ZF can be safely modified to accommodate the user's needs.

Representation Overlap in Set-Theoretic Formalisation. Translating human-written mathematics into ZF has complications. Every object in ZF's domain of discourse is a pure set, so objects of human-written text must be represented as pure sets. Objects that the mathematician views as distinct can have the same ZF representation. For example, consider formalising a function $g : (\mathbb{N}^2 \cup \mathcal{P}(\mathbb{N})) \to \{0, 1\}$ such that $g(\langle 0, 1 \rangle) = 0$ and $g(\{1, 2\}) = 1$. Let $(\,\cdot\,)^*$ be the translation of human-written mathematical objects into the domain of ZF. Typically, $\mathbb{N}$ is represented using the von Neumann ordinals, so $0^* := \emptyset$ and $(k{+}1)^* := k^* \cup \{k^*\}$. Also, ordered pairs are usually represented using Kuratowski's encoding where $\langle a, b \rangle^* := \{\{a^*\}, \{a^*, b^*\}\}$. Furthermore, sets of the human-written text usually get the naïve translation $\{x_1, \ldots, x_n\}^* = \{x_1^*, \ldots, x_n^*\}$. Using these representations, the ordered pair $\langle 0, 1 \rangle$ and the set $\{1, 2\}$ are represented in ZF by *the same pure set*: $\{\{\emptyset\}, \{\emptyset, \{\emptyset\}\}\}$. Thus, a naïve translation of the definition of g will require that $0^* = g(\langle 0, 1 \rangle^*) = g(\{1, 2\}^*) = 1^*$ and there will be no value for g satisfying its specification, i.e., the naïvely translated definition will fail to define anything. A standard set-theoretic solution is to not use $\mathbb{N}^2 \cup \mathcal{P}(\mathbb{N})$ as the domain of g but instead to use $(\{0\} \times \mathbb{N}^2) \cup (\{1\} \times \mathcal{P}(\mathbb{N}))$, i.e., tag every member of $\mathbb{N}^2$ with 0 and every member of $\mathcal{P}(\mathbb{N})$ with 1. This works because $\{0\} \times \mathbb{N}^2$ and $\{1\} \times \mathcal{P}(\mathbb{N})$ are disjoint. This requires complete foresight of the objects to be used, obscures the mathematics under a layer of tagging and untagging, and increases the costs of formalisation.

Furthermore, sometimes the mathematics needs a class (sometimes a proper class) of objects that are distinct from *all* sets, adding complication. And sometimes the objects that must be distinct from all sets can contain sets. The proper set-theoretic solution is to build a hierarchy in ZF to represent both the sets and the non-set objects of the human-written mathematics using a construction similar to the von Neumann cumulative hierarchy. An example of doing this is the set theory ZFP [5] which has proper classes of both sets and non-set ordered pairs. A model of ZFP can be built in ZF using tagged ZF sets to represent both ZFP sets and ZFP non-set ordered pairs.

Proper classes and tagging both involve awkward reasoning. Definitions, lemmas, and proofs quickly become messy. The user must redefine and reprove operations and relations, leaving them with duplicate symbols and concepts (e.g., the power set operation of ZF vs. the analogous operation on the tagged sets within ZF that represent the sets of the human-written mathematics). How to build these models is not obvious to most mathematicians.

Type Theory as an Alternative. Type theories typically avoid representation overlap by preventing operations that mix types. Operating on multiple types is done via sum types or inductive datatypes, and something equivalent to tagging and untagging happens in a type theory's underlying model theory, but the user is shielded from most details.

Unfortunately, formalising mathematics in type theory is not always the best option. Removing set-theoretic dependencies can transform a text in ways that take it far from the author's conception. As mathematics gets more complex, the typing combinations push the limits of human cognition. Type error messages can be beyond human comprehension. The typing rules of proof assistants can differ in significant ways from the human-readable documentation, and immense expertise in the implementation can be needed. Typing constraints can add proving obligations that are not relevant to the mathematics being formalised. Formalising mathematics in type theories can require awkward and expensive workarounds that sometimes seem infeasible. To address these issues, more sophisticated type systems are developed that can require more expertise to comprehend. Finally, some type-theoretic provers focus on constructive, non-classical reasoning, but much mathematics is non-constructive, and constructive reasoning can be an unnecessary burden.

An Arena for Custom Set Theories. We seek to retain the useful qualities of set theory whilst being able to have mathematical objects that are genuinely not sets. Some set theories (e.g., ZFA, KPU) have non-set objects called *urelements* which contain no set members (but are not the empty set) and can belong to sets. Typically urelements have no internal structure (an exception is Aczel's GST [1]). To avoid confusion with typical structure-free urelements, we use the phrase *non-set object* for members of a domain that are not sets. A set is *pure* iff all of its members are pure sets; other sets are *impure*. A *generalized set theory* (GST) is a theory that has pure sets and may also have non-sets that can have internal structure and impure sets. ZFP (mentioned above) is a GST with non-sets with internal structure.

If a set theory S can be shown to be consistent relative to ZF and S is a better match for some mathematicians' needs, it is reasonable that they use S instead of ZF as a foundation. So we ask: Is it possible to give each mathematician a foundation that matches their intuition and in which their mathematics is formally true in the original human-written form rather than only becoming formally true after substantial effort and transformation? With this aim in mind, we propose what we call an *arena* in which multiple different GSTs (including ZF) can co-exist and a toolkit to support showing relative consistency results. Our plan and its fulfillment in later sections of this paper is as follows.

We begin in Sect. 2 with a logical framework that supplies features needed for an arena for set theories. Our design is inspired by systems such as the combination of Isabelle/Pure with Isabelle/FOL that underlies Isabelle/ZF, but we have deliberately used a bare minimum of features. To cleanly support multiple GSTs simultaneously, we have a countably infinite set of *domain* types which are base types of individuals. We have function types to support definitions and set theory axiom schemas. In any given derivation, one domain type is designated as the *founder* domain type. We allow ∀-introduction only at the founder domain type. We allow ∀-elimination at the founder domain type and all non-domain types, and forbid ∀-elimination at all non-founder domain types. Reasoning in a derivation about a domain d_k other than the derivation's founder domain d_i is intended to work via a connection from d_k to a model for d_k in another domain; there should be a chain of connections from domains to their models which terminates in the founder domain. We supply axioms for using (eliminating) equality at all types but we only introduce equality at domain types and do so via domain-specific axioms like ZF's Axiom of Extensionality.

Section 3 axiomatizes example GSTs with non-set ordered pairs, non-set natural numbers, a non-set exception element that can not be inside any other object, and the combination of all of these features. This section gives a generalised specification of Zermelo-Fraenkel set theory (GZF) as a feature of GSTs. The GZF specification differs from ZF by (1) not expecting everything to be a set and (2) not specifying well-foundedness because this is handled by our toolkit for combining features to build a GST. The GZF specification is also used as a template where the $\forall$-quantifier may be replaced by a quantifier restricted to a model constructed within a domain.

Section 4 provides a toolkit for building and reasoning about models of GSTs. The user can build models of GSTs within any GST to verify the consistency of a GST or to explore what models are possible and what axiomatizations might be possible for those models. The main parameter of our model-building machinery is a constant called $\mathsf{Ops}_{i,j}$ which the user axiomatizes to specify the operations used to build in d_i the tiers of a cumulative model intended for use as domain d_j. Models are defined using transfinite recursion, the user-supplied axioms for $\mathsf{Ops}_{i,j}$, and tagging machinery. We show how a user can axiomatize $\mathsf{Ops}_{i,j}$ to yield a model satisfying GZF.

Section 5 defines how to connect to domain d_j a model built in domain d_i intended for domain d_j. Connection is achieved by axiomatizing an isomorphism between the model and the domain in the style of Gordon/HOL type definitions.

Section 6 builds models for the example GSTs given in Sect. 3 and connects these GSTs to their models as part of showing consistency.

Related Work. Isabelle/ZF [18] is an embedding of first-order logic and ZF in Isabelle/Pure, a simply-typed intuitionistic higher-order logic [17]. Isabelle/ZF's base library primarily proves theorems about set theory (functions, ordinals, recursion). IsarMathLib [9] is a library of mathematics in areas such as abstract algebra, analysis, and topology that is formalised in Isabelle/ZF. Mizar [2] provides a language for proving theorems in TG. A notable feature of Mizar is "weak typing" which gives some of the advantages of types. Metamath/ZFC [15] develops ZFC in a minimal framework without much proof automation.

Many have sought a middle ground between set theory and type theory. Krauss [10] worked on adding "soft types" to Isabelle/ZF, and this proposal was later developed into Isabelle/Set [11], an axiomatisation of TG. Brown [4] developed extended first-order logic (EFOL), which extends FOL with some higher-order convenience. The Egal prover [3] axiomatizes TG within EFOL. HOLZF [16] axiomatizes in Isabelle/HOL a type ZF of the pure sets of ZF and supports conversion between ZF sets and HOL sets of ZF sets.

$$
\begin{array}{l}
\delta \; \acute{\epsilon} \; \mathsf{Domain} \; ::= \; \mathsf{d_1} \mid \mathsf{d_2} \mid \mathsf{d_3} \mid \cdots \quad a, b, p, q, x, y, z \; \acute{\epsilon} \; \mathsf{Var} \quad ::= \; \mathsf{v_1} \mid \mathsf{v_2} \mid \mathsf{v_3} \mid \cdots \\
\sigma, \tau \; \acute{\epsilon} \; \mathsf{Type} \quad ::= \; \star \mid \delta \mid \sigma \Rightarrow \tau \qquad\qquad\quad c \; \acute{\epsilon} \; \mathsf{Const} \; ::= \; \rightarrow \mid \forall_\tau \mid \cdots \\
i, j \; \acute{\epsilon} \; \mathbb{N} \qquad\qquad\qquad\qquad\qquad\qquad\qquad \nu \; \acute{\epsilon} \; \mathsf{Var} \cup \mathsf{Const}
\end{array}
$$

$$
A, \ldots, Z \; \acute{\epsilon} \; \mathsf{Term} \; ::= \; x \mid c \mid B\,C \mid \lambda\,x : \tau\,.\,B \quad (\text{if } \mathsf{vtyp}(x) \equiv \tau)
$$

$$
\frac{}{x :: \mathsf{vtyp}(x)} \qquad \frac{}{c :: \mathsf{ctyp}(c)} \qquad \frac{B :: \sigma \quad \mathsf{vtyp}(x) \equiv \tau}{(\lambda\,x : \tau\,.\,B) :: \tau \Rightarrow \sigma} \qquad \frac{B :: \tau \Rightarrow \sigma \quad C :: \tau}{(B\,C) :: \sigma}
$$

Fig. 1. Syntax and typing rules

Aczel and Lunnon [1] worked on GSTs (and coined the phrase "GST"). It appears that their systems assume the Anti-Foundation axiom instead of ZF's Axiom of Foundation. They discuss model building but identify no axioms.

Kunčar and Popescu [8,12,13] developed and proved soundness of methods for connecting an entire abstract type τ to a subset of a concrete representation type τ' given by a predicate on τ'; our approach in Sect. 5 has a very similar essential core. Under the slogan "little theories", Farmer et al. [7] developed in the IMPS prover flexible meta-level methods for automatically generating and using theory interpretations for connecting abstract theories to concrete theories; here the emphasis is more on using the abstract theories to prove things in the concrete theories and less on using a trusted believed-to-be-consistent concrete theory to prove consistency of the abstract theory.

2 Logical Framework

Syntax. Figure 1 defines the meta-level sets Domain, Type, Var, and Const. Each type d_i is a *domain* (of FOL individuals). The *function type* constructor $\Rightarrow$ is right associative, i.e., $(\tau_1 \Rightarrow \tau_2 \Rightarrow \tau_3) \equiv (\tau_1 \Rightarrow (\tau_2 \Rightarrow \tau_3))$. The fixed *variable type* function vtyp maps every $x \epsilon \mathsf{Var}$ to some $\sigma \epsilon \mathsf{Type}$. For each $\tau \epsilon \mathsf{Type}$ there are infinitely many variables $y \epsilon \mathsf{Var}$ such that $\mathsf{vtyp}(y) \equiv \tau$. The fixed *constant type* function ctyp maps every member of Const to some $\sigma \epsilon \mathsf{Type}$ and it holds that $\mathsf{ctyp}(\rightarrow) \equiv \star \Rightarrow \star \Rightarrow \star$ and for every $\tau \epsilon \mathsf{Type}$ that $\mathsf{ctyp}(\forall_\tau) \equiv (\tau \Rightarrow \star) \Rightarrow \star$ and $\mathsf{ctyp}(=_\tau) \equiv \mathsf{ctyp}(\neq_\tau) \equiv \tau \Rightarrow \tau \Rightarrow \star$. For any $i \epsilon \mathbb{N}$, we abbreviate $\forall_{\mathsf{d}_i}$ as $\forall_i$. Fixed meta-level names for the other *constants* in Const and further details of ctyp will be revealed incrementally. Subscripts i and i, j on the meta-level names of constants are used to indicate a constant is relevant to domain d_i or both domains d_i and d_j; these subscripts are often light grey to help the reader not be distracted by them. Notation of the form $\mathcal{C} :\equiv (\xi_1 :: \tau_1, \ldots, \xi_n :: \tau_n)$ asserts for each $i \epsilon \{1, \ldots, n\}$ that $\xi_i \epsilon \mathsf{Const}$ (so the meta-metavariable ξ_i could have been written c_i) and $\mathsf{ctyp}(\xi_i) \equiv \tau_i$ and $\mathcal{C} \equiv \{\xi_1, \ldots, \xi_n\}$.

The rules in Fig. 1 define the meta-level set Term. As is standard for a λ-calculus, each *abstraction* $\lambda\,x : \sigma\,.\,C$ *binds* the variable x and this is the only way variables can be bound. We identify terms modulo α-equivalence. We then

$$
\begin{aligned}
&(\text{HYP}) \quad \{\varphi\} \vdash_i \varphi \\
&(\text{IMPI}) \quad \text{If } \Gamma \vdash_i \psi, \text{ then } \Gamma - \varphi \vdash_i \varphi \to \psi \\
&(\text{IMPE}) \quad \text{If } \Gamma \vdash_i \varphi \to \psi \text{ and } \Gamma' \vdash_i \varphi, \text{ then } \Gamma \cup \Gamma' \vdash_i \psi \\
&(\text{ALLI}_i) \quad \text{If } \Gamma \vdash_i \varphi, \; x :: \mathsf{d}_i, \text{ and } x \notin \mathsf{FV}[\Gamma], \text{ then } \Gamma \vdash_i \forall_i (\lambda\, x : \mathsf{d}_i \,.\, \varphi) \\
&(\text{ALLE}_i) \quad \text{If } \Gamma \vdash_i \forall_\tau P, \text{ and } B :: \tau, \text{ and } \forall\, j \neq i\,.\,\tau \neq \mathsf{d}_j, \text{ then } \Gamma \vdash_i P\,B
\end{aligned}
$$

$$
\begin{aligned}
\mathsf{Init} := &\left\{ \begin{array}{l} \forall\, p\,.\,\forall_\tau\, x, y\,.\, x = y \to (p\,x \leftrightarrow p\,y), \\ (\neq_\tau) = (\lambda\, x, y\,.\,\neg\,(x = y)) \end{array} \;\middle|\; \tau \in \mathsf{Type} \right\} \\
\cup\; &\{\, \forall_\star\, p, q\,.\,(\neg p \to \neg q) \to q \to p, \quad \forall_\star\, p, q\,.\,(p \leftrightarrow q) \to p \to q, \\
&\;\;\; \forall_\star\, p, q\,.\,(p \leftrightarrow q) \to q \to p, \quad \forall_\star\, p, q\,.\,(p \to q) \to (q \to p) \to (p \leftrightarrow q), \\
&\;\;\; \wedge = (\lambda\, p, q\,.\,\neg\,(p \to \neg q)), \; \vee = (\lambda\, p, q\,.\,\neg p \to q)\}
\end{aligned}
$$

$$
\mathsf{FOLQuants}_i := \{\, \exists_i = (\lambda\, p\,.\,\neg\,(\forall_i\,(\lambda\, x\,.\,\neg\,(p\,x)))), \; \forall_i[\cdot] = (\lambda\, p, q\,.\,\forall_i\, x\,.\,p\,x \to q\,x),
$$
$$
\exists_i^{\leq 1} = (\lambda\, p\,.\,\forall_i\, y, z\,.\,p\,y \wedge p\,z \to y = z), \exists_i[\cdot] = (\lambda\, p, q\,.\,\exists_i\, x\,.\,p\,x \wedge q\,x)\}
$$

Fig. 2. Inference rules, initial theory, and simple definitions for quantifiers

define the *free variable* function FV so that $\mathsf{FV}(B)$ is the set of variables free in the β-normal-form of B. We then further identify terms modulo β-equivalence and lift FV accordingly. Substitution $B[\nu := C]$ is defined as usual. Constants can not be bound by λ.

Figure 1 defines the typing relation :: between Term and Type. Inside a term expression $B :: \tau$ we allow omitting the type σ that is part of the name of an occurrence of $\forall_\sigma$, $=_\sigma$, or $\neq_\sigma$, or that is part of an abstraction $\lambda x : \sigma\,.\,C$, provided that σ can be uniquely determined by the other type information in or about B including what is known about the types of constants.

We say that a term B is a *formula* iff $B :: \star$. Let φ, ψ, γ range over formulas, and let Φ, Ψ, Γ range over sets of formulas. Let $\Gamma + \varphi$ denote $\Gamma \cup \{\varphi\}$ and let $\Gamma - \varphi$ denote $\Gamma \setminus \{\varphi\}$. Let $\mathsf{FV}[\Gamma]$ be the union of all $\mathsf{FV}(\varphi)$ for each $\varphi \in \Gamma$. Let $\Gamma[\nu := B]$ be the set of all $\varphi[\nu := B]$ for each $\varphi \in \Gamma$.

Propositional and First-Order Logic. A *sequent* is a syntactic object $\Gamma \vdash_i \varphi$ with *founder domain* d_i. Figure 2 give inference rules that define the entailment relation $\vdash_i$. We write $\Gamma \vdash_i \Psi$ iff $\Gamma \vdash_i \varphi$ for every $\varphi \in \Psi$. Note that $\vdash_i$ can only do $\forall$-introduction for $\forall_i$ (which abbreviates $\forall_{\mathsf{d}_i}$) and cannot do $\forall$-elimination for $\forall_j$ where $i \neq j$. We will later supply simple definitions for $\forall_j$ where $i \neq j$ that make these rules admissible:

$$
(\text{ALLI}_{i,j}) \quad \frac{\Gamma \vdash_i \varphi \quad x :: \mathsf{d}_j \quad x \notin \mathsf{FV}[\Gamma]}{\Gamma \vdash_i \forall_j (\lambda\, x : \mathsf{d}_j \,.\, \varphi)} \qquad\qquad (\text{ALLE}_{i,j}) \quad \frac{\Gamma \vdash_i \forall_j P \quad B :: \mathsf{d}_j}{\Gamma \vdash_i P\,B}
$$

We write $\Gamma \vdash_i (\text{ALLI}_{i,j}), (\text{ALLE}_{i,j})$ iff both $(\text{ALLI}_{i,j})$ and $(\text{ALLE}_{i,j})$ are admissible using Γ. The rule (ALLE_i) allows us to eliminate universal quantifications at d_i and any non-domain type, which supports simple definitions.

Figure 2 defines the *initial theory* Init that defines the other logic operators ($\neg$, $\leftrightarrow$, $\wedge$, $\vee$), and proves their usual introduction and elimination rules, establishes classical logic, and implements equality. A *simple definition* is a formula of the form $c =_\tau B$. The first axiom in Init allows *eliminating* equalities at all types, but we only *introduce* equalities via domain-specific axioms at domain types. The constants $=_\tau$, $\wedge$, $\vee$, $\leftrightarrow$, and $\rightarrow$ are all binary infix operators, listed in descending order of precedence. If c is infix, an application $(c\, X)\, Y$ may be written $X\, c\, Y$. If $B_1, \ldots, B_n, C$ are terms and $\sim$ is a binary infix operator, then we may write $B_1, \ldots, B_n \sim C$ for $B_1 \sim C \wedge \cdots \wedge B_n \sim C$. Negation ($\neg$) and function application take precedence over infix operators, e.g., $F\, x =_\tau G\, x$ is $(F\, x) =_\tau (G\, x)$.

If Q is a constant for a quantifier, then $Q\,(\lambda\, x : \tau\, .\, \varphi)$ may be written $Q\, x\, .\, \varphi$. The notation $Q\, x_1, \ldots, x_n\, .\, \varphi$ abbreviates the nested applications of quantifiers and abstractions $Q\,(\lambda x_1 : \tau\, .\, \cdots\, Q\,(\lambda x_n : \tau\, .\, \varphi))$. Quantification has lower precedence than all other logical constants. Thus, $\forall_0\, x\, .\, \varphi \rightarrow \psi$ is $\forall_0\, x\, .\, (\varphi \rightarrow \psi)$.

From each constant $\forall_i$ that represents a universal quantifier at type d_i, the set $\mathsf{FOLQuants}_i$ of simple definitions in Fig. 2 defines *existential* ($\exists$), *at-most-one* ($\exists^{\leq 1}$), and *bounded* (also called *restricted*) quantification ($\forall[\cdot], \exists[\cdot]$). Formulas of the form $(\forall[\cdot]\, P)\, Q$ and $(\exists[\cdot]\, P)\, Q$ may be written as $\forall[P]\, x\, .\, Q\, x$ and $\exists[P]\, x\, .\, Q\, x$ respectively. If $\sim$ is a binary infix operator, we may write $\forall\, x \sim B\, .\, \varphi$ and $\exists\, x \sim B\, .\, \varphi$ for $\forall[\lambda\, y\, .\, y \sim B]\, x\, .\, \varphi$ and $\exists[\lambda\, y\, .\, y \sim B]\, x\, .\, \varphi$ respectively, where y is fresh. If $\Gamma \vdash_i (\mathrm{ALLI}_{i,j}), (\mathrm{ALLE}_{i,j})$ and $\Gamma \vdash_i \mathsf{Init} \cup \mathsf{FOLQuants}_j$, then each quantifier satisfies its usual introduction and elimination rules on d_j.

3   Example Axiomatizations of Generalized Set Theories

This section axiomatizes five example GSTs. We define four example modular *features* that each characterise a kind of mathematical object. So the reader does not mix them up, we index features by odd numbers and later in Sect. 6 we index example domains by even numbers. Feature k in domain d_i is given by (1) a signature of constants sig_i^k, (2) a set of formulas theory_i^k that characterizes the constants in sig_i^k, (3) an unary predicate iden_i^k that identifies objects added by the feature, and (4) a binary predicate child_i^k that declares *internal* structure.

The **Set** feature provides sets. Figure 3 defines constants $\mathsf{GZFConsts}_i$ and formulas GZF_i. The feature's theory, signature, identification predicate, and structure predicate are given by $\mathsf{sig}_i^1 \equiv \mathsf{GZFConsts}_i$, and $\mathsf{theory}_i^1 \equiv \mathsf{GZF}_i$, and $\mathsf{iden}_i^1 \equiv \mathsf{Set}_i$, and $\mathsf{child}_i^1 \equiv \in_i$. The axioms in GZF_i allow non-sets. The Foundation axiom is missing from GZF_i and will be supplied when features are combined.

The **Pair** feature adds non-set ordered pairs. Figure 3 defines constants $\mathsf{PConsts}_i$ and formulas $\mathsf{PTheory}_i$. We define $\mathsf{sig}_i^3 \equiv \mathsf{PConsts}_i$, and $\mathsf{theory}_i^3 \equiv \mathsf{PTheory}_i$, and $\mathsf{iden}_i^3 \equiv \mathsf{Pair}_i$, and $\mathsf{child}_i^3 \equiv (\lambda\, x, p\, .\, \exists\, y\, .\, p =_{\mathsf{d}_i} (x, y) \vee p =_{\mathsf{d}_i} (y, x))$. The axioms include the standard *characteristic property of ordered pairs*.

The **Nat** feature adds non-set natural numbers obeying Peano Arithmetic. Figure 3 defines constants $\mathsf{NConsts}_i$ and formulas $\mathsf{NTheory}_i$. We define $\mathsf{sig}_i^5 \equiv \mathsf{NConsts}_i$, and $\mathsf{theory}_i^5 \equiv \mathsf{NTheory}_i$, and $\mathsf{iden}_i^5 \equiv \mathsf{Nat}$, and leave child_i^5 undefined.

The **Exception** feature adds a non-set exception element $\bullet_i$ and a definite description operator $\imath$ that uses $\bullet_i$ as its default. Figure 3 defines constants $\mathsf{EConsts}_i$ and formulas $\mathsf{ETheory}_i$. We define $\mathsf{sig}_i^7 \equiv \mathsf{EConsts}_i$, and $\mathsf{theory}_i^7 \equiv \mathsf{ETheory}_i$, and $\mathsf{iden}_i^7 \equiv (\lambda\, x\, .\, x =_{\mathsf{d}_i} \bullet_i)$, and we leave child_i^7 undefined. The only object this feature adds is $\bullet_i$, which has no internal structure.

$$\begin{aligned}
\mathsf{GZFConsts}_i :\equiv\ & (\in_i\ ::\ \mathsf{d}_i \Rightarrow \mathsf{d}_i \Rightarrow \star,\ \emptyset_i\ ::\ \mathsf{d}_i,\ \mathsf{Set}_i\ ::\ \mathsf{d}_i \Rightarrow \star,\ \textstyle\bigcup_i\ ::\ \mathsf{d}_i \Rightarrow \mathsf{d}_i, \\
& \subseteq_i\ ::\ \mathsf{d}_i \Rightarrow \mathsf{d}_i \Rightarrow \star,\ \mathcal{P}_i\ ::\ \mathsf{d}_i \Rightarrow \mathsf{d}_i,\ \mathsf{succ}_i\ ::\ \mathsf{d}_i \Rightarrow \mathsf{d}_i, \\
& \mathsf{Inf}_i\ ::\ \mathsf{d}_i,\ \mathcal{R}_i\ ::\ (\mathsf{d}_i \Rightarrow \mathsf{d}_i \Rightarrow \star) \Rightarrow \mathsf{d}_i \Rightarrow \mathsf{d}_i)
\end{aligned}$$

$$\begin{aligned}
\mathsf{GZF}_i :=\ \{\ & (\mathrm{EMP}_i)\ \forall_i\, a\,.\, a \notin_i \emptyset_i,\quad (\mathrm{SET}_i)\ \forall_i\, x\,.\, (\mathsf{Set}_i\, x) \leftrightarrow (x = \emptyset_i \vee \exists_i\, y\,.\, y \in_i x), \\
& (\mathrm{SUB}_i)\ \subseteq_i\, =\, (\lambda\, x, y\,.\, \mathsf{Set}_i\, x \wedge \mathsf{Set}_i\, y \wedge \forall_i\, a \in_i x\,.\, a \in_i y), \\
& (\mathrm{EXT}_i)\ \forall_i [\mathsf{Set}_i]\, x, y\,.\, (\forall_i\, a\,.\, a \in_i x \leftrightarrow a \in_i y) \rightarrow x = y, \\
& (\mathrm{UNI}_i)\ \forall_i [\mathsf{Set}_i]\, x\,.\, \mathsf{Set}_i\, (\textstyle\bigcup_i x) \wedge \forall_i\, a\,.\, a \in_i (\textstyle\bigcup_i x) \leftrightarrow (\exists_i\, z \in_i x\,.\, a \in_i z), \\
& (\mathrm{POW}_i)\ \forall_i [\mathsf{Set}_i]\, x\,.\, \forall_i\, z\,.\, z \in_i (\mathcal{P}_i\, x) \leftrightarrow z \subseteq_i x, \\
& (\mathrm{SUC}_i)\ \forall_i [\mathsf{Set}_i]\, x\,.\, \forall_i\, a\,.\, a \in_i (\mathsf{succ}_i\, x) \leftrightarrow (a \in_i x \vee a = x), \\
& (\mathrm{INF}_i)\ \emptyset_i \in_i \mathsf{Inf}_i \wedge \forall_i\, x \in_i \mathsf{Inf}_i\,.\, (\mathsf{succ}_i\, x) \in_i \mathsf{Inf}_i, \\
& (\mathrm{RPL}_i)\ \forall_{\mathsf{d}_i \Rightarrow \mathsf{d}_i \Rightarrow \star}\, p\,.\, \forall_i [\mathsf{Set}_i]\, x\,.\, (\forall_i\, a \in_i x\,.\, \exists_i^{\leq 1}\, b\,.\, p\, a\, b) \\
& \qquad\qquad \rightarrow (\mathsf{Set}_i\, (\mathcal{R}_i\, p\, x) \wedge \forall_i\, b\,.\, b \in_i (\mathcal{R}_i\, p\, x) \leftrightarrow \exists_i\, a \in_i x\,.\, p\, a\, b)\ \}
\end{aligned}$$

$$\begin{aligned}
\mathsf{PConsts}_i :\equiv\ & (\mathsf{pair}_i\ ::\ \mathsf{d}_i \Rightarrow \mathsf{d}_i \Rightarrow \mathsf{d}_i,\ \mathsf{Pair}_i\ ::\ \mathsf{d}_i \Rightarrow \star) \quad (X, Y)_i := \mathsf{pair}_i\, X\, Y \\
\mathsf{PTheory}_i :=\ & \{\ \forall_i\, a, b, x, y\,.\, (a, b)_i = (x, y)_i \leftrightarrow (a = x \wedge b = y), \\
& \ \forall_i\, p\,.\, \mathsf{Pair}_i\, p \leftrightarrow \exists_i\, x, y\,.\, p = (x, y)_i\ \} \\
\mathsf{NConsts}_i :\equiv\ & (\mathbf{0}_i\ ::\ \mathsf{d}_i,\ \mathbf{S}_i\ ::\ \mathsf{d}_i \Rightarrow \mathsf{d}_i,\ \mathsf{Nat}_i\ ::\ \mathsf{d}_i \Rightarrow \star) \\
\mathsf{NTheory}_i :=\ & \{\ \mathsf{Nat}_i\, \mathbf{0}_i,\quad \mathbf{0}_i = \mathbf{0}_i,\quad \forall_i [\mathsf{Nat}_i]\, x\,.\, \mathsf{Nat}_i\, (\mathbf{S}_i\, x), \\
& \ \forall_i [\mathsf{Nat}_i]\, x, y\,.\, x = y \leftrightarrow \mathbf{S}_i\, x = \mathbf{S}_i\, y, \\
& \ \forall_i [\mathsf{Nat}_i]\, x\,.\, \mathbf{S}_i\, x \neq \mathbf{0}_i, \\
& \ \forall_{\mathsf{d}_i \Rightarrow \star}\, p\,.\, p\, \mathbf{0}_i \rightarrow (\forall_i [\mathsf{Nat}_i]\, x\,.\, p\, x \rightarrow p\, (\mathbf{S}_i\, x)) \rightarrow \forall_i [\mathsf{Nat}_i]\, y\,.\, p\, y\ \} \\
\mathsf{EConsts}_i :\equiv\ & (\bullet_i\ ::\ \mathsf{d}_i,\ \imath_i\ ::\ (\mathsf{d}_i \Rightarrow \star) \Rightarrow \mathsf{d}_i) \\
\mathsf{ETheory}_i :=\ & \{\ \exists!_i = (\lambda\, p\,.\, \exists_i\, x\,.\, p\, x \wedge \exists_i^{\leq 1}\, x\,.\, p\, x), \\
& \ \forall_{\mathsf{d}_i \Rightarrow \star}\, p\,.\, (\exists!_i\, x\,.\, p\, x) \rightarrow (\forall_i\, y\,.\, p\, y \leftrightarrow y = (\imath_i\, z\,.\, p\, z)), \\
& \ \forall_{\mathsf{d}_i \Rightarrow \star}\, p\,.\, \neg\, (\exists!_i\, x\,.\, p\, x) \rightarrow (\imath_i\, z\,.\, p\, z) = \bullet_i\ \}
\end{aligned}$$

Fig. 3. Signatures and theories for the **Set**, **Pair**, **Nat**, and **Exception** features

To combine features to make a GST, Fig. 4 defines formulas that state that a combination of features is well behaved. The formula $\mathsf{Iden}(k_1, \ldots, k_n)$ states that every object in d_i belongs to at least one of the features k_1, ..., k_n, while the formula $\mathsf{AllDistinct}_i(k_1, \ldots, k_n)$ states that every such object belongs to exactly one such feature. The formula $\mathsf{WF}_i(k_1, \ldots, k_n)$ asserts the well-foundedness of the union of the internal structure relations given by $\mathsf{child}_i^{k_1}$, ..., $\mathsf{child}_i^{k_n}$. The formula $\mathsf{ExOutside}_i(k_1, \ldots, k_n)$ states that the exception element $\bullet_i$ is not a direct immediate child of any objects belonging to the features k_1, ..., k_n.

We define **ZF** in domain d_i via the axioms ZF_i in Fig. 4 as a GST that uses just the **Set** feature. Let PureZF_i be a traditional formulation of ZF obtained by replacing all bounded $\forall_i [\mathsf{Set}_i]$ quantifiers in GZF_i with unbounded $\forall_i$ quantifiers and adding the Axiom of Foundation. Because $\mathsf{Iden}_i(1)$ allows us to prove $\forall_i\, x\,.\, \mathsf{Set}_i\, x$, it follows that $\mathsf{ZF}_i \vdash_i \mathsf{PureZF}_i$ and also that $\mathsf{PureZF}_i \vdash_i \mathsf{ZF}_i$.

We define **ZFP** in d_i via the axioms ZFP_i as a GST with non-set ordered pairs that combines the **Set** and **Pair** features. Note that the non-set ordered pairs of **ZFP** do not have any extraneous properties.

We define **ZFN** in d_i via the axioms ZFN_i as a GST with non-set natural numbers that combines the **Set** and **Nat** features. Because $\mathsf{NTheory}_i$ only provides a predicate symbol Nat_i, the user of ZFN_i will want a set $\mathbb{N}$ containing

$$\mathsf{Iden}_i(k_1,\ldots,k_n) := \forall_i\, x\,.\,\mathsf{iden}_i^{k_1}\, x \vee \cdots \vee \mathsf{iden}_i^{k_n}\, x$$

$$\mathsf{distinct}_i(k,l) := \forall_i\, x\,.\,\neg\,\mathsf{iden}_i^{k}\, x \vee \neg\,\mathsf{iden}_i^{l}\, x$$

$$\mathsf{AllDistinct}_i(k_1,\ldots,k_n) := \mathsf{distinct}_i(k_1,k_2) \wedge \cdots \wedge \mathsf{distinct}_i(k_1,k_n)$$
$$\wedge \cdots \wedge \mathsf{distinct}_i(k_{n-1},k_n)$$

$$\mathsf{WF}_i(k_1,\ldots,k_n) := \forall_{d_i \Rightarrow *}\, p\,.\,(\forall_i\, x\,.\,\neg\, p\, x)$$
$$\vee (\exists_i\, [p]\, a\,.\,\neg\,\exists_i\, [p]\, b\,.\,\mathsf{child}_i^{k_1}\, b\, a \wedge \cdots \wedge \mathsf{child}_i^{k_n}\, b\, a)$$

$$\mathsf{ExOutside}_i(k_1,\ldots,k_n) := \forall_i\, x\,.\,\neg\,\mathsf{child}_i^{k_1}\, \bullet_i\, x \vee \cdots \vee \neg\,\mathsf{child}_i^{k_n}\, \bullet_i\, x$$

$$\mathbf{Base}_i := \mathsf{Init} \cup \mathsf{FOLQuants}_i \cup \mathsf{GZF}_i$$

$$\mathbf{ZF}_i := \mathsf{Base}_i + \mathsf{Iden}_i(1) + \mathsf{WF}_i(1)$$

$$\mathbf{ZFP}_i := \mathsf{Base}_i \cup \mathsf{PTheory}_i + \mathsf{Iden}_i(1,3) + \mathsf{AllDistinct}_i(1,3) + \mathsf{WF}_i(1,3)$$

$$\mathbf{ZFN}_i := \mathsf{Base}_i \cup \mathsf{NTheory}_i + \mathsf{Iden}_i(1,5) + \mathsf{AllDistinct}_i(1,5) + \mathsf{WF}_i(1)$$

$$\mathbf{ZFE}_i := \{\forall_i^{\neq\bullet} =_{(d_i \Rightarrow *) \Rightarrow *} (\lambda p\,.\,\forall_i\, x\,.\,x \neq_{d_i}\, \bullet_i \to p\, x)\}$$
$$\cup\ (\mathsf{Base}_i \cup \mathsf{ETheory}_i)[\forall_i := \forall_i^{\neq\bullet}]$$
$$+\ \mathsf{Iden}_i(1,7) + \mathsf{AllDistinct}_i(1,7) + \mathsf{WF}_i(1) + \mathsf{ExOutside}_i(1)$$

$$\mathbf{ZF}_i^+ := \{\forall_i^{\neq\bullet} =_{(d_i \Rightarrow *) \Rightarrow *} (\lambda p\,.\,\forall_i\, x\,.\,x \neq_{d_i}\, \bullet_i \to p\, x)\}$$
$$\cup\ (\mathsf{Base}_i \cup \mathsf{PTheory}_i \cup \mathsf{NTheory}_i \cup \mathsf{ETheory}_i)[\forall_i := \forall_i^{\neq\bullet}]$$
$$+\ \mathsf{Iden}(1,3,5,7) + \mathsf{AllDistinct}_i(1,3,5,7) + \mathsf{WF}_i(1,5) + \mathsf{ExOutside}_i(1,5)$$

Fig. 4. Operations for combining features, and axiomatisations of various GSTs

exactly all the objects that satisfy Nat_i (i.e., the non-set natural numbers), and this can be done via the axiom (RPL$_i$) and the von Neumann natural numbers.

We define **ZFE** in d_i via the axioms ZFE$_i$ as a GST with a non-set exception element that is excluded from the domain of quantifiers and is not contained in any set. It is intended that a ZFE user does not directly use the ALLI and ALLE rules, but instead uses a different quantifier $\forall_i^{\neq\bullet}$ (and other quantifiers derived from it) that excludes the exception element. Note that all occurrences of $\forall_i$ are replaced by $\forall_i^{\neq\bullet}$ in the formulas GZF$_i$ and FOLQuants$_i$.

We define **ZF$^+$** in d_i via the axioms ZF$_i^+$ as a GST that combines all four example features. Note that this uses the same $\forall_i^{\neq\bullet}$ quantifier as ZFE.

Remember the example specification from Sect. 1 of a function $g : (\mathbb{N}^2 \cup \mathcal{P}(\mathbb{N})) \to \{0,1\}$ such that $g(\langle 0,1 \rangle) = 0$ and $g(\{1,2\}) = 1$. How can g be handled in our five example GSTs? Assume we use non-set natural numbers if we have the **Nat** feature (ZFN, ZF$^+$) and otherwise we use the von Neumann naturals, and similarly we use non-set ordered pairs if we have the **Pair** feature (ZFP, ZF$^+$) and otherwise we use Kuratowski pairs. Represent g as the least set such that $\langle x,y \rangle \in g$ whenever input x should map to output y. In ZF, g is not a function because $\langle 0,1 \rangle = \{1,2\}$ and the set-function application binary infix operator '$_i$ can not make both $g\,{'}_i\,\langle 0,1 \rangle = 0$ and $g\,{'}_i\,\{1,2\} = 1$ true. Also, depending on how we "define" the "function" g, we might prove incorrect results or even make our entire system inconsistent. In ZFP, ZFN, and ZF$^+$ it holds that $\langle 0,1 \rangle \neq \{1,2\}$, so g is a function and we are happy. In ZFE, g is not a function but the **Exception** feature makes some failure-handling options a bit easier. One option uses the definite description operator $\imath_i$ in defining the set-function application operator

$$\{X,Y\}_i := \mathsf{upair}_i\, X\, Y, \qquad \{X\}_i := \{X,X\}_i, \qquad \langle X,Y\rangle_i := \mathsf{kpair}_i\, X\, Y,$$

$$0_i := \emptyset_i, \quad 1_i := \mathsf{succ}_i\, 0_i, \quad 2_i := \mathsf{succ}_i\, 1_i, \quad 3_i := \mathsf{succ}_i\, 2_i, \quad \ldots$$

$\mathsf{ZFUtils}_i := \{\, \bigcap_i = (\lambda\, x\,.\, \{\, y \in_i \bigcup_i x \mid \forall_i\, a \in_i x\,.\, y \in_i a\, \}),$

$\phi_i = (\lambda\, x, y, a, b\,.\, (a =_{\mathsf{d}_i} \emptyset_i \wedge b =_{\mathsf{d}_i} x) \vee (a =_{\mathsf{d}_i} \mathcal{P}_i\, \emptyset_i \wedge b =_{\mathsf{d}_i} y)),$

$\mathsf{upair}_i = (\lambda\, x, y\,.\, \mathcal{R}_i\, (\phi_i\, x\, y)\, (\mathcal{P}_i\, (\mathcal{P}_i\, \emptyset_i))),$

$\mathsf{kpair}_i = (\lambda\, x, y\,.\, \{\{x,y\}_i, \{x\}_i\}_i),$

$\pi_i^1 = (\lambda\, p\,.\, \bigcup_i \bigcap_i p), \quad \pi_i^2 = (\lambda\, p\,.\, \bigcup_i \{\, x \in_i \bigcup_i p \mid x \neq \pi_i^1\, p\, \}),$

$\times_i = (\lambda\, x, y\,.\, \bigcup_i \{\, z \mid \exists_i\, a \in_i x\,.\, z = \{\, p \mid \exists_i\, b \in_i y\,.\, p = \langle a, b\rangle_i\, \}\, \}),$

$\cup_i = (\lambda\, x, y\,.\, \bigcup_i \{x, y\}_i), \quad \mathsf{Tr}_i = (\lambda\, x\,.\, \mathsf{Set}_i\, X \wedge \forall_i\, y \in_i X\,.\, y \subseteq_i X),$

$\mathsf{Ord}_i = (\lambda\, x\,.\, \mathsf{Tr}_i\, x \wedge (\forall_i\, y \in_i x\,.\, \mathsf{Tr}_i\, y)),$

$<_i = (\lambda\, x, y\,.\, x \in_i y \wedge \mathsf{Ord}_i\, y),$

$\mathsf{Limit}_i = (\lambda\, x\,.\, \mathsf{Ord}_i\, x \wedge (0_i <_i x) \wedge (\forall_i\, y <_i x\,.\, \mathsf{succ}_i\, y <_i x)),$

$\omega_i = \bigcap_i \{\, x \in_i \mathcal{P}_i\, \mathsf{Inf}_i \mid \mathsf{Limit}_i\, x\, \},$

$\mathsf{TagSetMems}_i = (\lambda\, a, x\,.\, \{a\}_i \times_i x), \quad \mathsf{TagOf}_i = \pi_i^1,$

$\biguplus_i = \lambda\, y\,.\, \bigcup_i \{\, \mathsf{TagSetMems}_i\, b\, (y\, b) \mid b \in_i \omega_i\, \},$

$\mathsf{Part}_i = (\lambda\, a, x\,.\, \{\, y \in_i x \mid \mathsf{TagOf}_i\, y = a\, \}),$

$-_i = (\lambda\, x, y\,.\, \{\, a \in_i x \mid a \notin_i y\, \}),$

$\mathsf{OrdRec}_i =_{(\mathsf{d}_i \Rightarrow \mathsf{d}_i \Rightarrow \mathsf{d}_i) \Rightarrow \mathsf{d}_i \Rightarrow \mathsf{d}_i \Rightarrow \mathsf{d}_i} T_i\, \}$

Fig. 5. Set theoretic utilities

$'_i$ to be $(\lambda\, x, y\,.\, \eta_i\, z\,.\, \langle y, z\rangle \in_i x)$, which makes $g\, '_i\, x = \bullet_i$ if g is not functional at x. Another option is taking a predicate gSpec specifying a function with the desired input/output behavior for g and then defining g as $(\eta_i\, z\,.\, \mathsf{gSpec}\, z)$, which would evaluate to $\bullet_i$. The exception object $\bullet_i$ is useful in these cases because it can not accidentally get embedded inside larger results and can not equal a value tested by the $\forall_i^{\neq \bullet}$ quantifier.

4   Model Building Kit

This section defines tools for building within GZF-domains models of GSTs with the **Set** feature that can be specified to support additional features.

Set Theory Tools. We define three variants of *set comprehension* notation. If $a, b \notin \mathsf{FV}(P) \cup \mathsf{FV}(X)$, we write $\{\, b \mid \exists_i\, a \in_i X\,.\, P\, a\, b\, \}$ for $\mathcal{R}_i\, P\, X$, and $\{\, a \in_i X \mid P\, a\, \}$ for $\mathcal{R}_i\, (\lambda\, a, b\,.\, a =_{\mathsf{d}_i} b \wedge a \in_i X \wedge P\, a)\, X$. If $F :: \mathsf{d}_i \Rightarrow \mathsf{d}_i$ and $x, y \notin \mathsf{FV}(B) \cup \mathsf{FV}(F)$, we write $\{\, F\, x \mid x \in_i B,\, P\, x\, \}$ for $\{\, y \mid \exists_i\, x \in_i B\,.\, P\, x \wedge y =_{\mathsf{d}_i} F\, x\, \}$.

Figure 5 defines the set $\mathsf{ZFUtils}_i$ of simple definitions for operators including those related to ordered pairs, ordinals, and tagging. The operators π_i^1 and π_i^2, called the *left* and *right projections* (resp.), are defined such that if X and Y are sets, then $\langle X, Y\rangle_i =_{\mathsf{d}_i} \langle \pi_i^1\, \langle X, Y\rangle_i, \pi_i^2\, \langle X, Y\rangle_i\rangle$. A set X is *transitive* iff every set member of X is also a subset of X. A set X is an *ordinal* iff it is a transitive set whose set members are all transitive sets. We say that X is a *limit ordinal* iff $\mathsf{Limit}_i\, X$. The constant ω_i is defined as the intersection of all subsets of Inf_i that are limit ordinals. Thus, ω_i is the smallest limit ordinal.

$$
\begin{aligned}
(\mathsf{OrdRec}_i\, F\, A\, 0_i) &= A \\
\forall_i [\mathsf{Ord}_i]\, b\,.\; (\mathsf{OrdRec}_i\, F\, A\, (\mathsf{succ}_i\, b)) &= F\,(\mathsf{succ}_i\, b)\,(\mathsf{OrdRec}_i\, F\, A\, b) \\
\forall_i [\mathsf{Limit}_i]\, z\,.\; (\mathsf{OrdRec}_i\, F\, A\, z) &= \bigcup_i \{\, \mathsf{OrdRec}_i\, F\, A\, b \mid b \in_i z \,\}
\end{aligned}
$$

$$
\begin{aligned}
\mathsf{Model}_{i,j} := \{\; &\mathsf{Tier}_{i,j} = \mathsf{OrdRec}_i\, (\lambda\, z, x\,.\, x \cup_i \biguplus_i (\lambda\, y\,.\, \mathsf{Ops}_{i,j}\, y\, z\,(x -_i \mathsf{Ignored}_{i,j}))) \\
&(\biguplus_i (\lambda\, y\,.\, \mathsf{Ops}_{i,j}\, y\, 0_i\, \emptyset_i)), \\
&\mathsf{inModel}_{i,j} = (\lambda\, x\,.\, \exists_i [\mathsf{Ord}_i]\, a\,.\, x \in_i (\mathsf{Tier}_{i,j}\, a)), \\
&\overline{\forall}_{i,j} = (\lambda\, p\,.\, \forall_i [\mathsf{inModel}_{i,j}]\, x\,.\, p\, x) \,\}
\end{aligned}
$$

Fig. 6. Recursion equations, and simple definitions for building a model for d_j in d_i

If X is a set and A is an object, then $\mathsf{TagSetMems}_i\, A\, X$ is the set whose set members are exactly all ordered pairs $\langle A, Y \rangle_i$ where Y is a set member of X. If $X =_{\mathsf{d}_i} \langle A, Y \rangle_i$ for some A and Y, then $\mathsf{TagOf}_i\, X =_{\mathsf{d}_i} A$. We say that X is *tagged with* A or A-*tagged* iff $\mathsf{TagOf}_i\, X =_{\mathsf{d}_i} A$.

We now describe operators that use tagging to build disjoint unions and extract partitions from disjoint unions. Let S be a term such that $\Gamma \vdash_i A \in_i \omega_i \to \mathsf{Set}_i\,(S\, A)$, i.e., S has type $\mathsf{d}_i \Rightarrow \mathsf{d}_i$ and represents a sequence of sets indexed by von Neumann natural numbers. Then $\biguplus_i S$ is a set called the *disjoint union* of S, which is the result of tagging the members of each set in the sequence S with the set's index and collecting all the tagged objects. Hence $X \in_i \biguplus_i S$ iff $X =_{\mathsf{d}_i} \langle A, Y \rangle_i$ where $Y \in_i S\, A$ for some ordinal A. If X is a set containing objects with many different tags, then $\mathsf{Part}_i\, A\, X$ gives a set whose members are exactly all of the members of X tagged with A.

For any GZF-domain, we conjecture the existence of a term T_i such that the simple definition $\mathsf{OrdRec}_i =_\tau T_i$ defines OrdRec to do transfinite recursion on the ordinals.[1] The characterisation of OrdRec_i in Fig. 6 is equivalent to such a definition, where $A :: \mathsf{d}_i$ and $F :: \mathsf{d}_i \Rightarrow \mathsf{d}_i \Rightarrow \mathsf{d}_i$ is such that $\Gamma \vdash_i \forall_i [\mathsf{Ord}_i]\, b\,.\, \forall_i [\mathsf{Set}_i]\, x\,.\, \mathsf{Set}_i\,(F\, b\, x)$. The set A is used for the zero case, F is used for the successor case, and unions are taken at limit ordinals.

Model Framework. The constant $\mathsf{Ops}_{i,j}$ acts as a table of operations used for building in d_i the tiers of a model for d_j. The constant $\mathsf{Ignored}_{i,j}$ is a set of objects which are not to be used in building further objects. The user must axiomatize both of these constants. For this to work, if A and B are ordinals, then $\mathsf{Ops}_{i,j}\, A\, B$ must be an operator which returns a set when given a set. We call the A-indexed aspect of $\mathsf{Ops}_{i,j}$ the *slot* A. Each slot is used for a different kind of mathematical object, e.g., set, non-set ordered pair, non-set natural number, etc. When building a model, $\mathsf{Ops}_{i,j}\, A\, B$ is given the previous model tier minus the ignored objects and returns a set of objects, each of which is then tagged by A before being added to the next tier.

For each pair of domain types, $\mathsf{Model}_{i,j}$ in Fig. 6 is a set of simple definitions that builds a model in d_i for d_j and gives a membership predicate and a $\forall$-quantifier restricted to the model. The operator $\mathsf{Tier}_{i,j} :: \mathsf{d}_i \Rightarrow \mathsf{d}_i$ uses OrdRec_i to

---

[1] Our belief is based on tracing the expansion of uses of `transrec3` in Isabelle/ZF.

$$\mathsf{swap}_{i,j}(\star) := \star \qquad \mathsf{swap}_{i,j}(\mathsf{d}_i) := \mathsf{d}_j \qquad \mathsf{swap}_{i,j}(\mathsf{d}_j) := \mathsf{d}_i$$
$$\mathsf{swap}_{i,j}(\sigma \Rightarrow \tau) := \mathsf{swap}_{i,j}(\sigma) \Rightarrow \mathsf{swap}_{i,j}(\tau)$$

$$\mathsf{trans}_{i,j}(x, m) := m(x)$$
$$\mathsf{trans}_{i,j}(\forall_{\mathsf{d}_j}, m) := \overline{\forall}_{i,j}$$
$$\mathsf{trans}_{i,j}(\heartsuit_j, m) := \overline{\heartsuit}_{i,j} \quad \text{if } \heartsuit \in \{\imath, \forall^{\neq \bullet}\}$$
$$\mathsf{trans}_{i,j}(\heartsuit_j, m) := \overline{\heartsuit}_i \quad \text{otherwise, e.g., } \heartsuit_j \equiv \mathsf{Set}_j$$
$$\mathsf{trans}_{i,j}(\forall_\tau, m) := \forall_{\mathsf{swap}_{i,j}(\tau)} \quad \text{if } \tau \neq \mathsf{d}_k \text{ for any } k \in \mathbb{N}$$
$$\mathsf{trans}_{i,j}(=_\tau, m) := (=_{\mathsf{swap}_{i,j}(\tau)})$$
$$\mathsf{trans}_{i,j}(\neq_\tau, m) := (\neq_{\mathsf{swap}_{i,j}(\tau)})$$
$$\mathsf{trans}_{i,j}(B\,C, m) := \mathsf{trans}_{i,j}(B, m)\,\mathsf{trans}_{i,j}(C, m)$$
$$\mathsf{trans}_{i,j}(\lambda\,x : \tau\,.\,B, m) := \lambda\,y : \mathsf{swap}_{i,j}(\tau)\,.\,\mathsf{trans}_{i,j}(B, m[x \mapsto y])$$
$$\mathsf{trans}_{i,j}(\Gamma) := \{\,\mathsf{trans}_{i,j}(\varphi, \varnothing) \mid \varphi \in \Gamma\,\}$$

$$\mathsf{ZFOps}_{i,j} := \{\,\mathsf{Ops}_{i,j}\,1_i\,0_i = (\lambda\,x\,.\,\emptyset_i), \quad \forall_i[\mathsf{Ord}_i]\,b\,.\,\mathsf{Ops}_{i,j}\,1_i\,(\mathsf{succ}_i\,b) = \mathcal{P}_i\,\}$$

$$\mathsf{ZFModelDefs}_i := \{\,\overline{\emptyset}_i = \langle 1_i, \emptyset_i \rangle_i, \quad \overline{\mathsf{Set}}_i = (\lambda\,x\,.\,\mathsf{TagOf}_i\,x =_{\mathsf{d}_i} 1_i),$$
$$\overline{\in}_i = (\lambda\,x, y\,.\,\overline{\mathsf{Set}}_i\,y \wedge x \in_i (\pi_i^2\,y)),$$
$$\overline{\subseteq}_i = (\lambda\,x, y : \mathsf{d}_i\,.\,\overline{\mathsf{Set}}_i\,x \wedge \overline{\mathsf{Set}}_i\,y \wedge \forall_i\,a\,\overline{\in}_i\,x\,.\,a\,\overline{\in}_i\,y),$$
$$\overline{\mathcal{P}}_i = (\lambda\,x\,.\,\langle 1_i, \mathsf{TagSetMems}_i\,1_i\,(\mathcal{P}_i\,(\pi_i^2\,x)) \rangle_i),$$
$$\overline{\bigcup}_i = (\lambda\,x\,.\,\langle 1_i, \bigcup_i\,\{\,\pi_i^2\,y \mid y \in_i (\pi_i^2\,x)\,\} \rangle_i),$$
$$\overline{\mathsf{succ}}_i = (\lambda\,x\,.\,\overline{\bigcup}_i\,\langle 1_i, \{x, \langle 1_i, \{x\} \rangle_i\} \rangle_i),$$
$$\Theta_i = (\lambda\,a\,.\,\mathsf{OrdRec}_i\,(\lambda\,b, x\,.\,\{\,\overline{\mathsf{succ}}_i\,y \mid y \in_i x\,\})\,\{\langle 1_i, \emptyset_i \rangle_i\}_i\,a),$$
$$\overline{\mathsf{Inf}}_i = \langle 1_i \Theta_i\,\omega_i, , \rangle_i,$$
$$\overline{\mathcal{R}}_i = (\lambda\,p, x\,.\,\langle 1_i, \mathcal{R}_i\,p\,(\pi_i^2\,x) \rangle_i)\,\}$$

$$\mathsf{BuildModel}_{i,j} := \mathsf{ZFUtils}_i \cup \mathsf{ZFOps}_{i,j} \cup \mathsf{Model}_{i,j} \cup \mathsf{trans}_{i,j}(\mathsf{FOLQuants}_j) \cup \mathsf{ZFModelDefs}_i$$

Fig. 7. Definition of $\mathsf{swap}_{i,j}$ on types and $\mathsf{trans}_{i,j}$ and formula sets for model building

map d_i ordinals to model tiers. The formula $\mathsf{inModel}_{i,j}\,X$ holds if there exists an ordinal A such that $\Gamma \vdash_k X \in_i (\mathsf{Tier}_{i,j}\,A)$. The quantifier $\overline{\forall}_{i,j}$ allows quantification over the model by restricting $\forall_i$ to objects satisfying $\mathsf{inModel}_{i,j}$.

Figure 7 defines a function $\mathsf{trans}_{i,j}$ for translating formulas that speak about d_j to formulas that speak about the model in d_i for d_j. The function is defined recursively on terms mostly by translating constants to their "model versions". For example $\mathsf{trans}_{i,j}(\forall_j) \equiv \overline{\forall}_{i,j}$, and $\mathsf{trans}_{i,j}(\mathcal{P}_j) \equiv \overline{\mathcal{P}}_i$. Sets of formulas can also be translated. For example, we use $\mathsf{trans}_{i,j}(\mathsf{FOLQuants}_j)$ to generate extra quantifiers relativized to a model.

GZF Models. We now show how to configure the set slot of $\mathsf{Ops}_{i,j}$ to obtain a model satisfying GZF. We reserve slot 1 for sets. Each model tier must contain all subsets of all previous tiers, tagged with 1. Figure 7 defines the formula set $\mathsf{ZFOps}_{i,j}$ that specifies that $\mathsf{Ops}_{i,j}$ invokes the power set operator ($\mathcal{P}_i$) in slot 1 at each successor ordinal. The formulas in $\mathsf{ZFOps}_{i,j}$ allow proving that every 1-tagged set of model sets belongs to some model tier. A crucial fact used for demonstrating this is:

$$\Gamma \vdash_i \forall_i [\mathrm{Ord}]\, b \,.\, \{1_i\} \times_i (\mathcal{P}_i (\mathrm{Tier}_{i,j}\, b)) \subseteq_i \mathrm{Tier}_{i,j} (\mathrm{succ}_i\, b)$$

Figure 7 defines $\mathrm{ZFModelDefs}_i$ as a set of simple definitions for each model constant in $\mathrm{trans}_{i,j}(\mathrm{GZFConsts}_j)$. Because the definitions in $\mathrm{ZFModelDefs}_i$ only make use of the set slot of the model, they can be shared amongst all models we build in d_i. The constants in $\mathrm{trans}_{i,j}(\mathrm{GZFConsts}_j)$ act on the "model sets", and have been shown to satisfy the formulas in $\mathrm{trans}_{i,j}(\mathrm{GZF}_j)$ when used in a model. Figure 7 also defines $\mathrm{BuildModel}_{i,j}$ as a set of simple definitions for (1) set theoretic utilities for model building, including ordinal recursion, (2) specifying slot 1 of $\mathrm{Ops}_{i,j}$ to invoke ($\mathcal{P}_i$) at successor ordinals (3) building model tiers, checking model membership, quantifying over the model, (4) extra quantifiers relativized to the model, and (5) simple definitions for $\mathrm{trans}_{i,j}(\mathrm{GZFConsts}_j)$.

We say that Γ builds a *GZF-model* in d_i for d_j iff $\Gamma \vdash_k \mathrm{trans}_{i,j}(\mathrm{GZF}_j)$. We have proved that if $\Gamma \vdash_k (\mathrm{ALLI}_{k,i}), (\mathrm{ALLE}_{k,i})$ and $\Gamma \vdash_k \mathrm{Base}_i \cup \mathrm{BuildModel}_{i,j}$, then Γ builds a GZF-model in d_i for d_j.

5   Connecting Models to Domains

Section 3 showed how to axiomatize a GST in domain d_i directly using d_i as the founder domain. We now show how to combine an axiomatization Γ_i of a GST S_1 in domain d_i with model building definitions $\Psi_{i,j}$ to justify an axiomatization Γ_j of a GST S_2 in domain d_j so that $\Gamma_i \cup \Psi_{i,j} \vdash_i \Gamma_j$. This connects S_2 to a model for it built in S_1, which supports stating that S_2 is consistent if S_1 is.

Start by assuming that $\Gamma \vdash_k \mathrm{BuildModel}_{i,j}$ and we will connect the model built in d_i to d_j so we can prove things about d_j using $\vdash_k$. Figure 8 defines the set $\mathrm{Connection}_{i,j}$ that axiomatizes that the operators $\mathrm{Abs}_{i,j} :: \mathrm{d}_i \Rightarrow \mathrm{d}_j$ and $\mathrm{Rep}_{i,j} :: \mathrm{d}_j \Rightarrow \mathrm{d}_i$ are an isomorphism between the objects satisfying $\mathrm{Tier}_{i,j}$ and d_j. Figure 8 defines the meta-level function $\mathrm{swap}_{i,j}$ that translates terms with types involving the abstract domain d_j to corresponding terms with types involving the representation domain d_i, and vice versa. We also define $\mathrm{Delegate}_{i,j}$ to generate simple definitions for a set of constants for use in d_j in terms of the translation of those constants to corresponding constants for use with the model in d_i. In particular, swapping $\overline{\forall}_{i,j}$ supplies a definition for $\forall_j$ such that $(\mathrm{ALLI}_{i,j}), (\mathrm{ALLE}_{i,j})$ are admissible with $\vdash_i$.

If $\Gamma \vdash_k \mathrm{Base}_i \cup \mathrm{BuildModel}_{i,j}$, then we can give simple definitions for $\mathrm{GZFConsts}_j$ using $\mathrm{Delegate}_{i,j}(\mathrm{GZFConsts}_j)$. Hence we define $\mathrm{AbsModel}_{i,j}$ in Fig. 8 as the set of formulas which (1) axiomatizes an isomorphism between members of d_i satisfying $\mathrm{Tier}_{i,j}$ and d_j and (2) gives simple definitions for quantifiers over d_j and $\mathrm{GZFConsts}_j$ by swapping their model versions in d_i. To prove that the swapped constants and quantifiers form a GZF-domain, we show that if $\Gamma \vdash_k (\mathrm{ALLI}_{k,i}), (\mathrm{ALLE}_{k,i})$ and $\Gamma \vdash_k \mathrm{Base}_i \cup \mathrm{BuildModel}_{i,j} \cup \mathrm{AbsModel}_{i,j}$, then $\Gamma \vdash_k \mathrm{GZF}_j$. This is achieved by expanding the delegated definitions of $\mathrm{GZFConsts}_j$ in each formula of GZF_j. In practice, the instances of $\mathrm{Abs}_{i,j}$ and $\mathrm{Rep}_{i,j}$ in these formulas cancel each other out because the terms they are applied to always belong to the model. We are then left with exactly the formulas of

$$\text{Connection}_{i,j} := \{\,\overline{\forall}_{i,j}\, x\,.\,\text{Rep}_{i,j}\,(\text{Abs}_{i,j}\, x) = x, \quad \forall_j = \text{swap}_{i,j}(\overline{\forall}_{i,j}),$$
$$\forall_j\, y\,.\,\text{Abs}_{i,j}\,(\text{Rep}_{i,j}\, y) = y, \quad \forall_j\, y\,.\,\text{inModel}_{i,j}\,(\text{Rep}_{i,j}\, y)\,\}$$

$$\text{swap}_{i,j}(B) := \begin{cases} \text{swap}_{i,j}(C)\,\text{swap}_{i,j}(D) & \text{if } B :: \star,\, B = C\,D \\ B & \text{if } B :: \star,\, B \in \text{Var} \cup \text{Const} \\ \text{Abs}_{i,j}\, B & \text{if } B :: d_i \\ \text{Rep}_{i,j}\, B & \text{if } B :: d_j \\ (\lambda\, x : \text{swap}_{i,j}(\sigma)\,.\,\text{swap}_{i,j}(B\,(\text{swap}_{i,j}(x)))) & \text{if } B :: \sigma \Rightarrow \tau \end{cases}$$

$$\text{Delegate}_{i,j}(C) := \{\, c =_\tau \text{swap}_{i,j}(\text{trans}_{i,j}(c)) \mid c \in C, c :: \tau \,\}$$

$$\text{AbsModel}_{i,j} := \text{Connection}_{i,j} \cup \text{FOLQuants}_j \cup \text{Delegate}_{i,j}(\text{GZFConsts}_j)$$

Fig. 8. Formulas axiomatising $\text{Abs}_{i,j}$ and $\text{Rep}_{i,j}$, definitions of $\text{swap}_{i,j}$ on terms and $\text{Delegate}_{i,j}$, and formulas for connecting a model built in d_i to d_j

$\text{trans}_{i,j}(\text{GZF}_j)$, which hold because $\Gamma \vdash_k \text{BuildModel}_{i,j}$ can be shown to entail these formulas.

6   Examples of Models of GSTs

We now build models for each of the GSTs shown in Sect. 3. We use d_0 as our founder domain with ZF_0 as axioms.

We build a model of **ZF** in d_0 for d_2, then of **ZFP** in d_2 for d_4, then of **ZFN** in d_4 for d_6, then of **ZFE** in d_6 for d_8, and finally of $\text{\textbf{ZF}}^+$ in d_0 for d_{10}. First we define a meta-level function in Fig. 9 for building formulas which restrict $\text{Ops}_{i,j}$ to only invoke certain slots. We then define specifications of $\text{Ops}_{i,j}$ in Fig. 9 for the **Set**, **Nat** and **Exception** features, and simple definitions for the model translations of each constant in their signatures. The sets of formulas $\Psi_{\overline{\text{ZF}}}$, $\Psi_{\overline{\text{ZFP}}}$, $\Psi_{\overline{\text{ZFN}}}$, $\Psi_{\overline{\text{ZFE}}}$, and $\Psi_{\overline{\text{ZF}^+}}$ in Fig. 10 build models according to these specifications, including the simple definitions for acting on these models. The case for ZFE and ZF^+ is again more complex, requiring generation of definitions for model quantifiers using $\overline{\forall}_{i,j}^{\neq\bullet}$. Finally, we define the sets of formulas Ψ_{ZF}, Ψ_{ZFP}, Ψ_{ZFN}, Ψ_{ZFE}, and Ψ_{ZF^+} which connect each of the models to $d_2, d_4, d_6, d_8, d_{10}$ respectively, and delegate the constants of each signature.

We now briefly explain how to prove that $\Psi_{\text{ZF}} \vdash_0 \text{ZF}_2$, $\Psi_{\text{ZFP}} \vdash_0 \text{ZFP}_4$, $\Psi_{\text{ZFN}} \vdash_0 \text{ZFN}_6$, $\Psi_{\text{ZFE}} \vdash_0 \text{ZFE}_8$, and $\Psi_{\text{ZF}}^+ \vdash_0 \text{ZF}_8^+$. Because $\Psi_{\overline{\text{ZF}}} \vdash_0 (\text{ALLI}_{0,0}), (\text{ALLE}_{0,0})$ and $\Psi_{\overline{\text{ZF}}} \vdash_0 \text{BuildModel}_{0,2}$, we have that $\Psi_{\overline{\text{ZF}}} \vdash_0 \text{trans}_{0,2}(\text{GZF}_2)$. Then because $\Psi_{\text{ZF}} \vdash_0 \text{AbsModel}_{0,2}$, we have that $\Psi_{\text{ZF}} \vdash_0 \text{Base}_0$ and $\Psi_{\text{ZF}} \vdash_0 (\text{ALLI}_{0,2})$. The same argument can be repeated for the other instances of Ψ, with the exception of Ψ_{ZFE} and Ψ_{ZF^+} for which we are required to show $\Psi_{\text{ZFE}} \vdash_0 \text{Base}_8[\forall_8 := \forall_8^{\neq\bullet}]$ and $\Psi_{\text{ZF}^+} \vdash_0 \text{Base}_{10}[\forall_{10} := \forall_{10}^{\neq\bullet}]$. With some work, we can also show:

$$\Psi_{\overline{\text{ZFP}}} \vdash_0 \text{trans}_{2,4}(\text{PTheory}_4), \qquad \Psi_{\overline{\text{ZFN}}} \vdash_0 \text{trans}_{4,6}(\text{NTheory}_4),$$
$$\Psi_{\overline{\text{ZFE}}} \vdash_0 \text{trans}_{6,8}(\text{ETheory}_4),$$
$$\Psi_{\overline{\text{ZF}^+}} \vdash_0 \text{trans}_{8,10}(\text{PTheory}_{10} \cup \text{NTheory}_{10} \cup \text{ETheory}_{10})$$

$$\mathsf{RestrictOps}_{i,j}(\beta_1,\ldots,\beta_n) := \forall_i [\mathsf{Ord}_i]\,\alpha\,.\,(\alpha \neq \beta_1 \wedge \ldots \wedge \alpha \neq \beta_n)$$
$$\rightarrow \mathsf{Ops}_{i,j}\,\alpha\,=\,(\lambda\,\beta,x\,.\,\emptyset_i)$$

$$\mathsf{PairOps}_{i,j} := \{\,\mathsf{Ops}_{i,j}\,3_i\,0_i\,=\,(\lambda\,x\,.\,\emptyset_i),$$
$$\forall_i [\mathsf{Ord}_i]\,\beta <_i 0_i\,.\,\mathsf{Ops}_{i,j}\,3_i\,\beta\,=\,(\lambda\,x\,.\,x \times_i x)\,\}$$

$$\mathsf{NatOps}_{i,j} := \{\,\forall_i [\mathsf{Ord}_i]\,\beta <_i \omega_i\,.\,\mathsf{Ops}_{i,j}\,5_i\,\beta\,=\,(\lambda\,x\,.\,\{\beta\}_i),$$
$$\forall_i [\mathsf{Ord}_i]\,\omega_i <_i \beta\,.\,\mathsf{Ops}_{i,j}\,5_i\,\beta\,=\,(\lambda\,x\,.\,\emptyset_i)\,\}$$

$$\mathsf{ExOps}_{i,j} := \{\,\mathsf{Ops}_{i,j}\,7_i\,0_i\,=\,(\lambda\,x\,.\,\{\emptyset_i\}_i),$$
$$\forall_i [\mathsf{Ord}_i]\,\beta\,.\,\mathsf{Ops}_{i,j}\,7_i\,\beta^{+i}\,=\,(\lambda\,x\,.\,\emptyset_i)\,\}$$

$$\mathsf{PairModelDefs}_i := \{\,\overline{\mathsf{pair}}_i\,=\,(\lambda\,x,y\,.\,\langle 3_i,\langle x,y\rangle_i\rangle_i),$$
$$\overline{\mathsf{Pair}}_i\,=\,(\lambda\,p\,.\,\mathsf{TagOf}_i\,p\,=\,3_i)\,\}$$

$$\mathsf{NatModelDefs}_i := \{\,\overline{\mathsf{0}}_i\,=\,\langle 5_i,0_i\rangle_i$$
$$\overline{\mathsf{S}}_i\,=\,(\lambda\,x\,.\,\langle 5_i,\mathsf{succ}_i\,(\pi_i^2\,x)\rangle_i),$$
$$\overline{\mathsf{Nat}}_i\,=\,(\lambda\,n\,.\,\mathsf{TagOf}_i\,n\,=\,5_i)\,\}$$

$$\mathsf{ExModelDefs}_{i,j} := \{\,\overline{\bullet}_i\,=\,\langle 7_i,\emptyset_i\rangle_i,$$
$$\overline{\imath}_{i,j}\,=\,(\lambda\,p\,.\,\imath_i^{\mathsf{Set}}\,x\,.\,\mathsf{inModel}_{i,j}\,x \wedge p\,x),$$
$$\overline{\forall}_{i,j}^{\neq\bullet}\,=\,(\lambda\,p\,.\,\overline{\forall}_{i,j}\,x \neq \overline{\bullet}\,.\,p\,x)\,\}$$

Fig. 9. Specifications of $\mathsf{Ops}_{i,j}$ and simple definitions for model constants

The translations of AllDistinct and WF formulas are easy to prove from the structure of the model. After this, we have that $\Psi_{\mathsf{ZF}} \vdash_0 \mathsf{ZF}_2$, $\Psi_{\mathsf{ZFP}} \vdash_0 \mathsf{ZFP}_4$, $\Psi_{\mathsf{ZFN}} \vdash_0 \mathsf{ZFN}_6$, $\Psi_{\mathsf{ZFE}} \vdash_0 \mathsf{ZFE}_8$, and $\Psi_{\mathsf{ZF}}^+ \vdash_0 \mathsf{ZF}_{10}^+$.

We now argue that the reasoning above can be completed to conclude the consistency of ZF_2, ZFP_4, ZFN_6, ZFE_8, and ZF_{10}^+. We begin with belief in the consistency of first-order logic and ZF, which are embedded in our system as Base_0. We now discuss why we believe consistency is preserved by our methods of extending Base_0 to Ψ_{ZF}, Ψ_{ZF} to Ψ_{ZFP}, and so on. Most of the extensions are done by adding simple definitions, which preserve consistency. We have not yet written the term T_i in the simple definition for OrdRec_i, but we believe this can be done because Isabelle/ZF does it. Our specifications of $\mathsf{Ops}_{i,j}$ and $\mathsf{RestrictOps}_{i,j}$ are currently not simple definitions, but we believe we know how to reformulate them as simple definitions. The axiomatizations of $\mathsf{Abs}_{i,j}$ and $\mathsf{Rep}_{i,j}$ are not simple definitions, but this technique is widely used in Isabelle/HOL and has been argued to preserve consistency by Kunčar and Popescu [13].

7   Conclusion and Future Work

This paper presented methods for generating custom set theories intended to be more suitable for the formalisation of mathematics by being closer to mathematical practice. Our logical framework and toolkit supports reasoning about axiomatizations and models for a variety of GSTs. We show how to define ZF as a GST and give four examples of how to extend ZF with non-set features. We show how to use a GST via an axiomatization and also how to use it via a connection to a model.

$$\Psi_{\overline{\mathsf{ZF}}} := \mathsf{ZF}_0 \cup \mathsf{BuildModel}_{0,2} + \mathsf{RestrictOps}_{0,2}(1) + \mathsf{Ignored}_{0,2} = \emptyset_0$$

$$\Psi_{\overline{\mathsf{ZFP}}} := \Psi_{\overline{\mathsf{ZF}}} \cup \mathsf{BuildModel}_{2,4} \cup \mathsf{PairOps}_{2,4} \cup \mathsf{PairModelDefs}_2$$
$$+ \mathsf{RestrictOps}_{2,4}(1,3) + \mathsf{Ignored}_{2,4} = \emptyset_2$$

$$\Psi_{\overline{\mathsf{ZFN}}} := \Psi_{\overline{\mathsf{ZFP}}} \cup \mathsf{BuildModel}_{4,6} \cup \mathsf{NatOps}_{4,6} \cup \mathsf{NatModelDefs}_4$$
$$+ \mathsf{RestrictOps}_{4,6}(1,5) + \mathsf{Ignored}_{4,6} = \emptyset_4$$

$$\Psi_{\overline{\mathsf{ZFE}}} := \Psi_{\overline{\mathsf{ZFE}}} \cup \mathsf{BuildModel}_{6,8}[\overline{\mathsf{V}}_{6,8} := \overline{\mathsf{V}}_{6,8}^{\neq\bullet}] \cup \mathsf{ExOps}_{6,8} \cup \mathsf{ExModelDefs}_6$$
$$+ \mathsf{RestrictOps}_{6,8}(1,7) + \mathsf{Ignored}_{6,8} = \{\overline{\bullet}_6\}_6$$

$$\Psi_{\overline{\mathsf{ZF+}}} := \mathsf{ZF}_0 \cup \mathsf{BuildModel}_{0,10}[\overline{\mathsf{V}}_{0,10} := \overline{\mathsf{V}}_{0,10}^{\neq\bullet}]$$
$$\cup \mathsf{PairOps}_{0,10} \cup \mathsf{NatOps}_{0,10} \cup \mathsf{ExOps}_{0,10}$$
$$\cup \mathsf{PairModelDefs}_{10} \cup \mathsf{NatModelDefs}_{10} \cup \mathsf{ExModelDefs}_{10}$$
$$+ \mathsf{RestrictOps}_{0,10}(1,7) + \mathsf{Ignored}_{0,10} = \{\overline{\bullet}_0\}_0$$

$$\Psi_{\mathsf{ZF}} := \Psi_{\overline{\mathsf{ZF}}} \cup \mathsf{AbsModel}_{0,2}$$
$$\Psi_{\mathsf{ZFP}} := \Psi_{\overline{\mathsf{ZFP}}} \cup \mathsf{AbsModel}_{2,4} \cup \mathsf{Delegate}_{2,4}(\mathsf{PConsts}_4)$$
$$\Psi_{\mathsf{ZFN}} := \Psi_{\overline{\mathsf{ZFN}}} \cup \mathsf{AbsModel}_{4,6} \cup \mathsf{Delegate}_{2,4}(\mathsf{NConsts}_6)$$
$$\Psi_{\mathsf{ZFE}} := \Psi_{\overline{\mathsf{ZFE}}} \cup \mathsf{Connection}_{6,8} \cup \mathsf{Delegate}_{6,8}(\mathsf{GZFConsts}_8 \cup \mathsf{EConsts}_8)$$
$$\cup \{\forall_8^{\neq\bullet} =_{(d_8 \Rightarrow \star) \Rightarrow \star} \mathsf{swap}_{6,8}(\overline{\mathsf{V}}_{6,8}^{\neq\bullet})\} \cup \mathsf{FOLQuants}_8[\forall_8 := \forall_8^{\neq\bullet}]$$
$$\Psi_{\mathsf{ZF+}} := \Psi_{\overline{\mathsf{ZF+}}} \cup \mathsf{Connection}_{0,10}$$
$$\cup \mathsf{Delegate}_{0,10}(\mathsf{GZFConsts}_{10} \cup \mathsf{PConsts}_{10} \cup \mathsf{NConsts}_{10} \cup \mathsf{EConsts}_{10})$$
$$\cup \{\forall_{10}^{\neq\bullet} =_{(d_{10} \Rightarrow \star) \Rightarrow \star} \mathsf{swap}_{0,10}(\overline{\mathsf{V}}_{0,10}^{\neq\bullet})\} \cup \mathsf{FOLQuants}_{10}[\forall_{10} := \forall_{10}^{\neq\bullet}]$$

Fig. 10. Sets of formulas for building and abstracting models for GSTs

Toward an Isabelle Implementation. We aim to mechanize the results of this paper in Isabelle/Pure using locales and overloading with type classes. This includes adapting the development of transfinite ordinal recursion in the Isabelle/ZF library to our setting.

Toward User-Friendly GST Specification and Use. We aim that users should be able to construct a structure and specify some properties of the structure and request a fresh copy of it and the system should be able to generate a new GST domain where that structure exists as non-set objects with no other properties than those specified. We also aim that users should be able to specify identifications (e.g., quotienting) and then have a GST generated where those identifications are true. Ideally, there will be support for doing this locally within part of a formal development and the user should not need to be aware that they are temporarily operating in a new GST.

References

1. Aczel, P.: Generalised set theory. In: Logic, Language and Computation, vol. 1 of CSLI Lecture Notes (1996)
2. Bancerek, G., et al.: Mizar: state-of-the-art and beyond. In: Kerber, M., Carette, J., Kaliszyk, C., Rabe, F., Sorge, V. (eds.) CICM 2015. LNCS (LNAI), vol. 9150, pp. 261–279. Springer, Cham (2015). https://doi.org/10.1007/978-3-319-20615-8_17

3. Brown, C.E., Pak, K.: A tale of two set theories. In: Kaliszyk, C., Brady, E., Kohlhase, A., Sacerdoti Coen, C. (eds.) CICM 2019. LNCS (LNAI), vol. 11617, pp. 44–60. Springer, Cham (2019). https://doi.org/10.1007/978-3-030-23250-4_4

4. Brown, C.E., Smolka, G.: Extended first-order logic. In: Berghofer, S., Nipkow, T., Urban, C., Wenzel, M. (eds.) TPHOLs 2009. LNCS, vol. 5674, pp. 164–179. Springer, Heidelberg (2009). https://doi.org/10.1007/978-3-642-03359-9_13

5. Dunne, C., Wells, J.B., Kamareddine, F.: Adding an abstraction barrier to ZF set theory. In: Benzmüller, C., Miller, B. (eds.) CICM 2020. LNCS (LNAI), vol. 12236, pp. 89–104. Springer, Cham (2020). https://doi.org/10.1007/978-3-030-53518-6_6

6. Farmer, W.M.: Formalizing undefinedness arising in calculus. In: Basin, D., Rusinowitch, M. (eds.) IJCAR 2004. LNCS (LNAI), vol. 3097, pp. 475–489. Springer, Heidelberg (2004). https://doi.org/10.1007/978-3-540-25984-8_35

7. Farmer, W.M., Guttman, J.D., Javier Thayer, F.: Little theories. In: Kapur, D. (ed.) CADE 1992. LNCS, vol. 607, pp. 567–581. Springer, Heidelberg (1992). https://doi.org/10.1007/3-540-55602-8_192

8. Huffman, B., Kunčar, O.: Lifting and transfer: a modular design for quotients in Isabelle/HOL. In: Gonthier, G., Norrish, M. (eds.) CPP 2013. LNCS, vol. 8307, pp. 131–146. Springer, Cham (2013). https://doi.org/10.1007/978-3-319-03545-1_9

9. Kolodynski, S.: IsarMathLib (2021). https://isarmathlib.org/. Accessed 3 Mar 2021

10. Krauss, A.: https://www21.in.tum.de/~krauss/publication/2010-soft-types-note/. Adding soft types to Isabelle (2010)

11. Krauss, A., Chen, J., Kappelmann, K.: Isabelle/Set. https://bitbucket.org/cezaryka/tyset/src/master/

12. Kunčar, O., Popescu, A.: From types to sets by local type definitions in higher-order logic. In: Blanchette, J.C., Merz, S. (eds.) ITP 2016. LNCS, vol. 9807, pp. 200–218. Springer, Cham (2016). https://doi.org/10.1007/978-3-319-43144-4_13

13. Kunčar, O., Popescu, A.: A consistent foundation for Isabelle/HOL. J. Autom. Reasoning **62**(4), 531–555 (2019)

14. Maddy, P.: What do we want a foundation to do? In: Centrone, S., Kant, D., Sarikaya, D. (eds.) Reflections on the Foundations of Mathematics. SL, vol. 407, pp. 293–311. Springer, Cham (2019). https://doi.org/10.1007/978-3-030-15655-8_13

15. Megill, N., Wheeler, D.A.: Metamath: A Computer Language for Mathematical Proofs. LULU Press, Morrisville (2019)

16. Obua, S.: Partizan games in Isabelle/HOLZF. In: Barkaoui, K., Cavalcanti, A., Cerone, A. (eds.): ICTAC 2006. LNCS, vol. 4281. Springer, Heidelberg (2006). https://doi.org/10.1007/11921240

17. Paulson, L.C.: The foundation of a generic theorem prover. J. Autom. Reasoning **5**(3), 363–397 (1989)

18. Paulson, L.C.: Set theory for verification: I. From foundations to functions. J. Autom. Reasoning **11**(3), 353–389 (1993)

19. Wiedijk, F., Zwanenburg, J.: First order logic with domain conditions. In: Basin, D., Wolff, B. (eds.) TPHOLs 2003. LNCS, vol. 2758, pp. 221–237. Springer, Heidelberg (2003). https://doi.org/10.1007/10930755_15

CICM'21 Systems Entries

Martin Líška[1], Dávid Lupták[1(✉)], Vít Novotný[1], Michal Růžička[1],
Boris Shminke[2], Petr Sojka[1], Michal Štefánik[1], and Makarius Wenzel[3]

[1] Faculty of Informatics, Masaryk University, Brno, Czechia
dluptak@mail.muni.cz
[2] Université Côte d'Azur, CNRS, LJAD, Nice, France
[3] Augsburg, Germany

Abstract. This consolidated paper gives an overview of new tools and improvements of existing tools in the CICM domain that occurred since the last CICM conference.

WebMIaS

Dávid Lupták, Vít Novotný, Michal Štefánik, Petr Sojka, Michal Růžička, Martin Líška, Faculty of Informatics, Masaryk University, Brno

Tool:	WebMIaS
Version:	1.6.6-4.10.4
Impl. in:	Java
License:	Apache License 2.0
Download:	github.com/MIR-MU/WebMIaS

Description. MIAS (Math Indexer and Searcher) is a math-aware full-text search engine. It uses Apache Lucene under the hood; however, its maths processing capabilities are standalone and can be easily integrated into any Apache Lucene/Solr/Elasticsearch-based system, as in the European Digital Mathematics Library (EuDML) service.

WEBMIAS is a web interface for MIAS. WEBMIAS accepts math queries in the TEX or MathML format combined with text queries. Results contain snippets of the matching text and mathematical formulae.

MIAS and WEBMIAS have been containerized into separate Docker images named miratmu/mias and miratmu/webmias, respectively. The Docker images allow users to run both the indexing and the retrieval without a specific configuration of the environment. Resolving dependencies and building all modules of the system is up to the continuous integration:

F. Kamareddine and C. Sacerdoti Coen (Eds.): CICM 2021, LNAI 12833, pp. 245–248, 2021.
https://doi.org/10.1007/978-3-030-81097-9_20

Besides MIAS, the dependencies of WEBMIAS are: MATHMLCAN, which canonicalizes different MathML encodings of equivalent formulae, MATHMLUNIFICATOR, which generalizes distinct mathematical formulae so that they can be structurally unified, and MIASMATH, which adds math processing capabilities to Lucene or Solr.

After downloading a dataset to the working directory, users can index the dataset using MIAS and deploy WEBMIAS in a single line of code:

```
1  $ wget https://mir.fi.muni.cz/MREC/MREC2011.4.439.tar.bz2
2  $ mkdir dataset ; tar xj -f MREC2011.4.439.tar.bz2 -C dataset
3  $ docker run -v "$PWD"/dataset:/dataset:ro -v "$PWD"/index:/index:rw --rm
   ↪  miratmu/mias
4  $ docker run -v "$PWD"/dataset:/dataset:ro -v "$PWD"/index:/index:ro --rm
   ↪  --name webmias -d -p 127.0.0.1:8888:8080 miratmu/webmias
```

The WEBMIAS system will be running at http://localhost:8888/WebMIaS.

Applications. Any digital mathematics library or a website with mathematical content may benefit from the added value of a math-aware search. WEBMIAS has been deployed in production on the EuDML website for almost a decade now.

Changes from the Previous Version. We newly report the availability of the WEBMIAS Docker image with the latest versions of all components.

Python client for Isabelle server

Boris Shminke, Université Côte d'Azur, CNRS, LJAD, France

Tool:	Python client for Isabelle server
Version:	0.2.0
Impl. in:	Python
License:	Apache 2.0
Download:	https://pypi.org/project/isabelle-client

Description. Python client for Isabelle server gives researchers using Python as their primary programming language an opportunity to communicate with Isabelle server through TCP directly from a Python script. Since Python-based tools continue to dominate the machine learning (ML) frameworks [3], this package, installable from The Python Package Index, can help researchers from the ML community to use the power of Isabelle proof assistant in their studies. Also, in other research domains where Isabelle can be helpful, Python as scripting languages remains preferable [2]. Some pieces of software written in Python and related to Isabelle (e.g. [4]) can include code for communication with the server, but they are hard to find, not easily reusable and well-documented.

The client relies on a standard Python package `asyncio` for low-level communication with the server. It implements wrapper methods for all commands of Isabelle server listed in its manual [6]. The package also includes a function for starting Isabelle server from Python script.

Applications. At the moment, the package is being used by its author for research in AI for algebra. It helps to check hundreds of working hypotheses, auto-generated by other Python scripts.

Acknowledgements. This work has been supported by the French government, through the 3IA Côte d'Azur Investments in the Future project managed by the National Research Agency (ANR) with the reference number ANR-19-P3IA-0002.

Isabelle platform

Makarius Wenzel, Augsburg, ORCID 0000-0002-3753-8280

Tool:	Isabelle platform
Version:	2021
Impl. in:	ML, Scala, and others
License:	BSD, LGPL, GPL, and others
Download:	https://isabelle.in.tum.de

Description. The Isabelle platform supports theory and tool development for symbolic logic: usually simply-typed HOL, but untyped ZF is also available (dependently-typed languages are in principle possible, but rarely used). The core system is implemented in two distinctive languages: (1) Isabelle/ML for mathematical logic, and (2) Isabelle/Scala for connectivity to the physical world, e.g. editors or servers on the Java VM. The Isabelle/PIDE framework supports interactive processing of formal mathematical documents [8], consisting of logical definitions, statements, proofs, or snippets of functional programs, or other domain-specific formal languages. Isabelle/jEdit [7] is the best-developed PIDE application and standard user-interface of Isabelle: it acts like a sophisticated "spell-checker" for formal logic, with instantaneous feedback on user edits. Isabelle/VSCode[1] is an alternative editor front-end, but much less developed. Another interaction mode works under program control as "headless PIDE", either via Scala datatypes within the Java process, or via external programs in different languages using a JSON protocol [6, §4], for example Python.

Applications. Any language embedded into the Isabelle framework may count as an application. It is easy to get started by implementing parsing and type-checking in Isabelle/ML, even with Prover IDE markup for variable scopes, types, feedback messages etc. The best-known and most-developed application of the framework is Isabelle/HOL [5]: it provides a rich environment for specifications and proofs for Gordon-style HOL, with various add-ons like type-classes and heavy tooling like Sledgehammer. Applications of Isabelle/HOL are formal mathematical articles or books: some are distributed with Isabelle, but the majority is collected separately in the Archive of Formal Proofs (AFP) [1]. Isabelle/AFP is managed like a scientific journal, with fully formal checking and high-quality presentation in LaTeX. Its continued growth since 2004[2] usually drives further technological development of the underlying Isabelle framework.

---

[1] https://marketplace.visualstudio.com/items?itemName=makarius.Isabelle2021.

[2] https://www.isa-afp.org/statistics.html.

Changes from Previous Versions. Official Isabelle releases appear every 8–10 months. The release Isabelle2021 (February 2021) is notable for (1) integrating Isabelle/ML and Isabelle/Scala more tightly, (2) unifying batch-mode builds and PIDE processing more smoothly, (3) including up-to-date provers (ATPs and SMTs) managed by Isabelle/Scala, and (4) high-quality GUI look-and-feel on all platforms: Linux, Windows, macOS (Intel or Apple Silicon).

References

1. The Archive of Formal Proofs (AFP), 2004–2021
2. Dragomir, I., Preoteasa, V., Tripakis, S.: The refinement calculus of reactive systems toolset. Int. J. Softw. Tools Technol. Transf. **22**(6), 689–708 (2020)
3. Kaggle. State of data science and machine learning (2020). https://www.kaggle.com/kaggle-survey-2020
4. Wimmer, S., Haslbeck, M.P.L.: Platform for interactive theorem proving competitions. https://github.com/maxhaslbeck/proving-contest-backends
5. Paulson, L.C., Nipkow, T., Wenzel, M.: From LCF to Isabelle/HOL. Formal Aspects Comput. **31**, 675–698 (2019)
6. Wenzel, M.: The Isabelle System Manual. https://isabelle.in.tum.de/doc/system.pdf
7. Wenzel, M.: Isabelle/jEdit. https://isabelle.in.tum.de/doc/jedit.pdf
8. Kaliszyk, C., Brady, E., Kohlhase, A., Sacerdoti Coen, C. (eds.): CICM 2019. LNCS (LNAI), vol. 11617. Springer, Cham (2019). https://doi.org/10.1007/978-3-030-23250-4

Author Index

Printed in the United States
by Baker & Taylor Publisher Services